WITHDRAWN

D1087977

Stitches on Time

STITCHES ON TIME

Colonial Textures and Postcolonial Tangles

Saurabh Dube

DUKE UNIVERSITY PRESS   Durham and London 2004

©2004 Duke University Press

All rights reserved

Printed in the United States of America on acid-free paper ∞

Typeset in Quadraat by Keystone Typesetting, Inc.

Library of Congress Cataloging-in-Publication Data

appear on the last printed page of this book.

DS
341
.D82
2004

103106-7059 H6

FOR LEELA DUBE
mother and anthropologist

Contents

Abbreviations

AMC	Archives of the Mennonite Church, Goshen, Indiana
ARM	Annual Reports of Missionaries
BCRR	Bilaspur Collectorate Record Room
BDVSR	Bilaspur District Village Settlement Records
BMF	Bisrampur Malguzari File
CPG	Central Provinces Government
DA	Defense of the Accused
DDM	*Der Deutsche Missionsfreund*
DPW	Deposition of Prosecution Witness
DSCRR	District and Sessions Court Record Room, Raipur
EA	Examination of the Accused
EAL	Eden Archives and Library, Webster Groves, Missouri
FS	Folder on Satnamis
IMD	India Mission District
J	Judgment
MPDP	M. P. Davis Papers, Webster Groves, Missouri
MPSRR	Madhya Pradesh Secretariat Record Room, Bhopal
QRM	Quarterly Reports of Missionaries
ST	Sessions trial

Preface

The art that serves as the frontispiece to this book portrays a pre-colonial past mediated by colonial history and palpable in the postco-lonial present. It shows a fair man standing sideways between two dark figures. The fair form is a Brahman, evident from the tuft of hair at the back of his shaven pate, the insignia on his forehead, and the sacred thread across his body. No ordinary upper caste, this is an eighteenth-century Brahman-king, one of the Peshwas who ruled over western and central India. The dark figures are untouchables, a woman and a man. The untouchable woman appears on the left of the canvas, before the Peshwa, a pot painted with the caste-Hindu swastika slung from her neck in front of her body. The untouchable man stands behind the Brahman-king, also carrying around his torso and hanging from his neck a pot painted with the sacred om. Indeed, it is these pots that proclaim the untouchable identity of the dark figures. For the reference here is to the period of Peshwa rule when untouchables were allegedly made to carry pots of clay to spit into so that their saliva would not fall to the ground, accidentally polluting an upper-caste person. His left, impure arm upraised, a finger pointing to his front, the Brahman-king articulates an order of power and its productions that is founded on the wounds of caste and its formations. Several details, large and small, complete the composition. The oil on canvas, entitled *Peshwa in Pune*, a work by the contemporary expressionist artist Savi Sawar-kar, a Dalit, critically addresses issues of history, power, and difference, which are also present at the core of *Stitches on Time*.

Savi's formidable oeuvre approaches the subaltern and the dominant, ritual and politics, through a forceful expressionism. In *Peshwa in Pune*, the clearly delineated, burnished golden central figure of the Peshwa and the less well defined, brownish-black untouchable forms do not simply insinuate a black and white divide. Rather, the precise details of the work and its very composition—from the shifty glance of the Peshwa and the direct gaze of the untouchables, who face the viewer, to the presence of a crow, a sign of untouchability, on the exposed thigh and buttock of the Peshwa; the interrogation of the Brahman-king by another snakelike, palpable image of a bird at the top left of the canvas; the Peshwa's shamelessly exposed penis pointing toward the untouchable woman, insinuating the sexually predatory nature of the upper-caste man; and the precise placement of the Peshwa, who separates the untouchable couple, husband and wife—all announce the mutual entailments of these figures and their shared crises and coeval concerns. Each of these forms is a specter of the past, alive in the present. Together they are astute reminders of the constant crossings between authority and alterity—the dense desires of power and recalcitrance, the restless requirements of the dominant and the subaltern—and the contrary ways in which history and the here and now insinuate and inhabit each other. At the same time, the very ambiguity of other forms in *Peshwa in Pune*—the curious beast that seeks to enter a strange object above the untouchable woman, a large bubble containing a human likeness hanging over the untouchable man—equally indicate the importance of probing our own protocols of knowing. Having lived with images created by Savi for some years now, I have learned many lessons from them.

In this book, I attempt to track the incessant entanglements between power and difference, neither treating power as fetishized force, an abstract aesthetic, nor imagining difference as prior purity, an a priori alterity, but thinking their shared determinations and common denials down to the ground. This means attending to the textures and details of the past and present not only in empirical but in theoretical ways. Aware of the limits of simply demystifying or pointedly unmasking histories and subjects, beliefs and practices, the careful questioning, ethical articulation, and critical affirmation of social worlds that I offer in this work inhere in a history without warranty: procedures of understanding that unravel principally through cautiously querying the guarantee of progress, in the past and present, under regimes of modernity. Now, if the invocation of a history without warranty brings to mind Stuart Hall's celebrated call for "Marxism without guarantee," it equally intimates its own emphases. These reside in attempts to engage and extend both the recent ontological turn in political theory and the diverse yet connected critical understandings of history and modernity, state and nation, that characterize scholarship across a range of disciplines. Unsurprisingly, here are found considerations of the theoretical possibilities of the postcolonial as a critical category and recognition of the formidable conceit of this concept-entity, especially when it appears as a settled stage of history and/or a self-contained analytical terrain or (anti)disciplinary domain.

Such measures call into question forceful scandals—namely, those of the West and the nation—and the manner in which they often underlie other category-entities, the outrage of the postcolonial. Yet the protocols at stake do not treat such scandals as obtuse ideological aberrations or mere analytical phantasms, here now and gone tomorrow, deftly exorcised through prescient knowledge. The procedures recognize the dense ontological attributes of such scandals, their presence not only as objects of knowledge but as conditions of knowing, the stink and shame that are uneasily elided and fretfully forgotten, but the stench and disgrace that are also confronted and questioned, especially as the scandals find other expressions, heterogeneous articulations, among different subjects, not least because of their pervasiveness and persuasions. Clearly, all of this is neither to approach the notion of the scandal as signifying stark sensation nor to treat the existence of scandal as mere deviation from the social order. Instead it is to register the pervasive presence of the scandals under consideration as intimating the familiar state of social orders so that the more obviously sensational projections of the West and the nation themselves insinuate routine renewals of dominant norms and governmental commands. Put differently, to stay with the scandals that shore up our murky worlds is to trace the intricate interweaving of empire and modernity, the intimate interleaving of nation and history, and the uneasy braiding of colonial textures and postcolonial tangles.

The attempts made in this book to prudently probe our typical ways of understanding social worlds—of presupposing the past and prefiguring the present—rest on critical intersections between the cosmopolitan and the vernacular that have shaped my work and life. Over thirty years ago, as a fourth-grade student at St. Joseph's Convent School in Sagar, a provincial town in central India, my favorite teacher, Sister Mary, a nun from southern India, rendered the phrase "A stitch in time saves nine" as "A stitch on time saves nine." At the time, I didn't know which version was correct. I still don't. Therefore, I take liberty with cosmopolitan English not only to render the stitch in its plural, stitches, but to retain the rephrasing in vernacular English of the in as on. So Stitches on Time it must be, a work further divided into seven chapters and much introductory and supplementary material.

For permission to reproduce parts of previously published pieces, I thank Cambridge University Press for "Paternalism and Freedom: The Evangelical Encounter in Colonial Chhattisgarh, Central India," Modern Asian Studies 29 (1995): 171–201; Oxford University Press for "Colonial Law and Village Disputes: Two Cases from Chhattisgarh," in Social Conflict:

Oxford in India Readings in Sociology and Social Anthropology, edited by N. Jayaram and Satish Saberwal, 423–44 (Delhi: Oxford University Press, 1996); and Sage Publications for "Telling Tales and Trying Truths: Transgressions, Entitlements and Legalities in Village Disputes, Late Colonial Central India," *Studies in History* 13 (1996): 171–201.

The book has taken a long time to reach its conclusion, longer than I would have liked. But, as several subjects of the study would say, this is the way it happens. They must be right. I can now move to the pleasant matter of acknowledging those who made the work possible. As should be the case, I begin by thanking my friend Savi Sawarkar for painting *Peshwa in Pune* and for allowing me to reproduce it in *Stitches on Time*.

This is primarily a work of history and anthropology that pushes against the inherited ends of these disciplines while critically considering their configurations and possibilities. In the archives and the field, I would like to thank Dennis Stoesz of the Archives of the Mennonite Church of North America, Goshen, Indiana; John D. Thiessen of the Archives of the General Conference Mennonites, Newton, Kansas; Lowell Zuck of the Eden Archives and Seminary, Webster Groves, Missouri; Lois and Marion Deckert in Newton; Dorothy Yoder Nyce and John Nyce in Goshen; the (extended) families Martin, Das, and Chatterjee in Dhamtari; Pastor Nand in Champa; and the many people sustaining the study in Chhattisgarh, Nagpur, and the midwestern United States.

Stitches on Time was mainly written in Mexico, but two semesters in Ithaca were important for its gestation and completion. I gratefully acknowledge the institutional support of El Colegio de México and the invitations extended by the History Department and the South Asia Center at Cornell University. The inputs of my students at both institutions were significant for the work. Laura Carballido was a resourceful research assistant and remains a valuable graduate student. Different parts of the study were presented at conferences, seminars, and talks in Ann Arbor, Atlanta, Bogotá, Boston, Calcutta (now Kolkata), Cambridge (England and Massachusetts), Charlottesville, Chicago, Delhi (old and new), Guadalajara, Havana, Heidelberg, Iowa City, Ithaca, Kingston (Ontario), London, Madison, Mexico City, Minneapolis, New York, Orlando, Oxford, Rio de Janeiro, Shimla, and Toronto. I thank my interlocutors on these occasions.

Ken Wissoker of Duke University Press has been a supportive yet tough editor. His uncompromising insistence that I watch how (much) I write has made the book tighter and more focused. Christine Dahlin and Justin Faerber (also at the press) and Janet Opdyke helpfully, graciously sorted out matters. Arpita Das, Nitasha Devasar, and Anil Chandy of Oxford University Press, India, remain good friends and editorial allies. I cannot imagine better interlocutors than the two anonymous readers of the manuscript for

Duke University Press. Intellectually encouraging and theoretically critical, they alternately persuaded and forced me to rework the manuscript and recast its arguments, especially the introduction, making the study more meaningful, pointed, and relevant. The first reader's measured suggestions and the second's no holds barred critique complemented each other. Many thanks.

Not only this book but my different projects have been nurtured by the warm generosity and critical support of Shahid Amin, Gautam Bhadra, Craig Calhoun, Dipesh Chakrabarty, Partha Chatterjee, Bernard Cohn, Grant Farred, Ranajit Guha, Ann Gold, John Hutnyk, David Lorenzen, Walter Mignolo, Anupama Rao, Ajay Skaria, and Milind Wakankar. Over the years, many have influenced my thoughts and writing, including the arguments and materials presented in Stitches on Time, through their comments and kindness. Once more, simply registering names has its limits. The liability of forgetting a few makes matters worse. But while recognizing these costs I must gratefully acknowledge, in alphabetical order, Celma Agüero, Arjun Appadurai, David Arnold, Roger Bartra, Pratyusha Basu, Christopher Bayly, Ned Bertz, André Béteille, Sabyasachi Bhattacharya, Flora Botton, Rubén Chuaqui, Jean and John Comaroff, Fernando Coronil, Elisabetta Corsi, Fred Dallmayr, Valentine Daniel, Veena Das, Faisal Devji, Nicholas Dirks, Fernando Escalante, Romana Falcón, Shelley Feldman, Germán Franco, Suman Ghosh, Sandra Greene, Paul Greenough, William Grover, Anne Hardgrove, David Hardiman, Saidiya Hartman, Michael Herzfeld, Gordon Johnson, Indivar Kamtekar, Shruti Kapila, Hermann Kulke, David Lellyveld, Andrés Lira, T. N. Madan, Javed Majeed, McKim Marriot, John Marston, Shail Mayram, Uday Mehta, Chris Minkowski, Mrinal Miri, Dia Mohan, Satya Mohanty, Laurence Moore, Valentine Mudimbe, Ashis Nandy, Balmurli Natrajan, Gyanendra Pandey, Jonathan Parry, Prasannan Parthasarthi, Gyan Prakash, Chris Pinney, Benjamin Preciado, Arvind Rajagopal, Satish Saberwal, Sumit and Tanika Sarkar, Sudipta Sen, Mrinalini Sinha, Sanjay Subrahmaniam, Emma Tarlo, Mauricio Tenorillo, Romila Thapar, Michel-Rolph Trouillot, Denis Vidal, David Washbrook, Brackette Williams, Eleanor Zelliot, and Guillermo Zermeño.

At the end, several friends have sustained me with their warmth and concern. I trust they know who they are. Now and again, S. P. Banerjee and Gitasree Bandopadhyay had to suffer this study, which they did with cheerful fortitude. Ishita Banerjee has lived the work with me, especially through her own scholarship, in endless ways. The intersections and distinctions of our arguments and emphases, our lives and stories, course through the book. I owe her (another) one, as I do S. C. Dube. I only wish that he was around. I cannot begin to recount the contributions of Leela Dube as friend and mother, interlocutor and critic. Stitches on Time is dedicated to her.

Stitches on Time

Introduction

T his is a book of narrative and theory, history and anthropology, that explores questions and subjects of power and difference, the colony and the postcolony, empire and nation, and modernity and its margins. In Stitches on Time, my efforts entail critical conjunctions between social worlds and their academic apprehensions—between the field and the archive, fact and interpretation, reading and writing, and the past and the present—each casting doubt on the other, seeking not scandal but productive crises, reworking concepts, and rethinking entities. Along such tracks, I would like to begin by discussing a seductive ritual and secular drama, a critical event of contemporary vintage presenting colonial pasts and presaging postcolonial presents.

Multicultural Spectacles

During the dying days of the last millennium, intimating its terminal gasp, an inaugural moment of vital staginess captured the attention of the world at large. Assiduously broadcast on television, millions and millions of people witnessed the opening ceremony of the Olympic Games in Sydney in 2000. As event and image, this striking spectacle and its substantial stage hinged on history, a vision of antiquity and an optic of posterity held in place by the phantasm of progress—an idea and an imagining, singular and universal.

The show began with primordial images, first of fire, then of flowers. The desert landscape and aboriginal pathways were in perfect harmony, nature and culture collapsed together, a multicultural primitivist fantasy of primeval rhythms and colorful cadences endlessly insinuating a sylvan space sometimes known as Eden. To conjure this perfect past was to signal its eventual destruction. Captain Cook and English voyagers soon sailed into the arena with exploration at heart and discovery in mind. Here there was no riposte to, and little questioning of, colonial journeys. Not yet. Pilgrim forebears and adventuring ancestors command veneration. But then colonialism appeared, an ungainly beast, a mechanical monster that betokened an iron cage, traversing and transforming a faultless terrain, breaching and breaking with a pristine past. At once a finished maneuver of domination and a totalized term of power, colonialism emerged as uniformly efficacious, a clumsy but coordinated system that brooked no obstacle.

Unsurprisingly, the pristine gaze of the postcolonial present saw through the dense ravages of the colonial past, separated from and placed above its evil and pathetic trajectory. Precisely as the colonial behemoth moved through the middle of the Olympic stadium, a little child in virginal white was lifted into the Sydney sky. Hovering weightlessly above the spectacle of destruction enacted under her eyes, the untarnished innocence, celestial vision, and ethereal perspective of the child established the presence of guilelessness and virtue. On one hand, the scene suggested that Western purity and European innocence were essential attributes of empire, especially considering the place of the little girl gazing on this past, her position on history as it happened. On the other hand, the apparition implied that colonialism was a fleeting matter of an ambivalent history that is totally repudiated today. The sweet, incorruptible child—a famous music star, no less—descended to earth to offer the colonial beast an apple. Peace was made with the past. The colonial moment stood banished from the historical stage.

Now those on the margins moved to the center. The cultural minorities of a multicultural down under announced their presence. The panorama consisted of several distinct scenes. Brightly clad in "traditional" costumes and bearing the signs of "native" guise, the first inhabitants of the continent and the recent migrants to Australia danced and smiled, sang and laughed, separately but together. This was in tune with authoritative, everyday apprehensions of the culture concept, themselves drawing on persuasive prior anthropological projections of the category. Thus, the body of culture came to dwell in dress and dance, its heart to reside in color and costume, and its soul to inhere in myth and music, all enacted under the sign of the state, the mark of the majority. The minority cultures were many. The multicultural nation was one. The severalty secured the singularity, and the singularity stipulated the severalty—not only unity in diversity, but diversity in unity—contingent on the nation, complicit with the state, and predicated on progress.[1]

This idea of improvement, a palpable passage based on anterior advancements, found its culmination in the last tableau. Here progress kicked in through the depiction of hardworking Australians constructing a prefigured present and building a predestined future. Hard hats on their heads, visors shielding their faces, and tools in their hands, a young antipodal generation engendered a present and presented a posterity that was technologically sophisticated and materially handy. In the ultimate scenario in the Sydney Stadium, majoritarian premises shaped cherished ideals and populist representations of an industrious nation and a productive people—sort of working class and chiefly white.

The diverse tableaux and the singular strand of this media spectacle contain divergent truths, which come together with wide resonance. First, following the imperatives of the multicultural nation, *culture* signaled issues of (the) minority contained within reifications of tradition and community—enchanted spaces. Second, in tune with the determinations of statist-stagist progress, *history* signified attributes of (the) majority concatenated within representations of modernity and nation—modern places.[2] Finally, taken together, the precise separation of the enchanted and the modern, the reason of difference, conjoined these two metaphors and arenas in the exclusive passage of universal history, the fetish of progress.[3]

The opening ceremony of the Olympic Games in the Sydney Stadium is not an exotic exception or a rational rarity. On one hand, influential imaginings at the core of cultural politics and political cultures in the present rest on the putative divide between the enchanted and the modern, articulating difference and power, the postcolony and the colony. This involves implicit assumptions and explicit proclamations that a sensitive postcolonial order has emerged in the wake of evil empires and a caring multicultural sensibility has replaced the cruelties of corrupt colonialism. It also entails expressions binding ruses of difference of non-Western nations and communities with stipulations of Western progress and state and the battle of modern civilization against its savage enemy, or its many enemies, at once medieval and coeval. Today Kevin Costner's primary primitivism in *Dances with Wolves* and the dominant media presentation of the Gulf War recede into the recent past, proximate tidings of present history. At the same time, taking their place are the haunting tradition of *Once Were Warriors*, Stanley Kubrick's coupling of oriental rhythms and terrifying sexuality in *Eyes Wide Shut*, and the terrible attacks of September 11 and their unfortunate aftermath as event and image.[4] On the other hand, beyond media spectacles and statist visions, important strands of critical scholarship questioning modernity and interrogating the West find other uses for the split between power and difference. Sometimes straddling and sometimes subverting the twinned determinations of the enchanted and the modern, such endeavor can equally posit difference as an ethical a priori, the critics' cure to reason and answer to power.

I am suggesting, then, that the abiding enticements of the opening ceremony of the Sydney games, and their wide implications, raise critical questions. Beginning with presumed yet palpable projections of the singular passage from the colony to the postcolony, they urge consideration of the prior presence of colonial conceptions and the a priori persuasions of postcolonial propositions in the contemporary world, each intimately entwined with the hierarchies and oppositions of modernity. Indeed, these concerns themselves foreground issues of the linkages—mutual binds and shared exclusions—between power and difference, empire and modernity, nation and history, and the postcolony and the colony. It is such entangled strands that I now unravel.

Postcolonial Scandals

The problem with the postcolonial as a category is that its endless promises entail enduring postures, its many meanings register unproductive ambiguity, and its revelations and containments shadow each other. Not surprisingly, salient contributions to postcolonial understandings have pointed to the acute limits of the postcolonial concept as analytical conceit and historical trajectory. Here the issue does not simply concern how the terms of postcolonial discourse readily intimate a new "minority," often of privilege, in Western academic arenas and crucially insinuate novel struggles for turf and tenure in scholarly terrain, more broadly, processes that underlie the institutionalization of postcolonial scholarship. Significantly, it seems to me, criticisms of the postcolonial as a category-entity have highlighted its tendency to homogenize history and sanitize politics, resting on the divide between the colonial and the postcolonial and one totalized terrain leading to another, undifferentiated arena.[5] At the same time, however, abiding endeavors articulating postcolonial perspectives have also queried the place of the West as history, modernity, and destiny; unraveled the terms and limits of state and nation; and underscored the salience of critical difference in such distinct yet entangled terrain.[6]

Now, if the unproductive ambiguity and the residual stagism of the postcolonial as word and entity imply that my own thought and writings are not wedded to the notion, then the fruitful potential of the category, I feel, warrants staying with it longer. For even if scholars think hard enough, considering it an analytical nightmare, the postcolonial is unlikely to disappear and lurid theoretical scares are productive to ponder in any case.[7] Insinuating more than a pure perspective, the view from nowhere that becomes the vista for everywhere, these reflections follow from my presence at a center of research and teaching on Asia and Africa located in Latin America.

The rise to prominence of the postcolonial as a novel perspective, a critical stance, in history and anthropology coincided with the final phase of my doctoral work at the University of Cambridge and my subsequent return to India to teach at the University of Delhi.[8] In both places, my particular endeavor and wider disposition to combine history and anthropology and theory and narrative raised eyebrows and received encouragement. At the same time, my work broadly accorded with my interlocutors' inclination to give short shrift to the postcolonial ballyhoo, although I did not always share their desire to dismiss the category as merely a fashionable phantasm riding the success of the postmodern as word and orientation.[9] After three years in India, on moving to Mexico in 1995 all of this changed, at moments dramatically and at other times little by little.

At the Centro de Estudios de Asia y África of the El Colegio de México, among students and faculty, India—or China or Chad—frequently appeared as innately different, all too distant, and articulated by pervasive dualities of the Occident and the Orient, the West and the Rest, with Latin America positioned, uneasily yet readily, as part of *el Occidente*. This was not only true of my own research and teaching center, but it was characteristic of scholarly sentiments, quotidian conceptions, academic apprehensions, and their institutional manifestations in the Latin American world more generally. On one hand, Asia and Africa embodied a marvelous difference from the West, the mark of enchantment, *algo bello*, something beautiful. On the other hand, they concretized contaminated distance from the West, the sign of backwardness, *algo feo*, something ugly. At the same time, these twin dispositions rested on hierarchical oppositions of a singular modernity, splitting social worlds into enchanted spaces and modern places, while holding them together through the exclusive trajectory of universal history, scholarly traces and commonplace tracks in the shadow of the nation.

How were such grids to be queried? Asking and addressing the question, my prior critical considerations of analytical binaries—between myth and history, ritual and rationality, the magical and the modern, emotion and reason, East and West, community and state, and tradition and modernity—now assumed a formidable tangibility, a palpable force.[10] Slowly yet acutely, I came to realize that such dualities inhabited the interstices of theoretical blueprints *and* social worlds, spilling over from the one to the other. Aware of the active interchange between academic apprehensions and quotidian conceptions and registering the restless dynamic between colonialism and modernity, when I considered a possible dialogue between critical perspectives on South Asia and Latin America the postcolonial as a category presented itself as an apposite means of initiating such a conversation.

In Latin American and South Asian worlds, imperatives of empire and fabrications of nation have followed different chronologies, insinuating distinct trajectories. Unsurprisingly in scholarly schemes and everyday apprehensions, while in Latin America colonial power appears to be cast as an attribute of a distant past left behind by two centuries of formal independence, in South Asia the opposition to imperial effects through the means of national affects has carried greater and more proximate immediacy. Yet in both of these contexts the passage from imperial rule to independent state—and its diverse representations—crucially reflects the precepts of the colony on the work of the nation, variously implicating distinct idioms of social advance under empire and differentially envisioning the nation in the image of Western progress.

In the face of such categorical determinations, I found that engaging the postcolonial as a critical perspective called into question the persuasive presence in Latin America and South Asia of an aggrandizing West and its singular representations binding empire and nation, the colony and the postcolony, and history and modernity. At the same time, the very realization of such emphases was premised on querying the pretensions of the postcolonial as an exclusive viewpoint and casting it instead as one among related critical orientations—procedures and perspectives entailing the subaltern and the margin and ethnographic history and historical anthropology working in tandem with postcolonial propositions, with each stance engaging and extending the other disposition.[11]

The implications of this example extend even farther. The productive labor of the postcolonial as a category points toward two sets of scandals, each tied to burdens of colonial pasts, determinations of historical progress, and framings of universal history. The first concerns the scandal of the West, pervasive projections of an imaginary but tangible Europe, of a reified yet palpable West as the primary habitus of the modern, the enshrined space of modernity, democracy, reason, and history. The second entails the scandal of the nation—persistent propositions regarding state and nation as harbingers of progress and development, substantial or ephemeral, realized or failed, which anxiously elide and shamefully deny the broken promises of freedom and the undemocratic foundations of democracy under regimes of modernity in the colony, the postcolony, and the modern West. Brushing the category against the grain of its amorphousness and conceit, the possibilities of the postcolonial, I would submit, lie in carefully questioning this copula of scandals.

To register the scandals of the West and the nation does not imply their impatient, reckless dismissal, neither casting these outrages as obtuse ideological aberrations nor treating them as endless analytical specters and awaiting their inevitable ouster at the hands of pristine understandings. Rather, it is to acknowledge that they have pervasive ontological attributes, lying at the core of social worlds, that call for careful elaboration, especially through efforts aware of the analytical expressions and quotidian configurations that come together and fall apart. To speak of these scandals is to resist the desire to turn the West and the nation, modernity and empire, into monolithic manifestations of all-encompassing power and also resist the temptation to simply deprovincialize Western history and knowledge, to merely demystify the modern state and nation. Instead, it is to reencounter the parochialism of the West and the conceit of the nation, attending to the formative heterogeneity that produces *and* probes their exclusive claims, querying *and* affirming concepts and practices in the wake of these twin scandals.[12]

Such tasks require vigilance regarding the vanity of the postcolonial as entity and concept, readily implying a settled stage of history, an equipped proviso of progress, an inherently subversive knowledge, a predestined labor of cultural production, and a prefigured form of scholarly criticism. To draw on the resources of the postcolonial in order to think through the scandals of the West and the nation is to register the postcolonial as scandal from its formidable conceit to its lingering complicities in the artifice of the nation-state, from its bloated amorphousness to its pervasive access to an exclusive universal history. To acknowledge the outrages of the postcolonial is to sieve the category through critical filters, recognizing precisely the key containments of incisive postcolonial critiques, from the ways in which their ethical ends can simply point toward the presence of difference and the production of alterity as interrupting power in the colony and the postcolony, without staying longer with the burden of such difference, to their tendentious apprehensions of colonial cultures. At stake in the caution concerning the analytical arrogance of postcolonial propositions are mutual labors of distinct yet overlapping theoretical dispositions.

Against the current of its institutionalization within academe as a discrete knowledge or a novel discipline, and casting aside the search for the conceptual purity and the innate distinction of the category, in this book I approach the postcolonial as a critical rubric, especially in the sense of an analytical interpolation articulated by and itself animating other theoretical orientations.[13] In other words, I see postcolonial propositions as interlocutors in a wider debate, rethinking the nation-state and the West as concept and entity, process and destiny, history and modernity. Conceiving of the participants in this discussion as engaging each other in a critical yet constructive spirit, let me indicate four such overlapping orientations and salient sensibilities toward social worlds and analytical categories.[14]

First, for some time now critical scholarship has queried enduring oppositions between tradition and modernity, ritual and rationality, myth and history, and East and West that are formative of influential understandings of pasts and key conceptions of cultures. Such questioning has derived support from critiques of a subject-centered reason, a meaning-legislating rationality, and their hierarchical dualities within Enlightenment and post-Enlightenment traditions. Alternatively, it has expressed acute challenges to the analytical binaries of modern disciplines, interrogating enticing renderings of otherness and enduring projections of progress that are closely tied to the staging and production of modernity "as the West."[15] Second, in a related move, there have been imaginative explorations of distinct pasts and heterogeneous presents forged within wider, intermeshed matrices of power. Such emphases have put a question mark on the developmental imperatives of historical thought and the very nature of the academic archive, both bound to the totalizing templates of universal history and each envisioned in the likeness of a reified West.[16] Third, in recent years questions of modernity have increasingly escaped the limits of sociological formalism and exceeded the binds of a priori abstraction, emerging instead as matters of particular pasts and attributes of concrete histories defined by projects of power and molded by provisions of progress. Here there has been keen recognition not only of the divergent articulations of modernity and contending intimations of the modern but of the competing place within all modernities of exclusive images of Western modernity, where the singularity and universalism of the latter are differently engaged by the measures and horizons of the former. These distinct procedures shape and suture empire, nation, and globalization. As a result, modernity/modernities have themselves been revealed as contradictory and contingent processes of culture and control, as checkered and contested histories of meaning and mastery in their formation, sedimentation, and elaboration.[17] Finally, over the past two decades a variety of critical understandings have unraveled the sway and stipulations, the contentions and limits, of the modern state and the contemporary nation, especially as they bear powerful yet contending connections to provisos of historical progress, Western modernity, and universal history. Such considerations have ranged from the construal of the nation as an "imagined community" to the quotidian configurations and everyday apprehensions of state and nation, the attributes of difference and power articulated by anticolonial nationalism and the non-Western nation, and the dense embedding of nation-states within transnational processes.[18]

It warrants emphasis that such sensibilities and dispositions are not all of a piece, yet the arguments they announce are indicative of the questioning under way of categories and entities presupposed by typical ways of apprehending and acting in the contemporary world.[19] Circulating among such sets of questions, postcolonial propositions do not intimate a privileged purchase on, or unique access to, seeing and doing in the world today. Rather, as critical interlocutors in a larger conversation they register that the reflections of a singular Western modernity, the representations of an exclusive universal history, and the reifications of the modern state and nation are not mere specters from the past now exorcised by critical epistemologies and subversive knowledges. The postcolonial as critical rubric highlights the acute presence of these resilient mappings and their determinate redrawing, which articulate authoritative strains of contemporary knowledge and animate routine terms of everyday discourse—not only in an imaginary West but in inexhaustible contexts. But precisely these tasks also imply the recognition that even as a theoretical conceit the West, and nation, empire, and modernity, simply cannot exhaust each practice and every passion in the worlds of their doing and undoing, the domains they have worked over, formed yet transformed by their very subjects. The productive possibilities of postcolonial emphases, then, inhere in their prudently querying such scandals through the labor of critical interpolation in a wider debate, acutely open to questioning their own presumptions and predilections and pointing the way out of the postcolonial field as an academic ghetto.[20] These considerations shape my understanding and unraveling in this book of colonial textures and postcolonial tangles, tracking imaginative pathways and ragged networks of historical practice, chapters in an anthropological history.

Power and Difference

In speaking of the scandals of the West and the nation, I have noted that they constitute palpable vistas at the heart of the modern world. Precisely such recognition calls for critical engagement with projections of colonialism and modernity, state and nation, and the West and history as totalized fields of exclusive force while also carefully considering the quotidian configurations of these categories and entities. Rather than simply registering empirical exceptions to theoretical claims, at stake in this discussion are critical questions of power and difference.

More than a decade ago, in his synthetic survey of postmodern thought, the literary critic John McGowan argued that postmodernism

> begins from the fear . . . that we are witnessing the "apotheosis of capitalism." . . . Late capitalism constitutes the totalized terrain of contemporary life; the name of the despised totality is different in other postmodern texts, but the specter of patriarchy, or Western

metaphysics, or disciplinary power, or some other dominant social form haunts the postmodern imagination. This fear of a distopic totality is sometimes even embraced, partly in the heroic spirit of Nietzsche's and Freud's determination to face the worst truths without flinching, partly as a weapon to use against the hopes for autonomy found in modernist and avant-garde work, partly as a refutation of the liberal insistence that capitalism is not only compatible with, but actually productive of, pluralism. Thus the theoretical establishment of the monolith's existence is often a necessary step in postmodern work, although the desire to transform that monolith into a truly pluralistic society surfaces everywhere as the primary postmodern goal.[21]

There is much to ponder in this passage, to reconsider in this statement, and to revise in this assessment, but my purpose in recalling it primarily concerns the formulation and fear of the West and colonialism, the nation and history as dystopic totalities, schemes and scares that extend far beyond postmodern projections. Indeed, in influential analyses of colonial writing/culture and modern power/knowledge, colonialism, modernity, the West, and the nation can strikingly appear as "totalized terrain" of the past and the present, "another name of the despised totality" that constitutes history and the here and now. This has considerable import for current cultures of scholarship and contemporary politics of cultures.[22]

On one hand, in the best hands such orientations lead to the highlighting of the wide-ranging work of colonial knowledge and modern power in distinct and diffuse arenas and emphasizing the genealogies of present disciplines in their concatenation within both, authoritative apprehensions shaded by empire and dominant understandings in the shadow of the nation. Similar possibilities underlie ethical engagements of minority positions with overriding schemes of disciplinary knowledge and institutional power. In place here can be self-critical endeavors that question the privilege of categorical identities, forge other communities of debate and alter/native solidarities of struggle, and interrogate the majoritarian premises and statist assumptions underlying minority identities and ethnic statuses under the sign of the nation.[23]

On the other hand, I also wonder about the possibilities of understandings that attend to the spirit and sensibilities of critical thought that is ever suspicious of totalizing power and legislative reason but do not succumb to the tendency to render the "despised totality" as monolithic. Such dispositions, including my own, question the projection of power as "totalized terrain" and eschew the "celebration of difference wherever it appears," even as they reject the autonomy and integrity of the singular subject.[24] They position themselves alongside yet apart from both, influential tendencies that reproduce heterogeneity as "unrecuperated particulars," the antidote to the terms of power, and weighty dispositions that apprehend difference as produced by power but nevertheless instate alterity as an end in itself. Rather, they argue for the constitution of subjects within social relationships, defined by provisions of meaning and shaped within crucibles of power, tracing the sustained labor of difference within productions of power and the insistent expressions of power within formations of difference. Instead of submitting to the idea of difference as a priori inclusive intactness, ahead of the work of reason and in front of the productivity of power, or of projecting the presence of alterity within the interstices of authority as an analytical and ethical finale, the terms of heterogeneity and their limits are thus sown in the substance of social subjects and their constitution, meanings, and practices.

We might consider such stipulations of power and determinations of difference in relation to the terms of modernity. To begin with, modernity is not only an idea, ideal, or ideology; it is simultaneously the articulation of distinct historical processes. During the past five centuries, modernity has emerged elaborated within intersecting and disjunctive and authoritative and contested processes of meaning and power. I refer to processes entailing, for example, capital and consumption, industry and empire, nations and colonies, citizens and subjects, public spheres and private spaces, circumscribed religion(s) and disenchanted knowledge(s), resurgent faiths and reified traditions, normalizing states and disciplinary regimes, and enchantments of governance and the magic of the modern. As history, then, modernity is not singular; it is enacted instead in its plural, modernities. Yet this is not all. For, whether cast as modernity or modernities, the procedures entailed herein are neither seamless nor homogeneous, referring rather to decisively checkered, decidedly contingent, and distinctly contradictory processes. Indeed, it is within such contingency and contradiction that modernity's constitutive hierarchies, formative distinctions, and seductive productions, which insinuate the abiding enchantments of modernity—from the immaculate image of its origins and ends through to its pervasive oppositions, from the novel mythologies of empire and nation to the dense magic of money and markets—appear to be staged and elaborated. Put differently, the terms of modernity are assiduously articulated, yet they are also basically checkered and even out of joint with themselves.[25]

These processes are not subjectless procedures. Rather, they emerge expressed by subjects of modernity, subjects who have engaged and elaborated the terms, stipulations, and disciplines of modernity, history, and modernity as history. Here it is patently inadequate to conflate the *subject of modernity with the modern subject.* Time after time, subjects of modernity have revealed that there are different ways of being modern, now accessing and now exceeding the determinations of the modern subject, suggesting the need to rethink exclusive apprehensions of the latter entity—as image and as practice. Yet all too often subjects of modernity have also betrayed scant regard for the niceties of the modern subject while articulating the enduring terms of modernity; registering within their measures and meanings the formative contradictions, contentions, and contingencies of modernity/modernities; instating and inflecting power; and reiterating and re-working difference. To register the contingency and plurality of modernity is not merely to harp on alternative modernities but to stay with such modalities of power, formations of difference, and their restless interplay. This also means not turning away from but prudently unraveling the singular stipulations of an exclusive modernity that shapes the contentions and concatenations of all modernities, stipulations that are nonetheless set to work in different ways by social subjects, yielding expected outcomes and unexpected consequences.

If the constitutive practices of subjects of modernity emerge embedded within and enacted through the density of meaning and the gravity of power, such modalities of meaning and these profiles of power are rarely fully finished; they are ever subject to difference and displacement. Here it is important to trace the impassioned interest, incessant instability, and agonistic ambivalence at the heart of dominant projects of meaning and power, but it is equally significant to recognize that such operations are tied to the contradictory and constitutive actions of social subjects. In practice, spectacular recalcitrance can be conjoined with terms of power and quotidian routines can exceed dominant meanings, both subject to change and reworking and ever marked by possibilities of the intonations of older truths and the inflections of newer verities. Given the constant clamor for autonomy and agency, it bears pointing out that the very definition of *democracy*, the meanings of modernity, and the purposes of pluralism cannot be separated from the inherently different formations of social subjects in inescapably heterogeneous worlds shaped by the past and emergent in the present. Beyond vanguardist visions and technocratic blueprints, the terms for realizing and/or rejecting the possibilities of modernity, plurality, and democracy rest on ethics and politics that inhere in practices of social subjects in the here and now—tied to the past, turned to the present, and trafficking in the future.[26]

To emphasize the heterogeneity of empire and modernity, of the West and the nation as projects of power, then, involves more than the mere accretion of empirical detail, the patient addition of one new fact to another novel find, pure exercises in "academic refinement" of the scholarly picture of the past and the present. Rather, it entails the task of "locating the fields of force" within which colonial cultures and modern nations stand conceived and elaborated, including in transnational ways, and "counterhistories appear imagined and made."[27] This further suggests the salience of carefully considering the assumptions and entities that shore up our worlds. In other words, critical understandings of the complex fabrication, contradictory elaboration, and contingent character of colony and empire and the West and the nation lie at the heart of the contemporary politics of knowledge and culture. Much more than general solutions, I offer these observations as specific orientations set to work in this book in particular contexts and in distinct ways.

Colonial Cultures

Over the past two decades, questions of colony and issues of empire have made a striking appearance on the academic stage. Seminal texts and theoretical shifts have played a conjoint role here. Thus, across these years, if Edward Said's *Orientalism* (1978) put "colonialism into culture" and Johaness Fabian's *Time and the Other* (1982) put "culture into colonialism," so, too, have the broader moves toward process and power reinvigorated critical anthropology and the insurgent terms of subaltern studies helped us to rethink cultural history.[28] At the same time, the changing emphases of literary analyses and cultural criticism and the salient shifts in anthropology and history have not been oblivious to each other. Arguably, in debates on colony and empire today the contending positions rest not only on disciplinary dispositions but equally on theoretical predilections.

Conversing with and talking past each other, the new orientations toward colony and empire have assumed critical and conflicting consequences. Here critiques of literary/cultural analyses that accord extraordinary efficacy to colonial projects have been attended by questionings of anthropological/historical models postulating overarching colonial structures and overriding imperial systems. Such interrogation has highlighted the contradictory and contingent dynamic of empire driven by wide-ranging articulations of class and gender, caste and sexuality, and race and reason. It has foregrounded the contending locations and differing agendas of colonizing agents in the making of colonial cultures and underscored the ambivalent actions and contentious practices of colonized peoples in the shaping of colonial histories, treating the *colonizer* and the *colonized* as possessing unstable boundaries yet enduring as categories. Conversely, exactly these developments have been accompanied by apprehensions of colony and empire as monolithic, homogeneous endeavors, especially in varied domains of postcolonial theory, quite as the programmatic desire to consider the metropole and the margin, the colonizer and the colonized, as parts of conjoint analytical fields has frequently receded into the background in historical/anthropological practice.

But should this be surprising? The theoretical and empirical achievements of recent renderings of colony and empire are themselves bound to palpable tensions and distinct emphases in these arenas. It is critical to keep such distinctions in mind. Rather than seeking immanent resolutions and offering programmatic solutions, the precise plurality and consequent contention in the scholarship on colony and empire, it seems to me, can be a source of strength for asking and addressing new questions and revisiting and rethinking old issues. Far from a bland eclecticism, I point to the possibilities of thinking through analytical tensions, which are productive to ponder.[29]

Consider, for example, two major approaches toward colony and empire in historical writing on South Asia. On one hand, salient scholarship on the eighteenth and early nineteenth centuries in India, which has revised our understandings of this period, primarily predicates questions of colonial cultures on issues of state formation and processes of political economy.[30] On the other hand, in much of the influential, innovative work on Indian pasts that has come to lie at the heart of contemporary postcolonial scholarship the terms of colonial power frequently appear as unassailable propositions of history. In such writing, wider considerations of colonial cultures do not accord well with the presumed principles of imperial power, although once the terms of alien domination are assumed to be in place these analyses have yielded provocative understandings of Indian practices under colonial rule.[31] My sharp comments are far from dismissive, indicating caution toward both, the innate heuristic privilege afforded to continuities in state and society between Indian regimes and colonial rule and the a priori analytical prerogative accorded to ruptures introduced by colonial domination in subcontinental history, while addressing the questions they raise in discussions of meaning and power under empire.[32] Thus, I sieve the containments and conceits of these distinct dispositions through critical filters but also draw on them in order to trace the terms and textures of the colony and postcolony, finding in the former emphases the importance of attending to the specific attributes and limits of colonial processes and learning from the latter arguments the salience of probing the wider stipulations and effects of imperial power.

In taking up such tasks, I engage and extend the historical anthropology of colonial cultures, especially explorations of colonizing peoples at the cusp of ethnography and history—discussions of the representations and practices, the boundaries and contradictions, of imperial agents, settler communities, and evangelizing missionaries in various colonial locations.

First, such scholarship has highlighted the importance of fault lines between different agents of colonialism and diverse agendas of empire. Here the racial mythologies and home-fabricated lifestyles of the colonizers sought to blur the fault lines, but in distinct contexts their routine representations and quotidian practices could also foreground the divisions between different colonialist groups. Second, this corpus has revealed that just as distinct colonial projects often drew on each other's models and metaphors, imbuing them with varied and contrary salience, so, too, could the conflicting interests and contending visions of differentially located imperial agents drive a single colonial project.[33] Finally, such considerations point toward the close connections between the metropole and the margins, underscoring the fact that the impulse of empire and the pulse of the colony were critical to the definition of Western orders, unraveling conjunctions and contentions between efforts to discipline and normalize subject groups at home and attempts to civilize and control subject populations in the colonies.[34] Now I draw on these concerns to address particular procedures. Registering the inevitable distinctions among imperial agents and the shifty fault lines construed between the colonizer and the colonized, I place the burden of colonial histories on the practices and hierarchies detailed by subaltern subjects, articulating empire and modernity.

My efforts to think through contending scholarly orientations toward colonial cultures are crucial to this book. To begin with, tracking contingency and contradiction at the core of colonialism and culture, as the soul and substance of empire and modernity, not merely on empirical registers but in theoretical ways, itself foregrounds a host of critical considerations. These deliberations extend from the salience of revising the received wisdom and pervasive chronologies regarding global flows and hybrid identities, to questioning the dichotomous division of the colonial and the postcolonial, assumed to be in place across time and space, which serves to homogenize history and sanitize politics, and the importance of interrogating commonplace assumptions of the uniform efficacy and unbridled efficiency of colonialism as a stage of history and a modality of power. Such considerations stretch from the significance of rethinking the authoritative genealogies of social-scientific and humanist disciplines, to recognizing the palpable place and spectral presence of the dense profiles and diffuse pasts of empire, and rediscovering the categorical frames and social taxonomies fabricated by the colonial and the modern that have defined the violent prerogatives of race, empire, and nation and shaped the aggressive privileges of culture, reason, and civilization.[35] If the multiply textured histories of colonial subjects militate against their simple predication on any aggrandizing analytic of empire, so, too, is it imperative to think through the entanglements of colonialism and modernity, especially their mutual labors in the past and common productions in the present, and precisely recognize their heterogeneity as projects of power.

Drawing on different understandings of tensions of empire, textures of colonialism, and their modalities of power also allows me to explore particular issues of colonial histories that remain underenunciated in South Asian scholarship. The terms and subjects of evangelical entanglements, containing the interplay between colony and modernity, are salient here. Now contending specters of the missionary as surreptitious agent of empire and generous benefactor to the native, which once dominated historical and anthropological debates, increasingly return to haunt cultural politics and political cultures in India. But in recent years critical considerations have also thought through instrumentalist understandings of power, unraveling key linkages between the cultural forms and political implications of the mission project. Imaginative analyses of tensions of empire, acknowledging the contradictions of evangelical endeavors, have addressed the divisions between the models of colonization of imperial administrators and the images of empire of the missionaries, further highlighting the fact that missionary projections of civilization, modernity, and progress articulated and interrogated imperial power in frontier sites and metropolitan locations. In related moves, other writings have revealed that such processes of contention and contradiction assumed distinct configurations in the shaping of vernacular Christianity in diverse historical contexts.[36] Taken together, I find that these arguments point toward the fabrication of colonial cultures and the fashioning of vernacular faiths as entangled processes and enmeshed procedures, emphases that have wide implications. They underscore the significance of attending to quotidian configurations and negotiations of colonial power in discrete yet overlaying terrains: from heterogeneous questionings of interlocking hierarchies of colonial and indigenous authority to mutual articulations of colonial-modern law and popular-coeval legalities—critical conjunctions between colonialism and modernity in everyday arenas, expressed and enacted and queried and contested by agents and subjects of empire.

In Stitches on Time, I undertake four sets of tasks in order to understand such textures of empire and their interweaving with modernity on the ground. First, I define my considerations of colonial cultures in dialogue with recent critical perspectives on evangelization and empire and Christianity and colonialism, particularly by constructing entangled histories of the convert and the missionary in imperial India. These processes involved specific intersections and contradictions between evangelical projects and imperial agendas in the making of colonial cultures and shared determinations and denials between the evangelists and the converts in the fabrication of a vernacular Christianity. Second, the book traces the meshing of colonial-modern law and popular-coeval legalities, keeping in view both recent developments in legal anthropology and imaginative archival readings within critical histories, while simultaneously tying these considerations to questions of property, power, and the person and issues of gender, caste, and the nation. Third, I explore forms of power and terms of hegemony of colonial cultures within everyday arenas, including their inflections and articulations within practices constitutive of vernacular cultures, the work of subaltern subjects. In this endeavor, my analyses seek to join the quotidian practices surrounding food, marriage, and sexuality with the analytical domains of gender, kinship, and political economy. Finally, the book attends to pervasive mappings of social worlds that bear the imprint of imperial imaginings and modernity's hierarchies, the haunting of the postcolonial by the specter of the colonial at work and play in authoritative disciplines and the redemptive nation. Each of these considerations finds focused discussion in one or more chapters, but the implications of the congeries run throughout the book, entailing the colonial and the modern, the subaltern and the nation.

Nation and History

I have noted that in recent years acute analyses of nation, state, and nationalism have questioned familiar understandings of these categories and entities. Such writings are animated by distinct critical perspectives, yet they also share common antiessentialist sensibilities. While this scholarship has achieved much by treating nations and nationalisms as cultural artifacts and historical processes, it is also worth asking if it is enough, by means of combative antiessentialism, to simply reiterate the constructed nature of nationalisms and demystify nations as projects of power.[37]

Building on his ethnographic explorations of the nation-state, Michael Herzfeld has pointed to widespread analytical dispositions that frame nations and essentialisms as "distant, unreachable enemies."[38] It follows that such orientations refuse the challenge of thinking through the pervasive presence of nations and nationalisms—and of essentialist thought and binary thinking—as simultaneously bound to imperatives of power, determinations of difference, and their restless interplay, formative of social worlds. To take up this challenge is to call into question the scandal of the nation. It is to trace the construal of nations as "imagined communities" and attend to forgings and fabrications of states and nationalisms but equally to track how these very artifacts become forms of feeling, textures of experience, tangled tissues of people's lives and piercing sensibilities of citizens and subjects. It is to query claims of the innate naturalness of nations and nationalisms while recognizing their ontological traits, constitutive heterogeneities, and dispersed anxieties as projects of power. It is to reflect on pathways of anticolonial and subaltern nationalisms and consider quotidian configurations and everyday apprehensions of nations but without reading their distinctions as inherent attributes of insurgent alterity. It is, rather, to register their entailments of power and expressions of difference, reiterating authority and reworking domination—power and difference coming together yet also pulling apart along the weaves and at the seams of social worlds.[39]

Once more, this book takes up such challenges in specific ways. Discussing formations of subaltern nationalism in South Asia, my arguments especially engage critical efforts within subaltern studies. The initiation of this project led to rich explorations of the characteristic idioms of subalterns' diverse countercolonial initiatives. Breaking with nationalist propositions and instrumentalist projections concerning the politics of lower orders, such analyses showed that subaltern endeavors followed a creative process of straddling and subverting the ideas, symbols, and practices that defined dominant nationalism, reconstructing its ideologies as images and icons of their own understandings.

Demonstrating the importance and achievements of these accounts of subaltern history and politics and their distinct articulations of nation and nationalism, Stitches on Time also reads them against the grain of their constitutive assumptions. In particular, I unravel the tangles of postcolonial history, showing how such accounts emphasized the differences embodied by subaltern nationalism but also sieved them through seductive filters—teleological terms—of historical progress, which led to reified representations of subaltern cultures and resistant subalterns, all enacted under the sign of the nation. At the same time, I seek ways of critically rendering subaltern pasts without folding them into endless narratives of national history, exploring nation and nationalism as these were played out in evangelical encounters and legal entanglements in everyday arenas. Rather than allowing the aggressive analytics of the modern nation or the critical conceit of subaltern nationalism to stipulate the terms of historical narratives, I trace the weaving of motifs of nation and nationalism into patterns of gender and kinship, property and conflict. Here the detailed textures of obscure pasts often surprise us with their articulations of power and difference, binding state and community, the nation and the subaltern.

My emphases should themselves suggest that the nation cannot be exorcised from history through the mere expedient of turning our backs on its standardized past and monumental present. In case we still need to be cured of this illusion, it is enough to recall the overwhelming structuring of modern practices of history writing under the sign of the nation, which has distinct consequences for the manner in which the nation is taken for granted in the imagining of pasts and the organization of the discipline. Thus, if *Stitches on Time* seeks alternative terms for narrating nations and nationalisms, registering their authority and alterity and their homogenizing impulses and heterogeneous inflections, it also recognizes the requirements of gritty yet careful imaginings, ever aware of the incestuous couplings of nation and history under regimes of modernity. In this spirit, too, the book attempts to think through the ruses of history and the fetish of the nation.

On one hand, recent writing has explored the incessant complicities between the modern nation and its monumental history. Such critiques underscore critical possibilities, yet they also run the risk of reinstating the split between power and difference, approaching nation and history as undifferentiated projects of totalized force that are then interrogated through pasts and communities seen to embody innate alterity, bracketed and shielded from disciplinary dispositions (chapter 5). On the other hand, the rise to prominence of militant Hindu cultural nationalism in India has produced its own association of the past, the nation, and the modern. Here the homogenization of Hindu history works hand in hand with the fantasies of the Hindu state (chapter 6).

Let me present the dispositions of this book toward the interplay between history and nation in the form of four linked statements. First, to interrogate the homogeneous history and the bigoted nation of militant Hindu imaginings is not to simply cast them as political mistakes and ideological errors to be pointedly overcome by a prescient secular nation and a true disciplinary history, already in place, momentarily displaced, awaiting their resurrection. Instead, it is to enter the struggle over history and nation, tracking the interchange between their Hindu incarnations and liberal avatars and registering their constitutive heterogeneity, which coalesces into implicit exclusion and violent singularity to keep the minority and the subaltern in their places. Second, to query the procedures, pedagogies, and practices of the dominant Indian nation and its authoritative singular past(s) does not mean merely marking these off as essentialist productions of modern power. It means conducting such questioning by staying with and seizing on distinct—subaltern and quotidian, familiar and irregular—articulations of nation and history, not imbuing them with a priori alterity but recognizing the entanglements of the state and the subaltern, the nation and the community, which can yet engender critical difference. Third, this implies caution toward simply celebrating difference whenever it appears, whether construed as an answer to authority or apprehended as a production of power, carefully considering determinations of dominance within formations of difference, the mutual constitution of authority and alterity, from the "national modern" of Nehru's India to the "alternative universalism" of the Hindu Right's Bharat.[40] Finally, such considerations warrant extension to the writing of history, which reveals spillovers, ironies, and containments concerning theory and politics and conception and practice, from the recuperation of key distinctions of subaltern nationalisms by a young historiography itself elaborated under the mark of the nation to the search for nationalist difference ahead of a colonial governmentality that primarily predicates the former on the latter and postcolonial propositions that cast nationalist labors as pale likenesses of colonial productions.[41] My plea, then, is to allow adamant entanglements of power and difference, heterogeneity and singularity, and authority and alterity to cross our vision and burden our sight in critical reflection.

History without Warranty

Is there one rubric that might describe the different tasks undertaken in this book? Aware of the pitfalls of coining catchy terms, novel phrases that become defining buzzwords, some of the spirit and sensibility of Stitches on Time, it seems to me, inheres in its articulation of a history without warranty. The term bears clarification. In speaking of a history without warranty, I am neither demarcating a distinct domain (or discourse) of academic enterprise nor indicating a specific style (or school) of history writing. Rather, history without warranty refers to particular dispositions toward the past and the present, toward social worlds and their critical understandings.

Let us begin with the consideration that for a long time, in scholarly schemes and everyday apprehensions, the earnings and ends of progress in the past and entitlements and expectations of development in the present—as ways of seeing, methods of imagining, modes of feeling, structures of sentiment, and textures of experience—precisely constitute the guarantee of history under modernity. The terms and conditions of this guarantee inhere in, and shore up, the scandals of the West and the nation, the colony and the postcolony, discussed earlier. Engaging a history without warranty is a possible means of calling into question the guarantees of progress under regimes of modernity and thinking through the projections, presuppositions, scandals, and schemes that it produces and sustains.

What are the procedures at stake here? The dispositions of a history without warranty participate in wide, ongoing critical efforts that intimate a "recent ontological shift" in contemporary theory, "the result of a growing propensity to interrogate more carefully those 'entities' presupposed by our typical ways of seeing and doing in the modern world."[42] On one hand, the conceptions, propositions, and outrages queried by a history without warranty are neither cast as simple objects of knowledge nor treated as mere ideological aberrations awaiting their inevitable refinement or irrevocable exorcism at the hands of prescient knowledge(s), whether through the expedient of aggrandizing reason or through the convenience of critiques of ideology. Rather, they are understood as acutely intimating conditions of knowing, entities and coordinates that shore up our worlds and demand critical articulation. On the other hand, such understanding learns yet differs from "antifoundational" perspectives, which are primarily concerned with undoing the "foundations" of knowledge/power and deconstructing the "metaphysics" of power/knowledge, whether intimating stout resistance to murky worlds that have come to pass or insinuating heroic resignation before the terrible truths of today. This is to say that there is a certain shift of "intellectual burden from the preoccupation with what is opposed and deconstructed" to the equally engaging "what must be articulated, cultivated, and affirmed in its wake."[43]

Taken together, the dispositions of a history without warranty are intimately tied to the terms of a "weak ontology," acknowledging at once the contestable, contingent character *and* the unavoidable, necessary nature of "fundamental conceptualizations of self, other, and world."[44] Here there is no simple railing against the universal, no a priori championing of the particular, but close attention to their shared entailment and mutual production, their founding exclusions and constitutive contradictions, and their pervasive presence and urgent claims.[45] This further implies careful consideration of the analytical categories of an academic provenance by bringing them into conjunction with the quotidian configurations of these entities, the demanding terms of everyday worlds, not privileging one or the other but vigilantly unfolding both in view of their critical articulations. Through such procedures of prudent interrogation, affirmation in the wake of interrogation, an affirmation yet open to revision—each an actual enactment and not merely a programmatic pronouncement—a history without warranty opens the possibility of holding a mirror up to the assumptions, categories, and entities at the basis of social worlds, pointing to concatenations of distinct, coeval temporalities and overlapping, heterogeneous histories at the heart of the past and the present.

In this book, my specific elaborations of colonial textures and postcolonial tangles announce both the conceptions and entities that I query and affirm and the ways in which I take up such tasks. This further clarifies the title of the work, for the contingency and urgency implied by *Stitches on Time* are present in my efforts to entwine hermeneutic impulses and critical considerations, interlacing careful questionings of social worlds and their academic apprehensions with intimate accounts of the diversity and distinction of these terrains. To present historical fabrics—colonial textures and postcolonial tangles—in this way is neither to evacuate details by assimilating them into endless analytics of unpicking and unmasking nor to privilege particulars by presenting them as innate embodiments of alterity and difference.

Consider the discussions of evangelical and legal entanglements in the first part of the book. Here the dispositions of a history without warranty and the practice they invite do not recall and rescue a heroic subaltern subject split from power or simply doing its bidding. Rather, my purpose is to trace the manner whereby central Indian subjects of empire, evangelization, state law, and caste authority simultaneously thought through colonial categories *and* vernacular conceptions, tracking the practices through which they translated and recast the stipulations of evangelical Christianity and the terms of colonial law so that they did and undid the hierarchies of village life. This is to attend to the everyday lives of colonial power and evangelical authority, of nationalist persuasions and caste arrangements, and of the ways in which key projections of empire and evangelism, the law and the nation, and state and community were at once instated and made to bear unsanctioned and recalcitrant meanings by subaltern subjects. Such struggles to apprehend and act in the world through authoritative categories, vernacular frames, and their distinct uses, bound to each other, insinuate more than local color and exotic flavor, distant histories and strange stories, and mere exceptions to or simple exemplars of a larger analytical and historical record. Rather, they critically reveal the mapping and molding, the reiteration and reworking, of colonial cultures and vernacular practices, their constitutive contradictions and contentions, formative instability and ambivalence, and emergent distinction and novelty—the tensions and textures of empire and nationalism, history and modernity.

Such engagements bid us to ask what nationalist and radical conceit decrees that under empire the ethical work of Indians, and especially the moral labor of subalterns, consisted of flamboyantly challenging colonial power and native authority when this was rarely the case in practice. Must we simply shift our attention from dramatic moments of subaltern resistance to its everyday expressions? What is at stake in unraveling processes in which support for empire and evangelism was seemingly secured but colonial power and Christian truth were frequently configured in novel ways, in which modern law and village legalities were braided and reshaped in distinct expressions of order and pathology, authority and hierarchy, caste and community, state and subject? What does this tell us about colonial textures? What does this tell us about subaltern pasts?

My emphases query pervasive dichotomies between domination and subversion, power and protest, and collaboration and resistance that rear their restless heads each time they are banished from the scholarly stage, further questioning assertions on behalf of the contradictory and ambivalent subaltern, who in one instance complies with authority and in another challenges power. Such formulations tend to occlude exactly the conditions of power under which meanings are construed, practices are constructed, and action is elaborated. Conversely, I am not in ready compliance with influential positions that hold in place the singular sway of power and its productivity, whether as engendering mimesis or as constitutive of hybridity, the mimetic figure and the hybrid form accessing authority while scrambling power. Although such formulations reveal salient possibilities, they can also elide the burden of difference and distinctions of practice of heterogeneously constituted subjects, often exclusively predicating modalities of discourse and forms of action on the productivity of power.[46] Thus, my arguments imply more than just another effort to restore to the subaltern/native his or her voice/agency while also resisting tendencies that cast power as a totalized terrain, a fetishized force, an abstract aesthetic, or a dystopic totality. Instead, by tracking power and difference as embedded in social relationships, critically produced within particular processes, and entailing and shaping historical subjects, I wish to trace at the same time two inseparable movements: the place of difference within relationships, processes, and strategies of power; and the presence of power in the enactments, practices, and configurations of difference—the demand for critique accompanied by the desire to affirm.

The evangelical and legal entanglements elaborated within this book are measures of these movements, and their characteristic logic and salience are revealed in what Michel de Certeau has called the "details."[47] Such details are often discounted as mere nuance, strictly subordinate to the dramatic divisions instituted by historical knowledge and social science. The problem is not hard to see. If we stick to their distinctions, it is in the very nature of these details that they defy being gathered unto and contained by received schemes of the social sciences, familiar frames of historical understanding, and inherited terms of political thought, variously exceeding and escaping these categories and expectations. Specifically, the distinctions of the tales that are unraveled in this book lie in their singularity and details, produced as a contingent and contradictory amalgam of their protagonists acting on the world as it was given to them and improvising on what they have learned. Here are apprehensions and actions that are not easily digested. Yet these peoples did have their interlocutors, both friends and foes. And it is the specificity and strangeness of their conversations and contentions that make these subjects and stories important. If very few of their pronouncements and practices suit our own tastes and judgments, this is precisely the challenge of reading their apprehensions and actions.[48]

Here the rethinking and acknowledgment of categories and worlds of the past emerge bound to the querying and affirmation of concepts and entities in the present. Indeed, my endeavor is to critically engage the constitutive presumptions of academic apprehensions while attending to their textures and details. I hope that such procedures will be clarified by the wider emphases and particular explorations that this book carries. At the same time, let me turn briefly to a work with considerable import for my articulation of colonial cultures and a history without warranty, Ranajit Guha's influential book on dominance without hegemony in British India.[49] Simply put, there is much to be learned from Guha's discussion of the interplay between colonial power and indigenous authority, especially his insurgent interrogation of historiographical presuppositions. But such learning calls for critical consideration of the formative presuppositions of Guha's arguments and close attention to their tensions and textures.

In this work, Guha seeks to transcend liberal histories of bourgeois provenance, imperial and nationalist, finding that their pervasive projections bestow on colonial power a spurious hegemony. Thus, he not only gestures toward a surpassing of capitalism but shows how the universalizing tendencies of capital reached their limits in the colony, arguing that coercion far outstripped persuasion in the conduct of an authoritarian imperial regime. These apprehensions and their details reveal intriguing possibilities. Yet in making the case Guha equally posits an archetype of bourgeois hegemony, with persuasion outweighing coercion in the composition of its dominance. It is the classic prototype of the hegemonic liberal state representing a revolutionary bourgeoisie and democratic politics in metropolitan Britain, against which is contrasted the hapless instance of dominance without hegemony in colonial India. This casts the principal historical narrative of the subcontinent under colonial rule as one of failure and lack assiduously articulated by the bad faith of an autocratic imperial power and the ingrained limits of an ineffectual indigenous bourgeoisie—each envisioned in the immaculate image of a vigorous democratic culture and vital liberal politics of the West.

Rather than subscribing to the notion of an implacable breach, an innate contradiction, between a democratic regime at home and its endless omissions in the colony—or emphasizing the exceptionalism of imperial governmentality and colonial modernity—my efforts keep in view the mutual constitution and reciprocal labor of modernity and colonialism in the metropole and the margins. In other words, I question teleological projections of colonial pasts and metropolitan histories, the incomplete transitions of the former measured against the fulsome trajectories of the latter, with each shoring up the other. In taking up such tasks, and attentive to Guha's explorations of colonial power and subaltern endeavors, I also shift attention from larger than life protagonists of the historical archive, tracking instead the salient interplay between empire and modernity on the ground, processes enacted by apparently marginal actors—evangelical missionaries, native Christians, local authorities, and subaltern subjects.

Similarly, I recognize the analytical rigor of Guha's considerations of the logical, mutual entailments of domination and subordination driven by contingent, reciprocal implications of coercion and persuasion, collaboration and resistance. Here I especially acknowledge his incisive insight into shared transformations of matrices of power under colonial conditions. At the same time, my emphases also probe the allegorical and overriding cast of Guha's apprehensions of the interleaving and coalescing of British and Indian idioms of authority. Attending to the everyday life of colonial power and quotidian configurations of indigenous authority, I allow their singularity and details to hold a mirror up to familiar understandings of coercion and persuasion, collaboration and resistance, querying settled stipulations of these categories, and tracing their enmeshments not only in an empirical manner but in theoretical ways.[50] All told, my attempt is to place the burden of understanding on critical-affirmative reading and writing, in the esprit of Michel de Certeau, among others, enacting these procedures as inextricably conjoined endeavors, animated and articulated by different perspectives, that can bring each other to crisis. Such are the challenges of a history without warranty coursing through the pathways of this book.

Entangled Pathways

In Stitches on Time, my elaborations of colonial textures and tracings of postcolonial tangles are not marked off one from the other. Rather, they are premised on an active interchange between the archive and the field, fact and interpretation, and reading and writing, productive of critical associations. Along such tracks, chapters 1 through 4 discuss processes of evangelical and legal entanglements. They recall quotidian dramas staged within cultural fields where the nature of caste power and ritual dominance involved the intermeshing of principles of purity and pollution, cultural constructs of kingship, and the symbols and metaphors of colonial governance. On one hand, the enduring verities of colony, nation, state, and empire were refracted through the grids of vernacular cultures, acquiring a novel salience and new meanings in everyday arenas. On the other hand, the colonizers and colonized were bound to each other in myriad ways, so that apparently local dramas straddled and traversed the metropole and the margins, colonial modern law and popular coeval legalities.

In processes of evangelical enmeshment, discussed in chapters 1 and 2, the missionaries could lose the initiative, their endeavors tamed by vernacular understandings. At the same time, the converts' challenge to missionary authority was often construed through distinct work on the idioms of an evangelical Christianity. The missionaries rarely entered the domain of formal institutionalized politics, which was centered on the state in central India. Yet these evangelists often invested in the powerful idioms of Western domination because of the contradictory location of the mission project within colonial cultures of rule. While the converts fashioned their own uses for the arts of enlightenment and signs of civilization initiated by the mission project, the missionaries often unwittingly participated in the creation of a vernacular Christianity. The pooled resources of North American missionaries and central Indian converts underlay the creation of colonial cultures. This involved the institutionalization of myths and traditions, the fabrication of histories and truths, and the simultaneous formation of anthropological objects and the signifying practices of historical subjects.

The contradictory entailments of colonial entanglements are played differently out in chapters 3 and 4, which address the interlacing of colonial state law and popular coeval legalities. These tales are based on records of village disputes that were tried on the lower rungs of the imperial court hierarchy, a rare and rich archive. Here it is by working in the breach between the limited range of facts required by the judgment and the abundance of information offered by the depositions that it becomes possible to trace the interplay between the concerns of ordered state legalities and the processes of signification within village relationships. Far from the simple but insidious hermetic division between unchanging "traditional-folk-popular" disputing processes and dynamic "colonial-modern-state" legal systems, we find in these tales a formidable interplay among everyday norms, familiar desires, and alien legalities. On one hand, not unlike missionary verities, the imaginings and actions of colonial law were refracted and reworked to define new pathologies and fashion novel legalities within the quotidian lives of communities. On the other hand, the already framed notions of crime and emotion, property and the person, within the discourse(s) and practice(s) of modern law were quietly inflected by the recalcitrant presence of native "customs" and "traditions," the unsanctioned practices of subaltern subjects.

These explorations of empire and evangelism, modernity and nation, and the law and the West as these are commonly enacted and uncommonly articulated on the ground by the dominant and the subaltern set the stage for the second part of the book. Taking up contemporary formations of cultural history in South Asia—centering on histories from below and the subaltern studies project—chapter 5 locates this work in a transnational historiographical context. It traces the broad development and changing emphases of these genres and indicates some of the difficulties plaguing histories of subaltern subjects, problems concerning the binds among history, nation, conceptions of culture, and apprehensions of structure that can reify community and tradition. More recently, the writing of history has undergone critical transformations, which is also true of subaltern studies, and the chapter offers explorations of this newer articulation of postcolonial perspectives. Acknowledging the acute impact of current writing on state, nation, history, and modernity within subaltern studies, the discussion points equally toward other explorations of these questions through complementary yet critical filters. Taken together, my effort in this chapter is to critically attend to the details of the subaltern studies endeavor in order to convey a sense of the career and character and the possibilities and predicaments of the project, cultural histories that elaborate South Asian materials and animate wider sets of theoretical concerns.

Chapter 6 also explores cultures of history writing, though now through readings of histories produced by contemporary Hindu nationalists in India, and responses to these pasts from within the discipline of history. Here militant pasts of authoritative imaginings relentlessly draw together peoples and communities into a homogeneous history of the singular Hindu nation, their apocalyptic ends vested in a seamless Hindu state. Through a fantasy of the past and a fetish of the nation, the disavowal of difference proceeds hand in hand with the demonizing of the other, an eternal battle between Hindu/Indian native valor and minority/secular alien monstrosity. Such accounts and their interrogation have wide implications. First, they reveal the intense mutual attractions between the homogenization of history and the fetish of the nation. Second, they highlight the place of the past as an inevitably negotiable and inherently reworked resource. Third, they underscore the inextricably political nature of diverse modes of history writing—of the Left, the Right, and the center. Finally, they emphasize that in histories of the ethnographic persuasion fact and information have to be bound to the less conscious realm of images and icons, the subterranean simulations of popular imaginings.

The figurative schemes that underlie dominant mappings and everyday apprehensions of the world, shaped by invocations of tradition and images of the modern, the several seductions of enchanted spaces and modern places, are further unraveled in chapter 7. Beginning with the question, "Who speaks for Hinduism?" which was debated and discussed at a special forum at the meetings of the American Academy of Religion toward the end of 1998, it probes issues of voice, authority, and authenticity in the representation of other cultures and religions. I suggest that rather than imagining straw figures into existence, as foe or friend, it is important to consider the unsaid and underthought of academic deliberations. Here the figures of an already enchanted tradition and the forms of an always disenchanted modern lie before the privilege of vision and the distinction of voice in reading the past, writing the present, and imagining the future.

COLONIAL TEXTURES

1 Traveling Light

An immaculate conception of the epiphany of travel spells the end of memory. Yet memory strikes back—as empires have done, again and again—to be reunited with travel through a surplus of longing. Consider the following interchange: "Someone said to Socrates that a certain man had grown no better in his travels. 'I should think not,' he said. 'He took himself along with him.' "[1]

Overture

The light and baggage discussed in this chapter belong to the civilizing mission of God and the enlightened modernity of the Savior. Several years ago, Bernard Cohn invoked the image of "missionaries in the rowboat" to remind us of some of the ways in which memory, forgetting, and travel are bound to each other through excesses of longing. In the passage that follows, the anthropologist-historian is primarily questioning a model of anthropology as an ahistorical practice, but the metaphorical charge, critical force, and current implications of his writing extend rather wider. He writes that

> the missionary, the trader, the labor recruiter or the government official arrives with the bible, the mumu, tobacco, steel axes or other items of Western domination on an island whose society and culture are rocking along in the never never land of structural-functionalism [tradition], and with the onslaught of the new, the social structure, values and lifeways of the "happy" natives crumble. The anthropologist follows in the wake of the impacts caused by Western agents of

change, and then tries to recover what might have been. The anthropologist searches for the elders with the richest memories of days gone by, assiduously records their ethnographic texts. . . . The people of anthropologyland, like all God's Children got shoes, got structure.[2]

In tune with this testimony, my discussion of the worlds shaped by missionary travels questions the privilege accorded to Western origins of change—and queries the primacy given to Euro-American agents of transformation—in non-Western arenas. Indeed, by emphasizing the contradictory location of the mission project in the creation of colonial cultures of rule, I also seek to think through the imaginings of a singular West that simultaneously underwrite Eurocentric celebrations of a triumphant modernity and undergird nativist laments for ravaged traditions. The dialectic of enlightenment and empire *negotiated* enduring bonds between colonial power and evangelical knowledge, but the reworking of Western truths through vernacular apprehensions accompanied and interrogated such key complicities.

Second, in keeping with the tenor of *Stitches on Time*, this chapter traces quotidian cartographies defining spaces in time and places in history on the margins of the West. My reference is to mappings that probe the bloated typologies and immense reifications underlying authoritative imaginings of the metropole and the colony. The master languages of reason and race *contracted* lasting links between civilization and the Savior, but the recasting of European idioms through vernacular translations attended and subverted such close connections.

Finally, elaborating and extending the critical spirit of Bernard Cohn and carrying forward the combative concerns of other scholars, this chapter seeks to consider particular connections between the past and the present. I have in mind here possible complicities between the travels of many missionaries (and similar mandarins) and the journeys of certain anthropologists (and other academics). This last move rests on a retreat to Heidelberg, a journey to Germany that has to await the end of the chapter.

In the Shadow of the Cross

J. W. Shank was a pioneer Mennonite missionary who traveled from North America to northern Argentina in the early twentieth century. He was a participant—as witting apprentice and hapless journeyman—in the ceaseless trek of a traveling West. Here is what he wrote on the missionary as a civilizing agent in the *Christian Monitor*: "He opposes slavery, polygamy, cannibalism, and infanticide. He teaches the boys to be honest, sober, and thrifty; the girls to be pure, intelligent, and industrious. He induces the natives to cover their nakedness, to build houses. . . . It is hard to overthrow the long established heathenism, but slowly it yields to the new power and the beginning of civilized society gradually appears. In every country where mission work has been done we find that the first lasting changes for a higher social order began through missionary effort."[3]

The order of immanence and the design of transcendence that shore up this statement are both matters of temporality. This should not be surprising. At least since the Enlightenment, renderings of a universal history cast in the image of an exclusive Western civilization have rested on a critical opposition between sacral (enchanted) societies rooted in myth and ritual on one hand and dynamic (modern) orders grounded in history and reason on the other.[4] Here the many modes of colonial domination—a plethora of ideologies and hegemonies and varieties of epistemic and physical violence—are premised on a temporal privilege, a franchise for the future accorded to Western arts of civilization by the blueprint(s) of a universal history.

The idea that modern journeys shaped by such schemes simply forget the past and the present—or the place and the point—of their departure is disabling fiction. Actually, these trails lead us toward the immense monumentalization of a spectacular memory. A singular mapping of modern Western civilization plots the past and future of other peoples. Such cartographies reveal that beyond the self is more than the other, with the imaginary lines instead unraveling hierarchies of otherness. There is just one road to true modernity, but different peoples have reached its distinct milestones. Furthermore, these varieties of otherness share a similar logic with the severalty of Western selves. The fantasy of the absorption of the other through the rigors of travel is a ruse (and more) for discovering an ever enchanted past of the self—erased from contemporary memory through the disenchantment of the Western world—in the timeless presence of the primitive/native. Therefore, there can be striking symmetry between the evangelical persuasion of those who would convert Hindu heathens to Christianity in the last century and the sa(l)vage mind of those who today fetishize and freeze tradition to prevent the loss of a timeless primitive/native.

In discussing the light and the baggage of the civilizing mission of God and the enlightened modernity of the Savior, I focus here on evangelical enmeshments in central India in the nineteenth and twentieth centuries. The point is simple. If we wish to rethink dominant metageographies— "the set of spatial structures through which people order their knowledge of the world"—as a necessary condition of reconceptualizing colonial cultures and postcolonial pasts, we could do worse than think through the perspectives drawn from the margins.[5] The patterns of evangelical entanglements in the dim and dusty land of Chhattisgarh are no less important than the designs of dominance in the smart and spruce sites of London or Delhi for exploring the widest questions of meaning and power. It follows, too, that margins can invoke other mappings of the world. A story of the hegemonic worlds created by imperious journeys that excludes subordinate knowledges of subject peoples from within its folds runs the risk of reifying the place and power of Western institutions and imaginings—ever incomplete, always questioned, and already displaced in other realms—that it sets out to interrogate. These leitmotifs of margins run through the different movements of this piece.

Musical metaphors apart, this chapter and the one that follows combine critical theoretical concerns of recent explorations of evangelization and empire and crucial aspects of the ethnographic and historical record of Christianity in colonial Chhattisgarh in order to foreground important issues in the study of evangelical encounters. In central India, these entanglements were located at a critical intersection of meaning and power involving two simultaneous and overlapping processes: on one hand, the contradictory engagements of the mission project with colonial cultures of rule; and on the other the complex interleaving of Protestant theology, evangelical beliefs, and practices of missionaries with principles of caste-sect and dynamics of village life in the creation of a vernacular Christianity.[6] The missionaries, indigenous catechists, native congregations, and local populations were protagonists and players in dramas of divergent perceptions, actors and agents in theaters of contending practices.

This chapter and the next tell parts of this story. These tales concern the worlds fashioned by missionary travels and the reworking of these realms in quotidian arenas. Yet what I recall here are not merely disparate accounts chosen at random from the diverse stories on offer in a larger historical and ethnographic record. The fabric of the shared past of evangelical entanglements was woven from the interlacing of various threads, different designs, and many motifs—stitches on time made by evangelical missionaries and Indian converts. My task is to unravel the weave of these threads in order to present something of the tattered texture of empire.[7]

There is another critical agenda here. Just as the separation between enchanted spaces and modern places exercises its seductions in the here and now, long ago it set the agendas for the modern history and contemporary anthropology of South Asia. Indeed, according to a salient suggestion a classic division of academic labor has separated the historical study of colonial rule in South Asia from the anthropological analyses of indigenous society on the subcontinent.[8] *Stitches on Time* joins other critical exercises in the field to subvert the profoundly ideological division between the discrete desires of anthropology and the distinct longings of history while regarding the colonizers and the colonized and the metropole and the margins as part of a mutual terrain, interspersing modernity and empire.

A Journey

Theirs was but a short stay in Nagpur, the capital of the newly created Central Provinces of the British Indian empire, and now a few acquaintances had gathered to bid them farewell.[9] In the summer of 1868, on the morning of an oppressively hot day, with a small membership of the Free Church of Scotland in attendance, Rev. Oscar Lohr and his wife, deep in thought and prayer, arranged their three young children and carefully packed their belongings in specially rigged bullock carts. For the first missionary of the German Evangelical Mission Society, pursuing a path laid by Providence, this was the last leg of a long journey that had begun in Elizabeth, New Jersey (and even earlier in Laehn, Silesia). Oscar Lohr stood before the trail that stretched onward to Raipur, the administrative center of the Chhattisgarh region, and then beyond into the remote wilds of middle India. Would a guiding hand lead the missionary and his family to the heart of Chhattisgarh among the people he had come to serve?

Lohr could barely have known about the lasting effects of this arduous journey, carried out in three bullock carts across the "wilderness" of the central Indian plains (according to the missionary, a wilderness that was made up of relentless heat and overwhelming dust, an abundance of dangerous animals in the forests, and the lack of elementary civilization among the inhabitants). Of course, Lohr knew that he was a "pioneer." The structure of feelings and the forms of evocation that underlay this recognition were shaped by wider understandings of the ongoing colonization of the American West. More specifically, and rather closer to hand, much of Lohr's perception of being a pioneer derived from the express desire of the German Evangelical Mission Society that its first missionary carry out evangelical work among an Indian people who were yet to hear the Word.[10]

Yet the representations of the rigors of a remarkable journey emerged equally plotted onto—indeed, ceaselessly gathered unto and compulsively overlaid by—a grander, more masterly narrative. With the metaphorical figure of the pioneer exercising its many enchantments, Lohr's first-time travel to Chhattisgarh came to articulate tales of missionary vicissitudes in central India, cast much in the manner of similar stories from the Americas and Africa and orchestrated by the New Testament's account(s) of the struggles of the apostles. Were not the carts in which the family Lohr traveled mere "two wheeled conveyances, without springs or seats," with a thick layer of straw providing the sole cushioning and a top fashioned from bamboo matting the only cover? Did not dreadfully slow beasts of burden—

"bullocks capable of travelling at the most about four miles an hour"—pull these carts? Did not the Lohrs have to do their traveling by night, protected from panthers (and bandits, too) by a posse of policemen provided by a friendly British official, spending the day in government rest houses, which sheltered them from the sun and hot winds? Even so, could the Lohr family escape a horrid skin irritation that broke out in boils, "a condition caused both by the heat and the all-pervading dust which in the dry season is often a foot deep on country roads"? Indeed, in a contemporary oral testimony rendered by an Indian luminary of the Mennonite church, the rigors of Lohr's pioneering journey encapsulate the founding of Christianity in central India. Unsurprisingly, at its end the account proclaimed that Lohr was an "Apostle to the down-trodden of Chhattisgarh."[11]

Early Encounters

In the summer of 1868, Rev. Oscar Lohr of the German Evangelical Mission Society initiated mission work in Chhattisgarh, drawn to the region by the Satnamis. Lohr's preliminary inquiries had revealed that the Satnamis were heathens with a difference. They were a monotheistic group whose "creed" was opposed to idolatry and caste.[12] To the missionary, this was a providential connection willed by the Lord. Would it be long before the deliverance of the flock once it witnessed the Savior? Yet the Satnamis did not accept the arrival of the millennium. Declining its destiny, the community proved to be elusive for projects of conversion to Christianity.

The missionaries continued to till the field and to sow the seeds of faith. The halting enterprise of conversion gradually grew through ties of kinship and the prospects of a better life under the paternalist economy of mission stations. Over the next few decades, the missionary enterprise in the region expanded. Missionaries of other denominations—the American and General Conference Mennonites, the Disciples of Christ, the Methodists, and the Pentecostal Bands of the World—joined members of the German Evangelical Mission Society, and there were attempts to work with other communities. The converts continued to perceive missionary injunctions and interpret Christian truths through the filters of vernacular cultures. The "harvest" was never bountiful. The harvest was rather curious. The missionaries tended. The missionaries reaped. If they made headway, they also had to retrace their steps.

In recent years, we have had forceful reminders that Western man did not always command the initiative in processes of cultural encounter.[13] In 1868, Oscar Lohr visited the Satnami guru at his home in Bhandar during the community's "annual festival." The missionary described in detail how he was seated next to the guru and served "refreshments." He made the triumphant revelation to a "great mass" of Satnamis that the real *satyanam* (true name) was Jesus Christ. Elated by the warm welcome, Lohr ventured inadvertently into the realm of ethnographic representations and the pursuit of indigenous meanings, stating that the Satnamis had stroked his beard to show him great honor and affection in their "traditional way."[14]

Missionary hyperbole went on to order the event as one of monumental "historical significance."[15] But was the stroking of Lohr's flowing beard the enactment of a timeless, mysterious, and customary ritual or was it merely a display of Satnami curiosity? Was the serving of refreshments to the missionary by the guru an expression of deference to a *saheb* (white master)? Alternatively, did this extension of hospitality follow a different logic, signifying "the moral and conceptual subordination of the guest to the host?"[16] To the hundreds of Satnamis gathered in Bhandar, had Lohr's visit on the day of *guru puja* (worship of guru) unwittingly signified his acceptance of a subordinate role within the domain of the guru's authority? Three months later, the missionary unknowingly challenged a key principle of faith—the wearing of the sacred thread—within Satnampanth. The curiosity of the Satnamis did not lead to their conversion to Christianity, and hostility now replaced hospitality. The millenarian hopes of Lohr lay in ruins. The Satnamis became wary of the missionary enterprise.[17]

Missionary Idioms and Colonial Cultures

Recall here Bernard Cohn's ironic statement concerning the missionary as the agent of transformation of "traditional" societies. Implicitly, at the very least, it forces us to reflect on the plurality of Western travels for trade and treasure, evangelization and empire, and to think through the interplay between the colonizer and the colonized in the shaping of colonial cultures and evangelical entanglements. In other words, there is no escape from a tired question, which we must ask anew.

What were the connections between missionary endeavors and colonial rule? For a long time, the responses to this question reflected an epistemic breach, a political fault line. Rival caricatures of the evangelist as the crafty agent of empire and the missionary as the philanthropic apostle to the native did compulsive battle with each other. Here polemical positions dominated the debate over the linkages between Christianity and colonialism and evangelization and empire.[18] Jean and John Comaroff have pointed out that this debate remained confined to the issue of "Whose side was the missionary really on?" and by extension "Whose ends did he [or she] serve?" Thus, a complex question became a crude issue of cause and effect.[19]

Ever round the corner, the ghosts of academic debate bear no easy exorcism. It is hardly surprising, therefore, that these phantasms have returned to haunt the terrain of cultural politics and political cultures, especially Hindu nationalism in India today.[20] To think through the constricting conceptions framing discussions of evangelization and empire—and binding rabid projections within contemporary politics of the connections between Christianity and colonialism—it is important to turn to the contradictory enmeshments of the cultural forms and the political implications of the mission project while critically considering instrumentalist understandings of power.

It was not often that evangelical missionaries in central India intervened in the arena conventionally designated as "political," the domain of institutionalized power relations between the colonial state and its subjects. The key links between the mission project and colonialism lay elsewhere. To understand these connections, it is imperative to discard the profoundly disabling presuppositions that the idioms of dominance embedded within colonial cultures of rule stood seamlessly conjoined with the exercise of power through formal apparatuses of empire. In order to explore the myriad ways in which the constitution of colonial power, including missionary participation in these arenas, often exceeded imperial institutions, I suggest three lines of inquiry, presented in broad strokes here.

First, it is important to examine missionary participation in the fashioning of authoritative imperial inscriptions. Historians and theorists of colonial discourse often apprehend the construction of powerful images of the non-Western other by folding them into projections of a uniform Western mentality, which is understood to be the core of singular, conquering, colonial cultures.[21] Instead, there is a need to focus on the ambivalent location of the writings of missionaries within the field of imperial representations.[22] For example, to the missionaries the converts, as Christians, were equals in the "Kingdom of God." At the same time, the missionaries repeatedly emphasized the "satanic travesties" and "savage customs" of these "sons of wilderness."[23] Within these mutually contradictory proposals, the stock metaphors and routine images that structured missionary thought and writing constituted and reinforced—but also questioned and subverted—the powerful cultural idioms of colonial domination.

What, then, of the missionary rhetoric that frequently approved of British rule? Repeatedly, until the 1930s, the missionaries and the *sarkar bahadur* (colonial government), working in tandem, were depicted as the twin bearers of the light of the "Western lamp."[24] However, it must be stressed that such support did not simply insinuate a seamless community of colonial interests made up of metropolitan policymakers, provincial practitioners, local administrators, members of the armed forces, and missionaries. Rather, in order to understand the relation between the Euro-American evangelist and the colonial regime we need to turn to the tangled web of relations among the principles of mission work, the structure of Protestant beliefs, and the policies of British administrators. Put briefly, there seems to have been a linkage between two sets of processes. On one hand, there was the missionaries' stated commitment to the complementarity of church and state, of spiritual and temporal power; on the other, there was the post-Mutiny (the Indian Mutiny occurred in 1857) policy of the British administration, which attempted to effect a separation between religion and politics and served to critically augment imperial power.[25]

Finally, another set of tensions at the heart of missionary endeavors found its way into the wider field of colonial representations and imperial inscriptions. The missionaries invoked the precept of individual self-determination and the spiritual spectacle of the witnessing of Christ to argue for the religious freedom of the convert. At the same time, however, the missionaries regarded these converts as children struggling to grasp rational objective thought.[26] The wards of the mission project had to be guided, nurtured, and controlled within a paternalist enterprise.

Thus, within the interstices of these overlapping and tension-ridden movements, the missionaries participated, wittingly and unwittingly, in the construction of colonial mythologies of racial supremacy, the establishment of structures of paternalist authority, and the reinforcement of the legitimacy of colonial rule. All of this came about without the Euro-American evangelists' formal entry into the institutionalized power relations that centered on the colonial state. It is by looking beyond both the formal apparatuses of empire and a singular colonial discourse that we find the political implications and colonial connections of the mission project.

Home-Cooked Hegemonies

Along with other members of the British and Euro-American population in central India, the missionaries participated in the creation of colonial cultures of rule. These cultures, Ann Stoler has argued, were not direct translations of Western society planted in the colonies but "unique cultural configurations, homespun creations in which European [and North American] food, dress, housing and morality were given new political meanings in the particular social order of colonial rule."[27] Attention to the cultural forms borne and initiated by the mission project allows an exploration of two reciprocal processes.

The missionaries participated in new constructions of "Westernness" embedded in distinct lifestyles within the colonial order. A Mennonite historian has given us a detailed and sensitive description of missionary lifestyles in the late nineteenth century and the early twentieth in Chhattisgarh. Here is a short extract.

> Missionary dwellings . . . were large, one-storey houses of six to eight rooms. . . . The ceilings were high (14–16ft.) with a punkah [fan]. In the pre-electricity days, servants operated these fans. Most of the stations were surrounded with . . . glistening white walls. . . . Missionaries believed that their Western culture demanded a different approach to food, dress and houses from that of their Indian neighbors. . . . Dr. Esch [a Mennonite] reminded his fellow missionaries of their need to adapt to India. "The water isn't cold; the food isn't like American food; the people and especially the servants with whom one has to deal are not honest; the weather isn't pleasant—either too hot, too wet, or too dry." . . . [The missionary household] was operated by Indian servants . . . [who often included] a *pandit* (tutor), a cook, *dhobi* (launderer), *ayah* (nurse), [two or] three *tonga wallahs* (drivers-gardeners), milkman, *chaprassi* (errand boy), *punka wallah*, *kotwal* (watchman), several sweepers, and coolies. Most were paid very nominally. Missionaries . . . ordered canned foods and cereals from Calcutta and beef and pork when obtainable.[28]

All of this involved the conscious creation and fashioning of the boundaries of the "community" of white folk in Chhattisgarh. By emphasizing the similarities in lifestyles between the agents of the empire of Christ, the King of the World, and the imperial servants of Her Majesty, the Queen of England, these boundaries simultaneously served to underplay the internal differences between the Britons and Americans in central India.

At the same time, as an integral part of the evangelical project the missionary was also committed to civilizing converts through the initiation of a set of key practices revolving around building, clothes, writing, and the printed word. To return to the statement quoted earlier in this chapter, J. W. Shank was speaking of the role of the missionary as a civilizing agent across the entire non-Western world, and his vision was profoundly shaped by the writings of fellow missionaries in India. The evangelists in Chhattisgarh, in turn, saw the transformation of the world according to Shank as the doctrine that animated their labors in the wilderness of central India. The aim of these missionaries was to rationalize native peoples through the geometric grid of Western civilization.

We find two simultaneous processes here, a double trajectory, back and forth. On one hand, the missionaries participated in the constitution of distinct lifestyles in the novel context of central India as a measure of the Anglo-European community's distance from local cultures. On the other, the missionaries used many of the same signs of Western culture to civilize the heathen. Arguably, it was within the interstices of these contradictory yet mutual movements that the missionaries constructed a sense of belonging to a Western "community" in India while reinforcing the schemes of power that anchored the familiar symbols and routine signs of the cultural order of imperial rule.

The processes are strikingly illustrated by practices centering on food. These entailed issues of gender embedded within the entire missionary archive, simultaneously binding the contradictions of empire and evangelization in the quotidian key and the fashioning of colonial cultures of rule in everyday arenas. The preparation, preservation, serving, and distribution of food by the wives of missionaries were central to the valorization of the home as the focal site of the civilizing process of the mission project.[29] This complex of practices centering on food brought together the metropole and the colony by serving as a model for the reproduction of gendered Christian personhood(s) among Christian communities in central India, particularly through its clear demarcations of the "private" and the "public."[30] But the relational idiom of food simultaneously drew the boundaries of community of Euro-American folk in central India through distinctions of race and class.

Alimentary divisions elaborated these differences. During ceremonial feasts given by the native converts to celebrate a wedding or the birth of a child, the missionaries presided over the occasion, eating rice and chicken curry, often using their hands, and even sitting and squatting on the floor when chairs were not easily available. The native leaders—schoolteachers, catechists, and (later) pastors—among the Indian converts received tea when visiting the missionary bungalow. A few chosen converts could also be provided their first taste of ice cream by the missionary family, often inviting the mirth of the Western folk since the novel temperature and texture of ice cream so confounded the taste buds of the Indians that they found this delicacy of the sahebs to be much too hot. Yet this is exactly where the lines were most clearly drawn. No Indian convert joined the missionaries for hard-boiled eggs and cucumber sandwiches during Christian family picnics, which were strictly white affairs. At the formidable family table, covered with crisp white linen, there were no calls to an Indian pastor or church elder to break bread with the missionary household, whether the meal was roast chicken and meat loaf or dal (lentils) and rice.[31]

All this went beyond a mere tragedy of manners, where knives and forks were difficult to handle, and native belches stood frowned upon. The distinctions of the civilizing process ran deeper. I am suggesting that we are in the face of a wider creation of home-cooked hegemonies. At work were old recipes and novel ingredients, but also new blueprints and earlier elements. Such home-cooked hegemonies appeared articulated through cooks and cutlets, meats and marmalade, and arts of civilization and signs of enlightenment.

Arts of Civilization, Signs of Enlightenment

The authority of the evangelist was entwined with the Western arts and modern signs at the heart of the mission project. Yet this, too, was not a one-way process, for it was within the matrix of vernacular cultures that the missionaries were fashioned as sahebs.[32] An early map of Bisrampur, the first mission station of the German Evangelical Mission Society, places the missionary's imposing, square bungalow in the center. The other mission buildings are similarly neat square or rectangular structures, further emphasizing the symmetry of missionary designs and the clear demarcation of the area of their command.[33] A church built in 1873, positioned opposite the missionary's house, completes the picture.[34] The geometrical precision of mission buildings and the evangelist's close attention to the spatial organization of work accompanied each other. In September 1870, the missionary Oscar Lohr described the rhythms of his labor in running the mission station at Bisrampur, emphasizing the simultaneity between close attention to time in labor and the spatial organization of work.

> 9.00 A.M.: Lesson in school
> 9.45 A.M.: Breakfast at home
> 10.00 A.M.: Dispensary
> Afterwards till 2.00 P.M.: Lessons in school
> 2.00 P.M.: Lesson in catechism
> 3.00 P.M.: Supervision of work in fields
> 4.00 P.M.: Lunch at home
> 5.00 P.M.: Garden[35]

Clearly, the patterns of mission buildings and the spatial organization of work and discipline articulated the everyday definition and reinforcement of missionary authority, the saheb who owned and regulated the fields, the (occasional) forest, and the (ubiquitous) mission station, all placed with masterly discretion within his well-defined domain.

As part of the evangelical endeavor, the missionary controlled the production of the printed word. This needs to be set in a twinned context: the importance that Protestant evangelism attached to the convert's self-commitment to the Word and the Book as the mark of a true Christian; and apprehensions of the symbolic and substantive power of writing within oral traditions.[36] These overlapping emphases meant that the ability to inscribe and engender print served to underwrite missionary authority.[37]

Moreover, the missionary healed bodies using Western medicine. A number of conversions to Christianity in Chhattisgarh came about when individuals recovered from prolonged illnesses after successful treatment by missionaries.[38] Contemporary accounts suggest that perceptions of the regenerative powers of missionary medicine and Christ the Savior as embodying greater efficacy than the healing powers of Hindu deities and local specialists could prompt these individual conversions. Indeed, the missionaries' knowledge of writing worked together with their power to heal: the primers they produced and the cures they conjured compounded the Euro-American evangelists' command.

The missionary was the model in the moral discourse about Christian decency, bodily shame, and physical modesty. Shirts, trousers, jackets, and solar hats were the insignia of authority of the missionary saheb. Dresses, petticoats, boots, and bonnets configured the symbols of superiority of the missionary *memsaheb*. The saheb and the memsaheb presided over a public performance of propriety, as clothing became a distinctive sign of a vernacular Christianity.[39] The men wore pajamas and shirts. Some had shoes, too. The women donned five-yard saris. Most wore blouses as well. The little girls put on frocks. Generous benefactors usually sent these from across the seas. The little boys were the easiest to cover, including through surplus apparel and accessories. They were usually last in the luck of the draw.

Such sartorial signs of modern times were not always worn but to the Sunday service and the missionary bungalow certainly. At other moments, gestures of decency and modesty were enough. The days of loincloths, *lugdas* (short saris), uncovered breasts, and naked children lay in the past. Here the gains for the converts were at once material and symbolic, and they fashioned a distinctive understanding of missionary authority. A Satnami convert to Christianity when asked to perform a menial village duty replied, "No, I have become a Christian and am one of the Sahibs; I shall do no more *begar* [unremunerated labor]."[40] Indeed, the key social instruments of the mission project had contradictory consequences: the converts came to recognize these arts of civilization as attributes of the power of the missionaries, but they were also to deploy these signs of modernity in their questioning of missionary authority.

A Vernacular Christianity

The converts' refraction of missionary messages through the lens of vernacular understandings, each bound to colonial categories, underlay their uses of Christianity and their interrogation of the evangelists' authority. All of this entailed complex workings of hegemonies and intricate reworkings of power—processes clearly revealed in the manner in which the converts subverted the regulations laid down by the missionaries, the subject of the next chapter. Here, in order to illustrate the interplay between missionary authority and convert visions, I turn to the wresting of the initiative from Western evangelists by a vernacular Christianity played out in intriguing ways in the ideas and practices of native mission workers. The examples come from detailed daybooks of catechists, which record their daily trips to villages and bazaars, disclosing itinerant practices of proselytization followed by native Christian workers and divulging the terms of the Word as it wound its path and worked its way through familiar rhythms of life, labor, and leisure in colonial central India.[41]

In the beginning, the catechists' arguments seem to be little more than endless reiterations of the eternal verities of Christian faith. Yet to attend to the quotidian configurations of the catechists' chronicles is to trace the creation and contention, the distinction and dynamic, and the silence and salience of the colonial writings of a vernacular Christianity. Here the daybooks highlight the transformation of Western worlds through forms of local travel, revealing rearrangements, including alternative articulations, of Christian doctrines themselves closely bound to the catechists' constructions of Hinduism, Islam, and popular religions. To think through the routine details of the catechists' accounts, then, is to track their intimations of disjunctive verities and divergent veracities—of the providence of colony and the provenance of faith, of colonial provisions and vernacular prowess.

Consider how the catechists broached the critical distinction between "religion" and "politics." We have noted that in central India three overlapping, contradictory movements at the level of missionary precepts and practices crucially conjoined the purpose of evangelism and the project of empire. The catechists enacted their labor within this context, but their representations also confounded this structure. I provide a single instance.

> 1 *Friday October 1909.* Ganesh Chhatri a man of education met on the road to Kharora [village]. He was going to Raipur [town] with some other men, as he saw me, he thinking me that I was a Hindu began to talk about the Swadeshi Movement and deeply lamented the Government rule in India on account of many grievances the people have.[42] In reply I said that I am a Christian and have not concern with Swadeshi Movement because it is not carried on right principles, but to be a real Swadeshi [of one's own country/nation] is not bad in itself if there is no cause to complain against the Government. He said that you Christians are not on right lines[—]although you are born in this country, you always side with the rulers. I said it is good for us because the

Government defends us and you also with regard to religious liberty, if there were no Government such as this, you would try to exterminate the name of Christians from this land and Christians do not expect the least help from you. They are considered as an outcast by all who are not Christians, [although] only Christianity teaches the brotherhood of mankind. Your religion is not good for us while Christianity is good to all nations of the world. He said, look at the civil officers and the Missionaries, there is no difference between them, but a vast difference exists between you and them. You are not allowed to have guns nor any other weapons of defence, if a war broke out, you will not be helped by them, they will care for their European brethren whether Missionaries or not but they will not care at all for you. [What was the catechist's response?] I admit the racial difference and the prejudice they have for us. I do not look for an example to them. I know what you mean. I look to the teachings of the Bible. It does teach the brotherhood of mankind and where this is not there is war. Those who profess to be Christians whether rulers or the ruled, if they do not [rise] up to the Word of God and do not practice it daily in their lives, are simply like a sounding vessel making great noise and doing nothing. Their religion is vain, they have learnt only but cannot work up to it. Their religion is false. You need not follow such people. Simply read the Bible from where belief springs. Christ is the example for us.[43]

Conducted on the road, this seesaw argument about colonial rule and its nationalist disputations brings to the fore issues of liberal governance and racist practice. In the first part of the passage, the two protagonists debate the "right principles" of being *swadeshi* and the "right lines" of being Indian. Ganesh Chattri endorses the Swadeshi movement of Indian nationalism and criticizes the inequities of British governance soon after meeting the catechist, apparently because the well-educated and upper-caste man takes the native evangelist to be a Hindu. For his part, the catechist stridently confesses his faith, declaring at once his disagreement with the Swadeshi movement because it is not being conducted on the "right principles," and his agreement with being a "real" swadeshi, or Indian, which implies not opposing the government. Unsurprisingly, Ganesh Chhatri denounces the loyalism of native Christians, announcing that they are not acting on the "right lines": despite the country of their birth, Christians in India ever side with alien rulers.

Our intrepid evangelist is wholly unconvinced by this invocation of the land of one's birth as the ground of one's politics. His response entwines two simultaneous arguments. On one hand, the catechist highlights the unexceptionable principle of religious liberty for all subjects and faiths of the British Indian empire upheld by the "Government," particularly by stressing the terrible fate of Christians at the hands of the Hindus in the absence of such fair rule. On the other hand, collapsing the Word of God and the law of the state, he ineluctably braids religion and politics in order to emphasize the significance of Christianity as essential to "brotherhood of mankind" for the good of all nations.

Clearly, this response cannot satisfy Ganesh Chhatri. The Hindu man reminds the catechist of the force of racial distinctions under British rule, emphasizing the gulf that separates Indian Christians from Christian sahebs. Such difference has left all Indians, including native Christians, unarmed and defenseless: when war comes, European and American Christian superiors, officials and missionaries, will fend for one another, leaving in the lurch their coreligionists, the Indian Christians. With equanimity, the catechist admits the presence of racial discrimination, adding that rather than looking toward such prejudice and its beholders as models he finds his own inspiration in the Bible. For it is precisely the force of the "brotherhood of mankind," enshrined in the Book, that stands in the way of war. With ingenuity, the evangelist combines critical emphases of 1 Corinthians 13:1 with his rendering of the phrase "an empty vessel makes great sound," which also has resonance in Chhattisgarhi. He questions thereby all of those people—official or missionary, ruler or ruled—who profess Christianity but prevent the Word of God from entering their beings. Before the palpable figures of Western authority and beyond the urgent demands of Indian nationalism, the catechist's own faith lies in the Bible and rests on Jesus Christ, the former as the wellspring of belief and the latter as the exemplar of life.

The very literalism of the catechist's faith produced a surplus in relation to politics and religion, the temporal and the sacral, Western governance and Hindu rule, and Christian order and heathen disorder. I have shown elsewhere that bound to an unstable category of the "political" and distinct ruses of "religion" such excess acutely concerned two simultaneous spillovers. First, it scrambled and subverted the official stipulations of the colonial administrator and Euro-American missionary regarding the formal separation of religion and politics, the sacral and the temporal, in the work of empire and the labor of evangelism. Second, it held a mirror up to the hierarchies of heathen disorder and Christian order, and of Western rule and Indian misrule, that ceaselessly circulated in the discourse and practice of the official and the evangelist.[44]

Strikingly, the texts and times of the catechists acquired form and assumed substance in the very regularity and distinctive detail of such encounters—lives and worlds according to the native evangelists. Yet the precise routine and specific singularity of these experiences also registered the mapping and molding of other worlds through discrete terms of local travel—of the Word, the catechist, and the catechist's word. In these journeys, the past and the present ever appear as critical resources, ineluctably negotiated and inevitably reworked, underlying illustrations of tradition and representations of modernity debated and discussed through the retailing of a new faith and the retelling of old stories.

Signs of Science

Let me, then, rehearse two passages from the daybooks that deal with the critical concept metaphors of science and superstition.

> 4 *Saturday* [April 1908] Khaira. Narayan Gaura was engaged in making baskets, when I called on him his wife did not wish that I should interrupt him from work. Anyhow he put some questions regarding his own deity whom he worshipped ie. the Sun. I explained to him that the Sun is only a mass of great fire larger than the earth and man can make it by scientific methods, therefore anything made by man is not superior to man, therefore man will not worship anything that is inferior to him. On hearing so much Narayan heartily engaged himself to smoke opium (madak). 5 present.[45]

> 30 *Thursday* [April 1908] Torenga Parao. Banjaras are a trading class of people. On inquiry I found that they worship Aswari Deo to help them in their trade. They asked me about the Railway construction here also stating that the Railway car could not [be] drive[n] unless some animal was sacrificed to it. There is a red wagon (mail car) in it in which the Deo lives and he helps the motion of the train. I said that you are quite foolish to believe all such things without making inquiry. You see the Sewing Machine, is there any Deo who works in it? No. The Sewing Machine is nothing more than pieces of iron joined together, the intellect of man has made it and if you have intellect enough you can make it also. So is also [the case] with the engine which drives such a long train of wagons, there is nothing in it but coal, fire and water . . . how do you believe that there is an Aswari Deo whom you have not seen at all. There is only one Great God [who] is acknowledged by all and his existence is known to us because He has revealed Himself to man. He does not want your goat for sacrifice, the whole world belongs to Him.[46]

How are we to read these passages? In writing this section, in addition to the daybooks of the catechists, I have before me two essays, Homi Bhabha's celebrated piece "Signs Taken for Wonders" and Gyan Prakash's recent "Science between the Lines."[47] While Bhabha's ruminations begin and end with the strange case of Anand Messeh, "one of the first native catechists in India," Prakash considers the authorization and institution of Western science in colonial India as a matter of interlinear translation. It is not merely as wondrous signs of postcolonial times that these texts reached my desk.

Indeed, there is much that is valuable and suggestive in Bhabha's and Prakash's writing. Recall the debate on the connections between evangelization and empire that was discussed earlier. Bhabha's explorations of the ambivalent presence and agonistic authority of colonial cultural writing, including the productivity of colonial discourse, critically articulate this debate. Similarly, Prakash engages Bhabha's notion of the production of hybridity by means of colonial discourse, provocatively recasting the "second colonization" of India through science and modernity as a process of *translation* and raising interesting questions for the issues under discussion. Both of these writings critically complicate the efficacy of colonial power by tracing the effects and affects on it of hybridity and mimicry, contention and contingency. Yet this is also where the problems in these texts surface: Bhabha and Prakash predicate all the utterances, representations, and enunciations that they examine on colonial discourse and Western science, respectively. Ironically, their very attention to the splitting of cultural writings of colonialism and to fractures of the master script of Western science also turns these dominant discourses into bloated fields of force that orchestrate, overwhelm, calibrate, and contain each action and every enunciation in colonial locations.

So we return to the writings of the catechists: "I explained to him that the Sun is only a mass of great fire larger than the earth and man can make it by scientific methods." And, again, "So is also [the case] with the engine which drives such a long train of wagons, there is nothing in it but coal, fire and water . . . how do you believe that there is an Aswari Deo whom you have not seen at all. There is only one Great God [who] is acknowledged by all and his existence is known to us because He has revealed Himself to man." All of this is more than a matter of litany that turns Bhabha's catechist into both a metonymy of colonial presence and a subversive mask of colonial mimicry. Equally, there is rather more than colonial hybridity at work here. In these passages, science and faith appear as excess and fetish—excess and fetish that cannot be contained by the fetish of form and the aesthetic of power that mark the splitting image of Bhabha's colonial discourse and the ghostly double of Prakash's Western modernity.[48]

In a moment charged with rhetoric and irony, Bhabha closes his essay by asking two questions: "And what of the native discourse? Who can tell?"[49]

But perhaps we can. The catechists' chronicles suggest that the dialectic of empire and evangelism could forge enduring bonds between colonial power and Christian knowledge. But the intense literalism of these narratives—which reworked missionary truths through the force of vernacular translation—equally accompanied and interrogated such key complicities: "And what is the significance of the Bible? Who knows?"[50] But possibly we do. The catechists' writings indicate that the dynamic of reason and faith could establish lasting links between civilization and the Savior, but the dense surplus of these tales—which recast evangelical idioms through procedures of vernacular translation—simultaneously straddled and subverted such close connections.[51] Taken together, these accounts acquired form through vernacular work on the civilizing mission and assumed substance through colonial labor on a vernacular Christianity. Through their terms and agreements, idioms and inscriptions, and lives and stories, these texts seized and stipulated the evangelical encounter, reinstating and rewriting its salience.

Coda

Deploying vernacular idioms and traversing quotidian spaces, the journeys of the people of Chhattisgarh exceeded the designs of the evangelists' travels. They transformed the sojourns of the station-minded missionaries, who imagined their movement as a profound civilizational transformation. This has implications for the ways in which travelers, missionaries, and scholars see their work today. A salvage mentality is blind to asymmetrical movement. It erects fantasies around the forced thrust of a homogenizing civilization, now mourned as the debilitating cost of progress. Hence, we move to Heidelberg.

Heidelberg is a beautiful town with a character all its own. A place of history, it offers a rare site in which to discuss realms of knowledge and deliberate boundaries of disciplines. The marvelously restored Wissenschaftsforum, in the shadow of the Schloss (castle) that dominates the old town, overlooks the "philosopher's way" on the other side of the river Neckar. Here scholars of the sciences and savants of the humanities gather for colloquia and conferences several times a year. The early summer of 1997 was no different. Soon after the end of a workshop on plasticity in the physical sciences, in the third week of June, scholars and students from far and near converged on Heidelberg to deliberate the contours, continuities, and changes in the study of eastern India.

The deliberations on state, society, religion, and ritual in eastern India proceeded according to plan until something happened, at least for me. On the afternoon of the second day of the colloquium, someone presented an entirely professional paper on wall paintings in Soara huts drawn by these *adivasis* (literally, "original inhabitants") to communicate with their ancestors. During the course of the immaculate presentation, I found myself turning to the epiphany of travel, the end of memory, the excess of longing, and their endless enchantments, the motifs that opened this chapter. With the academic now cast as the pioneer and traveler, there was perhaps nothing surprising about my ruminations.

Indeed, the talk on Soara wall paintings began with the invocation of a journey. This journey carried the scholars of the Soara way of life to their destination. Here the evocation of a walk through difficult terrain over five hours to reach the highlanders of Orissa was all too reminiscent of the tropes that ordered Oscar Lohr's first trip through treacherous territory to arrive in the midst of the Satnamis of Chhattisgarh. If the Satnami guru served Lohr with refreshments, our intrepid traveling scholars had to suffer the fate of sharing the local hooch with tribal folk, the liquor quaffed with a small wince but no major qualms, all in the interest of ethnographic research.

The pain evinced at the disappearing "tradition" of wall paintings among the Soaras evoked the paternalism—albeit in a different guise—that we have encountered in the missionary vision and practice in central India. The Soaras, too, were like children, far removed from the rational and objective thought of the West. However, unlike the earlier missionaries' desire to guide, nurture, and control their wards within the confines of a paternalist enterprise, now the scholar's plea was to save the Soaras. More precisely, the ethnologist's call was to protect the tradition of wall paintings of the guileless Soaras from the relentless march of modernity, represented acutely (if ironically) by the presence of Baptist missionaries in the region.

Throughout the presentation, a tiny nod toward the crucial presence of cars and jeeps, planes and helicopters, in the slides of the Soara wall paintings signified the adaptability of the aesthetics of tradition: aesthetics and tradition animated now by the primitive's juvenile sensibility to draw on all objects of wonder from the West. The many ways in which the Soaras at once creatively appropriated and critically reworked these symbols of the power of the Indian state and the significata of domination of local superordinates to (re)draw in their wall paintings the relationship between life and death, the nether world and the domains above, did not enter the scholarly picture.[52]

During the discussion that followed the presentation, a participant brought up the gray landscape of Andrei Tarkovsky's feature film *The Sacrifice*, which is remarkably Lutheran in appearance. In the midst of this decor, at the end of the film a small boy puts a question to his towering father. Not with the wonder of beginnings, nor with the foreboding of ends, but rather with the acceptance of what has come to pass, the child asks, "In the beginning was the Word. Why was that Father?" The conference participant wondered: could the lush landscape of the Soaras not serve as a measure of distance and difference in the work of the Word? Was not the Word carried to southern Orissa by Baptist missionaries reinterpreted and reworked by the Soaras from rather different beginnings and toward different ends? (Or, as John Hutnyk, an anthropologist of a different stripe who was present at the meetings, put it more privately: what prevented the Soaras from smuggling a tiny image of the baby Jesus into their wall paintings?) The answer was a studied and sardonic silence. The circle stood fully drawn.

This circle intimates the presence and place of the timeless primitive/native, insinuating several complicities between the missionaries in Chhattisgarh in 1868 and the scholars of Orissa in 1997. Yet these missionaries and scholars are not mere exceptions. The problem has deep roots. For a long time now, as part of colonial, postcolonial, and Western modernities, apprehensions of the past and the present have endlessly entailed hierarchical oppositions of enchanted spaces and modern places, which split the world while holding it together. Here the telos of modernity, always envisioned exclusively, stands designated and dressed up, staged and rehearsed as history. On one hand, the modern condition rests on enduring imaginings that modernity as history has already happened elsewhere; on the other, the telos of modernity equally dictates that its embodied trajectory as universal history awaits enactment elsewhere, transforming terrain that awaits the touch of inexorable progress and unavoidable development in large doses or small measures. All peoples who seemingly refuse this trajectory, who apparently appear outside it, forsake claims on universal history, which is a matter of sorrow or celebration. Thus, reified representations of a singular modernity engender fear of tragedy or visions of triumph, and laments for ravaged tradition and community do battle with celebrations of modern progress and history.

It is important to carefully question these authoritative, competing conceptions, which valorize an exclusive modernity or glorify romanticized tradition in Western arenas and non-Western theaters. But to do so recognizing that, far from being mere ideological aberrations patiently awaiting their inevitable exorcism through superior knowledge, such schemes have pervasive ontological dimensions.[53] To undertake such steps is to underscore the possibilities of alternative articulations of pasts that question the conceit of a meaning-legislating reason in order to work through contending interpretive rationalities, elaborate plural understandings and interrogate the privileged trajectory of a singular, universal history. *Stitches on Time* articulates such possibilities.

T
his chapter shifts attention from the implications of missionary travel to issues of the mission station. In recent years, writings in historical anthropology have undertaken sustained explorations of colonial cultures. Analyses of Euro-American evangelism in imperial arenas and discussions of vernacular Christianity in colonial terrains have played an important role here. This second installment of the story of the evangelical encounter in middle India extends the emphases of this corpus, elaborating connected critical considerations. It seeks to unravel further textures of empire and modernity by tracing the pattern of quotidian contestations—featuring casts of gender, motifs of nationalism, and designs of governmentality—woven into the warp of a colonial and vernacular Christianity.

First Frames

We have seen that evangelical missionaries reached Chhattisgarh in the 1860s. Bisrampur was a key mission station established by the evangelists of the German Evangelical Mission Society in the region. In Bisrampur, the missionary combined the authority of the pastor and the malguzar, the owner-proprietor of the agricultural land and forest of the mission station. Here the division between the spiritual and temporal domains became blurred and finally lost. From the 1920s on, the missionaries took steps to end the converts' reliance on the economy of the mission station in order to foster a self-dependent congregation infused with the ideas and principles of Christian charity and fraternity. In 1929, they clearly separated the functions of the malguzar and the pastor in Bisrampur. This brought them into conflict with the converts of the mission station.

From the beginnings of the mission project, the central Indian converts had worked on the evangelists' messages through the grids of their own understandings within missionary-sponsored institutions and a colonial agrarian economy. This had shaped a vernacular Christianity, including idioms that interrogated the evangelists' authority. Faced with the steps undertaken by the missionaries in the 1920s, the converts defended the close connections between pastoral authority and landed power, the paternalist ties that had bound them to the evangelists. They turned the honor and chastity of women into an evocative metaphor for order within the community, asserted their self-dependence in a nationalist idiom, and instituted an independent church. Members of the Bisrampur church seized on Christian signs of civilization and elements of missionary rhetoric, working them into their own practice. Construed in a pastoral idiom and shaped by an evangelical governmentality, the converts' challenge to the missionaries featured distinct visions of gender and community, paternalism and freedom.

All of this raises larger questions of "hegemony" and "resistance" that are intimately entwined with wider considerations of colonial cultures. Instead of privileging hegemony and resistance as fully finished strategies, it is crucial to realize that they are at once social processes and the transitory ends of those processes. Rather than reifying resistance and hegemony as immaculate conceptions, it is important to understand their several renderings as historical practice and signifying action in specific arenas, determinate locales. In place of hypostatizing resistance and hegemony as starkly opposed entities, it is critical to recognize that the two mutually entail each other through provisions of power and containments of domination, always uncertain in their effects and already questioned by divergent imaginings.

Such concerns come alive in the tales that follow. Defying the rational assumptions of the missionaries and the progressive impulses of liberal scholars, the converts' assertions of novel forms of freedom from missionary authority could be inextricably bound to their avowal of earlier ties of dependence on the mission project. Exceeding the paternalist desires of colonial administrators and the logical schemes of social scientists, the converts' "mimicry" of the missionary within evangelical entanglements could trip up the civilizing vision of a colonial and checkered modernity in its own disorderliness.

Much more than univocal projects of overriding control, hegemonies—note that I render this critical category in the plural now—often work through saturated signs, dripping with dominance, which find their way into the interstices of subaltern communities. This was also true of the hegemony of the mission project. We are speaking here of blinkers that clouded the converts' vision in different directions and of binds that constrained their practices in several fields. Yet communities of converts also reworked the saturated signs that defined the hegemony of the mission project in everyday arenas. We are now talking about blinkers that left the converts' sight clear along various paths and binds that enabled their actions in diverse areas. It follows that in the remote theater featuring evangelical enmeshments in colonial central India the forms of resistance of the converts were contingent on wider symbolic and substantive schemes of domination but that these contestations and containments of authority further redrew the boundaries of meaning and power in the pasts of imperial entanglements.

These processes were inseparable. We forget at our own peril that power at once constrains and produces. We overlook at our own cost that such containments and productions feed each other. For a long time, fantasies have circulated of unimpaired political visions and unhampered cultural practices of social actors, fabrications that constitute truly "autonomous agents" in wide varieties of contemporary discourses of empowerment and current politics of identity. These imaginings reify human agency by rendering it as the purposive activity of purely individual actors, exorcising the conditions of power that make social action possible. Yet this is not all, for the notion of pure power, holding sway over subjectless processes, is an equally disabling device and possibly even a sign of analytical ennui and ethical exhaustion.[1]

Militating against relentless reifications of agency and increasing inflations of power, my discussion of missionaries and converts in central India also makes an incision on the body of writing on the evangelical encounter in South Asia. Church historians have generated a significant segment of the literature on Christianity in India. Many of these accounts provide us with chronicles of actions and events that are valuable for their detail.[2] Yet these histories also appear limited by some of their central assumptions, including their tendency to project the missionaries along the model of the New Testament accounts of the struggles of the apostles. Moreover, several other forays in the field are guided by similar simplistic suppositions. For example, they implicitly assume that except for the partial persistence of caste the converts to Christianity in India broke with "indigenous" institutions in the immaculate image of modernizing missionaries.[3] Finally, over the past decade critical writing has explored the meanings of *conversion*, discussing the articulation of missionaries, converts, and Christianity with indigenous schemes of rank, honor, caste, and sect in South Asia. Yet most of this work has focused on orthodox churches in South India.[4] Despite the appearance of a few new studies, the evangelical encounter in South Asia in the nineteenth and twentieth centuries remains a relatively neglected area of research.[5]

Beyond South Asia, recent writings on the evangelical encounter in historical anthropology and ethnographic history have reworked this terrain. We might trace two broad emphases here. On one hand, astute analyses of the contradictions at the heart of the mission project, themselves part of broader "tensions of empire," have underscored that models of modernity and projects of progress carried to the colonies by missionaries at once elaborated and questioned colonial power.[6] On the other hand, critical accounts of vernacular renderings of Christianity have put a question mark on the psychological prototype(s) and the Pauline model(s) of conversion to Christianity, also foregrounding the ways in which the "concept of conversion itself retains its commonsense European connotation."[7] Far from turning *conversion* into a privileged and self-contained analytical category, in this scholarship the multiple mediations and expressive experiences of becoming and being Christian are understood as part of a wider logic of the constitution of novel identities and the fashioning of newer verities.[8] Taken together, these intersecting departures raise a variety of questions, from the links between evangelical Christianity and the cultural construction of the colonial order to the converts' reiteration and refashioning of key practices of the mission project, missionary participation in the creation of a vernacular Christianity, and the interplay of the oral and the written in the making of myths, truths, and histories. The history and anthropology of South Asia have incorporated such questions only in fledgling and piecemeal ways.[9]

Not unlike the last chapter, but with somewhat different emphases, the narrative that follows explores a few of these questions. It traces the beginnings of missionary activity, the processes of conversion, the buildup of a paternalistic enterprise, and the drawing of the boundaries and contours of the Christian congregation in Bisrampur. This sets the stage for the next step, in which I unravel the unfolding of conflicts between missionaries and converts in Bisrampur in order to explore the missionary efforts to regulate the community of converts and the converts' reworking of evangelical idioms, nationalist rhetoric, and gendered boundaries in their articulations of a vernacular Christianity. Once more, the specificity of the historical and cultural case reveals the wider implications of evangelical entanglements.

Evangelists and Converts

Oscar Lohr was the pioneer missionary of the German Evangelical Mission Society in central India. The youngest son of a surgeon, Lohr was born in

Laehn, Silesia, on 28 March 1824.[10] He trained for three years as a surgeon at a private clinic and then completed a course in pharmacy at Dorpat University in Russia. He decided to become a missionary while at the university. Close contacts with the Moravian Brethren in Riga strengthened his resolve. In the autumn of 1849, he joined the Gossner Mission Society in Berlin. After six months of training, in March 1850, he was commissioned as a missionary among the Kol adivasis of Chota Nagpur. The young missionary's arrival in Ranchi in July 1850 coincided with the baptism of the first Kol converts. During the next seven years, as his mission work expanded, Lohr learned Hindi and applied his medical knowledge within evangelical endeavors. He also married the widow of a missionary in Ranchi. The proselytizing project proceeded at a fair clip. Lohr later recalled that by 1857 "over five hundred Kols had become Christians, and the number of inquirers grew day by day."[11] However, the fury of the mutiny of 1857 in the North Indian countryside interrupted these well-laid plans.

During the rebellion, the threat of an attack on the mission station by the adivasis of Chota Nagpur forced the missionaries of the Gossner Mission Society to flee to Calcutta. From Calcutta, Lohr and his wife sailed for North America, arriving in Boston in August 1858. In January 1859, Lohr was ordained and installed as a pastor in Elizabeth, New Jersey. Six years later, he provided "the first impulse" for the founding of the German Evangelical Mission Society.[12] Established on 9 March 1865 in New Jersey, the society was based on the principle of interdenominational cooperation in evangelical and mission work abroad, which was in keeping with the pattern of Protestant missionary organizations in North America at the time. Its membership represented six churches, namely, the German Reformed, Dutch Reformed, Evangelical, Lutheran, Moravian Brethren, and German Presbyterian denominations. The aim of the society was "to take the gospel to the heathen, preferably to the Hindus of East India, to the glory of God."[13] It also published a newspaper called *Der Deutsche Missionsfreund*. In October 1867, the society extended a call to Lohr to "begin work among the Santals or some other allied tribe in East India."[14]

Lohr reached Bombay at the end of April 1868. Bearing millenarian hopes and evangelical zeal and equipped with a knowledge of medicine and Hindi, all honed by his earlier experience in Chota Nagpur, the missionary had returned to India with his wife and three young children. A few weeks later, he attended a meeting of missionaries in Bombay where he heard of the Satnamis of Chhattisgarh. Rev. J. G. Cooper of the Free Church of Scotland in Nagpur had made an appeal for a missionary to work among "a peculiar sect of people" in Chhattisgarh. Colonel Balmain, the commissioner of the Chhattisgarh Division, had backed the appeal.

Lohr heard that the Satnamis spoke Hindi and that no missionary had ever worked among them. These were the two conditions laid down by the German Evangelical Mission Society for Lohr's missionary work in India. The Satnamis fit the bill. Lohr traveled to Nagpur and met Reverend Cooper, who informed him that the Satnamis had given up idol worship under the "leadership of an apparently inspired man of their caste." The Scottish Mission could not begin work among these people because of financial constraints. "Recognising the will of the Lord," Lohr decided to begin work in Chhattisgarh. A fortnight later, the missionary and his family were in Raipur, the capital of the Chhattisgarh Division.[15]

In Raipur, Lohr found a patron and ally in Colonel Balmain. In the aftermath of 1857, even as the colonial state sought to maintain its distance from the religions of its subjects, many individual officers took a keen interest in civilizing the heathen through the agency of missionaries and Christianity. Soon the chief commissioner advised Lohr to acquire a site for a mission station, informing him that a large tract of government wasteland comprising 1,544 acres was about to be put up for public auction. This dovetailed neatly with Lohr's plans to begin his work "out in the district right in the middle of these people." Receiving financial help from Colonel Balmain and other Britons in Raipur, Lohr bought the land. He named the place Bisrampur, "the abode of rest."[16]

Within a few months, Lohr's family had moved into a bungalow with outbuildings. The land included a deserted village called Ganeshpur. As part of the *malguzari* (village proprietorship) settlement initiated by the colonial regime in the 1860s, the missionary was registered as the malguzar of Bisrampur and Ganeshpur. From the start, his temporal power came to reside in proprietary rights that extended to the forest in Bisrampur and Ganeshpur. He was also the spiritual head at the mission station.[17]

Lohr baptized his first three converts soon after moving to Bisrampur. A thousand Satnamis had attended the Christmas service of 1868. The following Sunday a larger crowd gathered to witness the baptism of three Satnamis who had moved from Raipur to Bisrampur with the missionary. Lohr asked the Satnamis to remove their *janeu* (sacred thread).[18] These instructions created a furor. The converts, who had gone through the motions of a "public confession of their faith," recanted. The Satnamis launched an offensive.[19] On one hand, until the critical moment of the first baptism the basic principle of Lohr's teaching that a true Satnami had to believe in the "true name" of Jesus Christ was possibly perceived as an elaboration—a variation on the theme—of satnam within the structure of beliefs of the community. On the other hand, the missionary command to the Satnami converts to remove the janeu before baptism challenged a principle of faith within Satnampanth. As we have seen, the Satnamis became cautious regarding the evangelical enterprise, while the primary millenarian desires of Lohr were dashed.[20]

A year later, the missionary baptized four converts: two Satnamis, a Rawat (caste of village graziers), and a Brahman. The two Satnamis had moved with Lohr from Raipur to Bisrampur.[21] The Rawat had been in mission service for two years, and the Brahman had come in "a starving condition" at the time of the famine of 1868 and had then made rapid progress in learning at the training school.[22] The Rawat and the Brahman decided to become Christians after they survived prolonged illnesses that had brought them close to death. The previous chapter noted that the healing powers of missionary medicine and Christ the Savior embodied for some a greater efficacy than did local specialists and indigenous deities. The Lord's miraculous powers of healing continued to figure prominently in missionary accounts as a driving force that compelled people to embrace Christianity. At the same time, the missionary fixed on the "natural" ties of kinship as the basic building block for conversions: "The two Satnamis . . . [as] members of large families . . . will become instruments of the conversion of many of their kinsmen."[23]

The missionary's hopes were well founded. Kinship proved critical to the growth of the Christian congregation at Bisrampur. On 31 December 1871, Lohr wrote: "Today I have again led twelve souls to Jesus through baptism: all of them Satnamis. . . . Among the people baptised were the father and mother of Paulus [one of the two Satnamis who were first to be baptized], one of his sisters and his eight days old suckling baby—also his grand parents, daughter and uncle."[24] By July 1872, twenty-seven adults and seventeen children had been baptized and "the same number" was receiving religious instruction, "ready to embrace Christianity."[25] Almost a third of these converts and enquirers were members of one extended family, that of Anjori Paulus. This was part of a pattern. Their relatives generally followed the early settlers of Bisrampur.[26] The missionaries described the process as the growth of Christianity from within. They felt that the naturalness of ties of kinship acted as a counterweight to the materialist instincts of the converts.

The converts were part of a paternalistic economy that developed around the missionary and the mission station.[27] The mission employed the converts as coolies and servants. A household received four acres of land after it had saved enough to buy a pair of oxen. The converts who completed the course at the training school obtained employment as catechists and teachers in village schools and as scripture readers. The missionaries trained the converts as masons, smiths, and carpenters, most of whom were employed at the mission station. They engaged women converts as servants or employed them as Bible women who would present Christianity to women of other faiths. The converts at Bisrampur received loans at low rates of interest. Unlike other malguzars, the missionary did not exact *begar* (unremunerated labor), but paid the members of the Bisrampur community for labor on public works such as the building and repair of roads and irrigation tanks.[28] As owner-proprietor of Bisrampur and Ganeshpur, the missionary held together the economic system of the mission station.

The missionary was the master of the station. He combined the powers of the malguzar and the pastor, joining the provision of employment and aid to the converts with attempts to control and discipline the life of the congregation. Now, it bears little emphasis that in Protestant ideology marriage is a sacred contract between individuals and the monogamous household is the basic unit for the conduct of a Christian life. In order for civilization to flourish in the colony, the Holy Family of the Christian cosmos had to triumph over the moral murk, sloth, and chaos of the heathen world. The early evangelists had to direct their efforts against everyday customs and practices, the snares and traps of Satan, in the "primitive" terrain of Chhattisgarh.

Together with the catechists and schoolteachers, who comprised the "native leaders" of the Bisrampur converts, Oscar Lohr drew up a set of regulations meant to order the life of the congregation, the *Bisrampur Kalasiya ki Vishesh Agyayen* (Special Rules of the Congregation at Bisrampur).[29] These rules were printed on paper but were set on stone.[30] The regulations and institutions governing the community show marked continuities with the rules of caste and sect, particularly when viewed through the grids of Chhattisgarh kinship. The converts could only marry other Christians. To join the church was to become a member of another endogamous group. A marriage with a non-Christian was valid only if he or she had joined the church. Similarly, a wedding feast to which the extended kin group and members of the community were invited was critical to the sanctity of the marriage in the eyes of the converts. The feast signified the incorporation of a new member into a bounded group.[31] Of course, the evangelists' concern with monogamy and fear of adultery meant that they forbade the converts *churi* (secondary marriages).[32] Yet members of the Bisrampur congregation exercised considerable initiative in following prior practices and flouting missionary authority.[33] The institution of marriage among the community of converts drew on the principles of caste and sect in village life.

The concerns of purity and pollution informed the practices of the church. The members of the Bisrampur congregation had to avoid carrion because if eaten "Hindus and Satnamis look[ed] down upon us," and they were forbidden liquor, opium, and marijuana.[34] Although the missionary sponsored the writing and printing of the "Special Rules of the Bisrampur Church," the regulations it embodied did not mark the rupture with the past that was his chief desire. Indeed, the text itself suggests the contours of a community in which the rules governing its life in the past had been reworked, recast, and rearranged. To be sure, there was subversion of these rules and regulations, the transgressions punished through excommunication, which had its own particular twist, so that the offenders were considered as "outcaste" from the church.[35]

Not only purity and pollution but aspects of ritual kingship were critical for the constitution of the Christian congregations in central India.[36] To the converts at the mission station, viewing the nature of authority through grids that emphasized the indissoluble links between ritual and power, the missionary as the pastor and proprietor of the village could appear as *raja log*, a "kingly person," a dominant but benevolent figure.[37] Ultimately, the organization of the Bisrampur congregation was premised on the institutions of village life in colonial Chhattisgarh. Here the church council with its *prachin* (elders) paralleled the *panchayat* (caste adjudicatory body) with its *sayan* (wise men). It settled disputes and regulated the life of the congregation and its "outcaste" offenders.[38] In the face of threats to familiar norms, expectations, institutions, and practices, the church council of Bisrampur could also challenge the missionaries.

Paternalist Patterns

In the early 1930s, the well-oiled paternalist machine of Bisrampur ground to a halt. The conflict between the missionaries and the congregation had its apparent beginnings in a case of adultery. The villagers claimed that Boas Purti had had an adulterous relationship with one Rebecca. Employed as the *lambardar* or *mukhtiyar* (man in charge) of the malguzari by the mission, Boas Purti was an "outsider" who did not originally belong to Bisrampur. Rebecca was a "virgin Christian girl" of the mission station. Fat with money and flush with pride, Boas Purti had ensnared Rebecca in his "net of love." Rebecca had a baby. The child bore a resemblance to Boas Purti. The inhabitants of Bisrampur were incensed.

A meeting of the church council of Bisrampur in July 1933 found Boas Purti guilty. Only the missionary J. C. Koenig was not convinced of Purti's guilt. At the next meeting, the congregation forced the missionary to declare that Boas Purti was "out of caste."[39] Purti appealed to the India Mission District (IMD).[40] In August 1933, members of the district committee reached their decision. Boas was not out of caste. The church council had been partial and unjust. The angry members of the Bisrampur church fell out with the missionaries.[41] They set up an independent congregation and sent letters and reports to the Home Board of the mission in St. Louis. A little later they appointed an honorary pastor, who conducted Sunday services, baptized new members, and managed congregational matters.[42] The missionaries responded by locking the church at Ganeshpur, confiscating the treasury, resorting to punitive measures against infringements of missionary property, and closing avenues of employment within the mission station.[43] They repudiated all paternalist ties. We need to unravel the different threads of this Christian village drama.

I have noted that Bisrampur had developed as a paternalist institution. In a survey of Bisrampur conducted in 1925, the missionary Reverend Miller from Dhamtari sought to determine the economic status of people before they became Christians.[44] He divided the people of Bisrampur into three general categories: total charity cases, those able to earn their livelihood, and those able to provide for their livelihood. Miller's conclusion was that before their conversion to Christianity about 40 percent of the people had been total charity cases, 50 percent had been semi-independent, and 10 percent had an independent livelihood.[45] By 1926, according to Miller, there had been "a decided improvement" in the economic status of the Christian community at Bisrampur. Now only a few widows were charity cases; 23 percent (42 out of 183 families) were semi-independent; and 76 percent, who received an income of over ten rupees per month, were independent.[46] The mission station was the pivot of the local economy of Bisrampur. The missionary stood at center stage within the normative economy of the converts. Over time, the mission had built and dominated the economy of Bisrampur.[47]

At the same time, the missionaries had sought to discipline the lives of the converts, interventions geared to control the everyday matters of the congregation. In the pioneer mission station, the work of the evangelists appeared as an inexorable project of education, resembling the conduct of parents toward their children. The missionaries had projected themselves along the model of New Testament accounts of the struggles of the apostles.[48] Though equal in the Kingdom of God, the converts were childlike, struggling to grasp rational, objective thought. They had to be nurtured, guided, and controlled within the evangelical enterprise.

The converts and the missionaries were bound together by complex ties of dependence and control. In Bisrampur, the missionary occupied the figure of the ma-bap, the paternalistic master. The work of E. P. Thompson (among others) has reminded us that paternalism has at least two sides. The members of the Bisrampur congregation had their own vision of paternalistic ties. Their deference to the missionary was partly in the interest of self-preservation and partly the critical extraction of whatever was up for grabs. What is more, this deference emerged distilled through distinct filters. As they worked on the inextricable connections between ritual and power in quotidian arenas, to the inhabitants of the mission station the missionary's simultaneous command of pastoral authority and proprietary power turned him into a figure who joined in himself attributes of the saheb and a little king, in this case of Bisrampur. The converts of Bisrampur launched their critical initiative in the midst of the evangelists' efforts to dismantle paternalistic patterns and dependent ties in the mission station, which also threw a spanner into the works of the political sociology of the congregation.

Dismantling Dependence

The separation between spiritual and temporal domains organizes Protestant theology. However, in Bisrampur for almost sixty years the missionary had been pastor and malguzar, the master of the mission station. The distinction between the two domains had been lost in the evangelists' practice.[49] Further, as we have noted, this blurring of the spiritual and temporal domains fit well with the political sociology of the converts, which rested on close connections between ritual and power. An initiative in 1929 sought to reconstitute the two spheres. The missionary came to look after temporal matters, the realm of malguzari, in Bisrampur, while an Indian pastor took care of the spiritual life of the congregation. The evangelists wanted to make the congregation self-dependent. Now the members of the Bisrampur congregation were to pay for their pastor, maintain their church building, contribute to the construction of roads, and donate for Christian causes.[50]

In keeping with the pattern throughout most of Chhattisgarh, by the 1920s agriculture had reached the margins of cultivation in Bisrampur.[51] Within the mission station, the closing of avenues of employment compounded the problems of the lack of land. Functioning within the matrices of a paternalistic system, to the people of Bisrampur employment, land, and a regular cash flow lay at the heart of the missionary endeavor. This was also true of other "responsibilities" fulfilled by the mission project, from the supply of food during famines to the distribution of foreign goods, the construction of roads and houses, and the place of the missionary as the saheb who dispensed benevolence and controlled the congregation. Thus, the formal dismantling of paternalistic ties was a blow to the converts' normative economy, their sense of the proper functions and obligations of different members of the Bisrampur community, including the role of the missionary as raja log.

A number of specific measures undertaken by the missionaries aided the process. Faced with a situation of paucity of land and lack of employment, the members of the Bisrampur church felt that the evangelists were increasingly ignoring local people in making appointments to positions within the mission station.[52] Rather, "outsiders" to the American Evangelical Mission were receiving appointments as mission servants. Here it is significant that Boas Purti was the lambardar or *mukhtiyar* of the village of Bisrampur. Purti had come to Chhattisgarh from the Ranchi region in Bihar.[53] As lambardar/mukhtiyar, he was entrusted with the collection of payments from tenants and the collation of accounts of the lands of Bisrampur and Ganeshpur. He wielded considerable power, encoded within the malguzari system, over the tenants at the mission station.[54] In choosing Purti as the mukhtiyar, the missionary had appointed an "outsider" to an important position. But this was not all. Even after Purti's adulterous entanglement with Rebecca had become common knowledge, the missionary Koenig had defended him.

Second, in the eyes of the converts the missionaries had become increasingly inflexible with regard to use of the forest owned by the mission station. On one hand, in the annual reports of missionaries the forest appears as "a constant source of irritation" that could provide a missionary with his "most unpleasant experiences" in India:[55] "During the rainy season and the cold season the people graze their cattle and steal the grass, and during the hot season they steal the wood."[56] On the other hand, the villagers of Bisrampur and Ganeshpur had claimed that in grazing their cattle and collecting wood and grass from the forest for everyday use they were exercising their customary rights. Over the years, the missionaries had taken various preventive measures, but they had been unsuccessful. In the 1920s, the missionaries' tightened control of the forest accompanied their separation of the temporal and spiritual domains.[57] The evangelists resorted to prosecution. The converts brought into play their "customary" practices to criticize the highhandedness of the missionary: "Women are habituated to take wood for fuel from the Machinery Forest. The Machionery Saheb called the police for the inquiries to take the objections."[58]

Finally, in the past the missionary as malguzar had financed public works at the mission station, providing employment to the villagers of Bisrampur and Ganeshpur. Conversely, in other villages when the malguzar undertook "public work" it involved conscript labor or begar.[59] Here the missionary insistence that the Bisrampur congregation contribute to public works ran counter to the converts' normative economy. Such contributions appeared to them as a modified form of *bhet-begar*, free labor rendered under the pressure of "custom"—codified by the British administration—to the malguzar. Making this worse was the perception of the people of Bisrampur that the missionary was withholding "foreign gifts being sent for them."[60] In its efforts to foster a self-dependent congregation and separate temporal and congregational matters, the mission project invited "the opprobium in which the Malguzari system is held." The "outsider" employees in Bisrampur were termed illegitimate intruders, and the missionaries were fashioned as oppressive masters.[61]

Gender and Freedom: Virgin Sisters and Oppressive Masters

The trouble had been brewing for some time. In early 1932, "there was found fastened to the Imli [tamarind] tree near the [missionary] Bungalow a notice about *balwa* and *swatantrata*, revolution and freedom, the trend of which was to work for the removal of all employees from outside."[62] A little later the villagers came to hear about the "adulterous" relationship between Kenshwar Babu, an employee from another mission station, and Naomi, the daughter of Buth Burwha of Bisrampur. The church council had found Kenshwar guilty, leading to his excommunication and subsequent dismissal from mission service.[63] Less than a year later, Boas Purti appeared to follow Kenshwar in having an affair with a young woman of Bisrampur.

Unsurprisingly, the incident involving Boas Purti was projected as part of a larger pattern: "In American Mission Station Bisrampur there are servants as doctors, masters and clerks who have been called from other parts of India (outside mission) by your missionaries. Many of these have spoiled the character of our young Christian ladies."[64] Boas Purti had used his riches, accumulated in Bisrampur, and "spread a net of love to catch a Christian virgin girl, Rebecca. He enjoyed with her for many days. And when the girl had a womb [became pregnant] the secret was disclosed. At last the girl born a child."[65] Boas Purti was one among several outsiders who had "violated the honor of Christian sisters."[66] It was the missionary who appointed such outsiders as mission servants, employees who because of the "high salaries and favor of these missionaries had become proud." The missionaries "turned a blind eye" to the excesses of these outsiders. Indeed, they tried to hide their sins. As "the agent of [the missionary] Rev. J. Gass," Boas Purti confirmed the complicity between the missionaries and outsiders.[67]

From the late 1920s on, the growth of an independent church was an important part of missionary rhetoric in central India, underlying evangelical endeavors to separate the spiritual and temporal domains and foster a self-dependent congregation.[68] The converts of Bisrampur seized on the idea and worked it into their practice. Their enterprise involved playing with balwa and swatantrata. These twin signs were important elements in contemporary political-cultural discourse, particularly during the Civil Disobedience movement of 1929–32. The precise polysemy and polyphony of balwa and swatantrata meant that diverse social groups appropriated and deployed these critical figures in different ways.[69] Members of the Bisrampur congregation elaborated their vision of independence by rallying around the call for revolution and freedom to rid the mission station of outside employees.

All too frequently, in academic apprehensions and commonplace conceptions, state/nation and community/local are marked off, the one set from the other copula. Against this persistent tendency, Michael Herzfeld has pointed toward

> the essential homology between several levels of collective identity—village, ethnic group, district, nation. What goes for the family home also goes, at least by metaphorical extension, for the national territory. . . . For example, in the Rhodian village that I have named "Pefko" . . . a man who had raped a young woman was said to have "entered her father's house"—a metaphor that clearly illustrates the saliency as a component in the definition of social relations. In Pefko, again, the 1974 invasion of Cyprus was likened to a forcible entry into one's "house." . . . The Greek's conventional distrust of kseni (outsiders) from other villages translates easily into a comparable stance toward kseni in the sense of "foreigners." . . . the moral boundary between insiders and outsiders thus seems to be formally similar at several quite distinct levels of social identity.[70]

The actions of the members of the Bisrampur congregation were in tune with this wider logic, setting to work the homology that Herzfeld speaks of but in ways and through means that extended well beyond the initial formalism of his important observation.

The Bisrampur converts invoked the threat to the honor and chastity of the women of the community to question the presence and practices of the outsiders.[71] As we have noted, the Christian congregation of Bisrampur had drawn on principles of caste and sect and institutions of village life in Chhattisgarh in constituting itself as a community. Moreover, the converts were disallowed relationships outside the legitimate domain of Christian marriage. They had faced the ire of missionaries and excommunication by the church council for forming liaisons along the lines of churi.[72] Now members of the Bisrampur congregation brought together two distinct but overlapping emphases to sketch their understanding of the boundaries of gender and community.

On one hand, the converts underlined the need for maintenance of the boundaries of the community that underlay the rules of caste and sect. On the other, they brought to the fore the evangelical emphasis on adultery as sin to protest the intrusion of outsiders. Thus, the honor of the women of Bisrampur at once became an evocative metaphor for order within the community and a symbol that constructed its boundary. The Christian women of the mission station needed protection from violent acts of sexual transgression. The violation of their sexuality was a violation of the community's honor. Such transgressions by outsiders breached the boundary and disrupted the order of the community. Boas Purti's misdemeanor with Rebecca encapsulated the threat from the outsider and evoked disruption and disorder within Bisrampur.

The Bisrampur congregation's criticism of outsiders accompanied their questioning of the missionaries. The converts underscored missionary duplicity. At the meeting of the church council at which the case of Boas Purti and Rebecca was discussed, "Rev. Koenig knew the real fact yet he wanted to hide his [Purti's] fault."[73] At the biannual meeting of the church council, too, it was only under "the compulsion of the assemblage" that the missionary announced that "Boas was outcasted."[74] Yet Reverend Koenig also tricked the congregation. Before his announcement regarding the excommunication of Purti, he asked the assembled members of the church council if they would abide by the decision of the India Mission District. The council agreed. The missionary hurriedly convened a meeting of the IMD, less than a month later, in early August of 1933.

If Reverend Koenig did not wait until the middle of November, when the convention of the IMD that decided such cases met, it was also at the IMD meeting convened in August that the missionaries "solved the case and found Boas to be not guilty" without bothering to consult the church council. Even as the members of the church council waited outside on the "verandah" of the missionary bungalow, the meeting took place inside the home, surreptitiously arriving at a decision. The council further argued that the missionary members of the IMD, aware of their guilt and complicity, tried to run to a car at the back of the bungalow.[75] When asked for an explanation by the Bisrampur congregation, the president of the India Mission District, the missionary M. P. Davis, unwittingly confirmed the villainy of the missionary Koenig. According to the converts, M. P. Davis's speech "told us that Rev. J. C. Koenig forcibly made them [members of the IMD committee] to write the three sentences mentioned above." It was in keeping with his treachery and deceit that "Rev. J. C. Koenig reminded us [of] our promise and asked us to obey and to accept the justice of the IMD Committee."[76]

The converts drew a twofold distinction, projecting an unsullied church in confrontation with duplicitous outsiders and missionaries. Nothing less than "truth" was at issue in this struggle, a face-off inherently inflected with power. Here the "Church being weak could not fight with them [the missionaries] for truth."[77] On one hand, the converts offered the Home Board of the American Evangelical Mission in St. Louis written proof of the excesses of outsiders and missionary complicity, stating: "If you may like you may look at our minute book." This established both the legality and the truth behind their position. On the other hand, the missionaries had transgressed their authority, leaving them with little legitimacy. The rebels of Bisrampur argued that the judgment of the IMD "tells us that Boas cannot be outcasted for ever in any way. Now he [has] got a divine route from these members to enter in the heaven." It is hardly surprising that the decision was "full of insult [to] the Church Council. No civilised person will write or say like this."[78] The converts conducted their questioning of the missionaries in an evangelical idiom shaped by the reason and legality of pastoral power.[79]

The evangelists were construed as tyrannical masters. First, they had appeared "innocent and simple and faithful, but we the poor are being crushed by them. They have come to guide us in our lives' journey, to help the poor in spirit and body. They think quite opposite of it. By their doings it seems they have come to rule over us."[80] Second, the simplicity of the people of Bisrampur made the missionaries seem condescending: "They think, these people of Chhattisgarh are ignorant and mad. What can they do? They eat opium and do not know anything. These missionaries want to be apart from us."[81] Finally, it was the un-Christian character and bad behavior of the missionaries that had tainted Christianity, preventing the spread of the faith: "These missionaries come to us in the name of God and faith and dominate us. They are oppressive and irreligious because of which the neighboring Hindus reject us. This prevents a spread of the faith and we get a bad name and are criticised."[82] The twin traits of duplicity and domination distanced the missionaries from the people, setting them apart from the church, which was poor and concerned about its spiritual well-being and the spread of Christianity.

This oppressive and overwhelming present contrasted with a benevolent and benign past. The converts of Bisrampur invoked the kindly missionaries and the paternalist ties of earlier days. In the past, the converts were ignorant; they had lived in "darkness." But the earlier evangelists had "showed us the light of salvation and saved us from destruction." Therefore, the converts fondly remembered their "old masters (missionaries) who lived here fifteen years before."[83] Now all of this had changed. Looking into the situation at the Bisrampur station in the early 1930s, one missionary observed that, according to the converts, "there is no love left in the present missionaries."[84] The present no longer afforded a return to the past.

Independent Initiatives

Members of the Bisrampur congregation had fired their first salvo in the name of revolution and freedom. They worked on their independence by separating themselves from the missionaries and the India Mission District. After the converts had rejected the decision of the IMD committee, the first meeting of the church council took place in the Ganeshpur church on 10 August 1933.[85] The new mandli (congregation) appointed a new committee, with Premdas Master as president, Premprakash Tailor as secretary, and ten other members. The committee put forward eight resolutions, all of which were accepted by the congregation.

First, the Immanuel mandli separated itself from the IMD. Second, objecting to the rules and regulations of the IMD, the congregation became self-dependent. Third, it was resolved that the pastor sent by the IMD should be dismissed after a month's notice. Fourth, a person from another congregation could no longer be selected as the pastor of the Immanuel mandli. Fifth, the women of the congregation were not to work at the house of a person from another mandli. Sixth, if the women did such work they were to be excommunicated and made to pay a fine of ten rupees. Seventh, the Christians of Bisrampur who earlier had been turned out of the church because they had engaged in the "occupation of bones and skin" were to be reaccepted within the congregation. However, if they took up the trade in animal hides or ate carrion again they were to be punished heavily under new regulations. Eighth, the twelve prachins (elders) or members of the Immanuel congregation were to perform "all work of this Mandli except marriage matter."[86] These resolutions at the meeting in the Ganeshpur church sketched the main features of the independence of the new Immanuel congregation.

The letters that the new congregation sent to the Home Board in St. Louis clearly stated its desire for independence: "We request you to cut the name of our Church from your A. E. [American Evangelical] Mission and give us a transfer certificate that we may join in any other Mission. And if you please, you may have other inhabitants for the spot."[87] Even as it left the path for reconciliation open, leaders of the congregation were not making an empty threat to the Home Board.[88] The idea of an autonomous congregation and a church independent of missionary authority had become an important part of this venture. In January 1934, the "official" pastor of Bisrampur, appointed by the IMD, called a meeting of all members of the mission station. The meeting was disrupted by the "opposition group," namely, the members of the rebel Immanuel congregation. The missionary warned them that the IMD would take over the running of the church. This statement was greeted with joy: "The leaders of the opposition seemed to revel in the fact that the meeting could not continue." A few of the members called out, "Now we have no congregation, no constitution, and no pastor."[89]

The rebel converts from Bisrampur sought linkages outside the American Evangelical Mission. They had limited options. The close connections among the different missionary organizations in the Chhattisgarh region meant that members of the independent Immanuel congregation could not join another mission through the simple expedient of walking out of the I M D.[90] In an optimistic if mixed-up manner, they had shown their understanding of the situation when they asked the Home Board of the American Evangelical Mission in St. Louis for a transfer certificate. This was a bid to enable the independent congregation to join another missionary organization in the region. Of course, the certificate was not forthcoming.

Could these converts have returned to the fold of caste and sect? Nearly 97 percent of the people of Bisrampur had belonged to the Satnami caste-sect before their conversion to Christianity, but their relationship with the Satnamis was riddled with tension. On one hand, the people of Bisrampur considered themselves superior to the Satnamis. After an association of sixty years with the sahebs and the mission, to rejoin Satnampanth would have been to return to the "darkness" of the past, a condition from which the Immanuel congregation firmly believed it had extricated itself. On the other hand, during the 1920s and 1930s the Satnamis themselves were in the midst of reform initiatives sponsored by an organization called the Satnami Mahasabha, which drew new boundaries for the community through work on nationalist Hindu rhetoric and idioms of colonial governance.[91] The leadership of Satnampanth wished to maintain its distance from the "outcaste" Satnami converts to Christianity, who were doubly tainted with the stigma of engaging in the "hide and bone business," the trade in animal hides, and the eating of carrion. Clearly, a return to Satnampanth was not the way forward for the Immanuel mandli.

Rather, the rebel converts of Bisrampur turned to the local chapter of the Arya Samaj, an organization of Hindu revival and reform active in the Chhattisgarh region. An agitated evangelist wrote from the mission station, "I heard that the leaders of the group wrote to the Arya Samaj. . . . Brother Gass received a note from the police that a large number of Christians intended to turn to Arya Samaj and asking what the police should do about it."[92] To the independent Immanuel congregation, the Hindu proselytizing venture of the Arya Samaj offered a way to sever its connections with Christianity. Its members could then reenter the Hindu social order. But there was one condition. The members of the mandli had to quit the hide and bone business.[93]

The hide and bone business was at once an important resource and a significant strategy within the household economy of several families of Bisrampur and Ganeshpur. The people of Bisrampur continued to be marked by the stigma of the death pollution of the sacred cow because of their untouchable origins. They also stood outside the Hindu social order because of their conversion to Christianity. In this broader context, the proximity of Bisrampur to a *buchadkhana* (slaughterhouse) facilitated the trade in skins and bones of cattle conducted by many families at the mission station. It followed that such families also ate the flesh of the dead animals.

In 1929, the Bisrampur congregation had submitted a constitution to the India Mission District. It consisted of rules to regulate various matters pertaining to the congregation. According to the constitution, "members of the Church engaging in the hide and bone business" were to face excommunication.[94] A missionary noted that although the Satnamis had excommunicated members of their community who engaged in the bone and hide business many of the converts at Bisrampur persisted with the practice.[95] There were several efforts to put the relevant clause into effect. The official pastor of the Bisrampur congregation wrote that "In spite of great difficulties, the Church Council is trying to uphold the constitution. Furthermore, each member of the congregation is urged to obligate himself (or herself) to uphold the constitution by signing it . . . it will take sometime to get all of the signatures."[96]

The missionaries and the pastor were hoping for too much. The lapse of time did not bring in all the signatures. Rather, many members of the Christian community in Bisrampur and Ganeshpur were excommunicated for persisting with the trade in skins and bones of cattle and for eating carrion. Recall that one of the eight resolutions passed during the meeting that founded the independent Immanuel congregation was to readmit those people of Bisrampur and Ganeshpur who on these grounds had been put out of caste and excommunicated from the church. The hide and bone business was an important element in the articulation of independence by the Bisrampur converts. Of course, the resolution of the rebel Immanuel congregation had stipulated that its members should put an end to this business. At the same time, several members had continued with the trade. This further estranged them from the missionaries, distanced them from the Satnamis, and denied them entry into the Arya Samaj.

An Alternative Church

It was after the closure of the option of entering the Arya Samaj that the rebel converts set up an alternative, independent church. Prior to November 1934, the group had occasionally held its own services, but "only a few went and many attended here [the service in the main Bisrampur church], even occasionally some of the leaders."[97] A month later, the group became active. In December 1934, the rebels "had their own Christmas celebration in front of the chapel in Ganeshpur and on Christmas morning Premdas Jakub baptized about fifteen children, mainly children of such who because of the bone and hide trade had not been baptized and on the following Sunday gave communion to, as I hear, about 40 people."[98] The mandli was in earnest. It also started its own Sunday school in Ganeshpur. The missionary lamented, "I am sorry to say that the majority of children go to their Sunday school, there being about thirty left in ours."[99]

In a letter to the Home Board, the leaders of the independent Immanuel congregation reported that "When the missionaries separated us from them we appointed one from among ourselves as an honorary pastor and have continued the work of Faith. He baptized 17 children on 25 December 1934 and 4 children on 1 January 1935 and communion was given."[100] Like all official church bodies of the American Evangelical Mission, the mandli sent congregational reports to the Home Board. Its members also presented themselves as Christian martyrs, their faith unshaken by difficult and trying circumstances. "We are about seven hundred people who have been sitting in dust, sun and mud [praying for several months],"[101] they wrote, forced into this situation by the missionaries, who had "locked our Immanuel Church and confiscated our treasury."[102]

In order to sustain a parallel church, the rebel converts undertook keen efforts to reclaim both the chapel at Ganeshpur and the funds of the congregation. They collected signatures and money. The initiative had widespread support. A missionary conceded, "I understand they got the signatures of about three fourths of the people of Ganeshpur and several of those in Bisrampur."[103] The mandli sought out a Christian lawyer, one Mr. Chobbs of Raipur, to defend its interests. The missionaries in Bisrampur "received a notice from Mr. Chobbs as the 'pleader' for the Immanuel Congregation members who have severed their connection with the American Evangelical Mission. The notice is: to open the doors of the Ganeshpur Chapel and to turn over the funds of the congregation to his clients."[104] In a last ditch attempt, the rebels of Bisrampur had resorted to the law and were threatening to use the colonial court machinery. Yet the dice were loaded against them. The affairs of the Bisrampur congregation had been conducted in accordance with the constitution approved by the India Mission District. Premdas Jacob, the honorary pastor of the independent congregation, was the first signatory to the document. The independent Immanuel mandli did not carry through the idea of going to court. The group had made its last concerted move to establish an independent church and congregation.

In January 1935, after a meeting with Mr. Hodge, the secretary of the

National Christian Council, the rebel group decided to go to the negotiation table. On 12 February 1935, its members met Mr. Hodge and the missionaries on the IMD committee. The two sides agreed to reconcile their differences without conditions. The missionary J. C. Koenig was obviously satisfied: "I am very happy to report that the troubles in the large congregation at Bisrampur have ended. The important principle has been established, that the District has the power to overrule obviously unfair or harmful decisions of the individual congregation."[105] However, their problems were not over. In a letter to the Home Board written after the negotiations, Premdas Jacob complained that the matter concerning Boas Purti and Rebecca was festering like a sore. The missionaries had "forced conditions on us and force us to comply with them which is against our wishes and thoughts and in which we do not believe."[106] He persisted with the earlier critique of the missionaries, but his lone confrontational voice was silenced by the conciliatory tone of the other members of the congregation.

In early 1936, Reverend Goetsch from St. Louis visited the Indian missions as a representative of the Home Board of the American Evangelical Mission. During his visit, the members of the erstwhile independent Immanuel congregation presented him with a petition. The petition reiterated a number of their earlier demands, but it also eschewed any criticism of the missionaries. The invocation of the then/now distinction contrasted the flourishing state of the congregation in the past with what it had become, but there was only an oblique reference to the policies adopted by the present missionaries.[107] At the same time, the demands presented in the petition were more forthright.

The petition asked for greater educational care for the children in Bisrampur so that they could become reliable pillars of the church. It also sought financial assistance and free medicine for those who were seriously ill. The problem stemmed from unemployment and poverty. It was repeated again and again that rather than favoring outsiders the missionaries should appoint people from Bisrampur as catechists, preachers, Bible men, teachers, pastors, and other employees of the mission. The measure would end unemployment in the large congregation and would "strengthen the religious feeling of the people."[108] Nothing less than the question of the self-dependence of the congregation was at stake. The time for the congregation "to stand on its own feet" had come. Therefore, it was only logical that its own leaders should take positions of responsibility.

As in the past, these demands evoked the metaphor of the household. But the household received a different twist this time: "You know that in your time our household was small. But it is a matter of regret that now our household has grown larger than before and we have been removed from mission employment. We find it very difficult to look after ourselves and our household."[109] In a related petition, Premdas Jacob adopted a similar tack: "If you really want the progress of this congregation then (a) give us a capable Chhattisgarhi pastor (b) For you know that a household which has two women in it is destroyed. In the same way because there are people from two Missions in the congregation it is being destroyed."[110] The metaphor of the household served as a device of equivalence. It emphasized the solidarity of the Bisrampur converts as a group and made the evocative appeal of a family in distress. The petition from the people of Bisrampur ended on a dramatic note: "We should be freed from our bondage."[111]

The missionary response to the conflicts engendered by the case of Boas Purti and Rebecca was to revise those policies that they felt underlay the problem. Now a "paternalist relationship" stood "definitely repudiated."[112] As a corollary to this, the missionaries sought to consolidate a clear separation of temporal/mission and spiritual/congregational matters; their complete charge would be undertaken by the missionary and the pastor, respectively. Similarly, it was felt that the self-dependence of the congregation centered on its "intelligent and whole hearted participation in the affairs of the community" and on freeing the economy of Bisrampur from its dependence on the mission.[113] During the famine years of 1940–42, for instance, the mission handed out aid with a restrained hand.

And what of the converts' side of the story?[114] Their opposition to the severance of connections between pastoral authority and landed power and their own envisioning of paternalistic patterns underlay the converts' efforts to appoint the pastor of Bisrampur as the "submalguzar" of the mission station. This initiative failed in the face of opposition by the missionaries.[115] It is hardly surprising that to the converts the missionary continued to occupy the role of the oppressive malguzar. The people of Bisrampur negotiated and contested his authority by grabbing the land of the mission, staking customary claims on the wood and trees of the forest, and resorting to legal measures.[116] The malguzari was abolished in 1951.[117] The converts continued to articulate their "independence" through pastoral idioms, grids of an evangelical governmentality, demanding free education in colleges and training schools for their children and financial help and unemployment benefits for the members of the congregation.[118] The protagonists and players of the drama in Bisrampur had enacted the shared past of evangelical entanglements.

Conclusion

It remains to tie together the different strands of the accounts presented in chapters 1 and 2 and suggest some of the broader implications of evangelical entanglements in colonial central India. We have noted that these entanglements entailed critical intersections of meaning and power: the contradictory location of the mission project within colonial cultures of rule; and the interface of Protestant theology, evangelical beliefs, and the practices of missionaries with the principles of caste-sect and the dynamics of village life. Indeed, it was by elaborating the contradictions at the heart of the mission project that the evangelists constructed a sense of belonging to a community of Western folk in Chhattisgarh, reinforced the cultural order of colonial rule, invested in imperial mythologies of racial supremacy, and established structures of paternalistic authority. The cultural schemes and discursive agendas of the mission project unravel its colonial connections and political implications.

Who commanded the initiative in processes of evangelical entanglements? In early encounters, the evangelists appeared to be incorporated as affiliates in the domain of authority of gurus and deities, and the missionaries were fashioned as masters who commanded the practices initiated by the mission project within the matrices of vernacular cultures. There were deep enmeshments between the "arts of civilization" of the mission project and the everyday definition and reinforcement of the evangelists' authority, but the converts also deployed these signs and practices in their challenge to the missionaries. The examples discussed above suggest the presence of critical processes among communities of converts, entailing their particular apprehensions and refashioning of the Word and the Book, saints and martyrs, clothing and buildings, Western notations of time and spatial arrangements of work, and missionary medicine and Christ the Savior.

Ties of kinship and the paternalistic economies of mission stations proved critical to the growth of Christian congregations in central India. The missionary was the malguzar and the pastor of these villages, which obscured the division between temporal and spiritual power. The missionary along with the "native leaders" of the converts drew up rules to order the life of congregations. These regulations show continuities with the terms of caste and sect—mechanisms of incorporation and ostracism and concerns of purity/pollution and ritual kingship—and the institutions of village life, which acquired new meanings through their rearrangement within the relocated communities. As active agent and hapless victim, the missionary participated in the creation of a vernacular Christianity, including the scrambling of a key principle of Protestant theology.

The missionary preoccupation with monogamy and fear of adultery meant that the converts were disallowed secondary marriages. Indeed, the evangelists saw such arrangements as instances of the moral sloth of the world of "wilderness," seeking instead to impose marriage as a sacred contract between individuals. Yet the converts consistently flouted missionary authority in this area and continued to enter into secondary marriages, even though these were deemed adulterous by the evangelists. In the 1930s, the converts of Bisrampur drew on missionary injunctions against adultery and the principles of maintenance of boundaries of groups, embedded within rules of caste and sect, to invoke the threat to the chastity of "virgin Christian sisters." They turned the honor of women into an evocative metaphor for order within the community and a symbol that constituted its boundary. The converts defied the missionaries in fashioning their under-standing of sexual transgression.

The converts' criticism of the missionaries in the 1930s highlights their uses of Christianity filtered through the recasting of evangelical idioms, nationalist rhetoric, and governmental enchantments. Their initiative cen-tered on a pervasive "us and them," "community and outsider" divide. With the community forged around the converts of Bisrampur, all em-ployees who did not originally belong to the mission station were termed outsiders. Protested forthwith was the increasing intrusion of these out-siders into the affairs of the community. Moreover, efforts by missionaries to dismantle the ties of dependence of the converts and to make the con-gregation self-dependent were entangled with their defense of these out-siders. There was a disruption of the normative economy—the pattern of expectations and obligations—of the Christian community of Bisrampur. Through grids of understanding that underlined the inextricable ties be-tween pastoral authority and landed power, the figure of the missionary underwent transformations and turned from the benevolent ma-bap of the past into a tyrannical malguzar of the present. Finally, the assertion of independence by the Christian congregation of Bisrampur involved a de-fense of the "paternalistic" ties that had bound them to the missionaries through complex relations of dependence and control. Here, deference to the missionaries was one part self-preservation and one part the calculated extraction of land, employment, and charity. The converts employed both missionary and nationalist rhetoric in their practice, construing their chal-lenge to missionary authority in a Christian language through idioms of an evangelical governmentality. Together with the evangelists, in ways fa-miliar and unfamiliar, they articulated thereby the terms and textures of empire, nation, and modernity—provisos and patterns that found distinct configurations in legal entanglements within village life. This is the subject of the next two chapters.

Stories of the remotest of pasts have their beginnings in recent tales. Not so long ago, during a dull and dusty summer in central India, I was an optimistic youth, hopelessly haunting the local judicial record office in the city of Raipur. My search was for records that detailed the processes of conflicts between lower-caste tenants and upper-caste landlords in the Chhattisgarh region in the late nineteenth century. It was a characteristically naive thing to do. Almost a hundred years ago, the colonial government had destroyed these records.

Lost and Found

Just when all prospects appeared lost, I met Sattar. A Muslim from Maharashtra who had settled in Raipur, he worked in the record office as a peon. Now, Sattar was a lush. By eleven in the morning, he was pleasantly high; by one in the afternoon, he was reasonably—and sometimes unreasonably—drunk; and three hours later he was lost to the world. I had seen him when I first walked into the records office, then when I was pleading in vain to be allowed one look at the countless yellow-gray files lying in endless unhappy piles, and finally when my face had fallen, completely, totally, and (as it seemed then) irrevocably. On each occasion, poised strategically on a landing close by, Sattar had uttered the same sequence of sardonic sounds, a sigh followed by silence and then the laconic lament, "Aur ka karees" (What else to do)?

An earnest researcher, I had paid little attention to this funny but sad man, an anonymous alcoholic. This was to change one hot Friday afternoon as I stood near the records office waiting for a bus, a rickshaw, or a tempo, anything that would carry me away from my dashed desires turned to rubble, scattered at my feet and everywhere I looked. Sattar walked up, staggering a little, leaned over, and whispered confidentially, "There are records, records, records inside about murder, rape, murder."[1] The moment of high drama ended. Sattar retreated into himself, then sighed, fell silent, and inevitably announced, "Aur ka karees?" Yet my chase had begun. The many complicated dealings with Bade Babu—the somewhat cynical Brahman high priest of the records office—through which I gained access to and then permission to photocopy the records over several months is a tale within the tale best reserved for another time.

Sattar had led me to an ethnographic historian's gold mine. There were thousands upon thousands of pages of material on conflicts and the disputing process, often involving mayhem and murder between members of families, clans, castes, and communities in twentieth-century colonial Chhattisgarh. Routinely, the records should have met their end several decades ago. Saved because of administrative bungling, they suggested a large project entailing the interplay and interpenetration of "official-state" conceptions and "community-popular" contentions of crime and criminality, legality and property, and authority and morality, including rival constructions of the person. The records contain village stories, tales of transgressions and enmities, kinship and neighborhood, gender and age, authority and honor, caste and boundaries, and witchcraft and infanticide. On offer is an archive of the complex interchange and mutual constitution of everyday norms, familiar desires, and alien legalities: the reciprocal determinations of imperial law and village life and modernity and subalternity on the ground.

Sattar, I believe, has retired. Or, as it is sometimes said in Chhattisgarh, "Ab woh tire ho gaya hai" (He has [re]tired now). Yet I continue to work with a boon, the knowledge of a secret, which Sattar granted me. Let me then dedicate this chapter, and the one that follows, to Sattar, my comrade and coconspirator. Is this dedication theatrical? Is this dedication perverse? I am quite certain that Sattar would have said, "Aur ka karees?"

Reading Records

Out of the large corpus of legal materials, there emerge tales of four disputes in different villages of Bilaspur District in the Chhattisgarh region of middle India. These disputes from the 1920s and 1930s were located in the domain of the familiar and the quotidian in village life and were seized and fashioned into cases in the realm of the colonial district judiciary. They traversed and brought together the two arenas. Logics of kinship and neighborhood, involving a series of transgressions of the norms of the

Satnami community, informed the first two disputes, the subjects of this chapter. In chapter 4, I discuss two disputes that elaborated patterns of enmity over entitlements to property.

The body of the dispute materials is contained in what Simon Schama has condescendingly called "records of incrimination."[2] The Bilaspur District Sessions Trial cases produced capacious documents. Each case consists of the charge that sent the accused to trial at the Court of Session, the earlier examination of the accused before the committing magistrate, a descriptive list of exhibits, the documentary exhibits used, the depositions of witnesses for the prosecution and the defense, the examination of the accused, and finally the judgment in the Court of Session.

It is from this evidence that I reconstruct four stories of everyday life. The exercise is fraught with difficulties. The cases dealt with the events and features of a dispute by designating them as "crimes."[3] A dispute was fashioned into a "case" within the colonial judicial system through the privileging of an act—or a set of actions—with serious consequences, for example, a blow from an ax that led to a death. The act or actions came to be constructed as the key affair that defined the crime and occupied the center of the stage, while the other episodes and elements of the drama constituted the backdrop to this critical event.

The process turned on the discursive strategies of the law. The ordering of depositions of witnesses for the prosecution diverged from the actual sequence of events, arranged instead in an order that highlighted the central event of the crime. The depositions of witnesses began with descriptions of acts of murder, injury, or theft and then retraced their steps to earlier events and prior patterns in order to fill in the background of the crime. The questions posed during the examinations of the accused attempted to explicate the crime itself. The final, authoritative narrative of the judge drew on the different accounts rehearsed during the proceedings to present first a summary statement of the prehistory of the crime. Then it seized on the final act—its immediate circumstances, the intention underlying it, and the manner of its conduct—in order to determine, through the manifold requirements of judicial proof and legal evidence, the nature of the crime. There was much at work in the constitution of guilt and innocence.

However, it is also possible to pry open the cases, recovering what the disputes tell us about the play of relationships within village life in dialogue with state law.[4] Such a task requires a displacement. Rather than according the decisive act of the crime in question a position of privilege, this final moment now comes to be located alongside the diverse elements and distinct events of a dispute as only one part of a complex story. The sources allow us to effect such a displacement. We have noted that during their depositions the witnesses retraced their steps to fill in the background of the crime, particularly in the course of their cross-examination. Here the witnesses often constructed a rich and vivid picture of the social relationships, patterns of solidarity and enmity, and occurrences within the village that went into the making of disputes.

There was a gap between the limited range of facts required by the judgment and the abundance of information rehearsed during the depositions. It is important to mind this gap and work within it. By extracting the fine detail and seizing on the repetitions within the narratives of the witnesses, it is possible to trace the interplay between concerns of the normative order of the law and processes of signification within village relationships.[5] Through a curious logic, the examinations of the accused also come to our aid. The accused sought to establish enmity as the reason for his or her framing by the prosecution. Often the history of the dispute was narrated as both cause and proof of this enmity. This once again makes possible a rehearsal of the quotidian narratives of village life. Taken together, such readings of the evidence reveal the larger story of the interplay between "official-state" law and "popular-community" legalities.[6]

Dispute 1: A Case of Transgressions and Legalities

On the morning of 15 July 1927, an altercation and a fight between two families resulted in the death of a patriarch.[7] The families of Chandu and Itwari were *kashtkars* (cultivators) of the Satnami caste who lived in the village of Karkhena in the Bilsapur District of Chhattisgarh. Bound to each other through ties of kinship, they were neighbors in the village who also held adjoining fields. In the confrontation between the families of Chandu and Itwari, a singular, sanguinary statement played a critical role: "You have got us fined so we shall on this day bathe in your blood." The threads of this village drama warrant unraveling.

The Players

What do we know about the protagonists and the village? On one side, Chandu and Samaru were half brothers, "the sons of the same mother from different fathers": Chandu was the son of Sadhu and Samaru of Dina. Chandu was married to Sohgi and had two sons, Ramdayal and Sheodayal (see figure 1). On the other side, Itwari and Dukhiram were brothers: Hagru was born to Itwari and Banda to Dukhiram (see figure 2). As noted, the two groups shared kinship: Chandu and Dukhiram were cousins.[8] Finally, the two families were linked through the breakup of a marriage and the establishment of new conjugal ties. But more about this in a moment.

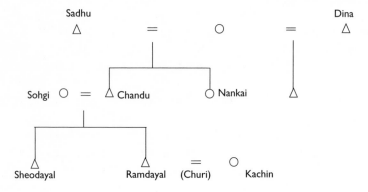

Figure 1   Chandu's family

The castes of Telis (customarily oil pressers, who were primarily agri-
culturists) and Satnamis mainly populated Karkhena. The village had a
substantial Muslim malguzar—with a landholding of 152.08 acres—who,
along with his brother and father, held full proprietary rights to the village.[9] In Karkhena, there were two plot proprietors, both of whom were
Kurmis with holdings of about 26 and 23 acres. In the village, 149 cultivators held land as tenants: 48 Telis, 37 Satnamis, 12 Kurmis, 12 Gonds, and
8 Chamars. The other castes represented in Karkhena were Lohar, Brahman, Dhobi, Muslim, Painka, Dhuri, one Christian, and a Kalar.

Itwari's family held nearly 30 acres of land: his sons owned 19.80 acres,
and Dukhiram owned 9.63. As for Chandu's family, Samaru owned 5.09
acres and Sheodayal and Ramdayal owned 6.83. Among other Satnamis
within the village, seventeen had holdings of less than 5 acres, four more
had holdings of between 5 and 8 acres, and another four had holdings of
between 8 and 12 acres. Apart from Itwari's family, six Satnamis had holdings of more than 12 acres. This is to say that Itwari's family ranked among
the most substantial Satnami cultivators in Karkhena, while Chandu's
group belonged to the third rung among Satnami cultivators, the poorer
agriculturalists in the village. All of this has significance for our reconstruction of the dispute.

A young woman called Kachrin occupied a key role in the drama. Kachrin was once married to Hagru, but the union did not last long. Kachrin left
Hagru and began living with Ramdayal. Ramdayal and Kachrin were married in the *churi* (secondary marriage) form (see figures 1 and 2). Now, churi
had been a widely prevalent form of secondary marriage in Chhattisgarh
among all but the highest castes of Brahmans, Rajputs, and Baniyas. Here a
married woman could marry another man if he gave her *churis* (bangles).
While the broad pattern was similar, specific practices regarding churi

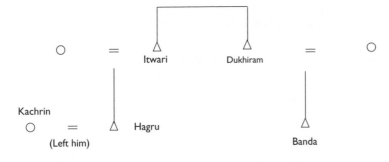

Figure 2   Itwari's family

varied across castes.[10] Among Satnamis, if churi took place with another member of the community, their caste panchayat deliberated the affair. They fixed a certain *behatri* (compensation for bride-price), which the new husband had to pay to the earlier husband and his family. The new husband also had to host a feast for the Satnamis, which symbolized the incorporation of the woman into his home and the acceptance of the marriage by the community. The earlier husband, in turn, had to feed the Satnamis within the village in the form of a *marti jeeti bhat*, a symbolic statement that the woman was dead to him. Finally, the new husband often paid a *dand* (punitive fine), a portion of which was kept for the guru of Satnampanth. The rest was used by the Satnamis in the village.

After the churi between Ramdayal and Kachrin, no Satnami panchayat was held to deliberate the matter. As a result, Ramdayal was not asked to provide the behatri, or compensation for the bride-price, that Hagru had paid earlier; no decision was taken regarding whether a dand was in order; and Hagru did not have to host a marti jeeti bhat. This is not surprising. Rather than having the Satnami panchayat adjudicate Kachrin's secondary marriage, Hagru had filed a complaint in the colonial Faujdari court, which imposed a fine on Chandu and Ramdayal. After a few days, Chandu and Ramdayal—along with Samaru and Sheodayal—had attacked Itwari in retribution for his machinations, which had led to Chandu's family being fined by the court. A dutiful son, Hagru in turn had filed another suit against Ramdayal for damages for having enticed his wife. The hearing for this lawsuit was to be held on 14 July 1927. Both groups traveled to town to attend the hearing, but there was an adjournment. The two groups returned to the village in the evening. The next day the bloody fight between the Satnami families of Itwari and Chandu broke out in Karkhena, ending in the death of a patriarch, the central event of the trial in the Court of Session.

On the morning of 15 July 1927, Itwari and Hagru, along with Dukhiram and Banda, went to work in their fields. Between them, they took three *nagars* (plows), three *lathis* (stout sticks), and three *tutaris* (sticks with sharp tips used to drive bullocks). According to the prosecution, the members of Itwari's group left their sticks on the *medh* (boundary) of one of their fields and began to work the plows. Meanwhile, Chandu, Sheodayal, Sohgi, and Nankai arrived at their fields with two plows. We have noted that some of the fields of the two groups adjoined each other. Chandu and Sheodayal were each carrying a lathi and tutari; Sohgi had brought a basket of seed grain, and Nankai carried two pickaxes and an ax. They began to sow one of their fields. After some time, Samaru and Ramdayal, both carrying sticks, arrived. As soon as they reached the fields, Sohgi moved across and removed the sticks of Itwari and his group, which were at some distance from them. Itwari noticed this and warned his "party" that there was trouble ahead. The men in Chandu's group then declared that Itwari's family "had got them fined so they would on that day bathe in their blood."[11]

On hearing this, the members of Itwari's group ran with their plows to the nearby field of Dukhiram but found that Chandu and his family were chasing them. Leaving their plows in this field, they ran to a field belonging to Kasi Panka. They asked Kasi to save them. When Chandu and his group arrived, Kasi remonstrated with them with folded hands. Chandu and his group did not heed his request. Instead, they repeated the statement about bathing in the blood of Itwari and his family.[12] Itwari and his men now ran to Girdhari's field, which offered greater safety, since there were eleven plowmen working there. When Chandu's family reached this field, the plowmen asked them why they were chasing Itwari's group. They replied that they had no evil intentions. Kodu, a laborer, stated that Chandu had said that they had taken the sticks of Itwari's group because there was no reason to bring them to the fields.[13] When the laborers asked the members of Chandu's group to return the sticks, they said that they would do so in the village before the panchayat and provided an assurance that they were returning. When Chandu and his group began to depart, the plowmen started working again. At that point, Chandu's group attacked Itwari's. Hagru was beaten with a lathi till he fell down, and Itwari was struck with an ax and a lathi and killed.

The defense of the "accused" hinged on self-defense. In their examination, the members of Chandu's family argued that when Chandu, Sheodayal, and Sohgi had begun working in the field they realized that they had not brought seeds with them. Sohgi started for home to get the seeds. On the way, Itwari confronted, rebuked, and abused her for enticing his daughter-in-law: "Bhosda chodi hamar palodu la lae havas" (Cunt fucker, you have taken away my daughter-in-law).[14] Itwari then struck Sohgi twice with a stick. On hearing the commotion, Chandu and Samaru moved toward Sohgi and Itwari. Nankai, Sheodayal, and Ramdayal were not present in the fields. Chandu asked Itwari not to hit the old woman. Itwari turned to Chandu and attacked him with a lathi. In his examination, Chandu stated that he was acting in self-defense when he first warded off Itwari's blows with a tutari and then used the tutari to hit him. He argued that somewhat later Samaru had joined him in hitting Itwari with a tutari. He could not be sure whether it was his or Samaru's blows that felled Itwari. Hagru, Dukhiram, and Boda soon reached the spot. With sticks, they attacked Chandu and Samaru, who defended themselves with their tutaris. Samaru and Hagru fell down. For his part, Samaru stated that he followed Chandu to the scene of the fight between Itwari and Sohgi: "I saw from a distance that Sohgi fell down on the ground on account of two blows which Itwari dealt her on the head. Hot words were being exchanged between Chandu and Itwari." At this point, the defense argued, Samaru was surrounded by Hagru, Dukhiram, and Banda, who all had sticks in their hands. They said to Samaru, "Bahen chod hamare Bap ko mare bar jat ho" (You sister fucker, you are going to hit my father), and then started hitting him with their sticks.[15] Samaru defended himself with his tutari and struck Hagru but fell down because of successive blows from Dukhiram and Hagru. Hagru sat on Samaru's chest and dealt with his fist blows until Samaru passed out. Samaru did not know what had happened next. He was sure of one fact: he "did not kill Itwari."

Kinship and Neighborhood
This dispute lay at an intersection of two axes: bonds of kinship and neighborhood and quotidian negotiations of legality and justice. We know from the deposition of Dukhiram that Chandu was a cousin. Not only were the families of the "accused" and the "victim" bound through ties of blood, but they were also neighbors, holding adjoining fields. Besides, the pattern of settlement of castes in a Chhattisgarhi village further meant that the families of Chandu and Itwari lived in the Satnami/Chamar para (neighborhood), which was also home to thirty-five other families of their caste. While the relations between the two families prior to Kachrin's leaving Hagru for Ramdayal are unknown to us, the dynamics of kinship and neighborhood informed what we know of the dispute.

In village society in Chhattisgarh, as elsewhere, relationships of affinity, friendship, and kinship are often double edged. On one hand, the ties that bind are the basis of mutual support in everyday life. On the other hand, these bonds are the most fraught with risk, posing possible danger to a person, family, group, or community. In a word, the relationships that constitute a network of solidarity are also pregnant with the threat of rivalry, envy, and disruption. A closure can breed and nourish the worst enmities.[16]

During my fieldwork in Chhattisgarh in the early 1990s, in the course of discussing this dispute with Satnamis (and members of other castes), almost all the people I talked to could identify with the tension inherent in the relationship between the families of Itwari and Chandu. Their quick affirmations—"ho" (yes) they had said, accompanied by a vigorous nod— assumed a succinct shape in Pitambar's pithy response: "This is the way it [always] happens." On other occasions, in efforts to follow up the strained relations between Satnami families that were neighbors and related to each other, I inquired about the reasons behind the tension. My query was usually met with good-humored laughter, which signified that I was asking about the obvious. Uttara was more tolerant about my patent naïveté and patiently explained, "Don't you know, neighbors always fight." I was asking about a norm and pattern that governed quotidian life. Moments of risk were a continuous presence structured into the relationship between the families of Chandu and Itwari.

The specific relationship between Ramdayal and Kachrin also contained a possible danger. Chandu and Dukhiram were cousins. Kachrin was Ramdayal's *bhauji* (brother's wife). Ramdayal was Kachrin's *dewar* (husband's younger brother). Kachrin and Ramdayal, bhauji and dewar, were bound by a "joking relationship." Indeed, the relationship between bhauji and dewar affords a high degree of freedom and license, replete with romantic and sexual overtones. This stands in contrast to the relationship of "avoidance" between a woman and her father-in-law and the husband's elder brother.

The joking relationship between bhauji and dewar has wide currency, particularly in patterns of northern and central Indian kinship. For example, the *dadaria*, an extremely popular genre of folk songs in Chhattisgarh, repeatedly work on the motif of the longing of bhauji and dewar for each other.

> Sweet rings of sugar
> The boys are eating
> Under every shade
> Bhauji awaits me
>
> Mother-in-law's comments
> Sister-in-law's jokes
> Because of the young Dewar
> My heart is not at rest[17]

Of course, there are well-defined limits to the jokes, the license, the longing, and attachments.[18] At the same time, within the caste it is only among close kin that a breach of these bonds constitutes a transgression of norms of kinship. On one hand, since Ramdayal and Kachrin were distant relatives, Kachrin's act of leaving Hagru and her secondary marriage to Ramdayal was no violation of the taboos of kinship. On the other hand, in keeping Kachrin *paithoo* (another term for the churi form a secondary marriage) and giving her bangles, Ramdayal worked on a possibility and confirmed a danger that was inherent in the nature of the relationship between the two families.

The retaliation by Itwari's family confirmed this enmity. The records do not tell us what Itwari's family actually made of Kachrin's decision to leave Hagru. During the proceedings, they underplayed considerations of her choice(s) when they held Chandu's family responsible for enticing their daughter-in-law. Denied volition of her own within the textual regimes of the law and silenced by the discursive claims of the prosecution, the defense, and the judgment alike, Kachrin had become a focal sign in the contest between the families of Chandu and Itwari.

Legalities and Transgressions
We have noted that the caste panchayat usually settles matters internal to the Satnami community, particularly those relating to marriage. Kachrin had not merely left Hagru. Rather, she and Ramdayal were married in the churi form. The Satnami panchayat would have considered this within the bounds of fair play. During fieldwork, among the people with whom I discussed the dispute—including several who act as *panchas* (council members) in caste panchayats—, none felt that Kachrin's marriage to Ramdayal constituted an outrage. Therefore, it is hardly surprising that Hagru did not take the matter of the secondary marriage between Kachrin and Ramdayal to the Satnami panchayat. Instead, he appealed to a colonial court. Here Itwari's family did not merely wish to recover behatri for the bride-price they had paid. Beyond the imposition of behatri and a possible dand on Chandu's family, they wished to avenge their loss of face in the village. The strategy of using the arbitrating agency of the colonial judicial system provided them with the answer. As substantial cultivators within Karkhena, they were better suited than Chandu's family to take the matter to court. At the very least, the move would financially embarrass their opponents. The strategy paid off, and the colonial court fined Chandu and Ramdayal.

The organizational structure of the Satnami community was premised on a fusion of the principles of caste and sect. I have shown elsewhere that the settlement of caste matters among the Satnamis was closely tied to the work of the organizational hierarchy of the sect of Satnampanth, with both defining the boundary of the community.[19] In tune with this logic, according to Chandu's group, the action of Itwari's family of taking the matter of a secondary marriage to court—and the subsequent sanction of a fine—crossed a well-defined boundary, namely, the settlement of internal matters of the caste in the Satnami panchayat.

To cross a boundary is to undermine it. The action of Itwari's family, according to its opponents, was a transgression of community norms of legality in everyday life. During his examination in the sessions trial, when asked if he had been fined in the colonial court, Chandu had said, "Han nalish ki thi aur jurmana hua tha; mor gavahi badal diye the" (Yes, there was a case and there was a fine imposed. My testimony/evidence had been changed)."[20] The statement arguably reveals the sharp feelings of Chandu and his family at having been tricked and wronged and the acute perception of the legality and correctness of their own position.

The four men of Chandu's family had consequently attacked Itwari. Following this fight, Itwari's family once more took their opponents to court, where they were fined a second time. Yet the matter did not end there. Hagru dragged Chandu's family to the law court for a third time, now filing a case against them for damages for having enticed his wife. The hearing of this case was to take place the day before the fight occurred. The adjournment of the hearing would have left Chandu's family not only uncertain over the outcome but angry about the expense and trouble Itwari's family—their well-off neighbors, relatives, and enemies—were causing them.

Blood Binds

"You have got us fined so we shall on this day bathe in your blood." The statement made by members of Chandu's family brought together the two axes outlined above: the logic of kinship and neighborhood and quotidian articulations of popular legalities with contingent negotiations of colonial law. In the eyes of Chandu's family, the fine sanctioned by the court was the result of a transgression. The transgression emerged from enmity. The enmity was rooted in ties of blood. The response to the transgression, characteristically, invoked and derived its motive force from the metaphor of blood. Itwari's family had stepped beyond the bounds of fair play, but Chandu arguably reaffirmed the norms of legality and justice of the Satnami community when he told the plowmen of Karkhena that his group would return the sticks of Itwari's family only before the Satnami panchayat. Then Chandu's family redressed a loss, avenged a defeat, and punished a transgression.

"You have got us fined so we shall on this day bathe in your blood." We are reminded here of Foucault's distinction between "customary" legal orders that seek to punish transgressions and "modern" regimes of justice that work toward establishing the intention behind a crime.[21] Yet this distinction needs to be rescued from the dualism of the "traditional" and the "modern," which conjures up an epistemic breach and a historical break, often pitting unsullied indigenous legalities against a singular colonial law.[22] Indeed, customs of the community could assiduously draw on symbols of the state. For example, in the late 1920s and the 1930s, the Satnami organizational hierarchy and the legalities of Satnampanth were altered and reordered through a recasting and reworking of the idioms of imperial governance and the languages of colonial law, an issue to which I will return.[23] The point is that the distinction between the emphasis on "transgressions" and the quest for "intentions" has a different provenance, a spectral presence in which the confrontations between the two are contingent in quality and coeval in character.

"You have got us fined so we shall on this day bathe in your blood." The statement of Chandu's family spoke of their construction and punishment of a transgression, but in their desire to seek revenge Itwari's family seized on the statement in order to establish their enemies' intention. Under the possible guidance of the counsel for the prosecution, they rehearsed and staged the statement to implicate all their enemies by seeking to establish the common intention of all members of Chandu's family to kill Itwari and Hagru. At the same time, the members of Itwari's family were not consistent in their depositions about this vital piece of evidence. In the universe of the familiar and the everyday—kinship and neighborhood—colonial courts and modern law simultaneously constituted alien legalities, resources for redefining order and pathologies within the community and strategies of settlement and revenge. In each case, the rules were difficult to master. This becomes clearer when we examine the next drama, the second dispute.

Dispute 2: A Tale of Authority and Conflict

Soon before the advent of the spring of 1940, a Satnami woman eloped with her young nephew from Darri village in the Janjgir Tahsil of Bilaspur District.[24] The matter precipitated a dispute in the village. In the dispute, motifs of kinship and community were interwoven with designs of inter-caste relations and entitlements to property. The opposed stands in the village panchayat on the issue of the elopement led to the formation of two "parties" in Darri. There was a link with earlier tensions over rival claims to ownership of land, which also entailed prior alliances of Satnamis with other castes within the village. Two groups of Satnamis clashed in Darri, and other members of the village joined the fray. On the night of 7 May

Table 1   The "Accused"

Caste	Name	Father's Name	Age
Brahman	Kunjbiharilal	Balakram Malguzar	22
Teli	Balaram	Jhagru Lambardar	42
Teli	Ramtyaloo	Sadasheo	40
Teli	Paltoo	Bhikari	55
Teli	Kanhaiya	Paltoo	20
Bhaina	Balli	Bahorak	45
Bhaina	Balmukund	Jaharoo	45
Rawat	Budga	Bhagat Rawat	55
Satnami	Pila	Kashiram	30
Satnami	Sahas	Kashiram	42
Satnami	Karman	Sahas	22
Satnami	Sukaloo	Gangaram	22
Satnami	Johan	Sangan	30
Satnami	Dasaram	Sangan	25

1940, a group consisting of one Brahman, five Telis, two Bhainas, one Rawat, and six Satnamis (see table 1 and figure 3) beat ten Satnamis belonging to the rival "party" in the village (see figure 4).[25] One of these Satnamis died, and the dispute was on its way to being fashioned into a case.

Darri was a small, mixed-caste village, its malguzari divided into equal parts among the four families of Balaram Lamabardar Teli, Bisahu Teli, Hiralal Brahman, and Balakram Brahman (see table 1). Among the fifty-six tenant-cultivator families listed as owning land in the village, the breakdown according to caste was eight Satnamis, ten Telis, nine Rawats, eight Bhainas, fourteen Marars, three Dhobis, three Brahmans, and one Bairagi. Brahmans and Telis dominated Darri village. Thus, of the four families of village proprietors, Hiralal Brahman, with a total landholding of 100.60 acres; Balakram Brahman, with 27 acres; Balaram Teli, with 30.29 acres; and Bisahu Teli, with 25.40 acres, owned much of the land in the village.[26] This pattern of landholdings—together with the designs of politics and the conflicts they engendered—have significance for the unfolding of the drama in Darri.

Kinship and Conflict

About three months before the fight on 7 May 1940, Dasaram's wife Bahartin had run away from Darri with Chait, her distant nephew by marriage (see fig. 3). Bahartin and Chait had stayed away from the village for two or three weeks. On their return, Dasaram had admitted Bahartin back into his

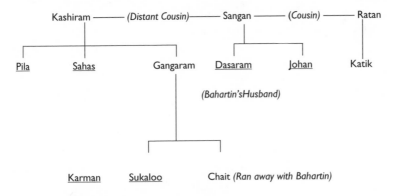

Figure 3   Relationships of Sahas Satnami's group

house, and Chait's actions were similarly condoned by the elders in his
family. To some Satnamis, the events of the elopement and its aftermath
were "scandalous" matters, and a group led by Gajaraj had put Bahartin
and Chait out of caste.[27] Significantly, kinship bound Gajaraj's group—
through Ratan, a cousin of Lala on one side and of Sangan on the other
(see figs. 3 and 4)—to the other main section of Satnamis in the village.
This section, together with several non-Satnami inhabitants of Darri, felt
that the excommunication of Chait and Bahartin was unnecessary, particularly after Dasaram had reestablished conjugal ties with his wife, apparently ignoring her indiscretion. All sides in the village agreed on the necessity of resolving questions of the readmission of Bahartin and Chait into
the caste after their excommunication by Gajaraj Satnami and his group.

A village panchayat consisting of Satnamis and six members of the other
castes met at Johan Satnami's house to decide the issue.[28] The defense of
Bahartin and Chait—and thereby of Dasaram's conduct in reestablishing
conjugal ties—lay in the hands of Dasaram, his brother Johan, Sahas (a
pancha), and his brother Pila. To represent the other Satnami group,
Ratan, Gajaraj, and Baldeo were summoned. When the three reached the
panchayat, they were informed by the panchas that no wrong had been
done by Chait and Bahartin. Apparently, the non-Satnami panchas colluded with Dasaram's group in denying the elopement, telling members
of Gajaraj's group that since Chait and Bahartin had not eloped their
excommunication was unjust, requiring their readmission into the caste
forthwith.

"There was no panchayat of our caste held to find out if Chait and
Dasaram's wife had really run away."[29] Ratan's statement directs us to his
group's acute feeling that there had been a series of violations of Satnami
norms of community, legality, and justice in the affair involving Bahartin,
Chait, and Dasaram. Dasaram had admitted Bahartin into their home

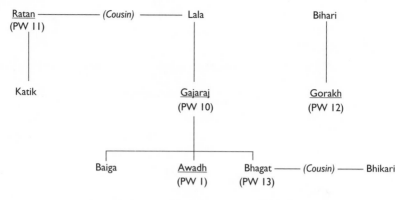

Figure 4   Relationships of Gajaraj Satnami's group

shortly after her return to Darri. Instead of a Satnami caste panchayat looking into this matter, a panchayat consisting mainly of members of other castes deliberated the issue. These panchas ostensibly colluded with Dasaram's group. As Awadh stated, "persons eloping are required to give a caste dinner" before they are readmitted into the caste.[30] However, in this case there were attempts to readmit Chait and Bahartin because the very fact of their having eloped was denied. There was, then, no question of following the norm of a feast for the caste to signify their (re)incorporation into the group. Ratan, Gajaraj, and Baldeo were unwilling to accept this decision.

Ratan, Baldeo, and Gajaraj, in fact, belonged to the five Satnami families that stayed in a separate neighborhood, apart from the other Satnami families of the village. Gajaraj made this clear: "There are five localities in the village. They are Bahman para, Bhama para, Raut para, Patel para, Chamar para, and Gajaraj para. Gajaraj para is the locality where families of us five persons myself, Gorakh, Ratan, Malikram and Katik have got houses. Dasaram also lives in my para and the other accused lived in Chamar para."[31] Members of these five closely knit families, tied through blood and the bonds of neighborhood, refused to accept the decision of the arbitrarily assembled village panchayat. They were unwilling to condone the actions of Dasaram.

Dasaram, a member of their locality, a neighbor, and a relative, had not taken the matter of his wife's elopement with Chait to a Satnami panchayat. He had also refused the suggestion of Gajaraj's group that he should avenge his loss of face by running away with Chait's sister-in-law. Instead, as Awadh stated, "Johan and Dasaram though related to me went over to the other side. Dasaram wanted to readmit his wife and in fact had admitted her in his house."[32] Finally, the five families disputed the authority of Gangaram and Sahas, the leaders of the other Satnami section, as the caste leaders of all Satnamis in Darri. "Ganagaram and Sahas are not the headmen of my caste. They are not the headmen of the whole caste but they are the headmen in our village."[33] Taken together, the five Satnami families of Gajaraj para had excommunicated Dasaram, also severing relations with the other Satnamis of Darri who were unwilling to follow this measure. At the same time, in refusing to abide by the decision of the panchayat to readmit Chait, Bahartin, and Dasaram into the caste, Gajaraj's group had challenged the opinion of dominant members of the village community, who partially excommunicated the five families of Gajaraj para.[34] Thus, an elopement crystallized into two "parties" in Darri.

There were other tensions in the village, the result of a *chekbandi* (consolidation of landholdings) carried out in 1939. Like many other villages in Chhattisgarh, the landholdings in Darri were extremely fragmented.[35] The consolidation of landholdings had been effected in the *falgun* (February–March) of 1939, and the relevant *parchas* (papers) were distributed a little later in *aghan* (November–December) and *pus* (December–January) that year.[36] Balaram Teli was the *sarpanch* (head of council) in the chekbandi proceedings. The other panchas were Budga Raut, Balmukund Bhaina, Bali Bhaina, Ramsai Marar, and Gajaraj Satnami.

Rival claims to land followed the consolidation of holdings, pitting the five Satnami families of Gajaraj para against the party of Satnamis and other castes in Darri. These five families felt that, despite the presence of Gajaraj at the land consolidation proceedings, the panchas had not been fair to them during the chekbandi. Here it is significant that the panchas in these proceedings were themselves the arbiters (or closely connected to key members) of the panchayat that had deliberated over the elopement of Chait and Bahartin. The five Satnami families of Gajaraj para had publicly raised doubts about the authority of these leading lights of Darri not once but twice.

An Altercation and Its Aftermath
It was against this background that there was a minor altercation in the village on the morning of 7 May 1940. Darri lies next to the River Son. In summer, the water would dry up and stagnant pools would form where the river had run. One of these pools supplied water to the villagers. The Satnamis used the southern end, while members of the other castes used the northern end. On the morning of 7 May, Malikram and Awadhram, both belonging to the five Satnami families of Gajaraj para (see fig. 4), had gone to the pool.[37] There Awadh took his buffaloes into the water, while Malikram sat on the bank washing his mouth. Once he finished washing the cattle, Awadh drove them out and began moving through the water toward the bank where Malikram sat. Malikram got up and entered the

water. The two began to bathe. At that moment, Paltoo Teli (see table 1), who sat not far away, toward the northern side of the pool, washing his mouth, reprimanded the two Satnamis: "He said to us as to why we were making the water dirty." Yet this was not all: "Paltoo then used abusive language towards us."[38]

When Awadh and Malikram protested, Paltoo became even more aggressive. He said that had it been another village the two Satnamis would have received five shoe blows each. Awadh and Malikram replied that other people fished in the river and washed their buffaloes there, so why was it that only they had to endure insults for making the water dirty? On hearing this, Paltoo turned furious. He picked up a stone with which to hit them, but changed his mind. Dropping the stone, he picked up his lathi, got into the water, and moved toward the two Satnamis. When Paltoo got close, Awadh snatched his stick and threw it toward the riverbank. By that time, other villagers had reached the river, and they intervened to stop the fight. Paltoo was about to go home, when his son, Rupcharan, reached the scene. Now Rupcharan tried to snatch the lathi from Paltoo, declaring that since Awadh and Malikram had used foul language against his father he would beat up the bastard Chamars.[39] Once more, other villagers prevented the quarrel from escalating. Soon the denizens of Darri returned to the village.

At noon that day, the malguzar, Kunjbiharilal (see table 1), went to Gajaraj para, meeting all the adult members of Gajaraj's group at Gorakh's house. Kunjbiharilal declared that he had heard of the quarrel near the river that morning, and it was advisable to put an end to such dissensions in the village. All the villagers were gathering for a panchayat in the evening. There they would effect a settlement. The Satnamis of Gajaraj para agreed to join these deliberations. Later that day the kotwar (village law and order functionary) announced in Darri that a panchayat would meet at the guddi (village meeting place). All the villagers were expected to attend. A second "proclamation" to this effect was made somewhat later in the evening. Finally, in a third announcement, around dusk, the time of the evening meal, the kotwar enjoined all the villagers of Darri to proceed to the panchayat forthwith, declaring that those who kept away would see their "mothers go wrong with sweepers." Gajaraj and his group reached the panchayat soon after finishing their evening meal. About fifty or sixty other people, including the Satnamis of the rival group, were already there.

Adjudicating Matters

The guddi was dark. There was no lantern. The panchayat attendees sat on the bank of a water tank. Gajaraj and his group squatted together, facing the other villagers. Balmukund Bhaina asked the reason why the villagers were meeting at the guddi. The malguzar, Kunjbiharilal, referred to the quarrel in the river that morning, adding that it was he who had called the meeting. He asked Gajaraj and his group to move closer to the other villagers. They moved nearer to the place where Kunjbiharilal sat with his supporters. Kunjbiharilal then said that he would select the panchas. Gajaraj's group agreed. Balmukund Bhaina, Balli Rawat, Budga Ganda, and Kachhi and Pila Satnami were named the panchas, and Kunjbiharilal was selected as the sarpanch. There were no objections to this choice of panchas.

Kunjbiharilal asked Paltoo about the quarrel near the river that morning. Paltoo replied that Bhola and Ramtyaloo were there as well. Bhola and Ramtyaloo then described the altercation, with Paltoo providing further details. Next Awadh and Malikram recounted their version. After this, Kunjbiharilal asked the panchas and Balaram Teli for their opinions. The panchas merely asked Kunjbiharilal to give his decision in his capacity as the sarpanch. Awadh later stated: "The panchas were not consulted and I do not know if they had consulted each other, but Kunjbihari gave out that we were fined. The panchas had not gone aside to consult each other. It was Kunjbihari who gave out of his own accord the decision."[40] Awadhram and Malikram were fined five rupees each, a large sum for a minor matter.

As the leader of his group, Gajaraj pleaded before the panchayat that the two boys, Awadhram and Malikram, had not committed an offense. He also stated that he was a poor man, arguing that the fine was much too harsh. These entreaties failed to move Kunjbiharilal. The malguzar announced that if the fine wasn't paid Gajaraj and his party would face further sanctions: complete excommunication from the village would replace their partial excommunication.

When Kunjbiharilal finished making this statement, the panchas turned to him and asked, "tabhin ki bat kaisan" (what about the previous talk/decision)? The records do not reveal the details of this conversation or of the decision taken earlier, but the moment he was asked the question Kunjbiharilal announced that those who would not beat the "chamars"— Gajaraj and his group—would go "wrong with their mothers." The panchayat seemed to have been waiting for this signal. Now the villagers of Darri gathered at the guddi attacked Gajaraj and his group.

In this attack, designated an "assault" at the Sessions trial, all the members of Gajaraj's party were beaten to the cries of "maro maro" (hit them, hit them). Caught in the midst of a small crowd, Malikram was savagely beaten with sticks. People bore down on him with further blows and kicks to the body. The attack on Gajaraj was also severe, but his son pulled him away. As Gajaraj's party retreated, Gorakh and Bhagatram, the only members of the group who carried sticks, defended themselves, warding off the aggressors' blows. Members of Gajaraj's group ran to Ratan's house in

Gajaraj para. Their opponents followed them and began throwing stones at Ratan's house and abusing Gajaraj and his group. As Ratan later testified: "After we returned home stones were thrown on my house. I did not see the persons throwing the stones but I recognised the voices of five persons who were giving abuses "Chamar saleman ko maro" [Hit the bloody Chamars]. . . . After this we drank water and we heard the crying of Bunkuwar."[41] Malikram had not been able to make it to Gajaraj para by himself.

Here is the testimony of Bunkuwar, the bereaved mother of Malikram, who had also gone to the panchayat.

> Kunjbihari gave the oath to all . . . for assaulting. All this while I was sitting on the platform under the pipal tree. I left my place on the platform when I heard the voice of my son calling oh mother and ran towards him. He was being assaulted near Dena's house near the lemon tree. . . . My son was lying on the ground face upwards. They were giving fist blows and lathi thrusts. They were repeatedly giving blows like pounding. They gave fist blows at times and stick blows also. All of them beat like that. I did not that time notice blood on my son but I noticed it when I found him lying near my house. Later on I alone went home. At that lane . . . I brought out light and saw the bleeding of my son. Myself and my daughter-in-law removed my son from the ground near the door inside the house. Later the people from the five families came up there.[42]

Malikram was dead.

Later that night Bunkuwar, Gajaraj, Awadh, and Katik started off for the police station house at Champa, about nine miles from the village, reaching it in the morning. Awadh was filing a report of the quarrel and the death of Malikram when Chinta Kotwar and Paltoo Teli from Darri reached the station house. According to their version, there had been a quarrel in the village but Malikram was alive and could be seen sitting in his house. Another line of argument underlay the defense of the aggressors of Darri before the District and Sessions judge. There they admitted that there were two parties among the Satnamis of the village, and some agreed that other castes had supported Sahas's group against Gajaraj's party. Further, they did not deny that there was an altercation on the morning of 7 May 1940. At the same time, all the "accused" refused to admit that there was a panchayat that night, also denying thereby that Gajaraj's group had been attacked after the meeting. A number of them claimed alibis, which were established through witnesses for the defense.

The defense argued that the fight in the morning had led to the injuries of Awadh, Gajaraj, Gorakh, Bhagat, and Bhikari, while Malikram had died because of an accidental fall. That morning the young man had been standing at some distance from the others on the riverbank. When the quarrel began, he started to run away but soon fell, fatally injuring himself. Gajaraj's group had deliberately implicated the accused in the trial because of previous enmity on account of the matters of Bahartin's elopement and the proceedings of the consolidation of landholdings. The additional Sessions judge did not buy this story and found that "all the fourteen accused had formed an unnatural assembly with the common object of assaulting Malikram, Gajaraj and the latter's followers who were called at the panchayat."[43]

Unraveling Stories

It would be unfortunate, indeed, if our histories were to end with mere judgments, for long after this dispute within Darri was fashioned into a case in the colonial courts and the judgment delivered processes involving the restitution of enmities, the recasting of transgressions, and the reworking of legalities would have been a part of the fabric of everyday life in the village. Indeed, one day I hope to develop this tale along such lines. Here let me move back and forth among the events and episodes of the narrative to tie up the different strands of this story.

Once upon a time, many fables were spun out of the simple but overarching opposition between (unchanging) traditional-folk-popular disputing processes and (dynamic) colonial-modern-state legal systems. There are, of course, newer stories being told now of different legal mechanisms and matrices.[44] Yet in the South Asian context accounts elaborating the imbrications and implications of modern law and popular legalities—critical attributes of colonial and postcolonial modernity—remain a rarity.[45] What compounds this problem is the assumption of a rather hermetical division between the colonial state (and modernity) and indigenous communities (and traditions) that shores up even the more imaginative considerations of these subjects.[46] It is important to think through such received dispositions.

"Gangaram and Sahas are not the headmen of my caste. They are not the headmen of the whole caste but they are the headmen in the village." With a small Satnami population, Darri did not have a Satnami panchayat in the village; rather, it formed one among a cluster of villages under the authority of a single caste panchayat. During the interwar years, the "traditional" organization of the Satnami panchayat was elaborated in novel ways, entailing the interplay between state and community.[47] Significantly, in the late 1920s and 1930s an organization called the Satnami Mahasabha drew on symbols and metaphors of colonial governance, situating them alongside key signs within Satnampanth, in order to constitute a new legality at once religious and political. This was an effort to reform, regulate, and recast the Satnamis. Here idioms of law, order, and command appeared to be closely bound to relationships of authority within the community. For example, there was the restructuring of the organizational hierarchy of Satnampanth, with its new ranks based primarily on colonial administrative categories, which reworked ritual control and adjudicatory mechanisms among the Satnamis. The tightening of the organization of the Satnami panchayat afforded an effective mode of intervention in the affairs of the community. The group of villages that had earlier deliberated matters arising in villages without their own Satnami panchayat now received a firm institutional basis, constituted as the *athgawana* (committee of eight villages).[48] Therefore, it is not surprising that Gajaraj's group did not accept Gangaram and Sahas as leaders of the caste. They considered that the real caste authority of the Satnami panchayat lay elsewhere, in the newly constituted athgawana of which Darri was a part.

"Gangaram and Sahas are not the headmen of my caste. They are not the headmen of the whole caste but they are the headmen in the village." Generally, all the members of a caste stay within one locale, a single para in a village, but the five Satnami families of Gajaraj's group did not live in the Satnami para—also known as Chamrapara—of Darri. Instead, the five households formed a separate Gajaraj para, named after Gajaraj, the leader of their group. Members of Gajaraj's group were among the substantial cultivators of Darri. Conversely, Sahas's group consisted of poorer cultivators and landless laborers who had ties to the dominant members of the village. On account of these ties, Gangaram and Sahas were projected as the headmen of the Satnamis within Darri. Yet this was not what Gajaraj and his group thought about the matter. Indeed, the questioning of the authority of Gangaram and Sahas as "the headmen of the whole caste" by Gajaraj's group emerged linked to the division among the Satnamis in the village. This division was tied to the endorsement of the authority of the athgawana—and of the Satnami Mahasabha—by Gajaraj's group, while the position of Gangaram and Sahas as leaders of the Satnamis within Darri rested on their ties to the dominant castes in the village. The elopement of Chait and Bahartin crystallized the division among the Satnamis of Darri.

Bahartin was married to Dasaram, and they lived in Gajaraj para. Kinship and neighborhood linked Dasaram and his wife to Gajaraj's group, while Chait was the nephew of Sahas, the leader of the other group of Satnamis. Recall the double-edged dynamic of kinship and neighborhood discussed earlier in this chapter. In keeping with this logic, the elopement of Chait and Bahartin confirmed a threat inherent in the nature of the relationship between the groups of Gajaraj and Sahas, and also constituted a challenge to solidarity rooted in kinship and neighborhood. Moreover, the elopement was a violation of the norms of kinship since Bahartin was Chait's aunt. Finally, Dasaram had not followed the suggestion of Gajaraj's group and avenged his loss of face by running away with Sukul's wife. He had accepted Bahartin into his house. Consequently, Dasaram had joined the other group. Prior bonds meant that the division between the rival Satnami parties was all the sharper.

We find two simultaneous movements here. On one hand, there was a challenge to, followed by a severance of, ties of kinship and neighborhood between the groups of Dasaram and Gajaraj. Awadh made this clear when he testified that "Johan and Dasaram though related to me went over to the other side. Dasaram wanted to readmit his wife and in fact had admitted her in his house." On the other hand, there were a series of transgressions of norms of caste and kinship. There was no customary feast for the caste after Chait and Bahartin returned to the village. A violation of kinship norms was not followed by an expiation of the offense, and a woman who had eloped and done "wrong" with her nephew had easily been readmitted into her husband's house. Indeed, in the eyes of Gajaraj and his group the most flagrant transgression derived from Dasaram's admitting Bahartin into his house without expiating the misdemeanor, premised on a denial of the elopement.

This was also the argument of the village panchayat that sought to settle the matter. Here the panchas decided that since there was no elopement all was to go on as before. By closing its eyes to the elopement, this panchayat denied a set of transgressions. It also poached in the arena—and itself transgressed the authority—of the Satnami panchayat, which should have adjudicated this matter: "There was no panchayat of our caste held to find out if Chait and Dasaram's wife had really run away." Clearly, Gajaraj's group was unwilling to accept the decision of the village panchayat.

There was a link here with earlier tensions in the village over chekbandi, the consolidation of landholdings. The statements of the witnesses and the accused underscore rival and disputed claims to ownership of land between Gajaraj's group and other members of the village following the chekbandi proceedings. The continued tensions over land alongside the suspicions harbored by Gajaraj's group about the fairness of chekbandi amounted to their questioning the authority of the non-Satnami panchas in charge of the consolidation of holdings. When Gajaraj's group did not accept the decision of the village panchayat over the issue of Chait and Bahartin's elopement, it was once more questioning the authority of the dominant members of Darri. Gajaraj was an important member of the village, the leader of his group who had a para named after him, and the families of Gajaraj and Itwari were among the handful of substantial cultivators, with over ten acres of land, in Darri.[49] To the dominant members of the village, the threat of insubordination from Gajaraj's group could not be any clearer.

There was a partial excommunication of Gajaraj's group, which denied them services of the village grazier and entailed other restrictions.[50] At the same time, there was a feeling among the villagers that these measures were not enough, since the indiscretions of Gajaraj's group were going unchecked. Paltoo Teli voiced this feeling when in the course of the fight on the morning of 7 May he said that had it been any other village the "Chamars," Malikram and Awadhram, would have received five shoe blows each. After the fight, during the day, it was resolved that members of Gajaraj's group would be fined and if they refused to accept the decision of the panchayat they would be beaten.[51] The dominant inhabitants of Darri were worried that Gajaraj's group would not attend the panchayat, given that they wanted the Satnami athgawana to settle the issue of the elopement. Unsurprisingly, the village watchman made three proclamations about the panchayat in the village; the last announcement, incorporating an "oath"—"those who do not come will have their mothers go wrong with sweepers"—was made solely in Gajaraj para.

At the panchayat, Gajaraj and his group felt that the decision announced by the malguzar, Kunjbiharilal, was far too severe. Yet the pleas of Gajaraj ended by questioning the authority of the village panchas for the third time. "Tabhin ki baat kaisan?" (What about the earlier decision?) The question invoked the decision that the villagers had taken earlier in the day. Kunjbiharilal made it clear that those who did not beat the "Chamars" (Gajaraj's group) would go wrong with their mothers. The authority and honor of the sarpanch and the panchas, of Kunjbiharilal and his influential allies in Darri was at stake. In order to punish and deter the repeated questioning of this authority and honor by the Satnamis of Gajaraj's group, the Chamars had to be beaten.

In the end, consider the many mix-ups, the critical contradictions, as the protagonists of this drama elaborated and extended the rules and processes of popular legalities and colonial law. Gajaraj and his group wanted a Satnami panchayat, in this case the athgawana, to deliberate the matter of Bahartin and Chait's elopement in order to reaffirm Satnami norms. Yet they also wanted Dasaram to avenge his loss of face by running away with Sukul's wife, an act that would have drawn the censure of the novel religious legalities fashioned in the interwar years, which often fueled the deliberations and decisions of the athgawanas.

As for Dasaram, his act of readmitting Bahartin to his home and hearth after she had returned to Darri was also part of a wider pattern in which Satnami men often chose to condone the sexual indiscretions of their wives, arriving at a settlement with fellow caste people by negotiating a minor expiation of the misdemeanor. Of course, it would have been difficult for Dasaram to settle the matter easily. First, there was the new emphasis on rigid norms governing conjugality, sexuality, and domesticity within the Satnami household, for from the late 1920s on a fixity of form had replaced the fluidity of the past, enforced through freshly constituted athgawanas and recently refurbished Satnami panchayats. Second, there lay the desire of Gajaraj's group to seek revenge on rival Satnamis within Darri, a response touched off by a raw, wounded morality of kinship since Chait (an enemy) was Bahartin's nephew. This said, Dasaram's arrival at a settlement with Gajaraj's group may have involved protracted negotiation, but it was also much the viable option. Indeed, disappointed as Gajaraj's group was that Dasaram had not run away with Sukul's wife, it actively desired expiation of the offense. It felt that Dasaram should give a feast—symbolizing the reincorporation of Bahartin into home, hearth, and community—and possibly pay a dand, of which a portion would be kept for the Satnami guru and the rest used to fund community activities within Darri.

Yet this is not what happened. In the wider context of the division among the Satnamis of Darri, Dasaram chose to break with Gajaraj's group and take the matter to the village panchayat. Dasaram's act of condoning Bahartin's brief elopement, upon her return to Darri, was not out of tune with Satnami "tradition." Dasaram's refusal to expiate the offense was out of tenor with Satnami norms. Dasaram's taking a matter internal to the community before the village panchayat was a transgression of Satnami moral legalities. What, then, of Kunjbiharilal and his influential allies in Darri? These men had beaten up Gajaraj's men to punish and deter the repeated questioning of their authority in everyday life within Darri. Yet in the colonial court they received deterrent punishment for "misusing their authority" in the village.[52]

Conclusion: The Silence of Women and the Gender of the Law

There is something missing in these stories. In the two disputes that we have discussed, the first turned on a secondary marriage and the second hinged on an elopement. Yet Kachrin and Bahartin, the women protagonists of the two stories, are virtually absent from the detailed dramas and dramatic details of these conflicts. There is much more than quick-fix invocations of "voice" and "agency" at stake here. More than a decade ago, Gayatri Spivak reminded us of the structure of interests and the chain of complicities that attend the difficult business of representing the subaltern.[53] With this warning in mind, the near absence of Kachrin and Bahartin in my account raises distinct, salient issues.

Of course, common sense dictates that Kachrin and Bahartin would have exercised their own choices, the former in her secondary marriage to Ramdayal and the latter in her elopement with Chait. At the same time, questions of the volition and actions of these two women warrant understanding as part of the wider arrangements of gender and kinship in Chhattisgarh, especially among the Satnamis. I have shown elsewhere that women of the Satnami community have a degree of autonomy and a measure of space in which to negotiate marriage(s), men, and motherhood within the larger constraints of patrilineal kinship. Over time, this relative autonomy emerged tied to the pattern of secondary marriages among the Satnamis and related to the nature of Satnampanth as premised on the principles of caste and sect.[54] Kachrin's secondary marriage to Ramdayal was in tune with this larger logic of kinship and community. Bahartin's brief elopement with Chait was in tenor with this broader dynamic of caste and gender. Yet Bahartin and Kachrin barely feature in the legal archive.

Should this be surprising? In a pioneering essay, "Chandra's Death," Ranajit Guha discusses the aftermath of the affair of a lower-caste Bagdi widow and her *nondoi* (husband's sister's husband) as engendering diverse responses from their kin.[55] Significant for our purposes are Guha's readings of colonial law and indigenous patriarchy, both of which are critical for his reconstruction of the fear, solidarity, and empathy surrounding the death of the Bagdi widow, Chandra. On one hand, the colonial judicial system dealt with all infractions of law and order by reducing their range of signification to a set of narrowly defined legalities, so that "crime" was the negativity of the "law." On the other hand, a complex interplay of fear and solidarity marked the transgressions of gender, kinship, and caste within indigenous patriarchy, defining the crushing subordination of women and leaving them with very few critical choices. In an innovative move, Guha rescues the collective crises of the Bagdi family from the impersonal determinations of colonial law. In a provocative maneuver, he recuperates from the dead hand of indigenous patriarchy the alternative solidarity, based on empathy, between Bagdi women kin. To recover the traces of gendered subaltern life in its passage through time is to read against the grain of these closures, but the twin structures of colonial law and indigenous patriarchy also impose their own schemes of silence. The dead woman and gendered subaltern, Chandra, cannot speak.

For all the elegance of these formulations, there is a disturbing edge to their implications. Once again, much more than the lack of recovery of the gendered subaltern Chandra's "voice" and "agency" it is Guha's reading of colonial law and indigenous patriarchy that bothers me here. This is particularly the case as we confront the mystery of the missing women, Bahartin and Kachrin, from the legal archive. Having learned much from Guha's readings of judicial discourse, I nonetheless suggest that there are limits to envisioning colonial law as solely possessed of a relentless desire to establish crime as negativity, which ever detached critical events of quotidian dramas from their contexts. Such apprehensions of colonial justice tend to underenunciate the wide-ranging patriarchy of modern law.

I submit, then, that the negative determinations of the law require reading alongside its overwhelming patriarchy. In the two disputes at hand, while establishing kinship connections as indispensable to determining the context of a "crime," the law traced the relationships of the "victim" and the "accused" through bonds of blood and ties of marriage among the male protagonists and players. As we have seen, this was also true of other events that defined the immediate background and the main drama that went into the making of a "crime." Bahartin and Kachrin appear in the judicial archive only when their involvement in dramas of illegalities assumed such density that for the law to ignore their presence would have been to compromise the basic plot of its own story. Yet these women remained in the shadow of their men. Indeed, leaving aside "cases" in which women decisively stole the stage from men, the patriarchy and the negativity of the law operated through unstated assumptions that it is the actions, relationships, and choices of men that matter, placing women on the margins of colonial justice and social order.

In doing this, the technologies of state law and the economies of modern justice—articulated by the judge and the police, advocates and assessors, and lawyers and clerks—drew in the participation and energies of village folk as victims, accused, and witnesses. Facing the law as a theater of power, at once an alien justice and legality and a procedure of settlement and revenge, the participation of colonial subjects could be reluctant and instrumental and their energies ambivalent and ancillary. Significantly, the patriarchy and negativity of the law often set the terms for this participation and these energies, entailing efforts to make the latter correspond to the former, at least within the space of colonial justice. There were several consequences, particularly for the issues under discussion, which are primarily raised as questions here.

Let us begin by thinking of gender relationships embedded within the structures of kinship in Chhattisgarh less as reflections of an unrelenting and seamless indigenous patriarchy and more as parts of inherently varied connections between patriliny and gender across South Asia and beyond.[56] Out of these varied binds, there follow different implications for the actions and practices of women within distinct arrangements of patrilineal kinship. Returning to the cases at hand, it was in keeping with its patriarchal and negative determinations that the law understood the constitutive ends of these dramas through rigid grids of patriarchal logic. This rode roughshod over the more fluid interplay between gender and kinship in everyday arenas in Chhattisgarh, further ruling out the volition of women. It followed that Bahartin and Kachrin became mere vectors of a patriarchal logic understood as governing the social order.

Yet, it would be hasty to consider these performances of modern law as sharply separated from the worlds of colonial subjects. If colonial judicial discourse gave a thorough working over to the narrative of the crime, the subjects of empire equally participated in processes of the law. On one hand, through the mediation of lawyers and advocates the victim, the accused, and the witness learned to frame their utterances in the syntax of modern law, distinct from the grammar of practical kinship. Along with the discursive operations of imperial justice, this led the colonial subjects to accede to the terms of the negative and patriarchal determinations of state law, especially in the domain of colonial courts. On the other hand, it is crucial that we also consider the consequences of such participation and these energies in newer articulations of order and gender, transformations of practical kinship, within arenas of popular legalities and quotidian illegalities through their work on state law. Novel verities lay beyond older truths.

In the end, acknowledging the complexity and intractability of subject retrieval and admitting the absences and fractures within dominant discourses, I raise a final question concerning Bahartin and Kachrin. Would it be too much to suggest that the disputes discussed in this chapter indicate an excess of meaning and power surrounding the actions of women and the articulations of gender, an excess hardly contained by the judicial archive, colonial law, patrilineal models, and academic discourse? It is hardly surprising that there is much of significance in the mutual constitution of colonial law, popular legalities, and quotidian illegalities that articulates empire and modernity. Such contradictions and contentions are further unraveled in the next chapter.

I n colonial representatives and South Asian perceptions, Indian peoples are peculiarly prone to litigation. It is easy to dismiss these descriptions as mere stereotypes. However, it is more important to consider the diverse histories that are contained by such "tropes that bind" of endlessly litigious subcontinental subjects. Here we find a gross mismatch between the scattered studies of the law and the abundant lives of legalities in India.

Joining a handful of critical exercises in the field, this chapter, like the one before it, seeks to elaborate the place of colonial-modern law and the play of popular-coeval legalities in South Asia.[1] Specifically, I discuss two disputes that featured patterns of enmity over entitlements to property in late colonial central India. An account of these disputes allows us to trace the competing conceptions of rights, legalities, and justice within quotidian encounters that shape subaltern and colonial histories. At stake are everyday negotiations and reworkings of state law. These entanglements extend from claims in the name of the subaltern person to contestations in terms of contingent communities, complicating both our ideas of the individual and our notions of the nation.

State and Subject

A few tentative remarks on the interplay between colonial law and popular legalities are in order at this point. These remarks emerge from my reading of the judicial archive in the last chapter. Equally, they frame my discussion of the two disputes that lie ahead. Bearing on power and personhood, these considerations suggest the simultaneous presence of critical distinctions and mutual binds between norms of colonial justice and practices of Indian subjects. Together such binds and distinctions, discourses and practices, shaped the articulations of empire and modernity on the ground in central India.[2] Two sets of considerations are salient here.

In the mid–nineteenth century, after the British acquired the territories of the raja of Nagpur, they created the Central Provinces, reconstituting the administration of this large province of the British Indian empire. I have shown elsewhere that down to the middle of the twentieth century the collection of land revenue and the maintenance of law and order together constituted the fulcrum of the interest of the colonial state in central India.[3] It was through ordered grids of property relations and the mechanisms of law and order that the colonial state primarily gained access to its subjects, also attempting through these measures to contain and control, define and discipline, and normalize and naturalize (central) Indian peoples. These matrices framed and articulated notions of the person and the subject.

In central India, the revenue system premised on the malguzari settlement tended to view persons as parts of the tenurial and proprietary arrangements within the village community. In contrast, the images mediating the notion of the "individual" in the criminal law courts were at once clearer and more complex. The process and discourses of colonial law articulated an inherited notion of the "person." Here the individual was envisioned as an integrated "whole," detachable from the matrix of social relationships and definable in terms of a discrete set of needs. We know that such a notion has a strong normative element. A construction of modern regimes of power, it is a way to distinguish pathologies, extend control over diffuse and intimate domains of social life, and produce normalized subjects. At the same time, however, in determining a crime colonial law could also attend to "indigenous" understandings, now and again drawing on the schemes of rank and honor of castes and communities and the patterns of local norms and practices. The establishment of guilt and constructions of the person within the practice and discourse of colonial law could not escape the mutual histories of imperial entanglements.

It is a truism that the emotions at work within a dispute did not merely emerge from the dynamic centers of awareness of individuals. These emotions were integrated elements of social experience and relationships. The contours of experience resonated with the force of cultural contingencies, the fiber of critical circumstances. To be in a dispute often involved a troubled inner state, anger, and a potential loss of honor. The emotions had to be addressed and the problem resolved. Moreover, we are dealing here with relationships of power structured by kinship and gender, caste and age, impinged on by colonial law and imperial authority. To act on emotions and redress problems by attacking the enemy—a relative, a neighbor, the spouse's paramour, a witch, a shaman—was to negotiate these relationships of power, avoid loss of face, and retain one's honor. Third, the reprisal avenging the violation of a person's place was far removed from that striking phrase invoked by colonial law (and made famous recently by Pink Floyd), "a momentary lapse of reason." Rather, such reprisals often appear to have been tuned in different ways to the meanings that underlay the everyday objects and quotidian conventions of the social order, variously upholding, contradicting, and exceeding these definitions. Fourth, as we shall see, the oft-repeated plea of "grave and sudden provocation" as the defense of the accused in the law court could straddle two sets of meanings. It could be a tactic, aided by the tutoring of witnesses by lawyers, to escape harsh punishment by using the grammar of colonial law, *and* it could be true, in a situational sense, since such "provocation" was the culmination of a particular mode of reasoning that was inseparable from emotion. Finally, the symbols, metaphors, and practices of colonial-modern law were simultaneously an alien legality, a strategy of settlement and revenge, and a pool of resources deployed selectively by Indian peoples to define new pathologies and fashion novel legalities within the domain of everyday life while also constructing fresh formulations of order within communities. These considerations inform my discussion of the nitty-gritty of community and conflict, power and personhood, in the two disputes before us.

Dispute 3: State and Nation in Everyday Arenas

The land revenue resettlement of the Bilaspur District between 1927 and 1932 led to the creation of two "parties" in Murlidih village: the "tenant party" and the "malguzar party."[4] The tenants belonged to different castes. The malguzars belonged to one family. The conflict centered on rival claims over the *gochar* (village waste) and the *barcha* (land adjoining the village pond used for growing sugarcane), questions of rent and interest, and the issues of repayment of debts and forced labor. Finally, there was the intrusion of the notion of *swaraj* (freedom/independence) as it was reworked and reinterpreted by the tenants. All this underlay a protracted battle of strategy and maneuver in the small village of Murlidih.

In the course of this long, drawn-out conflict, nine members of the tenant party—eight Rawats and one Satnami—were accused of taking a silver *chura* (ornament worn above the wrist) and a gold *bali* (ornament worn in the ear) from Govinda and Jagatram malguzars. When Govinda and Jagatram tried to get their possessions back by making a payment, the tenants kept the money but did not return the ornaments. The tenants also forced the malguzars to give them a receipt for *dhan* (un-husked paddy). This was

Table 2 Details of the "Tenant Party"

Name	Caste	Approximate Age	Occupation	Status within the Trial
Rendhia	Rawat	40	Tobacco seller	Accused
Orjhatia	Rawat	30	Cultivator	Accused
Sakharam	Satnami	30	Cultivator	Accused
Bhokna	Rawat	45	Cultivator	Accused
Balli	Rawat	45	Cultivator	Accused
Shivprasad	Rawat	40	Cultivator	Accused
Koli	Rawat	60	Cultivator	Accused
Mohan	Teli	32	Oil presser	Approver
Baijnathdass	Bairagi	50	Cultivator	Approver
Budga	Ganda	42	Cultivator	Prosecution witness

the prosecution's story. The defense claimed that the tenants had not stolen the ornaments or the money. The trial in the court of the additional Sessions judge, Raipur, was concerned with the facts of the "dacoity." The tensions between the malguzars and tenants constituted the antecedents of and background to this central event. However, it is possible to reverse this emphasis. The removal of the bali and chura, the acts that helped fashion the dispute as a "case" provide us with a point of entry with which to reconstruct the elaboration of a conflict between malguzars and tenants within village life in Murlidih.

Protagonists and Players
What do we know about the village and the family of malguzars? Murlidih was mainly populated by Rawats, the agricultural caste of village graziers. The other inhabitants of the village were Telis, Gandas, Bairagis, and Satnamis. The overwhelming majority of the tenants of Murlidih had meager landholdings: seven of the ten members of the tenant party, protagonists in the trial, had landholdings of between 1.5 and 3.75 acres. Koli Rawat owned 6.74 acres, Baijnathdass had 8.95 acres and Budga Ganda held no land at all.[5] Other details about the members of the tenant party are contained in table 2. The village proprietors of Murlidih belonged to the Chanahoo agricultural caste. The family had two branches. One lived in Murlidih and the other in nearby Karbadih. The family held the two villages jointly, but the two branches cultivated their lands separately (see fig. 5).

Two "Parties" and the State
The creation of the two "parties" in Murlidih was rooted in the land revenue resettlement of the district between 1927 and 1932. Malguzar Govinda

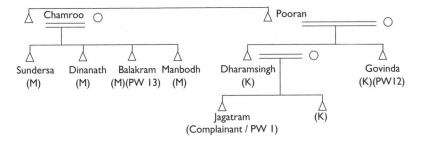

M = Murlidih; K = Karbadih; PW = Prosecution Witness

Figure 5   Family of Chanahoo malguzars

stated that "since last settlement the troubles between Malguzars and tenants have arisen."[6] The government announced the settlement in the two villages early in 1931. By August–September 1931, the malguzars and tenants stood divided in two parties. There were two major points of tension brought to the fore by the settlement operations: the gochar, or village wastelands for grazing; and the barcha, the land used for sugarcane cultivation in the village.

What did the settlement authority of the colonial state have to say about the two issues? Regarding village waste, the government argued the following:

> In the Khalsa of this district, definite areas of village waste have been exclusively reserved for the grazing of village cattle. The reservation of land for grazing purposes is an extremely controversial matter, but in view of the fact that much of the land reserved is practically unculturable and the consensus of opinion was in favour of such reservation, Government agreed to its continuance. But in order to preserve a certain degree of elasticity, it was ordered that power should be given to Deputy Commissioner to allow such changes during the currency of the settlement, as local circumstances might render desirable.[7]

The story of the sugarcane fields was a little different.

> The cane fields are either scattered plots situated in the holdings of individual agriculturists, or common lands locally known as barchas, which are appropriated permanently to the purpose and so situated as to facilitate irrigation from one of the village tanks. The barchas are either held by the Malguzar . . . and the tenants jointly, in which case each man has, each year, his plot from which he takes the rotation crop also in the following year, or it may entirely consist of the Mal-

guzar['s] . . . home farm where the rights of the tenants are limited to its use for growing cane only in alternate years, the owner of the land taking whole of the rotation crop. *In those villages, where the barchas have been divided into strips and held permanently in severalty the strips have been numbered and recorded separately according to possession.*[8]

Murlidih had witnessed that "certain degree of elasticity" left for government initiative in relation to gochar lands: "The tenants of the village used to demand from us the Malguzars that they should be given the pakka gochar lands for cultivation. They said they would pay rent."[9] Clearly, the gochar land in Murlidih was not "practically unculturable" or uncultivable. It was in keeping with these "local circumstances" that the government had allowed a change. The entire gochar of Murlidih came under the sole possession of the malguzars.[10] However, as we shall see, the measure went against the "consensus of opinion" of the tenants.

Concerning barcha, Murlidih was not among those villages where land for sugarcane cultivation had been "divided into strips and held in severalty." Before the settlement of 1932, the village malguzars alone used to occupy the barcha lands. It was their "home farm." However, after the settlement the barcha of the village was "surveyed, numbered and recorded separately": the strips of this land were now divided among the tenants and the malguzars of Murlidih for the cultivation of sugarcane.[11] Thus, "The tenants have been given rights for sugarcane and padti [gochar] land is allowed to the Malguzars by revenue officers."[12]

The decisions of the colonial settlement authority concerning the gochar and barcha in Murlidih marked a departure from the earlier practice in the village. The gochar on which all the villagers had once possessed grazing rights now became the sole property of the malguzars. The barcha earlier held only by the malguzars was distributed among the tenants and malguzars. Moreover, a certain ambiguity characterized these changes. There was a gap between what the settlement report said about gochar and barcha lands and what actually happened in Murlidih. In fact, the break with past practices—and the ambiguity surrounding these processes—created space for the contending claims of the two parties in the village.

Contending Claims
The conflicting claims of tenants and proprietors over gochar become clear from the statement of Jagatram the malguzar: "The tenants of the village used to demand from us the Malguzars that they should be given the Gochar . . . land for cultivation or else they would not allow us to cultivate the same. They said that they would pay rent and if the land was not given it may remain fallow. This year the idea became firm with the tenant."[13] The

malguzars refused to budge. "Applications were made to the Revenue Courts, but the tenants lost."[14] The loss would have been a disappointment, a blow. The claim of the tenants had legitimacy. If the gochar, the common property of the villagers in the recent past, was to be cultivated, then the tenants should have a right in cultivation—they were willing to pay rent. At the same time, if the tenants did not receive this right they would not let the malguzars cultivate—the lands would remain fallow.

There was in addition the question of the barcha. The tenants received rights in the barcha after the settlement. However, the malguzars were unwilling to part with what had been their land before the settlement: "Malguzar was also not giving sugarcane lands to tenants for cultivation."[15] Indeed, some of the tenants felt that the malguzars had lost their rights over both the gochar and the barcha, which bore testimony to the differential perceptions of the changes introduced by the land revenue settlement: "Since last settlement it is decided that all the tenants have a right to grow cane on lands reserved for it and also on Gochar lands. The Malguzars sole possession is refused by the settlement."[16]

The questions of the gochar and barcha found links with two other contested issues within Murlidih. The first of these was the payment of rent and interest to malguzar, and the second concerned begar or unpaid labor rendered under "custom"—codified by the colonial regime—by tenants to their malguzars. The trouble over rent went back in time. Dharamsingh, the resident malguzar of Karbadih, had got together with Sundersa of Murlidih. These two village proprietors had divided the tenants of Murlidih among themselves and separately collected rent from them. This arrangement had worked for a year. After that, the tenants had refused to pay rent for three years. At the time when the tension over the barcha and gochar in the village became serious, the malguzars were demanding rent with interest, but the tenant party was in no mood to pay: "Sundersa and Dharamsingh divided the tenantry privately and in one year they recovered the rent privately from their respective tenants. For three years next none of them received rents and then after that arrears with interest were demanded. The tenants declined to pay interest and on this account also there are two parties—one for the tenant and one for the Malguzar."[17]

Equally, the settlement of 1927–32 had formally done away with the institution of begar. The imperial settlement authority had declared that "Very little of the patriarchal idea now survives in the relations between landlords and tenants, and there is no reason why this relic of a medieval custom should be entered into the record of rights, particularly when there is so much cry against forced labour all over the world."[18] Govinda stated, "In the last settlement Bhet Begar has been stopped and the tenants now refuse to give Bhet Begar and [the issue] has made them rise against their

Malguzars."[19] While the malguzar was lamenting the final demise of "paternalistic" ties, the tenants were freed of a burden and a critical marker of their subordination to the malguzar: "This year we did not do Bhet Begar."[20] The lines of battle were clearly drawn.

The Tenants and Their Nation

The tenant initiative opened with the customary social boycott within village life, *nai dhobi bandh*, which entails depriving an offender of the critical assistance of the service castes, particularly the barber and the washerman: "The tenants stopped our servants and also barber and dhobis [washermen]. This was in last Kuar [September-October]."[21] The boycott was comprehensive. The shunning of the malguzars also involved a ban, enforced by oaths in the name of relatives, on verbal interaction with the malguzar: "The tenants had also the [other] tenants not to speak to the [malguzars] and had put oaths in the name of relatives."[22]

The social boycott was, of course, a form of censure, and this was also expressed in other ways. The tenants would smear the doors of the malguzars' houses with human excrement and throw the polluting substance into their compounds. They pelted the malguzars' houses with stones, uprooted the chili plants, and broke down the compound walls of their adversaries. These acts were intended to prevent the malguzars from showing their faces within the village. As the resident malguzar of Murlidih lamented, "We had to keep our doors closed. We used to come from the backdoor side. . . . We kept inside the house all day long."[23]

The tenants of Murlidih had initiated a major offensive. Over issues relating to the village as a whole, the malguzars ordinarily decided on matters of censure, also defining the network of relationships featuring service castes in quotidian life.[24] To initiate a complete social boycott of the malguzar therefore was to establish an alternative, oppositional center of authority. But this should not be surprising. The tenant enterprise was informed by the critical metaphor of swaraj—freedom, independence, and self-rule. Budga Ganda made this clear: "I was in the tenant party of Swaraj. The only persons excepted were Malguzars."[25] The repeated play with the metaphor of swaraj within the depositions of witnesses underscores the fact that the tenants believed that freedom had indeed come to Murlidih.

The dispute between tenants and malguzars in Murlidih was part of a larger pattern. Almost all over the Jaijaipur station area—in which Murlidih was located—there were tensions between malguzars and tenants. In his deposition, Niaz Ahmad, the circle inspector of police, stated that "In many other villages in the said station house area there are disputes between tenants and Malguzars." The police official had found out about the trouble in Murlidih when he was on tour, "making enquiries about the disputes" in the entire area.[26] In the first round of the Civil Disobedience movement, called by the Indian National Congress in 1930–31, there were numerous forest *satyagrahas* in the neighboring Raipur District, and the Congress organization was strong in the towns of Bilaspur District.[27] In the Jaijaipur station house area, tenant opposition to the malguzars was shaped by the articulation of generalized notions of challenge to authority and its displacement together with tensions rooted in processes of revenue resettlement that had begun in the late 1920s.

The tenants of Murlidih seized on the notion of swaraj within this matrix. We have noted that in recent years there have been forceful reminders of the need to understand swaraj as an inherently polysemic sign capable of generating and sustaining multiple perceptions. Apprehended and elaborated in varied ways, swaraj appeared to be differentially implicated in the practices of distinct social groups.[28] As Mohan Teli explains: "Swaraj in our village means that whoever can retain any article got should be allowed to retain that article as his own."[29]

Could an obscure oil presser's statement possibly have links to Antonio Gramsci's observation that popular currents of natural law are "the ensemble of opinions and beliefs concerning one's 'own' rights which circulate uninterruptedly among the popular masses and are continuously renewed under the pressure of real living conditions?"[30] At the same time, Mohan Teli had come up with what was only one of the definitions of swaraj in Murlidih. Swaraj opened up several possibilities reworked in practice by the tenant party of Murlidih. Indeed, swaraj informed an alternative, tenant locus of authority that launched and sustained a vigorous campaign of censure against the malguzars of Murlidih.

We get a glimpse of the shift in the nature of the tenant enterprise in the deposition of Jagatram the malguzar: "The disputes about Gochar land and other lands started from settlement time. The tenants used to damage our crops, since last Kartik [October–November] only. Before Kartik last ie. before taking the ornaments the tenants used to damage the crops by cattle and after that they gathered the crops themselves."[31] Mohan Teli added: "We were saying that Swaraj had come to our village and as Govinda and Jagat . . . were seeing the fields, we would call them and make them pay. This spirit has started since last Kartik."[32] The month of *kartik* was the point in time that inaugurated the shift. There was a change from merely damaging the malguzars' property to actually staking claim to it. Now the tenants did not allow the malguzars to gather their crops, reaping them themselves.

The shift also initiated an attack on the bonds that inscribed debts to malguzars. According to the village proprietor Balakram:

The tenants then held a meeting which all the accused attended. We four brothers were called. . . . Sundersa asked why they were summoned. Accused Sukharam, Bhaluwa and Rendhia then said that we should tear out all the bonds for debts and an agreement would be made. We wanted four days time for consideration. On that Orzatia said that they should go away and Malguzars would not tear away the bonds. The tenants went away one after the other and then we brothers came back. They began to throw night soil in the compound and we had to walk through it . . . the tenants began to trouble us more and more.[33]

The four brothers of which Balakram spoke were the four resident malguzars of Murlidih. In fact, the tenants of Murlidih did not take loans from moneylenders outside the village. It was the debt bonds to the malguzars of the village that the tenants had sought to destroy. This "territoriality" of the tenants brings us to the central event of the trial.

Open Events
According to the prosecution's story, on 20 November 1931 Rendhia, Orjhatia, Bhukua, Balli, Shivprasad, Koli, Sakharam, and Baijnathdass (see table 2) were sitting near the house of Koli Rawat. According to Mohan, "We were saying that Swaraj has come to our village and we will make them pay."[34] Jagat and Govinda malguzars were returning after spending a few hours in their fields within the village. They had reaped the crops the day before. The tenants summoned the two as they passed the house of Koli Rawat: "We went there and were asked to sit down."[35] Rendhia and Bhulwa said that Govinda and Jagatram should pay ten and fifteen rupees, respectively, if they wished to gather their crops. The malguzars stood up to leave, saying, why should they pay.[36] "The accused then said we should pay or else our fathers will pay and that would not do."[37] The two malguzars of Karbadih were surrounded with cries of "pakdo, pakdo" (catch them, catch them). Jagatram later stated: "I was caught hold of by Orjhatia and my uncle Govinda was caught by hand. All of them [the tenants] said 'chhino, chhino' [grab, grab]. Orjhatia then took out a silver Chura from my hands. . . . Rendhia took out a Bali from the ear of my uncle."[38] The tenants forbade Jagat and Govinda to enter Murlidih. The malguzars spoke about the affair with the kotwar of their village but did not report the matter to the police for fear that they would be killed if they talked about the incident. Jagat "refused to make a report for fear of life."[39] A week later Jagat and Govinda went to Murlidih. They paid eight rupees to Sakharam Satnami and asked for the ornaments. The money was kept, but the chura and the bali were not returned. About this time, the tenants also forced the two

malguzars to give them a receipt, which stated that malguzars had received their share of the paddy from the lands given to the tenants for cultivation.

These three acts of the tenants involved a play with territoriality. Jagat and Govinda were the nonresident malguzars of Murlidih: "As Jagat and Govinda were non-resident Malguzars we decided to take the money from them. The others lived in my village."[40] On 1 February 1932, the circle inspector of police, Niaz Ahmad, went to Murlidih for the second time within the month, making inquiries into the tensions between malguzars and tenants in the Jaijaipur station house area. During this visit, the malguzars reported the events of the "dacoity" to the circle inspector.

In their defense, the tenants denied that the three events had occurred. All of them claimed alibis, arguing that the bali and chura that had been seized by the police from Orjhatia and Rendhia belonged to the two Rawats. They argued that the malguzars were framing them out of *adawat* (enmity), which had its roots in the quarrel over the barcha and gochar lands and the tenants' refusal to pay rent for three years. Repeated by all the tenants in their examinations, the endorsement of enmity is significant for the reconstruction of this dispute.

In the judgment, which was delivered on 7 May 1932, the additional Sessions judge argued that the "prosecution consists of the testimony of eye witnesses only and it is a case of believing or not believing the prosecution witness." The judge went on to say that he believed the prosecution witnesses in "light of probabilities." The defense of the accused was "weak," the witnesses were "interested," and the case of the prosecution stood "unrebuked." At the same time, the judgment qualified the central event: "This is not a case of dacoity in the strict sense of the term, but is more or less technical dacoity. What the tenants really appeared to have desired was to coerce the Malguzars to subjugation." The seven accused received the sentence of rigorous imprisonment for seven months.[41]

If we believe the prosecution's story, the three central events of the "dacoity" were not exceptional occurrences. They were part of a pattern. The tenant party, inspired by the new possibilities opened up by swaraj, had begun making claims on village property. The tenants of Murlidih had taken the chura, the bali, the money, and the receipt from the malguzars because of their perception of what was their legitimate due and entitlement. Equally clearly, however, we do not have to believe the prosecution's story. It is quite possible, as the tenants argued in their defense, that their malguzar adversaries were implicating them on trumped up charges.

Here I would not like to assume the mantle of a masterful detective in order to sort out which of these versions of the story is true. Instead, let me suggest that even if we believe that the events of the dacoity did not take place this does not compromise the basic plot of the drama between the malguzars and the tenants of Murlidih. The tenants argued that the malguzars were framing them out of enmity. This enmity—which resulted in the creation of two parties—was rooted in the tensions and quarrels over the gochar and barcha lands and the refusal to pay rent and render begar. During their examination at the trial, all of the tenants admitted this. On being asked a pointed question about the way the tenants used to trouble the malguzars, a principal accused admitted that they had thrown excrement into the malguzar's house even as he made light of the event: "Thoda sa maila dere mein ek din phenk diya tha" (One day a bit of shit was thrown into the compound).[42] Indeed, the seven members of the tenant party turned the admission of their quarrel with the malguzars into their defense.

It is the nature and elaboration of this quarrel that I am after. The events of the so-called dacoity provide a point of entry at which we can reconstruct a struggle launched by the tenants of a barely known village in Bilaspur District. The point of entry also has to be the moment of closure, at the very least provisionally. My account of the dispute between the tenants and malguzars in Murlidih ends with the sentencing of seven tenants—six Rawats and one Satnami—to seven months of rigorous imprisonment.

Dispute 4: Migrant's Honor

Santram was a peasant, a tenant farmer who belonged to the Satnami caste. He lived in Kapisda village in the Janjgir Tahsil of Bilaspur District. Between agricultural seasons, Santram would migrate periodically to the koalari (coalfields) to the north and east, like tens of thousands of other Satnami cultivators, in search of labor and livelihood. On 8 November 1938, Santram fought with five Dhimar brothers in Kapisda village.[43] The fight was the culmination of a quarrel that had begun almost ten years earlier. This quarrel involved a debt, its repayment, and consequent tensions over rival claims to ownership of land.[44] On the morning of 8 November 1938, Motiram, one of the Dhimar brothers, had taunted Santram. In his statement to the police, Santram admitted that he had replied in anger. The verbal exchange became abusive and soon developed into an altercation in which Santram grappled with Panchram and Patiram Dhimar. Physically separated from the two brothers and his honor and self-respect at stake, Santram had struck Motiram with a lathi. Motiram died in the evening.

The village of Kapisda was mainly populated by the middle-ranking caste of Dhimars. The Satnamis ranked a close second in the caste composition of the village. Dhimars were the most substantial landholding caste in Kapisda, while the Satnamis were much poorer cultivators. In

1930–31, Santram and his brothers owned twenty pieces of land. Their largest holdings were 1.25 and 1.18 acres, and the rest were less than an acre. Their total holdings were 8.12 acres. There were only three Satnami families with holdings larger than those of Santram and his brothers. For their part, the Dhimar brothers owned 25.74 acres. They were among the more substantial cultivators in the village.[45]

Prosecution Truths and Accused Verities
The prosecution held that in 1929 Santram had borrowed Rs 100 from Sahasram, a Kostha cultivator and moneylender. His surety for the debt was Bisram, the *patwari* (accountant) of the village and the brother of Motiram, Patiram, and Panchram Dhimar. When the debt was not repaid, Sahasram filed a suit, obtained a decree, and received the money from Bisram, as Santram was not in a position to pay. On 29 October 1934, Sahasram issued the receipt in the name of Bisram. In order to satisfy his liability for the surety of Bisram, Santram Satnami had already sold him the tenancy rights to his five fields through an unregistered deed of sale on 28 July 1933. In 1933, Bisram and his four brothers cultivated the land and reaped the crops. In 1934, Santram reaped the crops sown by Bisram. The receipt from Sahasram and the unregistered deed of sale in hand, Bisram and his brothers now filed a suit to take possession of Santram's fields. A decree in their favor in civil suit no. 163 A of 1935 delivered the fields to the Dhimar brothers on 7 November 1937. The brothers sowed and cultivated them in *asad* (June-July) of 1938 and also reaped the crops of three of the fields, although Santram raised an objection. Indeed, Santram harvested the crops of one of the fields that had been cultivated and sowed by Bisram and his brothers, a fact reported by Patiram Dhimar at the Jaijaipur station house. The crop of one more field remained unharvested, but Santram did not reap it because it was not ripe.[46]

Santram's version of the long history of the quarrel and litigation was different. He admitted to borrowing money from Sahasram in 1929. But he argued that Bisram had not merely stood surety in this transaction. Actually, Santram and Bisram had together borrowed a sum of Rs 100—Rs 50 each—from Sahasram, although the officially stamped paper stated that the amount was Rs 200. In 1930, Santram had given Rs 30 to Bisram to give to Sahasram, but Bisram had pocketed the money. In 1931, Sahasram filed a case against Bisram and Santram. In 1932, Santram gave Bisram Rs 78, which once again did not reach Sahasram. In 1933, Sahasram and Bisram played foul. They persuaded Santram to sign an unregistered deed of sale when the Satnami actually wanted to obtain a mortgage deed. Santram reported this to the police, and the *thanedar* (subinspector of police) gave him permission to cultivate the fields. In 1933, 1934, and 1935, Santram reaped the harvest. In November 1935, Bisram filed a suit against Santram. Santram had gone to the coalfields to earn his living. He was ignorant of the result of the lawsuit. In 1936, no one cultivated the land. Santram came back in 1937. He told Bisram that if he and his brothers wished to cultivate the land they should pay the rent to the village proprietor, but they did not do so. Instead, Santram paid the rent and then sowed the fields. In 1938, Santram paid the rent once more, but Bisram's brothers did not allow him to sow the fields and fought with him. Santram still considered the lands to be his own. The Dhimar brothers would sow in the morning, and Santram would water fields in the evening. In *savan* (July–August) of 1938, Santram again went to the coalfields. On his return, as the time to reap the harvest approached, he told the Dhimar brothers that the matter of the ownership and use of the fields needed sorting out. However, Bisram and his brothers first reaped the crops of three fields and then of another field. On 6 November 1938, Santram reaped the crops of half of the one field still unreaped by the Dhimar brothers. Two days later, on 8 November, Bisram and his brothers sent a message to Santram that they had reaped the remaining crops of this holding. Santram had gone out on an errand. On the way back, he encountered the Dhimar brothers.[47]

According to the prosecution, Motiram was at the house of Shyamlal malguzar along with Kawal Prasad, Santram Marar, and Ramprasad. The "accused," Santram Satnami, approached from the right side. As he passed in front of the house, Motiram called out to Santram that if he was in search of witnesses to the reaping of crops he could take Ramprasad. Santram replied in anger that he did not want witnesses and he would not be cowed by the Dhimar brothers because of their numbers since he was a match for twenty like them. The verbal exchange turned abusive. Motiram entreated Santram not to quarrel and asked him to go away. Just then, Panchram and Patiram, the brothers of Motiram and Bisram, reached the house. Patiram had a bamboo stick in his hand. Now Panchram and Patiram Dhimar also asked Santram to go his own way rather than start a quarrel. They said that they had reaped the crops already and Santram could take legal steps. This provoked Santram further. There was an angry verbal exchange. Santram grappled with Panchram and Patiram, but Birichram and Kanwalprasad put an end to this fight. Once more, Motiram asked Santram to leave. At this point, Santram dealt Motiram a blow with a stick and took to his heels. Motiram was about to fall when Ramprasad caught him and lay him down under a tree. Patiram and Panchram followed Santram, striking him three times with their sticks as he ran. Then they returned to the place where Motiram was lying. He was taken to the family home, where he died that evening.[48]

As part of his defense, Santram admitted that on the morning of 8 November 1938, when he was passing the house of Shyamlal malguzar, he encountered Bisram's brothers. According to his first statement, recorded by the police, Santram had said that during the meeting the taunts of the Dhimar brothers had enraged him, particularly since their words had come in the wake of several prior insults. In anger, he had seized a stick from one of the men standing there and had struck Motiram with it. In his examination in the Court of Session, Santram stated that when Panchram called out and asked if he wanted a witness to their reaping of the crops he had declined and stated that he would get the crops through the *adalat*, the law court. Patiram then attacked, dealing him a blow on the forehead. Panchram also attacked, but Santram had warded off the blow. Next, all the brothers flung themselves on him from different sides. He had no stick with which to defend himself. He denied having struck Motiram. No, he could not say whose lathi had struck Motiram. Patiram, Bidyaram, and Judawan were his enemies. On this account, they had deposed against him.[49] At the same time, Santram's defense was that he had dealt a blow in self-defense and had not committed an offense. If he was found to have committed an offense, it would be the result of grave and sudden provocation.[50]

Two Tales
The major points in the contending accounts of this conflict require sorting out.

Santram's (Defense) Version	Bisram's (Prosecution) Version
1. Bisram and Santram together borrowed Rs 100–Rs 50 each—from Sahasram.	1. Santram borrowed Rs 100 from Sahasram; Bisram stood surety.
2. In 1930, Santram gave Rs 30 to Bisram to pay to Sahasram, but the money did not reach the moneylender.	2. Bisram made no mention of this transaction.
3. In 1932, Santram gave Rs 78— this amount included the interest on the capital borrowed—to Bisram, but it was not given to Sahasram.	3. Bisram made no mention of this transaction.
4. In 1933, Sahasram and Bisram tricked Santram. While he wanted a mortgage deed, they had an unregistered deed of sale written.	4. Santram's land was transferred through an unregistered deed of sale since he was not in a position to make even part of the payment.

5. There is no mention of a receipt given by Sahasram to Bisram. This was part of the conspiracy hatched later by Sahasram and Bisram.	5. In 1934, the receipt for the full payment of the debt was given by Sahasram to Bisram.
6. In 1933, 1934, and 1935, Santram sowed and reaped the crops on the orders of the police. In 1937, he again sowed and reaped the crops.	6. In 1933, Bisram and his brothers sowed and reaped the crops. In 1934, they sowed but Santram reaped the crops. There is no mention of who cultivated the fields in 1935.
7. Santram claimed ignorance of both the result of a lawsuit filed by Bisram and his brothers and delivery of the possession of his lands in 1937 since he was away working in the coalfields.	7. In 1934, Bisram and his brothers filed a suit. The court decreed in their favor in 1935, and in November 1937 they legally received Santram's lands.
8. In 1938, Bisram and his brothers took Santram's lands. They also reaped the crops of four fields. But Santram continued to water the fields.	8. In 1938, Bisram's brothers sowed all the fields. When Santram reaped the harvest of one field, Patiram reported it to the police.

There are certain similarities in these two tales of a debt, its repayment, and, when the debt was not paid back, rival claims to ownership of land. Well versed with the artifacts and vocabulary of the legal system, Bisram and his brothers staked their claims through receipts, deeds of sale, lawsuits, and the delivery of possession of land through a decree of the court. Santram Satnami in turn drew on the authority of an official who embodied the power of the colonial law and order machinery. It was on the orders of the thanedar, the subinspector of police, that he had sown and reaped his fields in 1933, 1934, 1935, and 1937.

Equally, in establishing the legitimacy of their claim over the land both sides used a related argument: a pattern of the use of land to assert a legitimate right, followed by a closure affected by the enemy through an intrusion. For their part, Bisram and his brothers claimed that in 1933 they had cultivated the land; in 1934, they had sowed but Santram had reaped the crops; and in 1938 Bisram's brothers had sowed the fields and Santram had reaped the crops of one of the fields. Santram, in turn, stated that he had cultivated the land in 1933, 1934, 1935, and 1937. Bisram's brothers had taken his land in 1938. Even so, the brothers would sow in the morning and Santram would water the fields in the evening. Bisram and his brothers had reaped the crops—including the unripe green crops of one field—of what in Santram Satnami's understanding continued to be his land.

There were also key differences of emphasis in the contending versions of the story. Bisram and his brothers made much of the documentary exhibits, legal artifacts that defined their sound position according to the requirements of civil law.[51] Santram countered the impersonal and abstract authority of mere "pieces of paper" by invoking the tangible and concrete power of the police embodied in the thanedar. The Satnami cultivator also questioned the legality of the position of the Dhimar brothers by suggesting that they had tricked him precisely through these pieces of paper, instruments of guile and power in the hands of adversaries who controlled documents. Bisram had not merely stood surety, but he was a codebtor who had twice pocketed the money meant for Sahasram. Further, it was Bisram's machinations, in league with Sahasram, that led up to the writing of the deed of sale when what Santram wanted was a mortgage deed.

In his examination, Santram voiced anger at these deceptions. The anger was coupled with a note of the tragic, a sense of pathos, when he spoke of his migration to the coalfields. He repeatedly emphasized that he was a poor man. He had been forced to go to the coalfields "jine khane ke liye" (to earn his livelihood).[52] It was during one such period of absence, brought about by the reduced circumstances of a poor and illiterate man, that Bisram's brothers had once again fudged, manipulated, and played foul. They claimed to have filed a suit and obtained a decree conferring on them the rights to Santram's land. Did Santram's statements that he was ignorant of the result of the lawsuit and the court decree express his skepticism regarding such legal procedures, a skepticism based on awareness of the purchase commanded by his enemies because of their superior understanding of legal documents? In Santram's understanding, were these maneuvers, assiduously staged and rehearsed by his opponents, anything but ruses for enactments of expropriation?[53] Indeed, Santram believed that his land still belonged to him. Even in 1938, Bisram and his brothers would sow his fields in the morning and Santram would water them in the evening.

Adding Insult to Injury

As far as Santram was concerned, there was more to the picture. Unlike Bisram and his brothers, who were content to control documents writ large with "legality," through all the years of conflict Santram had continued to pay the rent for his land to the malguzar. He explained that "1937 mein jamin boi aur 1938 mein bharna pataya" (In 1937, I sowed the fields and in 1938 paid the rent).[54] One of the Dhimar brothers, Patiram, stated: "I did not pay rent for the fields at any time. Bisram might be knowing that."[55] In his cross-examination, the village proprietor also declared: "The accused [Santram] paid the rent of the land before this year. Even after the delivery of possession to Bisram . . . the accused paid the rent."[56] For Santram, to sow, water, and pay the rent was to establish rights of use over land, but the five Dhimar brothers had harvested his crops. Compounding injury with insult, in a deliberate move the brothers had not even spared the unripe crops of half of a small field. Santram had been waiting to reap these crops.

In the fight on 8 November 1938, Santram had been repeatedly insulted. Told that members of a "timid caste" (the Dhimars) had grabbed the crops of a "proud Satnami," Santram was being deliberately taunted when asked whether he wanted Ramprasad to act as witness to the Dhimar brothers' reaping of his unripe crops. Santram had replied that "his green crops had been cut and he was being taunted."[57] He had also told Patiram that his unripe crops had been reaped, and now the Dhimars wanted to frighten him through sheer numbers. Following this, "The accused then became very angry and began to tremble with rage."[58]

Clearly, Santram's honor was at stake. His adversaries were in a strong position, since Motiram and Bisram belonged to a large family positioned on the top rung of cultivators in the village. Yet Santram, one of the four most affluent Satnami peasants in the village, was no pushover. Not surprisingly, the Satnami cultivator told Bisram and his brothers that he could take on twenty like them and that the force of numbers did not cow him. Santram declared that the Dhimar brothers "should not treat his field like some other persons and he would give them a lesson by beating them in their own house."[59] In the first report to the police, Santram went on record, saying that he had seized a stick and struck with it. In hitting Motiram, he had been responding to insult and injury and seeking to retain his honor. In the Sessions Court, Santram denied that he had challenged the Dhimars in anger, emphasizing that all along he had said that he would get the crops through the adalat, the court. Here he sought to establish that the Dhimar brothers had abused and beaten him. Passivity and belief in the adalat, the law and order machinery, had replaced the actions through which Santram redressed the grievance and avoided a loss of face.

Santram's claim that he had not committed an offense since he had acted in self-defense—but also that if he was found to have committed the offense of striking Motiram with a stick it was the result of "grave and sudden provocation"—did not cut much ice. The judgment found Santram guilty of culpable homicide not amounting to murder. He was sentenced to rigorous imprisonment for seven years.[60]

Grave Provocation

In the end, I would like to suggest that the plea of "grave and sudden provocation" as Santram's defense could straddle two sets of meanings. It was a tactic, possibly aided by the tutoring and arguments of Santram's lawyer, to escape harsh punishment by using the grammar of state law. The official procedures of the law construed Santram as a bounded center of reason and emotion: reason should allow him to keep his emotions in check, control his instincts, and balance his impulses and desires in light of the possible consequences. As a corollary to this, the long history of the quarrel and litigation was the background, while "grave and sudden provocation" was an event, an act, a word, that led to a momentary suspension of reason. According to the prosecution's story and the judgment, this was not what happened to Santram. When he struck Motiram with a stick, the "victim" was entreating him to go away. The judgment found Santram guilty of culpable homicide not amounting to murder.

At the same time, however, the plea of grave and sudden provocation was perhaps true in a situational sense. Santram's attack at once worked on and addressed emotions of anger and honor to negotiate relationships with his enemies in the village. Were Santram's emotions separable from his reason? Alternatively, was it not a fusion of reason and emotion that constituted and generated Santram's modes of thought and practice?[61] Was the long past of the dispute brought into sharp focus, foregrounded as it were, when the quarrel between Santram and the Dhimar brothers assumed a particularly intense form? Did not the weight and force of the dispute lie behind Santram's act? Was grave and sudden provocation—now understood as the sharp form that the conflict assumed because of an accumulation of insults—the culmination of modes of reasoning that were inseparable from emotion and the defense of honor? Was not Santram's plea of grave and sudden provocation in tune with his practice? The judgment sentenced Santram to rigorous imprisonment for seven years.

Conclusion

To conclude, I wish to raise a few questions around important statements regarding indigenous personhood and colonial power in South Asia connected to the issues of power and difference and empire and modernity discussed in this book. Far from being comprehensive, these comments are indicative of work that lies ahead.

For at least forty years now, anthropological literature on South Asia has discussed issues of the "individual" and concepts of the "person" in different ways. Louis Dumont's seminal exploration of renunciation in South Asian traditions hinges on his analytical opposition between "man in the world" (the householder) and "individual outside the world" (the re-nouncer). Further, holding this schema in place is the larger distinction that Dumont draws between *homo equalus* and *homo hierarchicus*, a distinction that itself points toward differential constructions of the individual and personhood. According to Dumont, the Euro-American world construes the person as an individual, ontologically prior to any collectivity, while regarding society as a whole "in principle [as] two things at once: a collection of individuals and a collective individual." On the other hand, in the Indian cultural order, which is governed by the overarching and encompassing opposition of the pure and the impure, the social whole is ontologically prior to all human beings. In the Euro-American "individualistic universe," the individual possesses all the possible attributes of humanity, while in the Indian "holistic universe" particular empirical actors are conceived of as bearers of different and unequal human attributes.[62]

McKim Marriott and his associates, particularly Ron Inden, elaborated these issues in distinct ways. They approached the issue of personhood in the holistic universe of India by focusing on the empirical human actor, cast somewhat preciously as the "dividual." Here the "dividual is a being who both manipulates and transmits blood purity and related codes of conduct, and is thus located as a kinsperson and a castemate." In South Asia, code appears to be fused with substance and modified by action; dividuals stand inextricably bound by systems of transaction, and transactions between actors lead to simultaneous transformations and transactions within each dividual.[63] With somewhat different emphases, Steve Barnett, Lina Fruzetti, and Akos Ostor initiated related accounts, accounts possibly closer to being "psycho-biological theories" of empirical actors than analyses of personhood in South Asia, a point justly made by Anthony Carter.[64]

In a different vein, working through the insights of Marriott and Peirce, Valentine Daniel's *Fluid Signs* skillfully unraveled a semiotic interpretation of Tamil villagers' understandings of themselves and their quotidian worlds by focusing on the "properties of substances"—of the village, the house, and the body, for example—within "daily, routine, everyday life."[65] Writing a few years later, Margaret Trawick elegantly elaborated the enactments of personhood within daily, quotidian life in other arenas of Tamil culture. Explored were expressions of love and ambiguity—motivations and emotions, feelings and desires—in the context of gender and age within a middle-class family.[66] Finally, more recently, and against the grain of much of the earlier writing on the subject, Mattison Mines has made an extended case for attending to the importance of "individuality" in history, culture, and society in South Asia. Combining archival research and fieldwork in Tamil Nadu, Mines discusses "expressions of individuality in public life" and in "private lives," which he sees as corresponding to the distinction in Tamil culture between the exterior (*akam*) and the interior (*puram*), to underscore the range and significance of Tamil "ideas about the nature of individuality and individual agency."[67]

Without claiming to have captured the complexities of the writings on personhood in South Asia, I nonetheless wish to point toward some of the ways in which such terms of debate might be extended through the perspectives of an ethnographic history of legal entanglements. At stake is that classic conundrum of ethnographic description and historical analysis: the competing claims of human universality and cultural particularity. On this, I have no immanent answer or transcendental solution to offer. Rather, the specific clues I wish to pursue are revealed in legal materials containing the encounters between the inherited, influential idea of the individual as an integrated whole and the diverse, negotiating practices of subaltern subjects variously enacting performances of personhood.

On one hand, far from the exclusive models of the Indian/Hindu—often Tamil—person of anthropology, I wish to explore issues of personhood within the historically layered entanglements among different orderings, distinct renderings, and rival definitions of the subject. On the other hand, I wish to move away from the harmony of the balancing "dividual" and the seamlessness of the balanced individual, the former struggling with the aggregation and disaggregation of "substances" and the latter straddling a priori "private" and "public" domains. Instead, I hope to explicate questions of personhood by locating them in the context of conflicts that were part of the everyday existence of subaltern subjects of empire and modernity.

The burden of colonial law is immense here. We have noted Ranajit Guha's argument that colonial judicial discourse trapped indigenous "crime" in its specificity "by reducing its range of signification to a set of narrowly defined legalities and by assimilating it to the existing order as one of its negative determinations." While there is much to ponder in this perceptive and provocative statement, its thrust is governed by Guha's wider understanding of colonial rule as constituting an "alien moment" of dominance, an autocratic regime "singularly incapable of relating to the society on which it had imposed itself."[68] As the introduction to this book has discussed—and the preceding three chapters will have clarified—my understanding of colonial cultures departs from Guha's somewhat singular reading of colonial dominance. Here I wish to reiterate my emphases regarding colonial law and popular legalities. The making of judicial discourse and legal practice under empire—and the fashioning of imperial rule itself—could not escape the impress of colonial subjects and popular legalities. This involved intersecting yet distinct energies, conjoint but contradictory resources of the colonizer and the colonized. Now, to argue in this vein is far from proposing a depoliticized dialogism of colonial encounters.[69] Rather, it is to mark the fractures and productivity and the terms and limitations—the fractured productivity and terminal limitations—of power, which inhered in colonial law and imperial dominance. There is also a corollary to this argument. The hegemony of the colonial state, including the place and the presence of the law, often rested on the fact that its symbols and practices, saturated with dominance, found their way into the interstices of the subjects of empire but the restless reworking of these saturated forms in "local" arenas prevented them from becoming the uniform currency of colonialism and capital.

Allow me to illustrate through a specific example the wider emphases and larger issues at stake in this discussion. Shahid Amin has provided us with a sensitive examination of the principles of construction of imperial judicial discourse through a detailed analysis of the central place of the "approver" within colonial law. By discussing the "figure" of Mir Shikari, the chief approver in the Chauri Chaura trials, Amin unravels the highly ordered and singularly productive nature of colonial judicial discourse.[70] Here, my reading of the testimony of two approvers in ST 22 of 1932, DSC RR, the first dispute discussed in this chapter, does not reveal the highly ordered principles of construction that, according to Amin, characterized the testimony of Mir Shikari. In this case, the two approvers, Mohan and Baijnathdass, did not become "agents of counterinsurgency." Indeed, we can hear the hesitant echoes of rebel voices in their depositions. Yet, much more than that disabling dichotomy of domination/resistance or approver-renegade/rebel-subaltern is at issue here. It is not just that the "balancing exercises" of the Judge in this Trial at Raipur hardly took recourse to the testimony of the two approvers. It is also that colonial judicial discourse did not always/already constitute the approver's testimony as "material for judgment." Such testimonies protected the prosecution story, but they could also defend the defense account along other grooves. Approver's testimony—alongside depositions for the prosecution and the defense, and examinations of accused—supported *and* subverted their official construction by judicial discourse, also carrying the consequences of such excess beyond the courts of empire to lay them before the tribunals of communities.[71] Such processes lay at the heart of colonial law, popular legalities, and their enmeshments.

In future work, I hope to address these questions of the contending constitution of evidence, the contradictory institution of guilt, and the competing definition of pathologies in the domain of colonial law and the arena of popular legalities by taking up two overlapping lines of inquiry. On one hand, I hope to explore the inextricably bound arenas of discursive strategies of the law and theaters of power of the modern judicial system indelibly marked by the presence of colonial subjects. On the other hand, I seek to probe the practices of subaltern subjects and the technologies of popular legalities, including the performances of personhood, innately inflected by the place of modern justice. To return to the beginning of the last chapter, a great deal lies before me if I am to articulate adequately Sattar's splendid gift of everyday pasts.

POSTCOLONIAL TANGLES

The story has done the rounds, but it bears another telling. During the second half of the 1970s, a small group of enthusiastic younger historians of South Asia, several of them in England, held a series of meetings with a distinguished senior scholar of colonial India, Ranajit Guha, who was teaching history at the University of Sussex. Those who met shared a mutual political sensibility, born of the events surrounding 1968 and the Maoist Naxalbari movement in eastern India, sustained by the unspectacular but determined radicalism of the 1970s, and sharpened by the police and administrative excesses that marked the state of political Emergency—prompted by Prime Minister Indira Gandhi—between 1975 and 1977 in India.[1] The purpose of these discussions in England and India was to thrash out a new agenda for the historiography of the subcontinent, an agenda that recognized the centrality of subordinate groups—rightful but disinherited protagonists—in the making of the past and thereby redressed the elitist imbalance of much of the writing on the subject. Thus, subaltern studies was born.[2] The ongoing historical-critical project has seen the publication of eleven volumes of essays alongside several books by members of the core collective that also form a part of the wider endeavor.[3]

In an opening programmatic statement, Ranajit Guha defined the aim of subaltern studies as an effort "to promote a systematic and informed discussion of subaltern themes in the field of South Asian Studies to rectify the elitist bias of much research and academic work."[4] Defying assumptions that economy, society, and culture in South Asia could be understood in terms of clear-cut divisions of class or explained through reified representations of caste, the project went on to elaborate the category of the subaltern, a term derived from the writings of Antonio Gramsci. Here the subaltern stood as a metaphor for the general attribute of subordination in South Asia expressed in terms of class, caste, age, gender, or office. Now, it was in the very nature of the catchall dimensions of the category that, rather more than a nuanced heuristic device, the notion of the subaltern could acquire the attributes of a substantive and singular historical and political entity. Yet, as an analytical shorthand, subaltern as a critical category also already held out the possibility of sustaining analyses that could elaborate the articulation of different, interlocked principles of social-economic division and political-cultural domination, including those of community and class, caste and race, and gender and nation.

Not surprisingly, in the development of the project the different renderings of the subaltern as a category have found interesting and intriguing manifestations. The earlier exercises within subaltern studies reconstructed the varied trajectories and modes of consciousness of the movements of subordinate groups in India in order to emphasize the autonomy and agency of these communities. To the considerable chagrin of the critics of the project, these endeavors precisely rendered the subaltern as a homogeneous category.[5] More recently, writings within subaltern studies have discussed the multiple mediations—social and epistemic in nature and cultural and discursive in character—that shore up the production of subaltern subjects. Confounding the claims of censors and commentators, these moves have turned the subaltern into a perspective and a metaphor with which to interrogate dominant knowledge(s) of empire and nation and state and modernity. In discussions of subaltern studies, critiques of the homogeneous staging of the subaltern, seen as romanticizing the past, are replaced with charges of a relentless heterogeneity understood as fragmenting history.[6] The project itself continues to find new meanings for subaltern as an analytical category and a critical perspective but equally as a historical metaphor and a theoretical verity.[7]

Either/Or

How are we to read subaltern studies? Is this venture a creative extension of the "histories from below" tradition, an endeavor that has now gone awry amid postmodern, poststructuralist, and postcolonial imperatives? Conversely, does subaltern studies designate yet another initiative, a distinct form of postcolonial criticism? Important interventions in the debate on subaltern studies reflect the polemical polarities at the heart of these questions.[8] But this should not be surprising. All too frequently, the subaltern studies endeavor has been read through resolutely overarching theoretical filters, riding roughshod over the tone and texture of the distinct bodies of writing within the project. In this chapter, my effort is to attend to the arguments and achievements, but also the differences and difficulties, of the work within subaltern studies. I focus particularly on early explorations of subaltern nationalism and politics and recent interrogations of the modern nation and history within this collective enterprise in order to explore critically the ways in which the project has animated and articulated different orientations, from histories from below through postcolonial perspectives.

The decades since the 1960s have witnessed the development of a transnational historiographical tendency variously known as "people's history," "history from below," and "history from the bottom up."[9] As part of the larger expansion of the critical writing of social history after World War II, this development became a significant historiographical move in India only in the late 1970s. The elaboration of the subaltern studies project played a critical role here. Now, subaltern studies is not only a specific form of history writing and cultural criticism in India but an integral part of broader transnational movements in historiography. This chapter discusses the formation of this project by locating it in the wider context of departures within histories from below, setting out the initial lines of development and emphases of this genre in India, and indicating some of the problems that have confronted the historiography of subordinate peoples.

Over the last fifteen years, ways of writing history have undergone further transformations in the world context, and Indian historiography has both followed suit and contributed critically to the wider changes under way.[10] Some of these shifts came about as historians and anthropologists lined up in increasingly large numbers to present their credentials to literary critics, the new chiefs of theoryland. Here several writings, including some from within subaltern studies, have conformed and contributed to a Left Bank meets East Village style of scholarship. Yet the project has also revealed an internal heterogeneity and a freshness of purpose in going about the task of critical understanding. The point is that there has been a shift of emphasis within the project from earlier constructions of the pasts of subordinate groups toward more recent interrogations of histories of the state and modernity.[11] This chapter explores the implications of this newer accent within subaltern studies, postcolonial inflections that are simultaneously a critical interrogation of reasons of state and a discursive register of states of mind.

Now, to argue in this vein is not to posit a radical rupture between the earlier and later orientations in subaltern studies, since this would be to overlook the elaboration of its emergent emphases over the course of the project, from its initial formulations through to its newer manifestations.

Recently, Dipesh Chakrabarty has made a forceful case for critical continuities in subaltern studies. Focusing on Ranajit Guha's seminal book, *Elementary Aspects of Peasant Insurgency in Colonial India*, Chakrabarty shows that from the start "subaltern historiography necessarily entailed (a) a relative separation of the history of power from any universalist histories of capital, (b) a critique of the nation-form, and (c) an interrogation of the relationship between power and knowledge (hence of archive itself and history as a form of knowledge)." These three fundamental features mean that Guha's work was different from English and European histories from below and that these differences defined "the beginnings of a new way of theorizing the intellectual agenda for post-colonial histories."[12] I find such a reading enabling because it is refreshingly candid regarding its own benefit of hindsight and because it critically considers the tensions within Guha's writing.

This chapter complements Chakrabarty's arguments, but it also has somewhat different emphases. First, while Chakrabarty spells out the "tension between a familiar narrative of capital and a more radical understanding of it" within *Elementary Aspects*, the burden of his argument rests on discussing the latter move, pointing toward "the specific differences in the histories of power in colonial India and in Europe." Here I am rather more interested in thinking through such tensions by staying with them somewhat longer. Specifically, I will show that the conditions of possibility in Guha's writing lie in its precise braiding of distinct orientations—the simultaneous discourse in separate tongues—concerning the terms of history. These discrete orientations straddle the critical force of Guha's analyses and traverse the inherited attributes of his understanding. It is important not to mark off the one from the other in Guha's extraordinary scholarship. This also has important implications for work within subaltern studies more generally, and I develop such considerations later, for one thing by highlighting the tension between moves toward postnationalist histories and the rehearsal of pasts under the sign of the nation within the field.

Second, it follows that much more than the mere refinement of the recent intellectual history of South Asia is at stake in this discussion. On one hand, my effort is to scramble the pervasive tendency to trace the career of subaltern studies as the unfolding of inherent and totalized orientations, including projections concerning both, the pristine past of the project as unfortunately overtaken by a murky present or its uncertain beginnings as increasingly overcome by confident ends. In the task of reading and writing, such tendentious and exclusive gestures put severe stress on the search for theoretical possibilities and the responsibility toward critical engagements. On the other hand, I see this chapter as supplementing Chakrabarty's genealogy of the "intellectual agenda for post-colonial histories," with its focus on immanent but emergent tendencies in subaltern studies, particularly by discussing the tensions within the project. This is not to legislate on but to learn from subaltern studies. If silences and strengths alongside gaps and distinctions have mutually entailed each other within the collective project, such entailments also bid us to think through changing historical cultures, discussing state and nation, modernity and history. Taken together, this chapter attempts to convey a sense of the career and character and the possibilities and predicaments of subaltern studies, cultural histories that work with Indian materials to articulate a wider set of concerns.

People's History / Histories from Below

Peter Burke has shown that the idea of people's history goes back to the later eighteenth century and the early nineteenth in Europe, when movements of "national self-discovery" and endeavors of the "discovery of the folk" generated histories of customs and traditions of "the people."[13] Moreover, the term *people's history* has covered writings varying enormously in their politics, their choice of subjects, and their treatment of themes. Through these differences, what has been common to various versions of people's history is their focus—assuming distinct, often contradictory forms—on common or "whole" people, ordinary or "everyday" folk.[14]

This is the meaning of *people's history* in its most inclusive, broadest sense. Here I use the term in a restricted way to refer to the moves toward the historical study of subordinate groups that have developed since the 1960s, recently finding newer meanings through the importance accorded to "minority" histories. Such a use of the term *people's history* or *histories from below* does not deny that these later studies can share continuities with past traditions and/or that they differ among themselves in method and politics. Rather, my point is that, unlike the disparate initiatives of the past, histories from below, in the specific political context of recent decades, emerged as something of an alternative historiography within institutions of academic learning (and outside them), establishing a remarkable historiographical discourse with an international presence.[15]

What was analytically distinctive and politically salient about such histories? Today it is critical orthodoxy that a persistent tendency within dominant understandings, which is also shared by historians, has viewed subordinate peoples—women and men of various ethnic groups, working classes, and subaltern communities—as objects devoid of consciousness, further casting them as the passive victims of history. As a corollary to this, the rebellions, revolts, and resistance of subordinate groups are explained (away) as a direct and mindless response to economic pressures. In a word, subalterns are not unlike a volcano—passive and dormant, the "masses" rise as a "mob" when the fires of the stomach begin to burn. The challenge to such conceptions of subordinate groups helped to constitute a major departure within histories from below. The critical work here envisioned subordinate groups as *conscious agents* of history, both shaping and shaped by social processes, as subject-actors who lived and made the past. Further, writing within this historiographical tradition went on to explore the modes of *culture* and *consciousness* of subaltern peoples. Underlying this twin focus was the premise that the characteristics of the culture and consciousness—voices and visions, utterances and practices—of subordinate groups entailed logic and rationality, the coherence of specific world-views and the validity of distinct experiences.

Let me discuss these conjoint emphases through specific examples.[16] According to the conventional historical picture, eighteenth-century England was a stable paternalistic society in which the values of the gentry had been internalized at all social levels. Not surprisingly, this made for the deference of the "lower orders." It was only in periods of acute dearth and scarcity that these plebian folk, responding to economic stimuli, clasped their hands to their stomachs and participated in food riots. At the very least, this was the historian's view from above. But studies of eighteenth-century England within the people's history tradition, particularly the work of E. P. Thompson, revealed a rich and autonomous popular culture.[17]

The subordinate groups in eighteenth-century England were creative participants in a vigorous "culture forming process from below."[18] At the same time, Thompson's work defined the "plebian" in relation to the "patrician" as part of a "field of force" articulated within the terms of domination and hegemony. Taken together, the plebian folk drew on their experiences of everyday labor, social relationships, and configurations of power to shape the symbolic universe of eighteenth-century plebian culture. Within this culture, deference appears as "one part necessary self preservation, one part the calculated extraction of whatever could be extracted from the rulers."[19]

It follows that crowd action during periods of scarcity in the eighteenth century cannot be predicated on economic pressures only to be dismissed through the use of terms such as *riot* and *mob*, categories that connote mindlessness, a spasmodic character, and lack of organization. Actually, most instances of crowd action did not lack in consciousness and organization; they were informed instead by the logic of a "moral economy"—a notion of norms and obligations defining the proper economic functions of different groups within the community—that was, according to Thompson, a central feature of eighteenth-century plebian culture.[20]

Finally, a distinct order also characterized other aspects of plebian culture. For example, with the immediate short-term demands of subsistence met, the patterns of consumption of subordinate groups in the eighteenth century involved extravagant expenditures in the interest of status, prestige, and luxury consumption. Was such behavior uneconomic and irrational? In a context of basic economic uncertainty and continually threatened losses, such expenditures helped to define the self-consciousness of subordinate groups. They strengthened bonds of kinship, neighborhood, and friendship within the domains of plebian culture.[21] The capital invested was at once monetary and emotional, producing and reproducing patterns of solidarity to which these subordinate groups had recourse in times of dearth and scarcity.[22]

Here is a second example. In discussions of African American slavery in the United States, there was a time when conservative historians spoke of the benevolent and paternalist aspects of the slave system, while liberal and radical historians emphasized its inhuman and oppressive character. Yet both these viewpoints treated the slave population as an object. Against such a picture, writings within the histories from below tradition emphasized that, although slavery was intensively oppressive, the African American slaves were not passive victims of this system.

In his pioneering study, *Roll, Jordan, Roll*, Eugene D. Genovese showed that African American bonded peoples did not uncritically accept Christianity, the religion that the masters sought to impose on their slaves, among other reasons as a mechanism of control. Rather, the African American slaves created distinct forms of faith through a process of selective borrowing of the motifs and idioms of the dominant religion.[23] Similarly, Lawrence Levine underlined the autonomy of black culture and consciousness as expressed in folktales, humor, and Negro spirituals. When the slaves sang, "Didn't my Lord deliver Daniel . . . then why not every man?" they were voicing their experience of subordination, its pain and humiliation, and their desire for freedom. The popular stories of the "animal trickster" that always gets the better of bigger animals through his cunning also reveal the contours of a consciousness that was unwilling to submit to blind obedience.[24] The cultures fashioned by the slaves at once articulated and sustained a "living space" in relationships of domination and subordination.[25]

Yet faced with the temptation to reify subaltern autonomy and exorcise terms of power, it is important to remember that the reinterpretation and subversion of symbols of authority by the slave population were accompanied by a critical acceptance of the discrete terms of domination and subordination that characterized slavery. Indeed, it would be hasty to consider these inextricably braided orientations toward authority as lying outside the modalities of power.[26] The interrogation of slavery by African American bonded peoples accompanied and exceeded their overt rebellions and spectacular revolts against this institution. According to Lears, the logic that informed slave culture was that of a "contradictory consciousness," which mixed approbation and apathy and resentment and resistance, simultaneously working through containments of power and contestations of domination.[27] A little later, I will return to questions of agency or practice, reading them through distinct, critical filters.

Shaping the political context that defined the initial emphases of histories from below was a wider disenchantment with dominant forms of leftist politics, particularly bureaucratically organized communist parties. In large measure, this followed from the questioning of Stalinist ideology and its institutions, structures, and systems. The ideal of a democratic state and egalitarian society that would respect its citizen-members instead of stifling their visions and silencing their voices, found expression in the writing of history. Work within histories from below turned to the past to recover libertarian and mass democratic movements that had asserted human dignity and subaltern solidarity in the face of tremendous odds and to recuperate the practices of peoples bracketed by established historical practice in socialist systems and capitalist states.[28]

Over the past three decades, this political context has been increasingly characterized by diverse efforts bearing a critical relationship with the terms of institutional power, including environmentalist and nuclear disarmament movements, feminist and factory floor initiatives, antiracist and gay liberation endeavors, and ethnic and Fourth World interventions. This has defined other important departures, extending and elaborating the critical emphases of histories from below. Two examples come to mind. In the first place, there have been various efforts to democratize the act of historical production by questioning its confinement within the academy, thereby enlarging the constituency of the authors of history. Women and men of different ethnic groups and laboring people have self-consciously reflected on and written about their own pasts; the imperatives of "minority" histories have expanded recently; and everyday subjects of dominant states have variously uncovered the hidden histories and quotidian cartographies of local places, generally against the grain of inherited understandings of past regimes and overweening nations.[29] Similarly, in the wake of feminist consciousness and organization, there followed varieties of writing of history by both women and men that focused on gender as a critical organizing principle of society and culture. If these departures have overlapped, they have also followed distinct pathways. Such developments have served to extend histories from below as an alternative practice, frequently following oppositional orientations toward the institutional implications of knowledge and power.

In India, the initial impetus for the development of histories from below came from debates concerning the place of peasant, worker, and adivasi initiatives within the Indian nationalist movement. Here several historians emphasized the greater militancy and relative autonomy of these popular endeavors in relation to the organization of the Indian National Congress, while the Congress leadership appeared to be imposing restraints on these initiatives.[30] However, the problem with most of the early contributions to this debate was that the Indian National Congress remained their sole point of reference. Explored and emphasized was the degree of autonomy of popular movements from the Congress organization. Consequently, insufficiently explored were arenas of the politics of subordinate groups, including their constitutive forms of consciousness. In overcoming such limitations, the subaltern studies enterprise played a significant role.

Rather than providing an inventory of the work carried out within subaltern studies, this chapter focuses on some of its key contributions concerning the critical domain of subaltern politics, writings that are representative of the departures signaled by the project. Such a reading can highlight the ways in which this historiographical endeavor has elaborated and extended the wider orientations of histories from below. At the same time, after I have presented the arguments of some of the earlier exercises within subaltern studies I also point out a few of the basic problems that beset these historical accounts. The difficulties relate to the manner in which these accounts were held in place by teleological schemes, their somewhat tenuous hold over the category of culture, and their curious and contradictory engagement with the mutual determinations of structure and practice.

Building on this discussion, later I will trace the shift within subaltern studies toward explorations of state, nation, and modernity in colonial and contemporary India, including the production and containment of subaltern subjects within the discursive orders of dominant domains. Once more, a critical spirit informs my efforts. While keeping in view the key achievements of the more recent writings within subaltern studies, I also read these accounts against the grain of some of their underlying assumptions, critical conceits, and methodological moves. I emphasize that such scholarship must guard against formulations that claim alterity and difference but imbue analyses with other strains of singularity and sameness, resisting yet reinstating given categories derivative of schemes of universal history. Having learned much from the critical spirit of subaltern studies, I extend critical reasoning to this historical and theoretical endeavor.

Subaltern Nationalisms

In discussing the earlier emphases within subaltern studies, let me begin with an essay located at the intersection of two distinct perspectives: the sociology of peasant protest in colonial India and an ecologically oriented study of history. Ramchandra Guha discusses the trajectory and idiom of social protest in the Kumaun region in North India in the early twentieth century.[31] Here the inception of commercial forestry by the colonial government disrupted the pattern of utilization of forest resources of the people of the hills. Further, the advent of the colonial forest department increased the incidence of begar. Taken together, the new laws and regulations threatened the considerable autonomy of the village community, transgressed the hill people's notions of the relationship between the ruler and the ruled, and clashed thereby with their notions of justice.

At stake, then, was a conflict between rival conceptions of property, a contradiction between separate worldviews. On one hand, there was the assertion by the colonial state of its monopoly over forests—a conception wholly grounded in exchange-value orientations, emphasizing a state monopoly used commercially. On the other hand, there was the right to the free use of forest resources by members of the village, which was sanctioned by custom and regulated by the community as a whole—a conception that operated outside developed notions of private property and was rooted in a subsistence economy with use-value orientations toward natural resources. This conflict and such contradictions resulted in discontent among the hill people, which manifested itself in different ways, from the desertion of villages to noncompliance with new rules, contravention of imposed regulations and the burning of forests. At an organizational level, village protest resulted in a radicalization of a body called the Kumaun Parishad. After the success of the Parishad's campaign against forced labor, under the leadership of Badridutt Pande the organization launched a movement against forest regulations characterized by the burning of forests.

The nature of resistance and the forms of protest in Kumaun were closely related to the political and economic structure of the region. First, the cohesion and the collective spirit of the village community provided the mainspring of political action. Second, the actual sociocultural idiom of resistance—the desertion of villages and the contravention of regulations— was marked by a relative absence of violence compared to the rebellious dramas of peasant uprising elsewhere in India. According to Ramchandra Guha, the absence of a culturally distinct buffer class in the highly autonomous village communities of Kumaun shaped such patterns of resistance. Finally, the sociocultural idiom of protest in the twentieth century and the distinctive history of peasant resistance in the region were bound to one another. At work were elaborations of the practice of *dhandak*, a form of protest sanctioned by "custom" to which the hill people could resort when their "traditional" notions of the *raja-praja* (ruler-ruled) relationship were transgressed.

Ramchandra Guha's work illustrates the double movement carried out by writings within subaltern studies. Reaching beyond the conventional Congress-centered studies of peasant and tribal movements, these accounts broke with analytical traditions that saw subaltern endeavors as straightforward expressions of major ruptures in the economy. This historiographical shift led to explorations of the causes, trajectories, characteristics, and idioms of diverse movements of subordinate groups—explorations carried out at the regional and local levels.[32] They also brought forth efforts to explore the complexities of culture and consciousness that defined the domains of subaltern politics.

Gyanendra Pandey's study of the Kisan Sabha (peasant collective) and Eka (unity) movements in Awadh in the North Indian countryside between 1919 and 1922 delineated the contours of the peasant perspective that went into the making of these initiatives.[33] These endeavors began with the setting up of Kisan Sabhas.[34] Caste solidarity and the authority of the caste panchayat played a significant role here. From the beginning, peasants defying the authority of the Kisan Sabhas faced the customary sanctions of local caste organizations, which enforced the practice of social boycott, *nai-dhobi band*, the stopping of the everyday services of the barber and the washerman. By the winter of 1920–21, when the Kisan Sabha movements had garnered support among tenants and laborers of different castes, the solidarities and practices surrounding caste continued to remain important within the organizational endeavors of the peasants of Awadh.

A pervasive religious symbolism marked the Awadh peasant movement. Baba Ramchandra, the best-known leader of the initiative, read excerpts from Tulsidas's epic *Ramcharitmanas* at the early peasant meetings. In the course of the movement, the salutation of *salaam* was replaced by *sita-ram*, a greeting that invoked the god-king Ram and his wife Sita. In the quotidian world of peasant social intercourse, usually a subordinate addressed a superior with salaam. Sita-ram did away with patterns of verbal deference. Now the greeting of sita-ram was also attributed with miraculous powers. Used by peasants of all communities, it became the chief rallying cry of the peasant movement.

According to Pandey, a religious mode of understanding the world underlay the idea of a just and moral struggle in the Awadh peasant movement, "fundamental to the peasants' acceptance of the necessity to revolt."[35] In the peasants' conception of the prescribed order of world, there were rulers (rajas) and ruled (praja). A true ruler was just. As for the ruled, their subordination was inevitable. At the same time, the "natural" relationship between the ruler and the ruled was premised on a contented subject population easily making its living and peacefully going about its business. This relationship did not brook transgression. Thus, it was only when the landlord decided to levy new and oppressive imposts in a period of considerable hardship for substantial sections of the peasantry that the Awadh peasants took up resistance as something that they regarded as both ethically correct and politically necessary.

The peasants' view of their rebellion and its leaders further articulated the notion of an alternative and truly just relationship between the rulers and the ruled: "Baba Ram Chandra ke rajwa, praja maja urawenai" (In the kingdom of Baba Ramachandra, the people will make merry).[36] Now, by arguing that during the course of the movement the Awadh peasants overcame some of their "traditionalist limitations," Pandey implicitly casts matters in terms of the telos of a progressive peasantry forging its way toward the modern nation. He ignores the fact that at work in these initiatives was not a radical transformation of peasant consciousness in the mirror of an imaginary modern but a reworking of peasant thought and action that involved complex renderings of ongoing traditions and contradictory articulations of a colonial modernity.[37]

By the early 1920s, as Pandey himself shows, in the course of the Eka movement, the Awadh peasants adopted a militant stand against the old order, yet the frames of reference of these rebellious peasants still articulated a "religious world-view" shaped by categories of the ruler and the ruled. Even after the Eka movement collapsed because of the lack of support from the Indian National Congress, the Awadh peasants did not fully comprehend this "betrayal" and lose their faith in Gandhi. They continued to look on Gandhi as part of the worlds of their imagination and practice, as a Mahatma, a Pandit, a Brahman, a great spirit, a learned man, and a (ritually) pure person.[38] My differences with Pandey on matters of emphases apart, his essay points toward the need to examine the varied perceptions of the Indian National Congress and its leadership, particularly of Gandhi and his message, fashioned by subordinate groups, and to explore the cultural frames of reference in which these visions were embedded.

Sumit Sarkar addressed these questions in the "system of correlations and oppositions, structures of collective mentality conducive to rebellion or its opposite," which he constructed by drawing on evidence of subaltern militancy in Bengal between 1905 and 1922.[39] According to Sarkar, perceptions of the breakdown of authority and domination were central to popular movements, undermining the hegemony and power of dominant groups. These perceptions of the breakdown of authority followed two pathways. First, a sudden change in the conditions of life of subalterns—for example, price rises, poor harvests, or the arrival in the community of "outsiders" who were seen as oppressors—brought forth resistance, characterized by an evocation of earlier norms, against circumstances perceived as new developments. Second, in the development of resistance, rumors of a breakdown of authority played a crucial role. Projections of an apparent breakdown either implied a conflict among superiors or assumed the collapse of existing authority and the emergence of a new symbolic power center, which would displace the old loci of control. According to Sarkar, in each case religiosity was central to perceptions of the breakdown of authority and defined other critical features of popular movements in the early Gandhian era in Bengal.

As a crucial part of anticolonial subaltern movements, rumors assumed three forms in this period in eastern India. The first kind of rumor presented Gandhi as an avatar, an incarnation. He was indestructible, broke the normal laws of nature, bestowed miraculous gifts on believers, relieved his followers of their individual ills, and punished those who did not accept his authority. In rumors of the second kind, the power of miracles was passed on to the followers of the Mahatma (Gandhi) and to minor local leaders. Rumors of the third kind embodied the theme of a sudden and miraculous total transformation, a world turned upside down. For example, throughout 1921 Gandhi's promise of *swaraj* (freedom) within a year led to predictions of dates when a complete reversal of the world would occur. The content of swaraj kept broadening, until by early 1922 the peasant perception of freedom embraced visions of a total repudiation of taxes, revenues, and payments of interest.

Sarkar argues that the emerging cult of Gandhi imposed ethical and ritual obligations on its devotees. A strong note of internal moral purification was prominent in many of these popular movements. Much of the appeal of Gandhi's antiliquor campaign lay in its purificatory role for the lower castes. The symbolic value of *khadi* (coarse handspun cloth) and *charkha* (rustic handloom) was far greater than the limited material gains that peasants could expect from the revival of these crafts. Indeed, Gandhi's appeal to the peasant imagination was closely connected to his evocation of the dispositions of renunciation, austerity, and sacrifice. According to Sarkar, unlike the concept and imagery of *puja* (ritual worship), which is integrally bound to the social and ritual hierarchies of Hinduism and variously excludes Muslims and the lower castes, the path of *sannyasa* (renunciation) is open to all, high and low. There have been innumerable holy men, local *sadhus* (Hindu ascetics), and *pirs* (Muslim ascetics), devotion to whom has cut across barriers of caste and creed. Furthermore, the virtues of austerity and sacrifice in the (early-twentieth-century) Indian context bear little emphasis.

Sarkar suggests that a specific combination of images and interests underlay the success of Gandhi in the peasant imagination. The popular image of Gandhi was that of a sannyasi. He had an established reputation for doing something effective about specific wrongs. And Gandhi was now promising change, swaraj within a year. This particular conjunction led the peasants to fashion Gandhi into a Mahatma, a great spirit. If Gandhi continued to remain important to the peasants despite his many "betrayals," the explanation lies in the fact that "part of the strength of a religious faith is derived from the kind of built-in explanation it tends to contain about failure."[40] When a devotee does not obtain the specific benefits he or she has been praying for, where does the fault lie? Does it lie with the deity, who can generally do little wrong? Conversely, does the fault lie with the devotee, who may not have observed the rites properly, or in a true spirit? According to Sarkar, the peasants relied on such modes of explanation, with Gandhi himself placing the responsibility for the retreats that he ordered on his—and his followers'—inadequacies in the areas of non-violence and untouchability.

Sumit Sarkar's arguments raise critical issues. The aims and methods of Gandhian movements were broad and accommodating enough to provide an appropriate context in which subordinate groups could conduct such initiatives in their own cultural idioms in order to achieve many particular ends. Another example serves to clarify the issue. Jitu Santal's movement between 1924 and 1928 in Malda in eastern India had several links with Bengali nationalist leaders, and it apparently rejected the Santal indigenous identity to strive instead for Hindu social status.[41] Yet Tanika Sarkar has argued that it would be a mistake to appropriate this movement to the grand narrative of the history of the freedom struggle or to see it as a straightforward "sanskritizing" movement.[42] The notion of a specifically Santal *desh* (land/country) informed Jitu Santal's conception of a new order, corresponding to an old Santal vision of a perfect state of freedom.[43] "Defying the political training brought to them by external leaders, defying even the stated aims (of Hinduization) of his [Jitu Santal's] own movement, the Santal thus returned to his indigenous code of belief. His understanding of national politics—be it that of Hindu Communalism or that of Gandhian Congress—was eventually framed by this code. Broader political forces were accepted through the filter of tribal logic and needs."[44] The reification of an unsullied "indigenous" aside, we are in the face of a creative cultural process of the reinterpretation, appropriation, and subversion of symbols, ideas, and practices by subordinate groups—a recasting deployed by these groups unto their own ends.

This analytical emphasis is carried forward in Shahid Amin's examination of how the idea of the Mahatma attached to Gandhi was thought out and reworked in the popular imagination in Gorakhpur in North India.[45] Amin bases his arguments on rumors associated with Gandhi that were reported in the regional Indian National Congress weekly, *Swadesh*, and in other dailies, in the months following Gandhi's visit to the region in February 1921. These stories discussed the miracle-working powers of Gandhi and described what happened to those who opposed the Mahatma and the Gandhian creed, particularly the taboos on drinking, smoking, and food. In Nainpur village, the long lost calf of a peasant returned to its peg because of a boon granted by Mahatmaji, and in Danariya village a man called Gandhiji names and consequently his eyelids became stuck. On 22 February 1921, a sadhu came to Godhbal village and began puffing at his marijuana pipe. When people tried reasoning with him he began to abuse Mahatmaji, and the next morning human excrement covered his entire body.[46] Amin argues that these stories indicate how "ideas about Gandhi's *pratap* [glory] and the appreciation of his message derived from popular Hindu beliefs and practices and the material culture of the peasantry."[47] Moreover, the name of the Mahatma used in public meetings and in pamphlets came to be inextricably linked to the notion of swaraj. Here the popular notion of Gandhiji's swaraj was distinct from the conception of swaraj of the regional leadership of the Congress in Gorakhpur. This popular and peasant notion of Gandhiji's swaraj implied a sort of peasant utopia of limited taxation and nominal rents. Similarly, the cry "Gandhi Maharaj ki jai" (Victory to Gandhi) assumed the function of such customary war cries as "Bam Bam Mahadeo" to become a rallying cry for direct action. Such action derived its legitimacy from the supposed orders of Gandhi.

Subaltern Insurgents

These attempts to uncover subaltern articulations of nationalism have formed part of a larger endeavor, the study of subaltern politics, involving explorations of modalities of culture and consciousness constitutive of subalternity in South Asia.[48] I now turn to an early and major departure in this field, Ranajit Guha's *Elementary Aspects of Peasant Insurgency in Colonial India*.[49] This pioneering work remains one of the most significant achievements of subaltern studies, a landmark in Indian historiography, and a seminal contribution to the study of peasant politics.

In *Elementary Aspects*, Guha's aim is to situate the peasant as a conscious and political subject-agent of history. To this end, he examines peasant rebellions in nineteenth-century India, identifying the "elementary aspects" of the common forms and the general ideas of insurgency, the consciousness that informed the activities of rebellious peasants. The starting point of Guha's enquiry is the principle of negation. In his words, "the peasant learnt to recognize himself not by the properties and attributes of his own social being but by a diminution, if not a negation of those of his superiors."[50] The peasants' revolt against authority derived much of its strength from the same awareness, intimating a project constituted negatively. The "negation" characteristic of insurgency followed two sets of principles, discrimination and inversion. The peasants used discrimination in selectively directing violence against particular targets, and negative consciousness of this type extended its domain by a process of analogy and transference. Inversion involved the peasants in turning the world upside down by violating the basic codes that governed relations of domination and subordination. Here norms of verbal deference and their corresponding structures of authority were demolished through abuse directed toward superordinates and the adoption of their modes of speech. The written word—a sign of the peasant's enemy and an exploitative device—was usually destroyed and appropriated symbolically in certain cases. Other nonverbal sign systems of authority—forms of body movements, gestures, and uses of space—were challenged intimately, and the palpable symbols of the dominant groups' authority, status, and power—clothing, homes, means of transport—were chosen as objects of attack. The rebel peasants destroyed and/or appropriated the signs of domination. In doing so, they sought to abolish the marks of their own subalternity.

Inversion was characteristic not only of insurgency but of certain forms of rural crime. There is a certain ambiguity here, since both the elitist and the peasant perspectives, for opposite reasons, could not distinguish between these two codes. A powerful peasant revolt tended to invest disparate attacks on property and person with new meanings and reconstitute them as a part of rebellion. This meant that the peasants tended to read all forms of defiance of the law as justifiable acts of social protest, while the elitist understanding spoke of insurgency as a more serious type of crime produced by conspiracy. At the same time, however, the very features that distinguished insurgency from crime actually constituted the modality of rebellion. Rebellion was necessarily an open and public event. In several cases, the rebels claimed to have the approval of a public authority, which both affirmed and legitimized their actions. With resistance armed with such putative approval, blessing, and support of (often the highest) public authority, it followed that in the perception of peasant rebels insurgent violence could assume the form of public service.

The mass communitarian aspect of peasant violence followed from its public and open character. A rebellion was a collective enterprise. It used communitarian processes and forms of mass mobilization, expressed mass violence in an idiom of communitarian labor, and encouraged communitarian appropriation of the fruits of pillage. To be sure, the ways in which such corporate violence undermined the authority of the peasant's enemies by destroying their resources—the insignia and the instrument of that authority—varied in different cases and distinct regions. At the same time, there were regularities of emphasis and pattern in this variety. These regularities reveal that there was discipline and order, a distinct logic, in what appears to be spontaneity and chaos, confusion and disorder.

Guha identifies four methods of resistance that were most conspicuous and prevalent in peasant rebellions during the nineteenth century: wrecking, burning, eating, and looting. Though analytically distinct, these forms of struggle actually constituted a total and integrated violence. In other words, during rebellion the four types of destructive activity lost their separate identities and functioned as connected elements of a single complex. This served to define the plural and total character of insurgent violence in the forms that it assumed and the objects it chose to attack.

What underlay the transmission of rebellion? The tendency in the discourse of colonial authorities, often reproduced by historians, is to describe and deal with the spread of peasant violence in terms of contagion. In brief, peasant rebellions resemble a disease or virus that spreads through the countryside. This defines both violence and its transmission as irrational, treating the two as natural phenomena. In sharp contrast, Guha argues that in nineteenth-century India the transmission of insurgency involved the energies of consciously acting peasant subjects. It had a distinct logic and rationality. Insurgency and its transmission constituted cultural facts of the social world.

At work here were processes involving means specific to primarily oral cultures that had a limited exposure to literacy. Thus, the transmission of rebellion assumed the basic forms of nonverbal and verbal communication. Nonverbal communication could be aural or visual, while verbal communication could be written or oral. In its aural form, the drum, the flute, and the horn were the most frequently used instruments. They acted as a surrogate for human speech and served to emphasize the family resemblance between fighting and other forms of communitarian labor. Visual signs constituted the second form of nonverbal communication, and insurgency extended the domain and added to the range of these sign systems.[51]

Although inseparable in practice from the nonverbal forms, verbal transmission of insurgency was distinctive enough to constitute a separate category. In its written form, the clearest examples took the shape of the kind of inscriptions self-consciously geared toward the spread of rebellion. However, this mode was not very prevalent in nineteenth-century India, being used primarily by members of the elite who were now allied with the rebels and by the few subaltern rebels who had acquired the means to read and write. Indeed, the high levels of illiteracy in the Indian countryside also meant that peasants often transformed written signs into purely visual ones, imbuing them with their own meanings.

The spoken word was much more important to the transmission of insurgency. Here a key role was played by authored spoken utterances, which could be traced back to known individuals, usually a charismatic leader. It is hardly surprising that this kind of speech constituted a critical component of the charisma of the leaders in worlds of subaltern insurrection. Such authored spoken utterances were composed of words and expressions with their referents in a universe beyond the practical domain of insurrection. They represented the desire for change in a religious idiom. Thus, insurgent leaders such as Titu Mir, Sido and Kanhu Santals, and Birsa Munda spoke the inspired language of prophets and reformers, their politics was conceived and expressed in religious terms, and not a few of these movements eventually ended up as exclusive "sects."

In its classic form of rumor, the category of anonymous spoken utterances also proved to be a powerful vehicle of the stuff that fired the minds of men, the perceptions of people. Rumor became the necessary instrument of the transmission of rebellion in its dual role as the trigger and mobilizer of the subaltern imagination. On one hand, such necessity derived from cultural conditions in which the peasants relied on visual and nongraphic forms of communication. On the other, it derived from the particular nature of rumor as a type of speech that seized on important issues in periods of social tension.[52] The transmission of rumor also generated solidarity. The socializing process of rumor brought people together and evoked comradeship, which contributed to its phenomenal speed. The origin of rumor in places such as bazaars, where people assembled in large numbers, along with the intimate association of verbal speech with ritually important exchanges tended to reaffirm the authority of rumor as a type of popular discourse.

The anonymity of rumor opened it as a receptacle for new inputs of meaning. Rumor functioned in situations of social tension as a distinct form liable to a considerable degree of improvisation. The additions, cuts, improvisations, and twists introduced to a rumor in the course of its circulation transformed its message, allowing for adjustment to variations within modes of popular expression and broadening its range of address. Truly, improvisation contributed directly to the efficiency and efficacy of rumor as an instrument of rebel mobilization. At the same time, rumor was improvised only to the extent permitted by the relevant codes of the cultures in which it functioned—cultural codes that gave it both shape and meaning.

The code of political thinking of subaltern insurgents rested on their knowledge and perceptions of the values and relationships of power in nineteenth-century India. This code could involve the peasants in conceptualizing all authority as "quasidivine." The peasants' understanding of the relations, institutions, and processes of power, and consequently of the vicissitudes of rebellion, were often rooted in religion. In Guha's view, this generated a certain kind of alienation. It made the peasants look on their destiny not as a function of their own will and action but as predicated on forces outside and independent of themselves. It followed that rumor served to transform minor agrarian disturbances into mass events by contributing to the extension of the domain of insurgency. But rumor also estranged the peasant rebel from seeing himself (or herself) as the purposive agent of historical change.

This duality was also characteristic of another defining feature of peasant insurgency, named by Guha "territoriality": a sense of belonging to a common lineage (consanguinity), a common habitat (contiguity), and the intertwining of these two bonds. Broadly understood, peasant uprisings until 1900 were "local" in character. In all of them, the rebels' view of the enemy as an alien to an ethnic and physical space provided the domain of resistance with critical determinations. Hostility toward foreigners was a prominent feature of tribal rebellions, demonstrated by the selective violence directed against the dikus (aliens/foreigners) by the Kol, Santal, and Munda insurgents. Indeed, the word diku retains its pejorative connotations to this day.

A tribe also used ideas relating to ethnicity in order to articulate its identity more positively. The notion of physical space enabled the insurgents to assert their identity in terms of their homeland. The idea of recovering a homeland lost to dikus fired the imagination of Santal rebels, also forming a central aim of Birsa Munda's campaign. A correlate of the category of space was the sense of time, in its most generalized form expressed as a contrasted pair of then and now, a good past negated by a bad present. At once a strategy and an imagining, this contrasted pair functioned to endow the struggle against the alien with the mission of recovering the past as the future.

Among the nontribal peasantry, the uprisings of 1857 reveal the role of territoriality as a force of rebel mobilization. These, too, were generally local affairs. They operated within discrete local vicinages, having their social bases in local areas with clearly recognized boundaries. The underlying caste consciousness that informed some of these uprisings helped emphasize their regionality and ethnicity. In nineteenth-century India, territoriality helped the spread of insurgency because the two spaces, ethnic and territorial, did not coincide even when they converged: "There were territorial limits which were home to more than one ethnic group and there were ethnic regions which extended over more than one territorial unit. A peasant uprising tended to fill in the gap by its own content and simulate a coincidence between community and habitat."[53] For example, the Santal rebellion of the 1850s came to assimilate lower-caste Hindus just as the Kol insurrection of the same period exceeded its geographical limits in the Chota Nagpur area and drew in fellow adivasis from neighboring regions. At the same time, territoriality also served as a brake on peasant insurgency. According to Guha, "localism" impeded the progress of insurgents at critical moments, particularly as caste fought against caste. Even when solidarity between ethnic groups triumphed over their separateness, it weakened under pressure from a common enemy.

Teleology and Culture

I have spent a long time in presenting these arguments. However, I can only barely claim to have brought out the variety, the texture, and the novelty of the earlier work conducted within the subaltern studies enterprise, which had diverse manifestations. First, engagements within subaltern studies revealed imaginative ways of reading historical materials—for example, conventional archival records, including reports of colonial administrators, but also earlier ethnographies as sources of history—to suggest in distinct ways that the study of South Asian pasts was a rich field with immense possibilities. On one hand, such readings problematized the nature of the historical archive itself. On the other, they initiated a dialogue with other disciplines and different orientations, particularly structural linguistics and critical theory.[54] Second, from the beginning, the energies and passions of the project were evident in its astute acknowledgment of the innately political character of the writing of history.[55] Finally, through its distinct readings of historical materials and its passionate politics, subaltern studies seized on a variety of subjects, articulating diverse themes of research, which critically animated and augmented the study of the subaltern and South Asia.[56]

At the risk of repeating a commonplace, subaltern studies raised new questions in the critical study of subalterns and South Asian history more generally. It followed that these developments also influenced and interacted with other analytical orientations—from feminist writing to labor studies and ethnographic inquiries—together underscoring scholarly convergences and theoretical debates of significance.[57] Aided by the approval of literary studies of colonial representations, writings within subaltern studies soon established themselves as important interlocutors in the transnational discourse on history and theory, colony and empire.[58]

Equally clearly, however, key problems, variously tied to the modern project of history, underlay the explorations of subaltern subjects within subaltern studies. It is in order to begin with the mutual determinations between teleological constructs—embodied in analytical categories, theoretical models, commonplace conceptions, and everyday apprehensions—and the writing of history. In its simplest sense, the work of teleology in the production of history implies that patterns of the past and the present appear as anticipating forms of the future. Such assimilation of the past and the present to overarching trajectories understands and frames events, persons, processes of history and the here and now in terms of orders of hierarchies, and even stages of succession, predicated on provisos of progress under regimes of modernity. All this does not simply entail a wider disregard for the specific and the singular at the heart of elaborations of cultures and histories. Significantly, the distinctions and disjunctions, contingencies and contradictions, of social worlds become grist for the mill of a preconfigured posterity. They insinuate salient cases or shadowy details in the tracks of a given, prior direction, an appointed, a priori destination of the passage of history.

Two simple but significant examples should suffice. In his wide-ranging survey of modern Indian history, Sumit Sarkar writes that the participation of women in the anticolonial Civil Disobedience movement of the early 1930s "marked in fact a major step forward in the emancipation of Indian women."[59] Here Sarkar implicitly situates women's participation in the nationalist movement on the axis of the overarching theme of the "emancipation of Indian womanhood."[60] On one hand, this assimilative procedure rides roughshod over the manner in which such participation was understood by middle-class and subaltern women and men, including as a "special form of sacrifice in an essentially religious process" that did not challenge the wider schemes of gender inequalities.[61] On the other hand, Sarkar's invocation of the telos of the emancipation of Indian womanhood not only overlooks the differences of caste and class in South Asia but elides the conditions of possibility, including the discursive containment, of women's participation in the nationalist movement.[62]

Similarly, resolutely overarching teleological blueprints have orchestrated the debate about the extent of autonomy of—and the place of leadership within—the anticolonial initiatives of subordinate groups in the Indian nationalist movement. Arguments shaped around visions of the "Indian national movement" or the "Indian freedom struggle" inherently propelled diverse anticolonial struggles in a definite direction and incessantly drove them to a determinate destination. Not surprisingly, despite ideological differences, such orientations have assumed a unitary meaning of the nation and nationalism for all social groups, ignoring thereby the various conceptions and several representations of independence and freedom, nation and state, within anticolonial initiatives in South Asia. Clearly, the writings within subaltern studies, including those presented earlier in this chapter, have issued critical challenges to such overwrought teleological schemes.

Yet the terms of teleology have a larger provenance and wider implications. The founding statement of subaltern studies, written by Ranajit Guha, set the aim of the project as the task of exploring *"the historic failure of the* [Indian] *nation to come into its own."*[63] Here the telos of history came to be located in the destiny of the nation, which had failed its poor citizens, dispossessed peoples, and subaltern subjects. This was symptomatic of the privilege accorded to the nation within subaltern studies. Thus, the discussions within the project, particularly those concerned with subaltern nationalism, were contained by the inherited terms of the nation-state and constrained by the modern coupling of history and nation. Although subaltern studies contested the claims of nationalist historiography, the very containments and constraints shaping the project circumscribed the space for other imaginings and alternative narrations of nation(s), and the endeavor continued to imagine distinct pasts through exclusive grids of national history.

Not surprisingly, within subaltern studies the key terms of national history emerged further conjoined with the modular forms of universal history, particularly the overarching designs of revolutionary pasts.[64] Thus, even as the project questioned teleological schemes denying the consciousness of the subaltern, the implicit, sustained presence of frames of universal history and designs of revolutionary pasts also led work within subaltern studies to understand Indian history in terms of lack, absence, and failure.[65] This is to say that the past and the present of India simply did not measure up to master blueprints and Ur-histories. Now, immaculate conceptions of history and theory are at once an established verity and an enduring enchantment. It is crucial to resist the temptation to exorcise such specters through analytical prescription and legislative theory. To reiterate, far from being mere dismissals of subaltern studies, my arguments seek to think through key tensions within the project, tensions that were critical for the sustained production of imaginative histories, tensions that are salient today.

The tensions in the earlier work within subaltern studies contain links to the place of the category of culture within the project. Here, culture often appeared as an a priori element rather than a critical category in the writing of history. On one hand, in this corpus cultures of subalterns remained somewhat static frameworks of belief and behavior, curiously corresponding to an earlier anthropological notion of culture as an "entire way of life," largely unchanging and broadly homogeneous blueprints of thought and action, which underlay the passivity and resistance of subordinate groups. On the other hand, through the preoccupation with the autonomy and agency of the subaltern, articulated by the duality between resistance and domination and subaltern and elite, meaningful practices of subordinate groups before authority appeared as simply opposing power, and therefore they lay outside its productivity. In different ways, these overlapping tendencies are evident in the various writings discussed above, which find complex conjunctions in Ranajit Guha's *Elementary Aspects*.

We have noted that in his pioneering text Guha focuses on the "elementary aspects" of subaltern insurgency, examining the common forms and general ideas of the consciousness that informed the activities of rebellious peasants. Guha reads and renders these common forms and general ideas of the consciousness that constituted insurgency in the manner of a code within a linguistic system. It is not only that this shared code underlay the diverse expressions—various utterances, as it were—of subaltern rebellion, the emancipatory and autonomous project of prescriptive reversal seeking to erase all signs of subalternity. It is also significant that, according to Guha, insurgent consciousness, the common code of the historical register of subaltern rebellion, was preeminently political in nature. Separately and taken together, these critical moves and analytical imperatives predicate the culture(s) of subordinate groups on the politics of peasant insurgency, which is understood as the essence of subaltern consciousness and initiatives.

Let us examine the consequences of such subordination of subaltern cultures to insurgent politics through two examples. First, discussing the principal modalities of subaltern insurgency—wrecking, burning, eating, and looting—Guha demonstrates that the use of fire and the consumption of food were critical elements in the work of rebellion. At the same time, Guha's analyses accord little importance to the differences of meaning and distinctions of practice in the use(s) of fire and the consumption(s) of foods during insurgency by culturally distinct groups—from the Hindu peasants of the Deccan to the adivasi Santals of eastern India and the Maplahs of the far south. Tied to the imperative of the code of insurgency, this analytical refusal in *Elementary Aspects* has broad implications. It simultaneously indexes and promotes a wider elision of the conventions of social life within subaltern cultures, which defined and produced meanings among subordinate groups, including apprehensions of fire and food during rebellion and resistance. Similarly, Guha's sharp distinction between passivity and resistance in the subaltern world is at once a symptom and a result of his bracketing of the several textures and specific hues of nineteenth-century peasant cultures. Once more, subaltern cultures that mixed deference, ambivalence, resentment, and rebellion appear sieved through exclusive filters of peasant insurgency.

The orientations and emphases of Elementary Aspects equally rest upon the structuralist assumptions and arguments of the text. Its analyses entail a series of sharp dualities between passivity and resistance, domination and subordination, and the elite and the subaltern, which posit singular disjunctions in the work of these opposed elements in colonial India. As a corollary to this, the emphasis on synchrony within Guha's text means not only that it presents the nineteenth century as a virtually unchanging period but it also frames peasant politics as defined by a wide-ranging yet static grid of subaltern insurgency. Of course, it is crucial to acknowledge the critical spirit and provocative force of Guha's writing, including the dialogue it initiated with structural linguistics and anthropology. Yet it is also important to consider that the dualities of Guha's analysis overlook the alchemy of approbation and apathy within subaltern cultures, its antinomies elide the distinctions within subaltern worlds, and its dichotomies disregard the multiple hierarchies of domination and subordination in nineteenth-century India. It follows that in Elementary Aspects patterns of the transformation of the agrarian world of nineteenth-century India, including the changes in subaltern cultures, the mutations in peasant consciousness, and the variations in the context of rebellion, remain at a remove from Guha's otherwise wide canvas.

In Elementary Aspects, the particular cast of its analytical grid also imbued the archival encounter between gender issues and subaltern historiography with a distinct salience. At a crucial moment in the text, Guha argues that communal modes of labor carried over into insurgency. During the Santal rebellion, for example, the men destroyed enemy property while the women gathered the loot. This division of labor was bound to the organization of kinship and everyday lives of communities, which entailed the subordination of women. Its continuation during rebellion reveals critical limits to key inversions during subaltern insurgencies. However, in his analysis of the Santal hool (rebellion), Guha ignores the implications of such a gendered division of labor. Similarly, from the sources that Guha consulted we know of the Santal practice of branding as witches the young girls who refused to participate in the rebellion. These materials also tell us that Sido and Kanho, as leaders of this Santal rebellion, had sexual access to women of the tribe. And these were only particular instances of the wider asymmetries of gender and power in subaltern arenas. Once more, Guha chooses not to speak about the gendered subaltern and the sexual exploitation of women.[66]

Although recent years have witnessed intense mutual engagements between anthropology and history, prompted by complex changes and shared emphases in both these disciplines, it would be hasty to assume that the dispositions of the past have disappeared in the face of new critical orientations. Through its emphasis on the first forms of underlying structures and collective consciousness, *Elementary Aspects* reveals the need to think through the older oppositions between structure and action. On one hand, my reading of Guha's text highlights the fact that in the dialogue between disciplines it is necessary to critically consider theoretical traditions and analytical models that predicate practice on underlying codes and collective structures. On the other hand, both Guha's work and my own arguments suggest that it is equally important to question methodological schemes that privilege agency by underplaying the conditions and limits, and particularly the stipulations of power, that make social action possible. Am I belaboring the obvious? As was suggested earlier, reifications of structure and romanticization of agency—now in the shape of constructs emphasizing the singular force of totalized power and conceptions privileging the ungoverned actions of individuated subjectivities—continue to pose challenges to the interplay between history and anthropology, narrative and theory. But I have no desire to offer programmatic pronouncements or final resolutions. Rather, I wish to emphasize that norms of narrative and terms of theory, including critical accounts of the mutual entailments of structure and practice, require their realization in the actual writing of history and the precise practice of anthropology—a doing of subjects that does not fear an undoing of disciplines.

Insurgent Subalterns

A few years ago, one among an exclusive group of high-powered theorists who had gathered in the sylvan surroundings of Shimla to ponder the grim contours of secularism in India, coined a catchy and charmingly indiscreet phrase. Over a ritual drink—and later in a more public ceremony—the philosopher Akeel Bilgrami referred to the "neurotic antistatism of Partha Chatterjee," implying that Chatterjee's very neuroses about the modern state have led to his obsession with this behemoth of modernity. The extent of the malaise and the existence of the pathology are open to debate. Yet over the past few years, countering the early charges of neglect of the colonial state leveled against the project, the core group of the subaltern studies endeavor has undertaken a series of explorations of the dynamics of power and the discursive agendas of state, nation, and modernity in South Asia in the nineteenth and twentieth centuries. This emphasis is an intimation of impressive, broad, and often freshly laid avenues of history, but it does not always highlight the rather more ragged bridle paths and murky dark alleys of the past. Is there perhaps an enduring irony here? Do fragments and margins run the risk of being orchestrated, even overwhelmed, by the sound and static of the center?

This chapter now explores the implications of this newer postcolonial accent, an accent that is at once a clipped interrogation of reasons of state and a tonal register of states of mind. A word on the form of my readings is in order. In the discussion that follows, I focus first on two critical texts that are representative of the newer emphases within subaltern studies: Partha Chatterjee's *The Nation and Its Fragments* and Dipesh Chakrabarty's "Postcoloniality and the Artifice of History." These writings have been enormously influential in the larger articulation of subaltern studies with postcolonial perspectives. My effort is to indicate the tone and the texture of these texts. This also sets the stage for the next step, in which I provide critical readings of another essay each by Chatterjee and Chakrabarty, which form part of *Subaltern Studies VIII*, straining these texts against some of their dominant assumptions. To reiterate, my endeavor is to provide a sense of the achievements and complexity, the difficulties and diversity, of the newer emphases within subaltern studies, which are closely connected to current discussions of postcoloniality.

Another Modern

In his seminal study *The Nation and Its Fragments*, Partha Chatterjee puts the spotlight on the modern state and anticolonial nationalism. Addressing Benedict Anderson's influential understanding of nation and nationalism as "imagined communities," featuring processes that center on "print capitalism," Chatterjee begins by posing a seemingly simple question with very wide implications.[67] Here is what he asks: following Anderson, if we accept that the "modular forms" of the nation as an imagined community were elaborated in the New World and Europe and then exported to the colonies, what was/is left of nation and nationalism for peoples of Asia and Africa to imagine?[68] Chatterjee's answer draws on materials from colonial and postcolonial India, particularly from the province of Bengal. He not only reveals the ways in which the "modular forms" of the nation imagined in the West were reworked in the colonies but shows that anticolonial nationalism was not confined to a political battle with the colonial state. Rather, one of the first steps that early anticolonial nationalism took was to divide the world into "spiritual" and "material" realms. The former was the space of tradition and culture of the East. The latter was the arena of state and politics of the West. Chatterjee argues that long before anti-colonial nationalism entered into political battle with the colonial state it imagined the sovereign nation in the inner, "spiritual" domain of culture and tradition.

Far from being a simple defense of anticolonial nationalism(s), Chatterjee's arguments interrogate the modern nation-state through a wide-ranging and sophisticated critique of the "grand narrative of capital" and a spirited defense of the "independent narrative of community," which defines regimes of modernity. He argues that the narrative of capital seeks to suppress the narrative of community, a suppression that also lies at the heart of modern European social theory. Thus, "If there is one great moment that turns the provincial thought of Europe to universal philosophy, the parochial history of Europe to universal history, it is the moment of capital—capital that is global in its territorial reach and universal in its conceptual domain. It is the narrative of capital that can turn the violence of mercantalist trade, war, genocide, conquest, and colonialism into a story of universal progress, development, modernization, and freedom."[69] On one hand, the modern state, embedded within this larger narrative of capital, "cannot recognize within its jurisdiction any form of community except the single, determinate, demographically enumerable form of the nation." On the other hand, "by its very nature, the idea of community marks a limit to the realm of disciplinary power."[70]

I have argued elsewhere that the sharp separation between state and community, which is characteristic of both the earlier and the later orientations within subaltern studies, stands in the way of comprehending the intricate relationships between symbols of the state and contours of the community.[71] Yet I would like to suggest that to register the interplay between state and community is not to exhaust the complexity and richness of Chatterjee's readings. A multilayered work, The Nation and Its Fragments is easily misread by critics and commentators. Therefore, two clarifications are pertinent. First, by locating narratives of community within regimes of modernity, rather than reifying them as instances of romanticized tradition or "pre-modern remnants that an absent-minded Enlightenment forgot to erase," Chatterjee takes an enormous step forward in our understanding of community and modernity. Second, in Chatterjee's analyses, community and state are not so much empirical categories as they are epistemological terms and ontological entities. Taken together, these characteristics provide Chatterjee's readings with the theoretical rigor and analytical force required to think through the categories of the state and civil society and the individual and the community in traditions of modern Western political theory. They allow Chatterjee to point toward the possibility of uncovering the contradiction between the two narratives of capital and community embedded within the idea of the nation, particularly anticolonial nationalism, and to suggest other imaginings of community, nation(s), and modernity.

Dipesh Chakrabarty further elaborates the new orientations within subaltern studies in a wide-ranging essay on postcolonial propositions and historical cultures, an essay that has justifiably acquired seminal status in contemporary discussions of postcoloniality.[72] Implicitly at the very least, Chakrabarty's point of departure is Heidegger's "second Coppernican revolution," interrogating the artifice of a meaning-legislating reason.[73] Focusing on "history" as a discourse that is produced at the institutional site of the university, Chakrabarty makes a compelling case for the ways in which Europe remains the sovereign theoretical subject of all histories. In other words, what are designated in academic and quotidian arenas as Indian, Brazilian, Chinese, or Mexican histories are variations on a master theme that can be called the "history of Europe." While admitting that *Europe* and *India* are "hyperreal" terms that refer to certain figures of the imagination, Chakrabarty critically points toward how a certain version of Europe stands reified and celebrated in the "phenomenal world of everyday relationships of power."[74] At once the site and the scene of the birth of the modern, Europe works as a silent referent that dominates the discourse of history.

Making his way through critical readings and imaginative renderings of European philosophy, Indian writing in English, British colonial representations, and radical South Asian histories, Chakrabarty unravels the consequences of the theoretical privileging of Europe as the universal centerpiece of modernity and history. In a word, the history of India emerges cast in terms of irrevocable principles of failure, lack, and absence, since it is always/already measured against the West. Against the grain of these dominant imaginings of Indian history as an incomplete transition to modernity, Chakrabarty rehearses a chapter in the pasts of bourgeois domesticity in colonial Bengal. He argues that the engagement of the Indian middle class with the project of modernity ushered in by the British Empire exceeded the trichotomous ideational division of modern political structures—into state, civil society, and family—by challenging and modifying the fundamental tenets of a nuclear family based on companionate marriage and the secular, historical construction of time. Struggling against overwhelming odds, Chakrabarty's arguments question the telos that makes all modernities and histories appear to be the same.

The arguments form part of Dipesh Chakrabarty's project of "provincializing Europe." This project is not a call for a simplistic rejection of modernity and science or reason and liberal values. Nor is it a plea for cultural relativism or the construction of a new nativism. Rather, the project of provincializing Europe entails the recognition that Europe's acquisition of its status as the foundational seat and primary habitus of the modern is an outcome of the dialectic between Enlightenment and empire(s). Second, this project is premised on the understanding that the equation of a certain version of Europe with visions of a singular modernity is a product of the joint energies and pooled resources of Western projects of progress and the modernizing ideologies of Third World nationalisms. Third, to provincialize Europe is to write into the history of modernity its attendant ambivalences and contradictions, violence and terror, ironies and tragedies. This includes the empowerment of marginal groups within sovereign states, but it equally involves the undemocratic foundations of democracy. Finally, the project of provincializing Europe embodies what Chakrabarty calls a "politics of despair." In other words, it is "a history that deliberately makes visible, within the very structure of its narrative forms, its own representative strategies and practices, the part it plays in collusion with narratives of citizenship in assimilating to the projects of the modern state all other possibilities of human solidarity."[75] The task of provincializing Europe points toward the social world as radically heterogeneous, pluralizing also the contradictory and checkered modernities of human histories over the past few centuries.

Clearly, this is an impressive achievement. Questioning aggressive Eurocentric imaginings and modular understandings of cultures and pasts, these writings highlight the telos that binds history, modernity, nation, and progress. Indeed, it is difficult to think of more abiding articulations of postcolonial perspectives. Yet the newer emphases within subaltern studies also require sieving through critical filters. To this end, I now turn to other writings by Partha Chatterjee and Dipesh Chakrabarty that are closely connected to the works by these scholars discussed above.

Other Histories

In his striking essay "Claims on the Past" Partha Chatterjee maps a genealogy of the historical claims of Hindutva, the driving force behind contemporary Hindu cultural nationalism.[76] Chatterjee notes that these claims emerge out of contestations of modes of colonial knowledge. They become possible only within the modern forms of historiography. Appropriately, the essay charts its course by rehearsing a set of fascinating histories contained mainly in textbooks written in nineteenth-century Bengal.

The account begins with a Puranic history written in the early 1800s by a Brahman scholar of Sanskrit. This Puranic past is articulated by divine will; its protagonists are not "people" but gods, demons, and kings; and in it myth, history, and the contemporary share the same conceptual space, jumbled together for the purpose of chronological (con)sequences. Next, the story deftly moves on to a complementary narrative, this time written by a Bengali Muslim in the 1870s. Rooted in the *puthi* (leaf manuscript) literature of village poets, this account follows much the same logic of mythic history.

This backdrop sets the stage for the step by step unfolding of several histories that were cobbled together by the English-educated Bengali middle-class in the second half of the nineteenth century. These accounts replaced divine will with the mortal pursuit of power, identified the Muslim as an enemy, and laid claim to a classical Hindu past. They drew on British histories at the same time as they contested colonial rule. The authors of the accounts transformed themselves from mere subjects, acted on by political events, into subject-agents who at once practiced the arts of politics and statecraft, further identifying themselves with the consciousness of a national solidarity that allegedly unraveled itself as history. Such histories are part of the larger scheme of modern forms of historiography, "which is necessarily constructed around the complex identity of a people-nation-state."[77] The very singularity (or singleness) of the idea of a national history of India—often bound to the claims of *raison d'état*—will always have at hand the resources of a single "national" history of the "Hindus." The triumphant march of this charged conception, which routinely presents the past by invoking its immaculate birth, has suppressed other imaginings of the nation—fragmentary glimmers governed by a more plural logic and (con)federal political assumptions—of nation(s), even as it continues to divide Indians from one another today.

Exploring the "difference-deferral" of another modern, Dipesh Chakrabarty questions the "narratological closures" that are afforded by nationalist narratives, imperial imaginings, and modernist musings, providing colonial modernity with a semblance of homogeneous unity.[78] Instead, he focuses on debates around domesticity, particularly those centering on the ideals of the Bengali *grihalaksmi* (housewife), "to understand how the question of difference was played out in [the] (re)construction of the domestic realm in *bhadralok* [Bengali middle-class] life," which was in turn bound to the fashioning and the nature of a colonial modernity in Bengal.[79] The essay is based on prescriptive texts on domestic life written by men and women in the nineteenth century, but it is equally made up of fancy footwork and foxy footnotes.

According to Chakrabarty, there were two radically different constructions of the social life of the "private" family as narrated in the "public" Bengali debates over new forms of domesticity. The first lent itself to a "civilizing" mission. Here domesticity and personhood were subordinated to the project of the creation of citizen-subjects and "the goals of the civil-political sphere which, in turn, were seen as the site of work for the acquisition of improvement and happiness." The second was "to imagine a connection between the domestic and a mytho-religious social . . . whereby the civil society itself became a problem, a constraint whose coercive nature was to be tolerated but never enjoyed."[80] These two contrary ways of articulating the domestic and the national, the "private" and the "public," the family and the civil-political, could only come together by bringing each other to crisis.

These movements cannot have a single, unitary history, for they exceed the "historicist" imagination of the historian. In fact, no adequate critique of Bengali modernity—with its central "neologism" of the grihalaksmi tied to the mytho-religious time of the *kula* (lineage)—can be "mounted or practiced from within secular historicist narratives alone."[81] Yet, even as the need for a more complete and nuanced critique of this modernity becomes a necessity, Chakrabarty also reminds us that colonial modernity in Bengal was marked by the order of difference and informed by the ideal of self-sacrifice in the spirit of subordination to the parochial principle of dharma. Indeed, involving a nonsecular and nonuniversal sense of aesthetics—or, an irreducible category of "beauty"—pointing to a certain *subject* of pleasure that was tied to a desire for the well-being of the kula, this modernity contained possibilities of other maneuvers, engendering utterances that looked beyond patriarchy. This ideal and spirit were more than a ruse for staging the secular-historicist project of the citizen-subject. The aesthetic, pleasure, and desire exceeded a straightforward bourgeois project of domesticating women. Finally, such statements of uncompromising resistance to duty resist assimilation to "the emancipatory visions [of] Eurocentric imaginations of civil-political life."[82]

Other Singularities

Once more, I have presented these distinct arguments at some length to bring out their theoretical texture and empirical variety. At the same time, this allows me to highlight the critical issues raised earlier. Let me begin, then, by asking three initial but broad questions concerning the critiques of homogenizing impulses of state, nation, modernity, and their historiography as these are mounted in the writings of Partha Chatterjee and Dipesh Chakrabarty. Do these critiques of singular strains also tend toward constructing other singularities? Is this because the essays replicate some of the key categories at the core of the very taxonomies that they set out to question and criticize? Do these writings obfuscate and obscure the diverse imaginative routes traversed by historical practice? Not wholly or in full measure but in some parts and certain ways, these charges stick to the two essays under discussion, also raising questions regarding the articulation between subaltern studies and postcolonial perspectives.

We have noted that Dipesh Chakrabarty queries the familiar and insidious conception of modernity as an all-encompassing, seamless behemoth. He seeks to "write difference into the history of our [Bengali/Indian] modernity in a mode that resists the assimilation of this history to the political imaginary of European-derived institutions . . . which dominate our lives."[83] However, the difficulty with this exploration of a colonial modernity lies in its replication of the givenness of several of the central elements that lie at the heart of the "epistemic violence" that Chakrabarty sets out to question. Thus, the "in your face" distinctions between the "public" and the "private," the "civil-political" and the "domestic," derived from an Ur-scheme of history, are configured as part of the natural order of all modernity/modernities. With the models in place, the unfolding of the past at once conforms to, deviates from, and (thereby) issues a challenge to the familiar designs of Eurocentric modernity. Indeed, Chakrabarty's plea is to "attend carefully to nineteenth century Bengali contestations over received bourgeois models for relating the personal to the public world of civil and political life."[84]

Yet we are compelled to ask what filters of understanding, what grids of reference, strained and shaped the reception of these bourgeois models. How did such frames of reference and bourgeois models mutually refashion each other? On what were the many "nineteenth century Bengali contestations," which Chakrabarty mentions, predicated, if not on modes of reception involving the reworking of both received models and inherited understandings? Can we really take for granted the meanings of the public and the civil-political and the personal and the domestic? Conversely, do these domains and categories require greater, context-bound elaboration? What are we to make of the suggestion in Chakrabarty's writing that the public and the civil-political bear a transparent quality, while the private and the domestic embody a concomitant dense opacity? Even while admitting that the "mytho-religious" within the domestic domain embodied particular, nonuniversal attributes, is an attribution of transcendence to this mytho-religious necessary to gestures that point out the limits of secular-historicist narratives?

Chakrabarty's busy essay darts about doing a great deal, a truly suggestive and provocative piece of writing. Nonetheless, I ask my questions in good faith. For these questions perhaps point to other possibilities in articulating pasts. A more satisfying alternate take—to borrow a recording studio phrase—on colonial modernities requires us to think through inherited categories. Needed here are alternative and fuller renderings of the gendered domains of the public and the domestic, the concepts of personhood and the civil-political, and indeed of that terribly fetishized category of the modern state. In any case, it is important to guard against the ease of playing variations on a master theme. The struggle against allowing all modernities to look the same has to be a matter of gritty improvisation.

Partha Chatterjee's forthright style is admirable, yet the clarity and finesse of the writing also underlie its difficulties. Chatterjee's discussion of the varied histories that make up his account has a much too linear, irrevocable step by step character. Here a somewhat static framework of sharp contrasts between mythic perceptions and modern conceptions of nationness, embedded in separate articulations of the past, orchestrates Chatterjee's construction of the similarities and differences between these tales. With these histories understood against a master blueprint, their different patterns, shocking colors, and many hues are rendered into a solemn set of contrasting designs in black and white, all grist for the mill of Chatterjee's account. This tends to obscure and shroud the relatively unexplored byways of the pasts that have been fabricated as part of colonial modernities.

There is a univocal quality to Chatterjee's conception of "*the form* of historical memory" before the implantation of modern European modes in the mind of the educated Bengali. This leads to the assertion that there "does not seem to be much difference in the mode of historical thinking" between the Puranic history of the early 1880s of Mrintunjay, the Pandit of Sanskrit, and the mythic history of Munshi Alimaddin, the Muslim poet from Barisal, steeped in the puthi style of village verse.[85] Now, I quite welcome and endorse the politics here. It is much more evocative than the routinely staged, saccharine invocations of "syncretism" in India. Yet is there also not a need to attend to the differences between these histories? These differences pertain to their dissimilar ways of reckoning time, imagining space, configuring the contemporary, constructing the apocalypse, and envisioning redemption, all of which are suggested by the fragments from these texts cited by Chatterjee. It seems to me that Chatterjee's essay admits of plurality in conceptions of the past, but it also suggests sameness in distinct imaginings of different mythic histories.

In Chatterjee's account, the modern followed the mythic, quite as night comes after day. Now new histories were produced as "the Bengali literati was schooled in the new colonial education" and "the modern European principles of social and political organization were deeply implanted in their minds."[86] (A bit like Chakrabarty, Chatterjee seems to take this process of "schooling" for granted. He does not really consider any critical reworking of "the modern European principles of political and social organization" apart from the more obvious contestations of the forms of colonial knowledge, and these, too, only after the modern principles are assumed to be in place.) The modern histories that Chatterjee rehearses exceed his analysis. These accounts did not always entirely jettison the "criteria of the divine will, religious values and the norms of right conduct in judging the rise and fall of kingdoms," not even in the course of writing the history of British rule in India.[87] All too frequently, the modes of construction of modern histories were critically entangled with mythic pasts.

Chatterjee has constructed a brilliant essay, one that provokes us to think through several complacent statist and centralist assumptions. Besides, it would be silly to expect any single writing to turn every conceivable trick, to perform all possible tasks. But there is perhaps a larger question here. Chatterjee's genealogy of Hindutva, tracing the fashioning of the basic materials of contemporary Hindu extremist political rhetoric back to the very birth of nationalist historiography, often obfuscates the diverse processes of construction that underlie the pasts that it rehearses. These processes involved the appearance and combination of (several) similarities and differences, (various) ruptures and continuities, and (diverse) oppositions and appositions, all constitutive of nationalist histories. And these appearances and combinations occurred at points and junctures, in patterns and ways, that are scarcely ordained by Chatterjee's overarching genealogical framework.

All of this has wider implications. Recall the discussion earlier of the difficulties surrounding renderings of power as a totalized terrain, a dystopic totality. Something similar is afoot here. On one hand, the terms of argument positing a singular connection between modernity and history treat the distinct extramodern pasts that they recall—"mythic history" or the "fragment"—as imbued with essential marks of alterity, the antidote to devices of power. On the other hand, such a singular connection between modernity and history cannot help attributing a relentless singularity to the plurality of pasts that it rehearses under the sign of the modern. Taken together, this tends toward presenting former pasts as unrecuperated particulars that are always different and portraying the latter histories as settled verities that are already the same. It follows that such terms of discourse locate difference and interrogate power, but they fall short of simultaneously recognizing and questioning the place of difference within power and the play of power within difference—in distinct sites, diverse arenas.

Conclusion

In the wake of the recent privilege accorded to postcoloniality within academe, itself tied to the current imperatives of multiculturalism in these arenas, it is easy to overlook the manner in which, over time, the subaltern studies endeavor has animated and articulated different perspectives, from histories from below through postcolonial propositions. At the same time, the purpose of this chapter was not only to show the empirical, analytical, theoretical, and conceptual variety of this project. My effort equally entailed tracing the difficult and contested passage through which subaltern studies has unraveled as an intellectual undertaking. This means critically engaging the constitutive presumptions of the project while attending to its textures and details and recognizing the plurality of the endeavor while registering its singularities. To do so is to articulate the procedures of a history without warranty, binding the impulse to question the imperative to affirm in dispositions toward the past and the present and social worlds and academic apprehensions, not only in order to track the imaginative pathways of human practice, including the dark alleys and the murky underworlds of pasts, but also to redraw the shifting boundaries and intricate relationships between the everyday and the nation, community and state, difference and power, and history and modernity. Such dispositions are further unraveled in the next chapter.

I f the past two decades have seen the prodigious production of critical scholarship on South Asia, these years have also witnessed the rise to prominence of an intolerant Hindu nationalism in India. Subsumed under the generic label of Hindutva, this newer articulation of Hindu cultural militancy is closely bound to processes of the institutionalized power relations of the modern Indian state. Indeed, at the heart of contemporary Hindutva lie conjunctions and contradictions between the programs and practices of a cluster of organizations of the Hindu Right, chiefly the Bharatiya Janata Party, the Rashtriya Svayamsevak Sangh, the Vishwa Hindu Parishad, the Shiv Sena, and their fronts and affiliates.[1] The ideology and the practice of Hindutva underlay the destruction of the Babri Masjid, a mosque in the town of Ayodhya in North India on 6 December 1992 and the large-scale sectarian violence that followed in its wake. Claims on history have been central to efforts that seek to establish the Hindu Right as the repository of a timeless Hindu tradition and the vanguard of a modern Hindu nation.[2] Not less than the new, theoretically challenging histories of South Asia, the aggressive construction and assiduous cultivation of the past within Hindu nationalism warrant critical readings.[3]

Homogeneous History

This chapter discusses a central segment of Hindutva's history. It is the story of the transformations of a god-king, Ram. It is the tale of the pasts of a place of pilgrimage, Ayodhya. The story and the tale do not exhaust Hindutva and/or its histories. Yet they suggest the intense mutual attractions between the homogenization of a singular history and the fetish of the modern nation.[4] The instantiation of the god-king Ram as the central deity of Hindutva has undergirded the current making of a Hindu modern. The claims on the history of Ayodhya have underwritten the contemporary construction of the modern Hindu. In the name of Ram and through the claims of history, the bellicose Hindutva has featured polemical and physical attacks against all alleged enemies of an undifferentiated community of Hindus in a bid to cleanse the body politic of modern Bharat (India) of its external impurities.

There is little to distinguish between the terror of state and a state of terror for many Muslim peoples and several Christian communities in India today. A hallmark of such aggression has been the intermeshing of the written word and the spoken symbol with visual images and violent acts. Here the Hindu Right's clarion calls of brutal belligerence, embodied in strident speeches and sanguinary scriptures of hysterical hatred, have seized and worked on the popular iconography of calendar art. This has led to significant transformations in the representations of the god-king Ram. Once a largely gentle deity fashioned within the interstices of oral traditions mainly through a rehearsal, reiteration, and reworking of the verses of medieval saint-poets, Ram has been transformed in recent years into a muscular, militant, and modern icon of Hindutva, at once symbol and savior carrying aggressively arranged implements of warfare.[5] These renderings of Ram as Rambo involve a particular construction of history. Ayodhya occupies a key place in this play with the past. A web of time and timelessness, Ayodhya is always/already present(ed) as the Hindu sacred desecrated by the Muslim profane. By disregarding diversity, discontinuity, and difference in the pasts of this place of pilgrimage, what is revealed, rather, is a singular and seamless history of Ayodhya.

Let us examine the main elements of this new account of Ayodhya and its association with Ram a little more closely. In a recent article, Gyanendra Pandey has identified the central aspects of the histories constructed by the Hindu Right over the past two decades.[6] These carefully plotted, assiduously rehearsed, and strategically staged "melodramas" do not recount a past of the region or the people of Ayodhya. They engineer, rather, the history of the destruction of a specific monument (the Ram temple, over whose ruins the Babri mosque is claimed to have been built) in a particular place (Ayodhya), as much in the past as in the present.[7] The newer narratives have effected a break with the "metaphorical" quality of earlier Hindu accounts of the pasts of Ayodhya, where Ram and Ayodhya were both metaphors that "stood for much more than the literal truth" of the god-king or the geographical and historical location of his capital. Thus, instead of the earlier "metaphorical" pasts there now stand hardheaded "real" histories that claim to present the "literal" and "comprehensive" truth.[8] On one hand, this newer narrative is in tune "with much of the 'modern' Indian effort since the nineteenth century to establish the historicity, rationality, masculinity—in a word, 'adulthood' in Western terms—of India and its religions." On the other hand, it carries the "positivism and literalism" of the fetish of the modern state much, much further.

There are two specific and simultaneous movements at the heart of the articulation of these accounts of Ayodhya. In the first place, verities of fact appear to be reinforced here by certainties of faith, so that the past "comes to be represented in a 'scientific' precision—of numbers, of dates, of geographical location—testifying to the literal truth of this 'history.' "[9] Indeed, in these histories the staging of science begins on the cover, with titles that proclaim their contents as "authentic" and "authoritative." As further proof, the front matter also displays the scholarly credentials of the authors, who are suitably armed with master's and doctoral degrees in archaeology and history. Next, the arrogation of authority and authenticity in these accounts is clinched through a rehearsal of chronologies, including the citation of definite numbers, dates, and hours. Two examples should suffice. First, "There were 76 battles fought by the Hindus against the Muslims between 1528 and 1932 [for the liberation of the Ram temple, which had been turned into a mosque] in Ayodhya." Second, and even more revealingly, "On June 9, 1528 A.D., at 2 P.M. Pandit Devi Prasad Pandey [a Brahman who had killed seven hundred soldiers of the emperor Babur's army in just three hours] breathed his last."[10]

The palpable accuracy and implied truth of these histories is now elaborated in an even more literal way. Casting aside the porous pasts of a people or a place, at stake here is the concrete history of a particular monument, the "Great Temple of Ram in Ayodhya."[11] The narrative begins with the destruction of this monument, only to return to this point repeatedly. The monumental history of the destruction and desecration of the Ram temple by the Muslims and its defense and preservation by the Hindus has a twin purpose, a double effect. It supplies an incontrovertible account of the innate evil of Islam in India and it provides an irrefutable history of the inherently indomitable Hindu spirit, Hindu people, and Hindu nation. Such fixing of the subject positions of Hindu heroes and Muslim monsters locked in mortal combat throughout history has close affinities with arrogant imperial imaginings and aggressive colonial conceptions of unchanging "national" cultures. According to Pandey, it follows that the newer Hindu histories of Ayodhya are fundamentally ahistorical. They do not allow for "process"—change and development—in the pasts of their protagonists, and they pay no attention to "context" in their relentless repetition of static stories regarding "foreign" (Muslim/Christian) aggression and "native" (Hindu/Indian) valor.[12]

This brings me to the second movement that has articulated the histories produced by Hindu cultural militancy over the past fifteen years. These accounts ceaselessly mix up and overlay the "scientific" with the "miraculous." The divine intervention of Ram orchestrates the past of Ayodhya from a million years ago (and before) through the new millennium (and beyond). Indeed, the circular nature of the narrative relentlessly draws together the mythic and the archaeological, the historical and the contemporary, to produce sameness in different orders of time.[13] This sameness is not at all at odds with the Hindutva-sponsored history's insistence on the literal truth of its assertions. Rather, the sameness of different conceptions of time and the literalness of truth claims work together in these accounts to point toward a single apocalyptic end, namely, the resolution of the conflict between Hindus and Muslims in the here and now.[14] At once informed by the logic of "legend" and the reason of "history," this resolution is nothing but the Hindu community realizing itself through the capture of state power. At the heart of the apocalypse now is the Hindu nation *becoming* the Hindu state.[15]

Interrogating History

How has this assiduous construction of history by the Hindu Right been questioned and challenged?[16] The main liberal and leftist democratic response—led by historians of the Jawaharlal Nehru University in New Delhi—has been to enter into a "public debate" over the claims of Hindutva on the history of Ayodhya.[17] The central strategy has been to argue that these claims rest on a distortion of historical "facts."[18] This line of criticism has successfully revealed the highly selective and intensely insidious ways in which the Hindu Right has gone about its business of fashioning history. At the same time, the chief problems of this approach also stem from its privileging of "historical evidence" in ways that turn history into a touchstone of truth.

In this understanding, the false claims on the past are shaped by political power, while the genuine article of true history appears to lie outside the domain of political choices. This leads to an implicit bracketing of the histories of the liberals and the Left from the wider existence of the past as a powerful negotiable and reworkable resource.[19] There are two consequences. On one hand, in contesting the claims of Hindutva these arguments tend to endorse the givenness of the "Indian secular nation," casting the entire debate within an inherited consensus that has developed around this category. On the other hand, as Peter Van der Veer suggests, such accounts can also lean toward a tendentious and in some respects disingenuous construction of history.[20] The effort to straighten the historical record can veer toward another homogenized history, a different sanitized past.[21]

It is not surprising, therefore, that the many valuable endeavors here have also fallen short of coming to terms with the challenges posed by a distinct response to the history produced by the Hindu Right. I refer to the important essay (published in Bengali and English) by Partha Chatterjee that constructs a "genealogy" of the historical claims of Hindutva. We have seen in the previous chapter that these historical claims were produced out of contestations of modes of colonial forms of knowledge and became possible only within the modern forms of historiography. Histories written by the English-educated Bengali middle-class men in the late nineteenth century marked a break with earlier mythic pasts. They replaced divine will with mortal pursuit of power, identified the Muslim as an enemy, laid claim to a classical Hindu past, and drew on British histories as they contested colonial rule. In these histories, the authors were not mere subjects acted on by political events. Rather, they emerged as subject-agents who practiced the arts of politics and statecraft, identifying themselves with the consciousness of the solidarity of the nation that allegedly acted itself out in history. Chatterjee argues that these histories are part of the larger scheme of the modern forms of historiography, which are "necessarily constructed around the complex identity of a people-nation-state." The singularity of the idea of one national history of India will always have at hand a single history of the Hindus.[22]

Partha Chatterjee has produced a challenging and compelling account. His interrogation of the singularity of a national history of India evokes other imaginings of nation(s). These are fragmentary glimmers governed by a plural logic and truly federal assumptions. Yet Chatterjee's overarching genealogical framework does not allow him to explore the ways in which the earlier elements of Hindu histories appear to have been drawn on and transformed in the construction of the modern myth of Muslim monstrosity and Hindu virtue in the new history fabricated by contemporary Hindutva. The undoubtedly valuable resources of a well-mapped genealogy of Hindutva, it seems to me, do not adequately interrogate the dark and terrible immediacy of rabid Hindu histories today.

Several decades ago, Walter Benjamin recognized a similar force of urgency regarding representations of the past. Written in the context of the rise of fascism in Europe, Benjamin's words are invoked so often that they bear repetition in a different time and another place that also feature the crisis of history.

To articulate the past historically does not mean to recognize it "the way it really was" (Ranke). It means to seize hold of a memory as it flashes up at a moment of danger. Historical materialism wishes to retain that image of the past which unexpectedly appears to man singled out by history at a moment of danger. The danger affects both the content of tradition and its receivers. The same threat hangs over both: that of becoming a tool of the ruling classes. In every era the attempt must be made anew to wrest tradition away from a conformism that is about to overpower it. The Messiah comes not only as the redeemer, he also comes as the subduer of Antichrist. Only that historian will have the gift of spanning the spark of hope in the past who is firmly convinced that *even the dead* will not be safe from the enemy if he wins. And this enemy has not ceased to be victorious.[23]

Of course, there is much to ponder in this passage, particularly in our time of a crisis of the democratic will, the success of populist nativisms, the elaboration of aggressive nationalisms, and the entrenchment of neo-neoliberal orthodoxies going for gung-ho globalization.[24] At the same time, my purpose in drawing on Benjamin's reflections is somewhat different.

Rather than relying on tacit assumptions regarding the transparent nature and inherent truth of "historical evidence," fact and information, I would submit, need to be bound to less conscious realms of subterranean images and everyday imaginings. Far from that romance of the merely quotidian, my call is for construing facts unexpected, which speak in the echoes of limiting doubt. This is particularly true with regard to political choices and intellectual moves to interrogate histories produced by Hindu nationalists. All of this also means that self-conscious historical interventions, political polemics, or Foucauldian genealogies (or however else we choose to describe these exercises) must not only recognize but also admit to seizing on the urgency and immediacy of memories that flash at the dark and dangerous moments in the here and now. To fly the banner of "true history" at the cost of rendering the past as lying outside the domain of political choices is to abdicate the struggle over histories. Yet this is no time to bicker simply about the fallacies of the liberals and the mistakes of the Left. An earlier version of this chapter, written in Hindi as a self-consciously political piece, joined the "public debate" initiated by liberal-leftist historians in India, even though it had important differences of emphases.[25] This chapter has also benefited from the arguments used in the struggle against the idea of a single national history that suppresses visions of more plural pasts. The emphases here eschew a sanitized and homogenized construction of history. In their stead, I now bring to the fore a few fragments of the fractured pasts of Ayodhya over the past four centuries.

Fractured History

The genealogical claim of the Hindu Right that Ayodhya belongs exclusively to a single lineage of the believers of Ram is founded on bad faith. The metaphor of one family of Hindus itself seeks to cover the differences and hide the contradictions within Hinduism. But let us leave aside this question and turn to the pilgrimage center that is said to be the birthplace of Ram.

Ayodhya is a sacred space in several different religious traditions. The Buddhists identify it with the ancient Saket. Local tradition has it that the Buddha meditated in Ayodhya, which figures among the oldest towns in Buddhist scriptures and contains an ancient Buddhist monument on Maniparvat. Ayodhya is also a site of pilgrimage for the votaries of the Jain faith. Both the Digambars and the Svetambars—the two main branches of the sect—believe that Rishabdev, their first tirthankar (preceptor), was born in the town, which has several important Jain temples. The religious significance of Ayodhya for Muslims stems from their popular belief that Noah lies buried in a grave here.

Queen Victoria, too, found incorporation into the Hindu pantheon in Ayodhya. A statue of the queen stood in a park named after her during the Raj. According to a local legend, when Nal, a general of Ram, fell in love with a girl who lived in these parts, his lord prophesied that the girl's children would gain fame and rule the world in kaliyuga, the epoch of evil. When Britannia ruled the waves, the pilgrims to Ayodhya worshiped Queen Victoria, who was transformed into both the symbolic mother of Britons and a latter-day incarnation of the local girl whose rise to dizzy heights Ram had foretold. Did her deification in a distant and dusty town amuse the dour queen?[26]

These legends appear to be bound to the great prestige held by Ayodhya through its identification as the birthplace of the god-king Ram. At the same time, even this identification is not entirely free from ambiguities. Ayodhya is a sacred site for both hereditary Brahman priests and ascetics belonging to the Ramanandi order. The pandas (priests) and the open category of sadhus (Hindu ascetics) who respectively preside over a Brahmanical ritual complex and a monastic spiritual complex each have had different uses for Ayodhya. In fact, the interests and identities of these religious specialists, as Peter Van der Veer has shown, have altered over time with processes of state formation and socioeconomic change in North

Indian society.[27] In brief, in the face of the aggressive marketing of Ram by Hindutva it is easy to forget that Ayodhya is characterized by the congruence of interests of varied religions and different specialists of the sacred.

The contemporary political fantasies of power brokers that pawn Ram in the modern market freeze the past when, according to legend, the Babri Masjid was constructed over the ruins of the temple at the birthplace of the deity. However, popular fables of the past weave a richer tapestry. Local history presented the birthplace of Ram as a site frequented by Hindu and Muslim ascetics, where ordinary members of both faiths brought their children to increase their life span. Similarly, according to a popular local legend, if the Muslim saint Khwaja Fazal Abbas Ashkhan was a prime mover in the building of the Babri mosque, he also has an ambiguous, contradictory role in the past of Ayodhya.

Here Khwaja Fazal Abbas Ashkhan appeared as a disciple of the Hindu ascetic Syamanand. Indeed, the *faqir* (saint) Khwaja realized his goals of Yoga by uttering a Muslim mantra. All this bears testimony to the highly syncretic nature of popular religious traditions. At the same time, as the legend continued, after gaining spiritual power, the saint Khwaja got together with faqir Jalal Shah to advise Babur, the first Mughal emperor, that he should destroy the temple of Ram in Ayodhya and build a mosque in its place. When Babur's general Mir Baqi failed to destroy the temple after repeated attempts, the saint Khwaja dreamed that the sanctum of the temple was the wrong place over which to build the mosque. Then he suggested a spot somewhat behind the *garbha* (sanctum). The command of the saint led to the building of the mosque in such a way that the sanctum of the temple remained open and formed a pit into which Hindus threw flowers for centuries.[28]

Of course, it is true that this legend, collected by the anthropologist Peter Van der Veer in the 1970s, has been incorporated since—in a sufficiently selective and sanitized manner—by the Vishwa Hindu Parishad into its history of the Hindu nation.[29] This definitely politicizes the issue in new ways. At the same time, my point is that we cannot shy away from such local legends. Even the most partisan and one-sided of such stories presents a richer picture of the past than the histories of the Hindu Right. Indeed, these fractured pasts and fading fragments can serve as a means of interrogating the order of homogenized histories.

Besides, fragmentary written evidence from the late sixteenth through to the eighteenth centuries reveals that Hindu worship continued at the site under Mughal rule. The European traveler William Finch, for instance, visited Ayodhya sometime between 1608 and 1611 and wrote a brief description.

A city of ancient note, and seat of a Potan [Pathan: Muslim], now much ruined, the castle built foure hundred yeeres agoe. Here are also the ruines of . . . [Ram's] castle and houses, which the Indian ac-knowled(g)e for the great God, saying that he tooke flesh upon him to see the tamasha [show] of the world. In these ruins remaine certaine Brahmenes, who record the names of all such Indians who wash themselves in the river running thereby, which custome, they say, hath continued four lacke of yeeres (which is three hundred ninetie four thousand and five hundred yeeres before the world's creation).[30]

Against the tenor of histories inspired by Hindutva, it is important to point out that this account and other documents reveal that under Mughal rule Hindu pilgrims visited Ayodhya and Brahmans functioned as ritual priests for their *jajmans* (patrons of the sacrifice), the latter being petty kings and landlords in North India.[31]

This is not to make a case for the seamless stitching of inherent toler-ance toward other religions into the fabric of precolonial kingship in India. Indeed, given present-day debates on the nature of secularism in South Asia, it is important to recognize the close ties between "religion" and "politics" in pasts of kingship and the histories of empire on the subconti-nent. Put briefly, religion and politics were inextricably bound to each other in different ways under varied versions of Hindu kingship, Islamic empire, and colonial rule in India. I only wish to suggest that local legends and meager written evidence from the past point to variegated patterns of fables and critical continuities of faith in Ayodhya under Mughal rule. They exceed a vision of history that fixes its gaze on a single moment of destruc-tion, obliterating life and endorsing death.

Ayodhya's emergence as a pilgrimage center of importance had to wait until the eighteenth century. Its background lay in the consolidation of the Mughal empire in the seventeenth century, which led to an expansion of communications. This provided a stimulus both to the growth of trade and to Hindu pilgrimage. In fact, the two phenomena were closely connected. The work of Bernard Cohn and Chris Bayly has shown that in the eigh-teenth century different groups of ascetics combined military and commer-cial power to use their cycle of pilgrimage through the Gangetic Plain, from Haridwar in the north to Jagannath Puri and Bengal on the eastern coast, as a network of long-distance trade. They linked areas of supply and demand in the stable and productive zones, provided protection on the difficult terrain and routes in between, and used their corporate savings with great efficiency. Indeed, during the eighteenth century ascetic orders emerged as the principal traders and dominant moneylending and property-owning groups in several parts of North India.[32] Among the most important of these itinerant ascetic groups was that of the Ramanandi ascetics, who acted as military entrepreneurs and traders, engaging in commerce and moneylending.

The Ramanandis "rediscovered" Ayodhya in the eighteenth century and established it as a significant center of pilgrimage. Until the seventeenth century, the Ramanandi ascetics had been confined principally to western India, particularly Rajasthan. During the eighteenth century, the territory and network of operations of this ascetic order expanded all over India. It established monasteries in present day Uttar Pradesh, Bihar, and the Terai region of Nepal. In Ayodhya, Ramanandi *akharas* (divisions of fighting ascetics) first appeared in the early eighteenth century and rapidly grew in number over the next eight decades. Aided by the Ramanandi ascetics' activities as traders and mercenaries, this process was accompanied by the Ramanandi rediscovery of sacred sites associated with the legends of Ram and his wife Sita.

Richard Burghart has shown the manner of identification of Janakpur in the Terai region as the birthplace of Sita and the site of her marriage to Ram, which together underlay the establishment of Janakpur as an important Ramanandi center. There were different steps here, from the belief that Janakpur had disappeared in an earlier epoch to its rediscovery through a celestial vision by Sur Kisor, a Ramanandi ascetic from Jaipur; the Ramanandi struggle with the rival Dasnami sect, long established in the area, over the sacred space of Janakpur; the Ramanandi displacement of preexistent modes of worship, establishing the supremacy of their own myths and icons; and their winning the support and patronage of local rulers.[33] At the same time, none of this was peculiar to the Ramanandis or confined to Janakpur. Charlotte Vaudeville's work underscores the enactment of a very similar process in Braj in Uttar Pradesh after the Madhav Gauriya, a community of believers in the god Krishna from Bengal, came to settle in the region.[34]

In other words, the Ramanandi "rediscovery" of Ayodhya in the eighteenth century formed part of a larger pattern of the mechanism of expansion of ascetic orders and the construction of religious traditions. Now sacred sites identified as having been lost in a previous epoch were reclaimed and infused with new meanings. At the same time, there was a twist to the particular manner of the "rediscovery" of Ayodhya. Since the town was associated with the legend of Ram, the construction of new temples by the Ramanandis in the eighteenth century emerged as a task of "repair" and "restoration," and these new temples were represented as replicas of buildings from the time of Ram.[35] A projection of timelessness informed the rebuilding of pristine Ayodhya. Yet this abolition of the temporal was not out of time in the pasts of Ayodhya.

Actually, the Ramanandi endeavor was a sign of the times. It could not have been possible without the ascetic order's acquisition of the patronage of the Muslim *nawabs* (rulers) of Awadh. Richard Barnett has shown that in the eighteenth century Awadh under its nawabs—who were Shia (as distinct from the much more numerous Sunni) Muslims—underwent a transformation. The Mughal province now became an autonomous regional successor state, which doubled its size, began to attain a distinct historical and cultural identity, and acquired considerable economic and political power. The rule of the Shia nawabs of Awadh rested on the successful collaboration of Hindus and Muslims. Hindu participation in political and military domains was critical. On one hand, the administrative control of this successor state lay in the hands of Hindu Khatri and Kayasth families of scribes and clerics. On the other, for their military power, the nawabs relied principally on two warrior-ascetic groups, and their armies were made up of regiments of Dasnami Naga ascetics and Gosain sadhu generals.

In the eighteenth century, the growing prosperity of Ayodhya and its increasing prominence as a pilgrimage center were both results of the patronage of the nawabi court and the upward mobility of Hindu groups in the expanding state system of Awadh. The existing documents kept by some Brahman priests and Ramanandi ascetics in Ayodhya reveal that the Hindu *diwans* (chief ministers) of the nawabs built and repaired several temples. Moreover, Muslim officials of the nawabi courts gave gifts for rituals performed by the priests. Finally, it was the nawab Safdarjung, a ruler of Awadh, who gave land on Hanuman's Hill to the Nirwana group of the Dasnami fighting ascetics for the construction of a temple. This grant later led to the building of the temple-fortress of Hanumangarhi with the help of Tikayat Ray, the Hindu minister of Asaf-ud-Daulah.[36] Therefore, far from being blighted by "Muslim rule," as the proponents of Hindutva assert, the expansion of the Ramanandis and the growth of Ayodhya over the eighteenth century were stimulated by the character of the court of the Muslim nawabs of Awadh, including the patronage extended by these rulers to different Hindu ascetic orders.

The nineteenth century witnessed further changes in the character of Ayodhya. The first half of the century saw the gradual erosion of the power of the Awadh nawabs because of the increasing influence of the East India Company in the politics of the state. According to Peter Van der Veer, these developments came to threaten the patterns of coexistence of Hindus and Muslims in Ayodhya. In the mid–nineteenth century, during the reign of Wajid Ali Shah, Sunni leaders began to militate against the Shia nawabs. In 1855, they claimed that earlier there had been another mosque within the precincts of the temple-fortress of Hanumangarhi, arguing that it should be reopened for Muslim worship. This led to violent clashes between the

Ramanandi Naga ascetics and the Sunni Muslims. The Nagas killed seventy Muslims. The Sunni leaders continued to press for jihad against the Nagas in defiance of the explicit orders of the nawab. It was against this background that the British, after the annexation of the kingdom of Awadh in 1856, put a railing around the Babri mosque and raised a platform outside the fence. Now the Muslims worshiped inside the mosque, and the Hindus made their offerings from the platform.

After the mid–nineteenth century, other developments had a significant impact on the shape of Ayodhya. The patronage of petty kings and landed gentry, who were Hindus, replaced that of the nawabs and their officials. These groups came to invest heavily in the building and maintenance of temples in Ayodhya. This was part of a pan-Indian development, which followed different trajectories. On one hand, Nicholas Dirks has shown that colonial rule effected a separation between ritual and politics that had defined the bases of power of Indian kingship. As "little kings" lost effective political power, they came to invest heavily in royal ritual, including the maintenance and building of temples, a pattern that underlay their increasingly "hollow crowns."[37] On the other hand, as Shail Mayaram has argued, in states such as Alwar and Bharatpur in princely India, kingly sponsorship of temple building could enhance Hindu regal power.[38] At any rate, unlike in the past, the members of the landed gentry who patronized Ayodhya did not support the Ramanandi ascetics, appointing instead their own Brahman priests in the temples they constructed. At the same time, the building of such temples proceeded at a rapid pace and continued into the early twentieth century. By the 1930s, the fortunes of these groups had begun to decline, and increasingly they could no longer afford to maintain their temples. Indeed, a large number of the ruins in Ayodhya projected as belonging to the time of Ram are constructions of the nineteenth century.[39]

Such designs of the form of history and the content of tradition bring me to the twentieth century. It is the events of this century—leading up to the demolition of the Babri mosque and the subsequent fallout—that have turned Ayodhya from a relative political backwater into one of the most contentious arenas in Indian politics. This centrality underwent upswings and downswings in the very recent past. These events have been extensively analyzed.[40] Here I point toward a less discussed development in Ayodhya in this century. Under colonial rule, there was a heightened emphasis on caste identities, which consequently grew more rigid. This has led to the construction of a large number of temples and pilgrims' lodges in Ayodhya for the exclusive use of lower and untouchable castes since the early part of the twentieth century. Beyond status mobility and displays of respectability, this development has also involved the expression of pilgrimage as a form of devotion. For example, lower-caste lay Ramanandis—a sect that retains caste distinctions within its internal organization—have a Ramanandi ascetic of their community who acts as preceptor and often as manager of their caste institutions in Ayodhya. Alternatively, the caste group of Marwari merchants, which rationalizes its patronage along lines of bureaucratic and business organization, has increasingly replaced the landed elite as the major religious patron in Ayodhya. The pious lifestyles of these merchants involve the meetings of religious trusts that simultaneously serve to establish business contacts.[41] Over time, then, Ayodhya has been invested with and become constitutive of multiple meanings.

Ends and Beginnings

"Part of the importance of the 'fragmentary' point of view lies in this, that it resists the drive for a shallow homogenization and struggles for other, potentially richer definitions of the 'nation' and the future political community."[42] Hardly heroic and barely decisive, these words appeared in print around the same time that the marauding forces of Hindutva destroyed the Babri mosque in Ayodhya in the winter of 1992. This chapter has sought to join Pandey's emphasis on the fragment and Benjamin's injunction to the historian to span the "spark of hope in the past" by being "firmly convinced that *even the dead* will not be safe from the enemy." By further laying these orientations alongside procedures of a history without warranty, I have attempted to perform two tasks. On one hand, I hope to have shown that the invocation of the eternal verities of the sacred space of the birthplace of Ram in the assiduous construction of a standardized history by Hindu nationalism is actually an exclusive reinvention of Ayodhya. Such singular accounts flatten all traces of the diversity, discontinuity, and difference that in fact characterize the pasts of this town. On the other hand, I have sought to unravel and question the mutual binds between the homogenization of history and the fetish of the nation. This latter task entails thinking through the persistence of enchanted spaces and modern places, a concern further elaborated in the next chapter.

7   The Enchanted and the Modern

The cry of "discipline in crisis" is not new. Recently, such spiraling crises appear to have claimed another casualty. Designate them a discipline or deem them a domain, "Western studies of Hinduism," many of their proponents have asserted with vigor, are under threat from vociferous critiques of a postcolonial provenance. These postcolonial claims, such scholars further suggest, deny Western academics the right to speak about Hinduism.

In November 1998, on another humid day at the Disney resort in Orlando, at the annual meetings of the American Academy of Religion, a roundtable met to discuss issues of "voice" and "authority" (read, *authenticity*) in the study of Hinduism. Unsurprisingly, the roundtable bore the title "Who Speaks for Hinduism?" As the different panelists spoke, it became clear that at stake in this forum was not a debate but a defense of Western studies of Hinduism. Of course, there is nothing wrong with defense in itself. Yet terms of discourse matter. At the roundtable, for many panelists, to claim voice and authority in speaking for Hinduism, it was sufficient to be Hindu—Hindu by birth or Hindu by becoming, South Asian Hindu or Western Hindu. As for the few panelists who touched on postcolonial propositions in their presentations, it seems to me that rigid polarities were already in place and the beast of "postcoloniality" was always a given. Taken together, a live enemy appeared fabricated and an imagined interlocutor was demolished.[1] As a panelist at the roundtable and even more today, I believe that there are other terms of discourse, distinct questions of understanding, that lie behind and before the putative polarity between Western studies of Hinduism and postcolonial critiques of Western knowledge and power. Indeed, the stipulations of voice and the seductions of authority themselves bear unraveling.

Who Speaks for Hinduism?

In addressing this question, I worry about the large conceit behind different claims to speak *for* Hinduism. This worry does not simply concern the mystical unknowability of Hinduism. Rather, my agitation directly addresses issues of voice and authority at the heart of the question under discussion. Many speak *about* Hinduism. Some speak *around* Hinduism. For a few, it is perhaps possible to speak *from* within Hinduism(s). But speaking *for* Hinduism? I am not nitpicking here. Without putting too fine a point on the matter, claims to speak *for* Hinduism generally tend toward endorsing different conceptions of a singular Hinduism, discrete objects of the votaries' desires. Further, various explicit and implicit endorsements of positions that there can be "authentic" ways of speaking *for* Hinduism—on grounds of national origin, religious persuasion, or scholarly understanding—tend to remain trapped, in inherently different ways, within the political premises of exclusive identitarian truth(s), which have conservative incarnations, liberal faces, scholarly embodiments, and radical avatars.[2]

It is certain versions of these politics that seem to suggest an intemperate attack along the following lines: if you are of Western origin, and white to boot, your representations are rooted in an entire archive of domination grounded in the inescapable connections between knowledge and power. Rooted in privilege and authority, your contamination and complicities are final. On what grounds, then, do you speak for (or indeed about) another culture? Of course, there can be conservative takes on this theme, cast in different idioms but sharing related premises. Stated thus, such propositions and positions deny possibilities of understanding itself. They employ an epistemological nihilism, setting up an opposition between imagined incommensurable subject positions that are always there, already in place. They set into play relentless reifications of a homogeneous and singular West and romanticized representations of an authentic and heroic non-West. At stake, then, is denial of dialogue in its widest sense, founded on the logic of essential differences across rigid binaries, a rejection of possibilities of conversation.

Yet do propositions and positions that deny the claims of the Western academic, particularly the Euro-American intellectual, to speak about Hinduism truly exist? It is here that I would like to muddle the picture. In contemporary India, as in other parts of the globe, from the First World through to the Fourth, invocations of nationalism and evocations of national culture are often a ruse (and more) for authoritarian governments, populist regimes, and their academic mouthpieces to endorse nativisms and engender ideologies founded on a rhetoric of innate cultural difference. These nativisms and ideologies simultaneously showcase, albeit as representations in a mirror, the ideals of historical progress and the idioms of a masculinist adulthood, which are the signs of a mature state in the reified image of Western modernity. It seems to me that any scholar, particularly a Western academic authority, projecting the picture of a wholesome Hinduism—or, at the very least, all academics who do not challenge the carefully cultivated picture of a majoritarian Hindu nation—would be welcome in statist centers in India today.

What, then, of radical critics in different locations who would deny Western scholars the right to represent other cultures, peoples, genders, and ethnicities, the lines of criticism that are the subject of our discussion? Without altogether denying the existence and challenge of such separatist positions, I would like to suggest that, in discussions of Hinduism and South Asian religions, the picture is much more mixed and rather too complex to be captured in terms of a simple opposition between Western studies of Hinduism and radical postcolonial rejections of such scholarship. To begin with, just as there are varieties of studies of Hinduism, there are several strains of the newer critical scholarship of South Asia, and sometimes these bodies of writing overlap.[3] The issue is salient, clarifying, for example, that today the term *postcolonial* often appears as a privileged category/stage of history but also is debated as a perspective, its ambivalences and possibilities matters of critical discussion. This is not unlike the ways in which the category of Hinduism can be a fully fabricated, given object in certain understandings and a contentious heuristic device, a contested analytical terrain, in other analyses.[4] At the same time, beyond this necessary invocation of critical differences within bodies of scholarship, I have five interlinked propositions to offer on issues of colored suspicions and fair anxieties in the apparent postcolonial rejection of the Western scholarship on Hinduism.

First, significant writings associated with what is widely understood as postcolonial scholarship have been variously concerned with issues of naturalized representations of non-Western worlds and with questions of Eurocentrism, which is understood as the projection of the West as history, modernity, and destiny. In these endeavors, the key complicities of modern scholarship with enduring blueprints of colonial knowledge(s) have been demonstrated *not* on grounds of race and nationality, cast as black and white binaries, but through the unraveling of taxonomical schemes, foundational frameworks, and categorical imperatives. Such writings have entailed interrogations of different universalizing modes of explanation and diverse essentializing genealogies of representation. For example, they have broken down the singular subject of a universal woman, put a question mark on the discursive politics of subaltern representations in Western and non-Western arenas, and revealed the limits of knee-jerk nativisms that lay claim to romanticized traditions through ready rejections of complex histories and mixed-up modernities.[5]

At the same time—I come to the second point here—oppositional positions tend to inversely reproduce the terms of the dominant discourse they set out to question. These representations in reverse are particularly true of positions articulated in the heat of epistemic confrontation.[6] At times, this generates slippages. Now challenges to Eurocentric knowledge(s) simultaneously suggest a questioning of the "authority" of contemporary Western scholarship to "represent" non-Western religions and cultures, in this case Hinduism.

Third, such slippages in fact emerge marked by acute intersections between the distinct meanings of the terms *representation* and *authority*.[7] Seizing on the battle lines that are drawn between an allegedly "orientalist" study of Hinduism and a self-consciously radical engagement with South Asia, such slippages can equally involve the strident staging of politics of combative South Asian identities in the Western academy. On one hand, called in to question is the authority of Western scholarship on Hinduism to represent India. On the other, played out here are South Asian identities that in different ways claim to represent and authorize the subcontinent.[8]

Fourth, while implicitly present in practices of reading and writing, everyday entanglements in academic arenas, including quotidian encounters in seminars and conferences, rehearse these twin moves more rigorously. Yet we must bear in mind a related dimension of such staging of academic politics. It is also in the familiar intellectual spaces noted above that those who are seen (and who see themselves) as standing on the other side of an epistemic breach and a political divide equally play out rivalries and forge solidarities on distinct but overlapping grounds.

Finally, it follows that to project a radical postcolonial position rejecting contemporary Western scholarship on Hinduism on grounds of the race/ nationality of its authorship is to set up an imaginary interlocutor and fabricate a live enemy that simply does not exist, especially in its designated singularity. Rather, the image of such a concerted onslaught on—the idea of this blanket rejection of—Western scholarship is much more a function of anxieties and aggressions produced within everyday encounters and quotidian confrontations in academic arenas. This tends to overlook series of dispersed effects in scholarly terrain that flow from different negotiations of politics of identities and cultures of scholarship today. Straw figures make for misleading enemies and hopeless friends.

I am suggesting that the challenges posed by the question "Who speaks

for Hinduism?" compel us to think through the ambiguities and ambivalences, contradictions and challenges, and predicaments and possibilities
at the heart of the current cultural politics of identities and the contemporary political cultures of scholarship. This may be a large agenda, but it is
not an impossible endeavor. Indeed, the very difficulty of finding conve-
nient talking cures to these problems suggests the prospect of making
particular incisions on the body of issues at stake.[9] It follows that I take one
such specific step in the next section.

Speaking against the Grain

The beast of postcoloniality is a curious creature. In order to indicate the
nature of this beast, and to suggest what the creature might have to say
about the issues under discussion, I turn to a text that has acquired a
seminal status in contemporary discussions of postcolonial apprehensions. I refer to Dipesh Chakrabarty's "Postcoloniality and the Artifice of
History: Who Speaks for 'Indian' Pasts?"[10] Both the title of the essay and its
contrapuntal reading of history have important implications for discussions of the question "Who speaks for Hinduism?"

We have seen that in the essay, which is implicitly constructed against
the backdrop of Heidegger's interrogation of the artifice of a meaning-
legislating reason, Chakrabarty focuses on "history" as a discourse that is
produced at the institutional site of the university. He makes a compelling
case for the ways in which Europe remains the sovereign theoretical subject
of all histories, where different pasts appear sieved through the master
blueprint of the "history of Europe." Admitting that Europe and India
are "hyperreal" terms that refer to certain figures of the imagination,
Chakrabarty critically points toward how—in the "phenomenal world of
everyday relationships of power"—Europe is reified and celebrated as the
site and scene of the birth of the modern.

This is to say that Europe works as a silent referent that dominates the
discourse of history.[11] The essay makes its way through critical readings
and imaginative renderings of European philosophy (Husserl and Marx),
Indian writing in English (Michael Madhusudan Dutta and Nirad Chau-
dhari), British colonial representations (Alexander Dow and James Mill),
and radical South Asian histories (the subaltern studies endeavor). Thus,
Chakrabarty unravels the consequences of the theoretical privileging of
Europe as the universal centerpiece of modernity and history; the past and
present of India are cast in terms of irrevocable principles of failure, lack,
and absence, since they are always/already measured against the West.[12]

It should be clear that this questioning of the epistemological privilege
accorded to Europe as the celebrated site of modernity has nothing to do

with a hasty rejection of Western scholarship on grounds of the race/ nationality of its authorship. Yet this is not all. The critical emphasis that I derive from Chakrabarty's answer to the question "Who speaks for 'Indian' pasts?" concerns the importance of querying the undersaid of academic disciplines and interrogating the underthought of intellectual-political positions. Extending this emphasis to the issues under discussion, I cast my net fairly wide.

For a very long time now, in Western spaces and non-Western arenas, authoritative understandings of patterns of the past and influential conceptions of designs of societies have been shaped by an enduring separation between traditional (often but not only non-Western) communities, on one hand, and modern (generally but not exclusively Western) societies on the other. These antinomies are at once a lasting legacy of the European Enlightenment's idea of universal history and an aggrandizing representation of a Western modernity, each seeking to remake the world in its singular image. Over time, this analytical and ideological separation has appeared variously elaborated in post-Enlightenment traditions (and contemporary scholarship) and differently reworked within non-Western modernities (and current critiques of the West). On offer have been diverse castigations and celebrations of tradition and distinct reifications and rejections of modernity.

Yet these disparate positions are bound to each other through their implicit reliance on and explicit reproduction of overriding oppositions— between tradition and modernity, ritual and rationality, myth and history, community and state, magic and the modern, and emotion and reason.[13] While broadly homologous to each other, these oppositions have been expressed in various permutations and diverse combinations, quite as their constitutive elements have been imbued with contradictory value and contrary salience. More pertinently, the formative agendas of the disciplines in the humanities and the social sciences can be seen as predicated on these binaries.

Aware of the complex genealogies of disciplines in the humanities and appreciative of the dense stemma of developments in the social sciences, I speak here of broad orientations of modern learning toward the social world, particularly over the past century. On one hand, key conceptions of religions (and anthropology, as the study of the irremediable other) long favored the study of ritual, magic, and myth as marked off from the modern. On the other hand, influential understandings of politics (and history when it is cast in the image of a hard social science) directed toward modern states, rational individuals, maximization of interests, and linear chronologies continued to take the opposite route.[14] Here, concerning each copula, the celebration of one category accompanied the lessening of the other.

At the same time, the terms thus exorcised or undervalued by disciplinary distinctions and scientific strategies did not lose their spectral place and transcendental presence in defining the division of labor between disciplines. Rather, they tended to hold in place (and to place on hold) the sanctioned dispositions (and the transgressive ambitions) within disciplines. Mutually shaping each other, the absent elements and the present terms of the binaries of social theory at once animated and were orchestrated by a master blueprint of past, present, and posterity shaped around the polarities of enchanted spaces and modern places. These enduring enchantments persist in the here and now.

Far from being mere building blocks for symbolically charged but normatively benign representations solely within academe, these authoritative antinomies have occupied an influential place and an insidious presence in fabrications of tradition and makings of modernity in Western places and non-Western spaces. After all, the Ur-narratives in which these binaries are embedded were motivated projects "not simply of looking and recording but of recording and remaking" the world in their likeness of universal history and their image of a singular modernity.[15] Here cultural differences were rendered in terms of principles of order and stages of succession to be turned into hierarchies of otherness, which were variously exotic and erotic, durable and dangerous. At the same time, invocations of a common humanity often contained the dialectic of race and reason, which served, for example, to issue a challenge to slavery but also to speak through categories of the "primitive" and the "civilized."[16]

Meanwhile, in non-Western theaters, to take but one example, anticolonial nationalisms reworked Enlightenment principles and Western knowledges to creatively translate and actively transform the ideals of the sovereign nation and the free citizen by mapping them onto powerful constructions of the subjugated homeland and the colonized subject. Here the nation equally often was elaborated in diverse communitarian ways. Taken together, such pasts and constructions question singular and univocal Eurocentric conceptions of nations and nationalisms.[17] At the same time, however, these communitarian imaginings of the nation and dominant visions of the modern state in the non-Western world bear critical readings, for they have both been crucially shaped by the influential binaries at the heart of narratives of universal history and Western modernity.[18]

Nor should it surprise us that singular ideas of universal history and reified images of exclusive modernity, in reordered and different guises, continue to lead a charmed life at the beginning of the twenty-first century.

Elaborating novel versions of hierarchies of otherness even as they transform critical difference into mind-numbing sameness, these ideas and
images have diverse manifestations. They work together in diverse but
tangled domains from the movements of transnational capital through
global markets to the policies of the International Monetary Fund and the
World Bank, the programs of Third World modernization, the endless
celebrations of a Brave New World of globalized cultures and hybrid identities, and the militarist-masculinist agendas of the Hindu and Islamic
bombs. These different endeavors and diverse ideologies all lay claims on
an aggressive likeness of modernity in the tangible mirror of a reified West.
Here modernity is rendered and represented as a self-realizing project of
progress and a self-evident embodiment of development. In a word, modernity inexorably propels states and relentlessly pushes societies from a
traditional (and colonial) past to a modern (and postcolonial) present and
increasingly into a postmodern (and global) future-present where this path
marks both the trajectory and the end of universal history.[19]

At the End

This schematic survey of the effects and affects of overriding oppositions is
not meant to suggest that the "foundations" of these dualities in the image
of Western modernity exhaust the range of meanings of human action and
scholarship that have animated these antinomies.[20] Nor does this brief
sketch imply that the "origins" of these designs of the past in the Enlightenment idea of universal history consign to a rubbish heap the varieties of
historical practice and writing trapped in the telos of progress. To do so
would be to exorcise from imagination and understanding diverse human
energies and enormous historical passions that I cannot even begin to
recount here. It could also be to adopt facile strains of anti-Enlightenment
rhetoric, rejecting the (often unrealized) possibilities of democracy and
modernity, including their critical rethinking, and leaving in their place an
elitist nihilism. It might even be to attribute blame and confer guilt on
people on the grounds of their racial/national origin through an academic
politics of victimhood, an ethically pernicious move that is also beside the
point.

I am suggesting, rather, that the implications of these binaries and the
seductions of this blueprint have constituted the undersaid and the underthought of academic disciplines, a part of reigning metageographies. They
inculcate dispositions toward mapping modern peoples and places in history and charting traditional communities and customs out of time. They
cultivate inclinations toward plotting native peoples in their passage to
progress, the grand transition from enchantment to disenchantment, from

tradition to modernity. They generate sensibilities toward rendering "authentic" communities as changeless and entranced, already before history and always beyond the modern. They foster fondness for reifications of a singular modernity as magical Midas or beastly behemoth. They spawn sentiments for envisioning a seamless community as embodied virtue or inconvenient impediment. There are many moves here, but the various images reflect each other.

It is not only that urgency marks the task of exploring the roles played by the overriding oppositions that I have discussed in constructions of various understandings of Hinduism and of other religions and cultures. It is also that I find it imperative to recast issues of voice and authority at the heart of the question "Who speaks for Hinduism?" by asking three crucial questions. Behind diverse theoretical frameworks, what implicit cartographies of enchanted spaces and modern places *authorize* the different yet shared conceptions of religions, including Hinduism? Beyond particular subject positions, what underlying mappings of the sacral and the temporal *speak* through the several specific analyses of cultures, here of Hinduism? In other words, what anterior idea and which prior image imbue representations of societies, including pictures of Hindu orders, with the distinction of voice and the privilege of vision?

It hardly bears emphasis that these questions articulate my minor conceit of speaking against the grain and, indeed, of writing *Stitches on Time*. Returning to the initial submissions and subsequent suggestions of this book, to register the deep play of enchanted spaces and modern places is not to simply banish such seductive schemes from the historical record and social worlds, revealing and surpassing the ideological fault line they insinuate through protocols and procedures of disenchanting knowledge. Rather, it is to face their many lives as categorical dispositions and ontological entities, the enchantments of modernity and the basis of social worlds, in order to carefully question, critically unravel, and ethically articulate the past and the present. Recognizing this, a primary task of thinking through the provenance and prevalence of enchanted spaces and modern places, it seems to me, entails exploring the interplay of power and difference—tracing the presence of power in the labor of difference, and tracking the place of difference in the work of power, the two together, ever entwined.

It follows that the roundtable in Orlando entitled "Who Speaks for Hinduism?" may have other lessons to offer. Arguably, there is wide agreement today that intellectual discussions and scholarly debate cannot merely proceed as though they are located outside the realms and relationships of power, beyond the regimes of disciplinary truths. This is to say that we might speak of a critical consensus that academic work takes place within wider contexts of power and politics. Yet my point is not about contexts of power as things out there, as matter both in and out of place. Rather, my critical comments concern apprehensions of the contexts of academic work as those great overarching structures that we acknowledge with a perfunctory nod, only to banish them from our study so that we can get on with our writing, thinking, and speaking. In these familiar gestures of denial and affirmation—of denial in affirmation—contexts of power and politics are ever outside.

Thus, we remain secure in the knowledge that these contexts will not come round uncomfortably knocking on the doors of our study, messing up our lectures and upsetting our well-laid plans. Yet we only need to think about the horror films *Exorcist I* (and the possessed Linda Blair) and its sequel *Exorcist II* (and the big bad wolf). These films are reminders that to exorcise a devil is not to get rid of it. Moreover, the devil strikes by being within us. In tune with these testimonies from mass culture, the realms of power relations and the regimes of disciplinary truths that haunt the academy are not merely contexts out there, somewhere. Rather, they exist within the interstices of the academy, moving through the capillaries of our bodies of knowledge, inhabiting the study and the seminar, stalking our lectures and talks, and defining our articles and books.

This is not to argue that we have arrived at that profoundly disabling moment when an undifferentiated notion of power freezes all activity, turning us into vectors and victims of power's exclusive discursive and institutional force. Rather, my advocacy of a critical recognition of the play of power at the heart of academe refers to rather different realities. Eschewing elitism but also discarding populism, it is a call for making sense of the different modes of authority—including the metageographies that shore up our everyday worlds—at work in academic arenas. It is a plea for an awareness of how as teachers, researchers, scholars, and activists we reproduce forms of hierarchy within scholarly spaces such as classrooms and bookshops but over beer and coffee too. Finally, it suggests the importance of recognizing not only the ways in which the realms of intellectual politics are complicit with wider cultures of power but also the manner in which the sites of higher education engender and breed their own forms of pulpit-pounding politics.

Afterword

n the last quarter of 2001, the breathless ringing in of the new millennium having wound down, two millennial projections, dramatically opposed and mutually entailed twin images, severely shook our worlds at large. In their wake, it would be a travesty to submit the suffering of lives shattered to the bump and grind of analytics as usual. Yet, just as endless memories born of pain cannot be stowed safely in distant recesses, so, too, is there no escaping the shadowy but tangible apparitions of history and the here and now.

Recognizing this, many years ago, through the medium of Paul Klee's painting *Angelus Novus*, Walter Benjamin brought an angel into the world— "His eyes are staring, his mouth is open, his wings are spread."[1] How can we forget the angel of progress, an angel propelled into the future, his face "turned towards the past," by a storm "blowing from Paradise," the storm that "we call progress"? Was this critical likeness not an acute reflection of modernity and history, darkly? Did not the storm claim Benjamin's life? Has the angel left the earth?

On the morning of 11 September 2001, from high above New York, is the angel of progress staring stupefied at the inaugural, airborne strike of unremitting terror? Is he witness to the burning tower, to the cameras focused on it, to the air thick with smoke and stunned disbelief, and to the second plane, a giant bird of predatory destruction, crashing into the other tower? Unable to close his own wings because the storm of progress is caught in them with ferocious violence, does the angel recognize the storm and the violence—both bearing a disjunctive likeness of cultural hierarchies and historical progress at the heart of modernity—caught in the wings of these technological creatures and carrying them to their deadly ends? What is the angel of progress at this moment "about to move away from"—the depredations of progress as usual? What is it that the angel is now "fixedly contemplating"—contending imaginings of progress avenging inherited verities of progress? Hurtling backward into the future, watching the pile of debris grow before him, does the reenchanted but disenchanted angel register how time after time, yet ever with difference, in the unraveling of progress revenge and redemption, prophecy and prediction, betoken and bind each other through their mutual elisions and shared determinations? Wanting to but unable to "stay, awaken the dead, and make whole what has been smashed," is the beleaguered angel of progress trying hard, very hard, to catch the drift of the swirling, swelling storm that is not only in front but all around him? What truth and which secret does the angel discover in the defacement of a (national-global) monument, a monument to the spirit of liberty and the world of capital, and in the obliteration of the lives it contains, tracking what surplus of negative energy and which labor of the negative arousing from within the object desecrated and the lives destroyed?[2] And not much later, how, indeed, does the angel apprehend Operation Enduring Freedom—as phrase and program—grounded in the oppositions, hierarchies, and enchantments of modernity; conducted in the name of civilization and through the designation of the nation; and directed against the evil, an enemy coeval and medieval?

To ask these questions is to stay with Walter Benjamin's testimony, calling into question the scandals of the West and the nation, brushing pasts against the grain of progress, confronting the seductions of power, facing the romance of difference, and tracking their mutual enmeshments. It is to query the place of development in the image of history and the reflection of modernity, including possibly in Benjamin's own likeness of the storm of progress, ever remembering our responsibility to the past, its burden in the present, the gravity of loss, and the stake of suffering.

Thus, the category of the postcolonial has not appeared in *Stitches on Time* as a stage of history that follows the colonial, quite as day comes after night. In these pages, *postcolonial* refers to a critical rubric that carries possibilities of carefully questioning the enduring viewpoint of the West as history, modernity, and destiny, the enticing vision of progress and development along the grooves of the nation-state, recognizing that such imaginings are pervasive attributes of social worlds. At the same time, it should also be clear that the postcolonial signifies neither a privileged perception nor an exclusive knowledge, tendencies that often turn the colonial and postcolonial into theoretical and empirical ghettoes. Instead, in this book the postcolonial as rubric articulates overlapping but distinct orientations—involving ethnographic histories, historical anthropologies, and critical theory and entailing subaltern subjects, recalcitrant margins, and quotidian pasts—all working together but also bringing each other to crisis. Such dispositions and procedures of a history without warranty take up the task of thinking through the terms of a singular modernity and its universal history, querying the prior presence of colonial/modern apprehensions within contemporary knowledge, probing the conditions and possibilities of modernity, and interrogating the limits and stipulations of state and nation. Tracking the shared determinations and common denials of power and difference, analytical categories and social worlds, colonial textures and postcolonial tangles, *Stitches on Time* has undertaken such tasks in small, specific steps.

Notes

Introduction

1 My discussion of this transnational theater needs to be read together with Elizabeth
Povinelli's important argument concerning how, as an ideology and practice of governance, Australian settler liberal multiculturalism works by "inspiring subaltern and
minority subjects to identify with the impossible object of an authentic self-identity . . .
[so that] indigenous subjects are called on to perform an authentic difference in exchange for the good feelings of the nation and the reparative legislation of the state."
This entwining of multicultural recognition of cultural difference, with a strong emphasis on national unity, "does not simply produce good theater, rather it inspires
impossible desires: to be this impossible object" among indigenous subjects. The spectacle in Sydney shows the tragic theater of stagist-statist progress produced by multicultural domination, although I confess to not even approaching the ways in which
majority and minority subjects—in Australia or elsewhere—experienced this liberal
drama. At the same time, I feel that Povinelli is somewhat hasty in differentiating
"postcolonial struggles" from "multicultural ones," with the former suggesting how
colonial domination worked by inspiring in colonized subjects a desire to identify with
their colonizers and the latter revealing the requirement that subaltern subjects perform
their true difference. Indeed, those involved in postcolonial struggles have also thought
through demands for enactments of difference—often braided with inspirations toward
identification between the colonized and the colonizer, the "minority" subject and the
"majority" citizen—in the colony and the postcolony and of a settler and nonsettler
provenance, extending historically from Mexico to South Asia and Africa. See Elizabeth A. Povinelli, *The Cunning of Recognition: Indigenous Alterities and the Making of Australian
Multiculturalism* (Durham: Duke University Press, 2002), 6, emphasis in the original. On
issues of incitements to difference and identification in distinct historical epochs, see,
for example, María Josefina Saldaña-Portillo, "Reading a Silence: The 'Indian' in the Era
of Zapatismo," in *Critical Conjunctions: Foundations of Colony and Formations of Modernity*,
edited by Saurabh Dube, Ishita Banerjee Dube, and Edgardo Lander, special issue of
Nepantla: Views from South 3, no. 2 (2002): 287–314; Kaushik Ghosh, "A Market for
Aboriginality: Primitivism and Race Classification in the Indentured Labor Market of

Colonial India," in *Subaltern Studies X: Writings on South Asian History and Society*, edited by Gautam Bhadra, Gyan Prakash, and Susie Tharu, 8–48 (New Delhi: Oxford University Press, 1999); and Mahmood Mamdani, *Citizen and Subject: Decentralized Despotism and the Legacy of Late Colonialism* (Princeton: Princeton University Press, 1996).

2 Two clarifications are in order. First, although it may appear that I use the terms *space* and *place* interchangeably, this is not the case. In general, the tendency is to deploy *place* to refer to a particular, determinate locale, while *space* connotes at once a more abstract and developed idea and/or entity. Following such usage, one would speak of *enchanted places* and *modern spaces*. Instead, I wish to put a question mark on the telos entailed by such measures by emphasizing the dense interconnectedness between the abstract and the concrete in the naming of places and spaces. Therefore, I speak in this book of *enchanted spaces* and *modern places*. Second, as should be clear, such mappings are connected to dominant apprehensions of the "disenchantment of the world," which constitutes the watershed between custom-bound "tradition" and rationality-driven "modernity," something of a horizon of the modern subject, whether in scholarly schemes or commonplace conceptions. This means that the *enchantments* of enchanted spaces certainly refer to a happy, fairy tale universe within, say, strains of nativist and primitivist projections and certain romantic and antimodernist understandings, but they equally connote superstition and backwardness or the precise other of a celebrated reason. By the same token, for some centuries now the *modern* of modern places has been construed as a privileged terrain acutely reflecting the bright light of reason and Western civilization and instituted as the fundamental fall of humanity under modernity. Without claiming that modernity begins only in the eighteenth century in "North Europe"—aware, indeed, of prior formations of the "modern/colonial world" (Walter Mignolo), the "first modernity" (Enrique Dussel), and the "coloniality of power" (Aníbal Quijano)—this introduction and the other chapters of *Stitches on Time* consider how the antithetical usages and contending elaborations of enchanted spaces and modern places are bound to each other, revealing the constitutive conjunctions between these charged antinomies. See Walter Mignolo, *Local Histories/Global Designs: Coloniality, Subaltern Knowledges, and Border Thinking* (Princeton: Princeton University Press, 2000); Enrique Dussel, "World-system and 'Trans'-modernity," in Dube, Banerjee Dube, and Lander, *Critical Conjunctions*, 222–29; and Aníbal Quijano, "Colonialidad del poder, eurocentrismo y América Latina," in *La Colonialidad del Saber: Eurocentrismo y ciencas sociales, perspectivas latinoamericanas*, edited by Edgardo Lander, 201–46 (Buenos Aires: Consejo Latinoamericano de Ciencias Sociales, 2000).

3 Arguably, such conjunction was also evident in the ceremonial bearing of the Olympic torch by Australian women athletes and the eventual lighting of the Olympic flame by Kathy Freeman, an athlete of aboriginal ancestry—the last a touching if token gesture that was hugely troubling, too, particularly in the manner of its claim on Freeman's body. I owe this point to Sara Ahmed.

4 In Stanley Kubrick's *Eyes Wide Shut*, the extended sequence of an orgy filmed as terror is accompanied by a soundtrack containing a worked over version of a *shloka* (verse) from the sacred *Bhagwad Geeta*. Not surprisingly, considering the politics of "tradition," a group of liberal Hindus based in the United States launched an e-mail signature campaign in the summer of 1999 to register its protest before Warner Brothers, asking the producer to take effective steps regarding the offensive portion of the soundtrack. Of course, Kubrick could not respond, as he had died earlier in the year. The producers made no revisions. It seems to me that both this segment of the feature and its critics drew on fantasies of the Orient in different ways and to distinct ends. *Once Were Warriors*, a

powerful feature from New Zealand, at once reveals the possibilities and reifications of a politics charged with primitivism, particularly by casting the past as the desire for the future. From the perspective of a historical anthropology of colonial cultures, for interesting discussions of *Dances with Wolves* and the media coverage of the Gulf War see Nicholas Thomas, *Colonialism's Culture: Anthropology, Travel, and Government* (Princeton: Princeton University Press, 1994), 95–96, 178–83.

5 This is a large field, a veritable minefield. A few—very few—of the important critiques that have influenced my own thought include Anne McClintock, *Imperial Leather: Race, Gender, and Sexuality in the Colonial Contest* (New York: Routledge, 1995), especially 9–16, 391–96; Ella Shohat, "Notes on the Post-colonial," in *Contemporary Postcolonial Theory: A Reader*, edited by Padmini Mongia, 32–34 (London: Arnold, 1996); and Gayatri Chakravorty Spivak, *A Critique of Postcolonial Reason: Toward a History of the Vanishing Present* (Cambridge: Harvard University Press, 1999), 1 and passim. See also Arif Dirlik, "The Postcolonial Aura: Third World Criticism in the Age of Global Capitalism," in Mongia, *Contemporary Postcolonial Theory*, 294–320.

6 Examples include Dipesh Chakrabarty, *Provincializing Europe: Postcolonial Thought and Historical Difference* (Princeton: Princeton University Press, 2000); Partha Chatterjee, *The Nation and Its Fragments: Colonial and Postcolonial Histories* (Princeton: Princeton University Press, 1993); Homi Bhabha, *The Location of Culture* (New York: Routledge, 1994); Mamdani, *Citizen and Subject*; Mignolo, *Local Histories/Global Designs*; and Gyanendra Pandey, *Remembering Partition: Violence, Nationalism and History in India* (Cambridge: Cambridge University Press, 2001). See also Achille Mbembe, "The Banality of Power and the Aesthetics of Vulgarity in the Postcolony," *Public Culture* 4 (1992): 1–30; and Ashis Nandy, *Traditions, Tyranny, and Utopias: Essays in the Politics of Awareness* (Delhi: Oxford University Press, 1992).

7 Thus, I wonder whether replacing "postcolonial studies" with "colonial studies" to designate domains of scholarly inquiry—as suggested by Frederick Cooper and Ann Laura Stoler—does not entail its own problems. For example, while "colonial studies" may pass muster, when Cooper and Stoler speak of their work as "colonial history" that rehearses "colonial readings," the terminological difficulties and conceptual-political problems become evident. Clearly, I am not invoking a knee-jerk nationalism. My point is much more about giving up turf battles. There are larger issues at stake. See Ann Laura Stoler and Frederick Cooper, "Between Metropole and Colony: Rethinking a Research Agenda," in *Tensions of Empire: Colonial Cultures in a Bourgeois World*, edited by Frederick Cooper and Ann Laura Stoler (Berkeley: University of California Press, 1997), 34. See also Frederick Cooper, "Conflict and Connection: Rethinking Colonial African History," *American Historical Review* 99 (1994): 1527.

8 Gyan Prakash, "Subaltern Studies as Postcolonial Criticism," *American Historical Review* 99 (1994): 1475–94; Dipesh Chakrabarty, "Postcoloniality and the Artifice of History: Who Speaks for 'Indian' Pasts?" *Representations* 37 (winter 1992): 1–26; Chatterjee, *The Nation and Its Fragments*. See also Gyan Prakash, "Writing Post-orientalist Histories of the Third World: Indian Historiography is Good to Think," in *Colonialism and Culture*, edited by Nicholas Dirks, 353–88 (Ann Arbor: University of Michigan Press, 1992); and Carol A. Breckenridge and Peter Van der Veer, eds., *Orientalism and the Postcolonial Predicament: Perspectives on South Asia* (Philadelphia: University of Pennsylvania Press, 1993).

9 For example, see Saurabh Dube, "Myths, Symbols and Community: Satnampanth of Chhattisgarh," in *Subaltern Studies VII: Writings on South Asian History and Society*, edited by Partha Chatterjee and Gyanendra Pandey, 121–56 (Delhi: Oxford University Press, 1992); and "Issues of Christianity in Colonial Chhattisgarh," *Sociological Bulletin* 41 (1992): 37–63.

10 See Saurabh Dube, *Untouchable Pasts: Religion, Identity and Power among a Central Indian Community, 1780–1950* (Albany: State University of New York Press, 1998).

11 Saurabh Dube, ed., *Pasados poscoloniales: Colección de ensayos sobre la nueva historia y etnografía de la India* (Mexico City: El Colegio de México, 1999). Conducted through a wider discussion of the colony and the postcolony, nation and history, and modernity and its margins, the burden of this conversation initially rested on presenting to a Latin American readership in Spanish translation salient work within subaltern studies and historical anthropology, critical developments in South Asian scholarship. I also need to admit the sometimes hazy ways in which I encountered and expressed mutual considerations of South Asia and Latin America, which my account has not been able to capture. For a more recent expression of the terms of this dialogue, consider Saurabh Dube, "Introduction: Colonialism, Modernity, Colonial Modernities," in Dube, Banerjee Dube, and Lander, *Critical Conjunctions*, 197–219. See also John Kraniauskas and Guillermo Zermeño, eds., *Historia y subalternidad*, a special issue of *Historia y grafia* 12 (1999): 7–176; Silvia Rivera Cusicanqui and Rosa Barragan, eds., *Debates PostColoniales: Una Introducción a los Estudios de la Subalternidad* (La Paz: Ediciones Aruwiyiri, 1997); Saurabh Dube, *Sujetos subalternos: Capitulos de una historia antropologica*, translated by Germán Franco and Ari Bartra (Mexico City: El Colegio de México, 2001); John Beverley, *Subalternity and Representation: Arguments in Cultural Theory* (Durham: Duke University Press, 1999); and Ileana Rodríguez, ed., *The Latin American Subaltern Studies Reader* (Durham: Duke University Press, 2001).

12 Such emphases are critical to my arguments, and I return to them in different ways, concerning distinct issues, especially in this introduction. See also Timothy Mitchell, ed., *Questions of Modernity* (Minneapolis: University of Minnesota Press, 2000), viii, xii–xiii.

13 For efforts elaborating wide critical considerations while affirming and questioning postcolonial propositions, see, for example, P. Radhakrishnan, "Postmodernism and the Rest of the World," in *The Pre-occupation of Postcolonial Studies*, edited by Fawzia Afzal-Khan and Kalpana Seshadri-Crooks, 37–70 (Durham: Duke University Press, 2000); Gaurav Desai, *Subject to Colonialism: African Self-Fashioning and the Colonial Library* (Durham: Duke University Press, 2001); Spivak, *A Critique of Postcolonial Reason*; and Chakrabarty, *Provincializing Europe*. Consider also Saurabh Dube, ed., *Postcolonial Passages: A Handbook of Contemporary History-Writing on India* (New Delhi: Oxford University Press, 2004); and David Scott, *Refashioning Futures: Criticism after Postcoloniality* (Princeton: Princeton University Press, 1999).

14 My reference is to dispositions that have been expressed in a variety of ways, constituting an enormous corpus. The works cited provide a few representative examples. Note also that I have my disagreements with specific emphases and particular projections of these different writings, a fact significant for the terms of conversation that I propose and explore. To spell out these divergences would require a long chapter if not a short book.

15 Timothy Mitchell, "The Stage of Modernity," in Mitchell, *Questions of Modernity*, 15, emphasis in the original; Lander, *La Colonialidad del Saber*; Talal Asad, *Genealogies of Religion: Discipline and Reasons of Power in Christianity and Islam* (Baltimore: Johns Hopkins University Press, 1993); Enrique Dussel, *The Invention of the Americas: Eclipse of "the Other" and the Myth of Modernity* (New York: Continuum, 1995); Zygmunt Bauman, *Intimations of Postmodernity* (London: Routledge, 1992); John Comaroff and Jean Comaroff, *Ethnography and the Historical Imagination* (Boulder: Westview, 1992); Shelly Errington, *The Death of Authentic Primitive Art and Other Tales of Progress* (Berkeley: University of California Press, 1998); John Gray, *Enlightenment's Wake: Politics and Culture at the Close of the Modern Age* (New

York: Routledge, 1995). See also Edward Said, *Orientalism* (New York: Pantheon, 1978); and Ashis Nandy, *The Savage Freud and Other Essays on Possible and Retrievable Selves* (Princeton: Princeton University Press, 1995).

16 Johannes Fabian, *Out of Our Minds: Reason and Madness in the Exploration of Central Africa* (Berkeley: University of California Press, 2000); Ashis Nandy, *An Ambiguous Journey to the City: The Village and Other Odd Remains of the Self in the Indian Imagination* (New Delhi: Oxford University Press, 2001); Nancy Florida, *Writing the Past, Inscribing the Future: History as Prophecy in Colonial Java* (Durham: Duke University Press, 1995); Saidiya H. Hartman, *Scenes of Subjection: Terror, Slavery, and Self-Making in Nineteenth-Century America* (New York: Oxford University Press, 1997); Kerwin Lee Klein, *Frontiers of the Historical Imagination: Narrating the European Conquest of Native America, 1890–1990* (Berkeley: University of California Press, 1999); Walter Mignolo, *The Darker Side of the Renaissance: Literacy, Territoriality, and Colonization* (Ann Arbor: University of Michigan Press, 1995); Richard Price, *The Convict and the Colonel: A Story of Colonialism and Resistance in the Caribbean* (Boston: Beacon Press, 1998); Joanne Rappaport, *Cumbe Reborn: An Andean Ethnography of History* (Chicago: University of Chicago Press, 1994); Chakrabarty, *Provincializing Europe*; Dube, *Untouchable Pasts*; Ajay Skaria, *Hybrid Histories: Forests, Frontiers, and Wildness in Western India* (New Delhi: Oxford University Press, 1999); Michel-Rolph Trouillot, *Silencing the Past: Power and the Production of History* (Boston: Beacon Press, 1995).

17 Peter Redfield, *Space in the Tropics: From Convicts to Rockets in French Guiana* (Berkeley: University of California Press, 2000); Donald Donham, *Marxist Modern: An Ethnographic History of the Ethiopian Revolution* (Berkeley: University of California Press, 1999); Mitchell, *Questions of Modernity*; James Ferguson, *Expectations of Modernity: Myths and Meanings of Urban Life on the Zambian Copperbelt* (Berkeley: University of California Press, 1999); John Comaroff and Jean Comaroff, *Of Revelation and Revolution: The Dialectics of Modernity on a South African Frontier*, vol. 2 (Chicago: University of Chicago Press, 1997); Dilip P. Gaonkar, ed., *Alternative Modernities* (Durham: Duke University Press, 2001); Lisa Rofel, *Other Modernities: Gendered Yearnings in China after Socialism* (Berkeley: University of California Press, 1998); Saurabh Dube, ed., *Enduring Enchantments*, special issue of *South Atlantic Quarterly* 101, no. 4 (2002). See also Paul Gilroy, *The Black Atlantic: Modernity and Double Consciousness* (Cambridge: Harvard University Press, 1993); Arjun Appadurai, *Modernity at Large: Cultural Dimensions of Globalization* (Minneapolis: University of Minnesota Press, 1996); Harry Harootunian, *Overcome by Modernity: History, Culture, and Community in Interwar Japan* (Princeton: Princeton University Press, 2000); Aihwa Ong, *Flexible Citizenship: The Cultural Logics of Transnationality* (Durham: Duke University Press, 1999); Gyan Prakash, *Another Reason: Science and the Imagination of Modern India* (Princeton: Princeton University Press, 1999); and Charles Piot, *Remotely Global: Village Modernity in West Africa* (Chicago: University of Chicago Press, 1999).

18 Benedict Anderson, *Imagined Communities: Reflections on the Origin and Spread of Nationalism* (London: Verso, 1983); Chatterjee, *The Nation and Its Fragments*; Ana Maria Alonso, "The Politics of Space, Time, and Substance: State Formation, Nationalism, and Ethnicity," *Annual Review of Anthropology* 23 (1994): 379–400; Shahid Amin, *Event, Metaphor, Memory: Chauri Chaura, 1922–1992* (Berkeley: University of California Press, 1995); Michael Herzfeld, *Cultural Intimacy: Social Poetics in the Nation-State* (New York and London: Routledge, 1997); Claudio Lomnitz-Adler, *Exits from the Labyrinth: Culture and Ideology in Mexican National Space* (Berkeley: University of California Press, 1992); Thomas Blom Hansen and Finn Stepputat, eds., *States of Imagination: Ethnographic Explorations of the Postcolonial State* (Durham: Duke University Press, 2001); Partha Chatterjee, *Nationalist Thought and the Colonial World: A Derivative Discourse?* (London: Zed Press, 1986); Pandey, *Remembering*

Partition; Shail Mayaram, *Resisting Regimes: Myth, Memory and the Shaping of a Muslim Identity* (Delhi: Oxford University Press, 1997), 53–92, 162–220; Fernando Coronil, *The Magical State: Nature, Money, and Modernity in Venezuela* (Chicago: University of Chicago Press, 1997); Brian Axel, *The Nation's Tortured Body: Violence, Representation, and the Formation of the Sikh "Diaspora"* (Durham: Duke University Press, 2001). See also Craig Calhoun, *Nationalism* (Minneapolis: University of Minnesota Press, 1997); Achille Mbembe, *On the Postcolony* (Berkeley: University of California Press, 2001); and Rosalva Aída Hernández Castillo, *La otra frontera: Identidades multiples en el Chiapas poscolonial* (Mexico City: Centro de Investigaciones y Estudios Superiores en Antropología Social, 2001).

19 Indeed, such interrogation intersects with what Stephen White has identified as the "ontological shift" in contemporary political theory, discussed later in this introduction. See Stephen White, *Sustaining Affirmation: The Strengths of Weak Ontology in Political Theory* (Princeton: Princeton University Press, 2000).

20 Kalpana Seshadri-Crooks has proposed recently that since postcolonial criticism is unable "to commit itself to canon revision, which is essentially a minoritarian project," it differs from ethnic or minority studies. At the same time, as is well known, issues of "location" in the production of knowledge have haunted postcolonial claims from the earliest moment of their enunciation. Here I wonder about approaching such questions in ways that neither pigeonhole the institutional site of academic labor nor privilege the national origin of scholarly endeavor. This means keeping in view the geopolitical fault lines of knowledge production—critically yet differently highlighted by Edward Said and Walter Mignolo, for example—while attending to their ambivalence and blurring and further questioning the wider terms of what Pierre Bourdieu has called "scholastic reason," the "disposition," and the "perspective" entailing "(active or passive) igorance not only of what happens in the world of practice . . . but also of what it is to exist, quite simply, in the world." We do not have to agree with Bourdieu's implicitly instrumentalist understanding of the limits of reflection in "the lower regions of the social space," his gratuitously polemical dismissal of philosophy, or his assertion that in each instance the scholastic "view" necessarily "implies more or less triumphant ignorance of [its] ignorance." Rather, it is important to recognize that Bourdieu put his finger on how such dispositions often bracket their conditions of possibility, insufficiently probing their own presuppositions and insinuating, in the words of Johanes Fabian, the "progressive disembodiment of reason and knowledge" that frequently rests on an "ascetic withdrawal from the world" as it is experienced through the senses, a "sense-less" science. My point is not only that each of these emphases calls for querying projections of the disembodied vision from nowhere that becomes the palpable perspective for everywhere but that (self-)questionings of premises and propositions of knowledge are salient here. It is such interrogation that firmly underwrites my plea for mutual engagements between salient postcolonial orientations and other critical dispositions toward the West and the nation—indicating in this book, for the present, my provisional procedure for thinking through questions of the locus and location of the productive labor of postcolonial propositions. See Kalpana Seshadri-Crooks, "At the Margins of Postcolonial Studies, Part I," in Afzal-Khan and Seshadri-Crooks, *The Pre-occupation of Postcolonial Studies*, 3–4; Said, *Orientalism*; Mignolo, *Local Histories/Global Designs*; Pierre Bourdieu, *Pascalian Meditations*, translated by Richard Nice (Cambridge: Polity Press, 2000), 15, 17, and passim; and Fabian, *Out of Our Minds*, xii–xiii.

21 John McGowan, *Postmodernism and Its Critics* (Ithaca: Cornell University Press, 1991), 16 and passim.

22 I am referring to broad dispositions toward the past and present of social worlds,

drawing in and reaching beyond the scholarly deliberations explicitly expressed and implicitly endorsed today in various permutations and combinations. To critically consider such orientations is not to dismiss their particular possibilities, a point that I develop through examples in both Saurabh Dube, "Introduction: Enchantments of Modernity," in Dube, Enduring Enchantments, 741–43; and "Introduction: Colonialism, Modernity, Colonial Modernities," 203–5.

23 I find such efforts acutely present in the work of Savi Sawarkar, an expressionist Dalit artist from India. See Saurabh Dube, "Auguring Art: The Iconography of a Radical Imagination," manuscript; and Brackette Williams, "A Class Act: Anthropology and Race to Nation across Ethnic Terrain," Annual Review of Anthropology 18 (1989): 401–44.

24 I recognize that there can be distinct quests for difference. For instance, Michael Roth has argued that "When deconstruction shows that something or the other escapes the metaphysical attempt to subsume it to the logic of metaphysics, it shows us that there is otherness. . . . Deconstruction does not champion difference in this move, it merely shows there is difference . . . Difference. Something that is not metaphysics, that is different from metaphysics and escapes its logic, something that positions itself differently, that differs from metaphysics, that is not dominated or determined or predetermined by metaphysics, that is other to it." Leaving aside questions of the status and virtue of such a formulation of difference—although I sense that the exclusivity implied by this projection may not be of this world, or at least should not be—my critical comments are directed toward the substantialization and celebration of difference, of its traces, as absolute alterity. See Michael Roth, The Poetics of Resistance: Heidegger's Line (Evanston: Northwestern University Press, 1996), 12.

25 The arguments in this paragraph and the next draw on Dube, "Introduction: Enchantments of Modernity."

26 To argue in this vein is to stay with Elizabeth Povinelli's suggestion to critically reaffirm, "a sociological science of the ought in order to develop an ethnography not simply of exiting states of mood and modality, of propositionality and obligation, and of moral possibility and necessity, but also of the conditions of their emergence and transformation"—registering, especially, that in social worlds "the unimaginable is imagined." Povinelli, Cunning of Recognition, 31. See also John Gray, Two Faces of Liberalism (New York: The New Press, 2000), particularly 105–39.

27 Stoler and Cooper, "Between Metropole and Colony," 6, 29.

28 On this double move concerning colonialism and culture, see Thomas, Colonialism's Culture, 18.

29 These considerations are based on my wider discussion of shifts and transformations in historical/anthropological understandings and literary/cultural analyses of colonial cultures over the past three decades. See Dube, "Introduction: Terms That Bind: Colony, Nation, Modernity," in Dube, Postcolonial Passages.

30 C. A. Bayly, Indian Society and the Making of the British Empire (Cambridge: Cambridge University Press, 1988); C. A. Bayly, Rulers, Townsmen and Bazaars: North Indian Society in the Age of British Expansion, 1770–1870 (Cambridge: Cambridge University Press, 1983); David Washbrook, "Progress and Problems: South Asian Economic and Social History," Modern Asian Studies 22 (1988): 57–96.

31 I have in mind, for example, important work within subaltern studies, discussed later, yet consider, too, Nicholas B. Dirks, Castes of Mind: Colonialism and the Making of Modern India (Princeton: Princeton University Press, 2001).

32 Of course, both of these approaches are marked by internal heterogeneity in their explorations of colony and empire. Concerning histories of colonial transitions, see Radhika

Singha, *A Despotism of Law: Crime and Justice in Early Colonial India* (Delhi: Oxford University Press, 1998); Seema Alavi, *The Sepoys and the Company: Tradition and Transition in Northern India, 1770–1830* (Delhi: Oxford University Press, 1995); and C. A. Bayly, *Empire and Information: Intelligence Gathering and Social Communication in India, 1780–1870* (Cambridge: Cambridge University Press, 1997). Within the subaltern studies project, consider David Arnold, *Colonizing the Body: State Medicine and Epidemic Disease in Nineteenth-Century India* (Delhi: Oxford University Press, 1993); and Prakash, *Another Reason*. Works engaging both of these orientations include Skaria, *Hybrid Histories*; and Dube, *Untouchable Pasts*. See also, K. Sivaramakrishnan, *Making Forests: Statemaking and Environmental Change in Colonial Eastern India* (New Delhi: Oxford University Press, 1999).

33 On these twin emphases, see, for example, John Comaroff, "Images of Empire, Contests of Conscience: Models of Colonial Domination in South Africa," *American Ethnologist* 16 (1989): 661–85; Ann Laura Stoler, *Carnal Knowledge and Imperial Power: Race and the Intimate in Colonial Rule* (Berkeley: University of California Press, 2002); Stoler and Cooper, "Between Metropole and Colony"; and Jean Comaroff and John Comaroff, *Of Revelation and Revolution: Christianity, Colonialism, and Consciousness in South Africa*, vol. 1 (Chicago: University of Chicago Press, 1991). See also Thomas, *Colonialism's Culture*; Ann Laura Stoler, "Perceptions of Protest: Defining the Dangerous in Colonial Sumatra," *American Ethnologist* 12 (1985): 642–58; and Patrick Wolfe, *Settler Colonialism and the Transformation of Anthropology: The Politics and Poetics of an Ethnographic Event* (London: Cassell, 1999).

34 Anna Davin, "Imperialism and Motherhood," *History Workshop* 5 (1978): 9–65; Susan Thorne, "The Conversion of Englishmen and the Conversion of the World Inseparable": Missionary imperialism and the languages of class in early industrial Britain, in Cooper and Stoler, *Tensions of Empire*, 238–62; Redfield, *Space in the Tropics*; Comaroff and Comaroff, *Of Revelation and Revolution*, vol. 2; and Comaroff and Comaroff, *Ethnography and the Historical Imagination*, 265–95. See also Ann Laura Stoler, *Race and the Education of Desire: Foucault's History of Sexuality and the Colonial Order of Things* (Durham: Duke University Press, 1995); Sally Engle Merry, *Colonizing Hawai'i: The Cultural Power of Law* (Princeton: Princeton University Press, 2000); McClintock, *Imperial Leather*; Uday Singh Mehta, *Liberalism and Empire: A Study in Nineteenth-Century British Liberal Thought* (Chicago: University of Chicago Press, 1999); Mignolo, *The Darker Side of the Renaissance*; Lora Widenthal, "Race, Gender, and Citizenship in the German Colonial Empire," in Cooper and Stoler, *Tensions of Empire*, 263–83; Peter E. Hoffenberg, *An Empire on Display: English, Indian, and Australian Exhibitions from the Crystal Palace to the Great War* (Berkeley: University of California Press, 2001); and Mrinalini Sinha, *Colonial Masculinity: The "Manly Englishman" and the "Effeminate Bengali" in the Late Nineteenth Century* (Manchester: Manchester University Press, 1995).

35 Dube, "Introduction: Terms That Bind."

36 See the discussion in chapter 2, which cites representative writings that elaborate these emphases.

37 Dube, "Introduction: Terms That Bind," elaborates the questions raised here.

38 Herzfeld, *Cultural Intimacy*, 1–2, 165.

39 These considerations keep in view impressive recent writings on nation, state, and nationalism in India, works that include Urvashi Butalia, *The Other Side of Silence: Voices from the Partition of India* (New Delhi: Viking Penguin, 1998); Ritu Menon and Kamla Bhasin, *Borders and Boundaries: Women in India's Partition* (New Delhi: Kali for Women, 1998); Veena Das, *Critical Events: An Anthropological Perspective on Contemporary India* (Delhi: Oxford University Press, 1995); Hansen, *The Saffron Wave*; Akhil Gupta, *Postcolonial Developments: Agriculture in the Making of Modern India* (Durham: Duke University Press, 1998);

C. J. Fuller and Véronique Bénéï, eds., *The Everyday State and Society in Modern India* (New Delhi: Social Science Press, 2000); Amin, *Event, Metaphor, Memory*; and Pandey, *Remembering Partition*. I develop such issues in Dube, "Introduction: Terms That Bind." See also Prasenjit Duara, *Rescuing History from the Nation: Questioning Narratives of Modern China* (Chicago: University of Chicago Press, 1996).

40 Consider, for instance, Prakash, *Another Reason*, 202–14; and Hansen, *The Saffron Wave*, 229–34.

41 For works expressing such spillovers, ironies, and containments, consider the first six volumes of *Subaltern Studies: Writings on South Asian History and Society*, all edited by Ranajit Guha and published in Delhi by Oxford University Press between 1982 and 1989; Prakash, *Another Reason*; and Dirks, *Castes of Mind*.

42 Such a shift, then, implies even more than the "ontological turn" that both considers what "entities are presupposed" by theories and takes on "a commitment to the existence of certain entities" entailed in the affirmation of a theory (White, *Sustaining Affirmation*, 4–5). Recall my suggestion that critical work in the social sciences and the socially inflected humanities today can intersect with the kind of questioning that defines the recent ontological shift under discussion. To register this is far from denying the salience of distinctive procedures of interrogation and affirmation in contemporary political theory. Rather, it is to prudently engage them in order to address related concerns, especially articulating worlds beyond the West. Finally, such terms of discussion reach beyond facile polarities between the "realist" and "constructivist" positions ably disaggregated and unraveled in George Steinmetz, "Critical Realism and Historical Sociology," *Comparative Studies in Society and History* 40 (1998): 170–86.

43 White, *Sustaining Affirmation*, 8.

44 Ibid. This further means that my proposal for a history without warranty, engaging the terms of a weak ontology, draws on but also extends the sensibilities and steps of "postfoundational" criticism (sensitively discussed in Desai, *Subject to Colonialism*, 10–13).

45 For rather different expressions of such dispositions compare Chakrabarty's *Provincializing Europe* and Stephen White's emphasis on figurations of "universal constitutives of human being," which is premised on the recognition that the persuasiveness of these existential universals "can never be fully disentangled from an interpretation of present historical circumstances," so that "gaining access to something universal about human being and world is always also a construction that cannot rid itself of a historical dimension" (White, *Sustaining Affirmation*, 9). See also Saurabh Dube, "Presence of Europe: An Interview with Dipesh Chakrabarty," in Dube, *Enduring Enchantments*, 859–68; Mitchell, "The Stage of Modernity"; and Michel-Rolph Trouillot, "North Atlantic Universals: Analytical Fictions," 1492–1945, in Dube, *Enduring Enchantments*, 840–57. It seems to me that these distinct considerations equally suggest shared horizons crucial to both the interrogation and affirmation at the core of a history without warranty.

46 Bhabha, *Location of Culture*; Gyan Prakash, "Science between the Lines," in *Subaltern Studies IX: Writings on South Asian History and Society*, edited by Shahid Amin and Dipesh Chakrabarty (Delhi: Oxford University Press, 1996), 59–82. Yet see also Christopher Pinney, "Indian Magical Realism: Notes on Popular Visual Culture," in *Subaltern Studies X: Writings on South Asian History and Society*, edited by Gautam Bhadra, Gyan Prakash, and Susie Tharu (Delhi: Oxford University Press, 1999), 201–33. Bhabha has recently clarified his "attachment to poetic justice" while announcing the tension that his work sets up between the translatability and untranslatability of a concept. These are interesting

considerations, but I doubt whether they deflect or blunt the terms of my criticism. See Kalpana Seshadri-Crooks, "Surviving Theory: A Conversation with Homi Bhabha," in Afzal-Khan and Seshadri-Crooks, *The Pre-occupation of Postcolonial Studies*, 370–72. Finally, the use of concepts such as *hybridity* in finely textured historical/ethnographic analyses can work as a discursive shorthand or descriptive categories, but I wonder if they are adequate to the richness of the materials they present. See, for instance, Nancy Rose Hunt, *A Colonial Lexicon of Birth Ritual, Medicalization, and Mobility in the Congo* (Durham: Duke University Press, 1999); and Birgit Meyer, *Translating the Devil: Religion and Modernity among the Ewe in Ghana* (Trenton, N.J.: Africa World Press, 1999).

47 Michel de Certeau, *The Practice of Everyday Life*, translated by Steven Rendall (Berkeley: University of California Press, 1984), ix and passim.

48 For works intimating related emphases see, for example, Norman Brown, *Life against Death: The Psychoanalytical Meaning of History* (London: Routledge and Kegan Paul, 1959); Luise White, *Speaking with Vampires: Rumor and History in Colonial Africa* (Berkeley: University of California Press, 2000); and Mbembe, *On the Postcolony*. Consider also Partha Chatterjee, *A Princely Impostor? The Strange and Universal History of the Kumar of Bhawal* (Princeton: Princeton University Press, 2002); and Lisa Lowe and David Lloyd, eds., *The Politics of Culture in the Shadow of Capital* (Durham: Duke University Press, 1997).

49 Ranajit Guha, *Dominance without Hegemony: History and Power in Colonial India* (Cambridge: Harvard University Press, 1997), chap. 1.

50 It should be clear that just as there is nothing disparaging about such procedures—indeed, I offer these comments in a spirit of gratitude to Guha—so, too, the desire to question and affirm should not simply surface as an exceptional measure, a one-off oddity. Unsurprisingly, something similar is afoot in what I have learned from Ashis Nandy's ethical extensions of democratic horizons through claims on tradition and Enrique Dussel's interrogation of Eurocentric framings of modernity, while I cautiously question their distinct proclamations of innocence and autonomy ahead of modernity and power. See Ashis Nandy, *The Intimate Enemy: Loss and Recovery of Self under Colonialism* (Delhi: Oxford University Press, 1983); Nandy, *Traditions, Tyranny, and Utopias*; Enrique Dussel, "Eurocentrism and Modernity," *Boundary 2* 20 (1993): 65–76; and Dussel, World-system and "trans"-modernity. See also Dipesh Chakrabarty, *Habitations of Modernity: Essays in the Wake of Subaltern Studies* (Chicago: University of Chicago Press, 2002), 38–47.

1 Traveling Light

1 In this interchange, a monumental forgetting becomes the transcendental trick of the true traveler. Here it is possible to mark the reification of a heroic self—exorcised through its will to know yet reinstated later through its acquisition of betterment—losing and finding itself in travel, a construction that fatally fuels alienated adventurisms on offer today. At the same time, it is equally conceivable that we can uncover from this fragment the importance of interrogating the self in order to make the familiar strange and render the strange familiar, putting a question mark on both strangeness and familiarity. These are matters of readings and questions of emphasis. My point is that a surplus of longing underwrites travel even in this passage. Thus, the fabulous fictions of the traveler's spectacular exorcism of the self and assiduous absorption of the other can share a similar logic with the dark desires of the traveler's dominant construction of the other and singular celebration of the self. See Pierre Clastres, *Society against the State: Essays in Political Anthropology*, translated by Robert Hurley (New York: Zone Books, 1989), 7. Clastres is quoting Montaigne on Socrates on travel here.

2   Bernard Cohn, "History and Anthropology: The State of Play," *Comparative Studies in Society and History* 22 (1980): 199.

3   J. W. Shank, "The missionary as civilizing agent," *Christian Monitor*, January 1910, 394.

4   The introduction to this volume suggested that my use of *enchanted spaces* and *modern places* does not imply that modernity begins only in the latter half of the eighteenth century in "North Europe," ignoring the critical presence of an anterior Spain, a prior Portugal, and the "New World" in formations of what Walter Mignolo describes as the "modern/colonial world" and Enrique Dussel as the moment of the "first modernity." Nor do I overlook the fact that related antinomies—for, example, between the "barbaric" and the "civilized"—have formed part of the modern/colonial world since the sixteenth century, a point implied by Aníbal Quijano's notion of the "coloniality of power" as being central to this terrain. Indeed, it would be interesting to explore the stipulations of exclusion that defined the coloniality of power within the first modernity in conjunction with the "liberal strategies of exclusion" that Uday Mehta describes as fundamental to nineteenth-century British India. Here it is important to keep in view the connections as well as the disjunctions among the terms, criteria, and imperatives of exclusion in these distinct contexts, particularly the ways in which the very exclusions of different colonial projects were variously premised on civilizing the colonized and thereby "including" these subjects through particular procedures in emergent hierarchies of otherness and civilization. My efforts in this book primarily concern the ways in which certain dualities in their distilled form have haunted mappings of the world over the past two centuries. Given the nature of the exercise, I confess to not having examined the transformations over time of the enchanted and the modern. See Mignolo, *Local Histories/Global Designs*; Dussel, "World-system and 'Trans'-modernity"; Quijano, "Colonialidad del poder"; and Mehta, *Liberalism and Empire*.

5   Martin Lewis and Karen Wigen, *The Myth of the Continents: A Critique of Metageography* (Berkeley: University of California Press, 1997), ix.

6   These overlapping processes articulate critical, intersecting, and recent departures in the ethnography and history of evangelical entanglements. Mentioned in the introduction, they are elaborated in chapter 2, where I also indicate the relation of my own work to studies of Christianity in South Asia.

7   Fuller accounts of the detailed dramas and tangled theaters of evangelical entanglements in nineteenth- and twentieth-century central India form part of my ongoing research and writing. A few expressions of this larger project include Saurabh Dube, "Native Witness: Colonial Writings of a Vernacular Christianity," manuscript; *Genealogías del presente: Conversión, colonialismo, cultura* (Mexico City: El Colegio de México, 2003; and "Conversion to Translation: Unbound Registers of a Vernacular Christianity," in Dube, *Enduring Enchantments*, 807–37.

8   Nicholas B. Dirks, "Foreword" to *Colonialism and Its Forms of Knowledge: The British in India*, by Bernard Cohn (Princeton: Princeton University Press, 1996), ix–xvii.

9   The account in the following three paragraphs is primarily based on the "Autobiography of Oscar Lohr" (manuscript written in German in 1902 and translated into English in 1971), typescript, EAL. See also Theodore Seybold, *God's Guiding Hand: A History of the Central Indian Mission, 1868–1967* (Philadelphia: United Church Board for the World Ministries of the United Church of Christ, 1971).

10 See chapter 2.

11 Oral testimony of Bishop J. G. Malagar, Dhamtari, January 1995.

12 Ghasidas, a farm servant, initiated Satnampanth primarily among the Chamars (customarily leatherworkers but in practice agriculturalists) of Chhattisgarh in the first half

of the nineteenth century. The Chamars—and a few hundred members of other castes who joined Satnampanth—became Satnamis. They rejected the deities and idols of the Hindu pantheon and had no temples, believing only in a formless god, *satnam* (true name). There were to be no distinctions of caste within Satnampanth. With Ghasidas, there began a guru *parampara* (tradition), which was hereditary. Satnampanth developed a stock of myths, rituals, and practices and an organizational hierarchy that were closely associated with the gurus. Combining the features of a caste and a sect, the Satnamis are still a significant presence in Chhattisgarh. I construct an anthropological history of the Satnamis from the 1780s through to the 1990s in Dube, *Untouchable Pasts*.

13 See, for example, Pier Larson, "Capacities and Modes of Thinking: Intellectual Engagements and Subaltern Hegemony in the Early History of Malgasy Christianity," *American Historical Review* 102 (1997): 968–1002; Gwyn Prins, *The Hidden Hippopotamus: Reappraisals in African History* (Cambridge: Cambridge University Press, 1980); Andrew Apter, *Black Critics and Kings: The Hermeneutics of Power in Yoruba Society* (Chicago: University of Chicago Press, 1993); and Marshall Sahlins, *Islands of History* (Chicago: University of Chicago Press, 1985). At the same time, consider the exchange that takes place between Gananath Obeyesekere, *The Apotheosis of Captain Cook* (Princeton: Princeton University Press, 1992); Marshall Sahlins, *How "Natives" Think: About Captain Cook, for Example* (Chicago: University of Chicago Press, 1995); and Greg Dening, *Performances* (Chicago: University of Chicago Press, 1995), 64–78.

14 *Der Friedensbote* 79, no. 20 (1928): 309–15, EAL.

15 Notrott, Typescript history of Mission, 5, EAL.

16 I derive this suggestion from the anthropologist Michael Herzfeld. Elaborated in the context of a Mediterranean culture, his arguments have rather wider implications: "At the level of collective representations . . . [hospitality] signifies the moral and conceptual *subordination* of the guest to the host. In this way, it 'englobes' the visitor, to the substituting moral advantage for political subordination. . . . The act of hospitality can thus become a means of expressing and reversing a pattern of domination at one and the same time. The stance that the host takes toward the guest reproduces collective attitudes to the social or cultural group that the latter represents." See Michael Herzfeld, "As in Your Own House: Hospitality, Ethnography, and the Stereotype of the Mediterranean Society," in *Honor and Shame and the Unity of the Mediterranean*, edited by David Gilmore (Washington, D.C.: American Anthropological Association, 1987), 77, emphasis in the original.

17 This is one tale. There are other stories. For details see chapter 2.

18 For a succinct discussion, see Jean Comaroff and John Comaroff, "Christianity and Colonialism in South Africa," *American Ethnologist* 13 (1986): 1–22. Yet such terms of debate are far from dead, as is evident in recent works on South Asia that reflect prior positions. On the missionary as benefactor of native, consider Aparna Basu, "Mary Anne Cooke to Mother Teresa: Christian Missionary Women and the Indian Response," in *Women and Missions, Past and Present: Anthropological and Historical Perceptions*, edited by Fiona Bowie, Deborah Kirkwood and Shirley Ardener (Oxford: Berg Publishers, 1993), 187–208. Conversely, see Tejaswini Niranjana, *Siting Translation: History, Post-structuralism and the Colonial Context* (Berkeley: University of California Press, 1992). In the public discourse on history, opposed conceptions regarding the role of the foreign missionary have long been routine on the Indian subcontinent, albeit becoming more striking in recent years. For example, concerning the missionary turned anthropologist turned administrator, Verrier Elwin, see Ramchandra Guha, *Savaging the Civilized: Verrier Elwin, His Tribals, and India* (New Delhi: Oxford University Press, 1999). Compare also Maina Chawla Singh,

Gender, Religion, and "Heathen Lands": American Missionary Women in South Asia (1860s–1940s) (New York: Garland, 2000); and Dirks, *Castes of Mind*, particularly chapters 7 and 8.

19 Comaroff and Comaroff, "Christianity and Colonialism."

20 For a discussion of such issues—including the stipulations, limits, and mutual binds of *conversion* and (Indian/Hindu) *civilization* as categories—see Dube, "Conversion to Translation"; and Saurabh Dube and Ishita Banerjee Dube, "Spectres of Conversion: Transformation of Caste and Sect in India," in *Conversion in India: Modes, Motivations, and Meanings*, edited by Rowena Robinson and Sathianathan Clarke (New Delhi: Oxford University Press, 2003).

21 Rather more than an explicitly stated agenda, such conceptions appear as implicit assumptions that then guide the analyses of an exclusive colonial discourse. See, for instance, Gyanendra Pandey. "The colonial construction of 'communalism': British writings on Banaras," in *Subaltern Studies VI: Writings on South Asian History and Society*, edited by Ranajit Guha (Delhi: Oxford University Press, 1989), 132–68. As I discuss later, the work of Homi Bhabha skillfully and strikingly opens up the different registers of colonial representations, but here, too, the "pluralities" remain internal to a binding colonial discourse.

22 Clearly, such contradictions are quite distinct from the "tensions" that Kate Teltscher, for instance, explores in the context of European representations and British writings. See her *India Inscribed: European and British Writing on India, 1600–1800* (Delhi: Oxford University Press, 1997).

23 Such representations are routine and pervasive in nineteenth-century missionary writings. See *DDM*, 1875–1890, EAL; and Th. Von Tanner, *Im Lande der Hindus oder Kulturschilderungen aus Indien* (St. Louis: German Evangelical Synod of North America, 1894).

24 For example, M. M. Paul, *Satyanami Panth aur Ghasidas Girodvasi* (Raipur, 1936), 35.

25 See, particularly, Nicholas B. Dirks, *The Hollow Crown: Ethnohistory of an Indian Kingdom* (Cambridge: Cambridge University Press, 1987).

26 Annual Reports of the Chuttesgurh Mission, 1872–1879, ARM, EAL; Bisrampur Malguzari File [1925–55], EAL.

27 Stoler, *Carnal Knowledge and Imperial Power*, 24.

28 J. A. Lapp, *The Mennonite Church in India* (Scottsdale: Herald Press, 1972), 74–75.

29 See, for example, Correspondence of Missionaries, Menzel, E. W. and Ida, 82–16b MIS 69, EAL; Hist Mss I–117, J. A. and Lina Zook Ressler Correspondence—Lina, 1887–1903 (Box I), AMC.

30 Hist Mss I–117, J. A. and Lina Zook Ressler Correspondence—J. A. (Box 2), AMC.

31 Correspondence of Missionaries, Menzel, E. W. and Ida, 82–16b MIS 69, EAL. This discussion also draws on my conversations (in the midwestern United States in the late 1990s) with older ex-missionaries who had grown up in Chhattisgarh in the 1920s and 1930s as the offspring of evangelists. From the late 1940s on, such implicit terms of interaction, especially those concerning food, between Euro-American missionaries and Indian Christians gradually became more relaxed. It also warrants emphasis that exclusions surrounding commensality were not a prerogative of the British and the Americans in colonial India. Exclusion equally characterized relations of purity/pollution in the caste order, including stipulations of segregation with respect to Euro-American evangelists and Indian Christians. Both the differences between these separate forms of exclusion, including disjunctive articulations of "race" and "custom" and the "domestic" and the "private," and their conjoint implications for lower-caste converts raise important questions, which I hope to address in my ongoing work on evangelical entanglements.

32 See the detailed discussion in chapter 2.

33 *DDM*, 9, 7 (July 1873), p. 48, EAL.

34 *DDM*, 10, 8 (August 1874), p. 57; *DDM*, 8, 4 (April 1872), p. 26, EAL.

35 *DDM*, 6, 12 (December 1870), pp. 89–90, EAL. The account is incomplete.

36 For a critical discussion of writing in the colonial context in South Asia, see Ajay Skaria, "Writing, Orality and Power in the Dangs, Western India, 1880s–1920s," in *Subaltern Studies IX: Writings on South Asian History and Society*, edited by Shahid Amin and Dipesh Chakrabarty (Delhi: Oxford University Press, 1996), 13–58. See also Skaria, *Hybrid Histories*; and Dube, *Untouchable Pasts*.

37 *DDM*, 6, 4 (April 1870), p. 3; *DDM*, 8, 11 (November 1872), p. 82; *DDM*, 13, 2 (February 1877), p. 11; *DDM*, 10, 10 (October 1874), p. 74; *DDM*, 11, 2 (February 1875), p. 13, EAL; Annual Report on the Chuttesgurh Mission, 1874–75, pp. 10–14, ARM, EAL.

38 Annual Reports of the Chuttesgurh Mission, 1874–1879, ARM, EAL.

39 *DDM*, 8, 7 (July 1872), p. 50; *DDM*, 8, 11 (November 1872), p. 85; *DDM*, 9, 8 (August 1873), p. 58 EAL. See also the photographs of missionaries and converts in Julius Lohr, *Bilder aus Chhattisgarh und den Central Provinzen Ostindiens* (n.p., 1899).

40 C. P. *Ethnographic Survey XVII, Draft Articles on Hindustani Castes*, first series (Nagpur: Government Press, 1914), 57.

41 For a detailed discussion of these early-twentieth-century manuscripts and their enactment of colonial apprehensions and vernacular translations, the one bound to the other, see Dube, "Conversion to Translation"; and "Native Witness."

42 With its beginnings in political endeavors of the 1890s, the Swadeshi movement within Indian anticolonial nationalism was at its height between 1905 and 1908, especially in the large imperial province of Bengal. By the time of this encounter of the catechist, the Swadeshi movement was already in decline, but its spirit lived on in remote regions such as Chhattisgarh. See Sumit Sarkar, *Modern India, 1885–1947* (Delhi: Macmillan, 1983), 96–100, 105–35.

43 Entry for 1 October 1909 from the daybook of a catechist (not named), manuscript, 83–5, EAL.

44 Dube, "Conversion to Translation."

45 Entry for 4 April 1908 from the daybook of a catechist (not named), manuscript, 83–5, EAL.

46 Entry for 30 April 1908 from the daybook of a catechist (not named), manuscript, 83–5, EAL.

47 Homi Bhabha, "Signs Taken for Wonders: Questions of Ambivalence and Authority under a Tree Outside Delhi, May 1817," in *The Location of Culture*, 102–22; Prakash, "Science between the Lines."

48 See also McClintock, *Imperial Leather*, 63.

49 Bhabha, "Signs Taken for Wonders," 121.

50 Ibid.

51 I discuss critical procedures of vernacular translation in Dube, "Native Witness"; and "Conversion to Translation."

52 A revised version of this presentation has now appeared in print. See Cornelia Mallebrein, "Constructing a 'House Within the House': Reading the Wall-paintings of the Lanjia Sora from Recitations," in *Jagannath Revisited: Studying Society, Religion, and the State in Orissa*, edited by Hermann Kulke and Burkhard Schnepel (New Delhi: Manohar, 2001).

53 Here there are issues not only of "alternative" modernities but of modernity's "enchantments." These find context-bound elaboration in Dube, "Introduction: Enchantments of Modernity."

2 Evangelical Entanglements

1 Works that shape these considerations include Michel de Certeau, *The Practice of Everyday Life*; Michel Foucault, "Governmentality," in *The Foucault Effect: Studies in Governmentality*, edited by Graham Burcell, Colin Gordon, and Peter Mills (Chicago: University of Chicago Press, 1991), 87–104; Antonio Gramsci, *Selections from the Prison Notebooks of Antonio Gramsci*, translated by Q. Hoare and N. Smith (London: Lawrence and Wishart, 1971); V. N. Voloshinov [Mikhail Bakhtin], *Marxism and the Philosophy of Language*, translated by L. Matejka and I. R. Titunik (Cambridge: Harvard University Press, 1984); Sherry Ortner, "Resistance and the Problem of Ethnographic Refusal," *Comparative Studies in Society and History* 37 (1995): 173–93; E. P. Thompson, *Customs in Common: Studies in Traditional Popular Culture* (New York: New Press, 1993); and Asad, *Genealogies of Religion*. See also Florencia Mallon, *Peasant and Nation: The Making of Postcolonial Mexico and Peru* (Berkeley: University of California Press, 1995); and Michael Taussig, *Shamanism, Colonialism, and the Wild Man: A Study in Terror and Healing* (Chicago: University of Chicago Press, 1987).

2 For central India, see James Juhnke, *A People of Mission: A History of the General Conference Mennonite Overseas Mission* (Newton: Faith and Life Press, 1979); Lapp, *Mennonite Church in India*; and Seybold, *God's Guiding Hand*. See also Lohr, *Bilder aus Chhattisgarh*; and Tanner, *Im Lande der Hindus*.

3 See, for example, James C. Manor, "Testing the Barrier between Caste and Outcaste: The Andhra Evangelical Lutheran Church in Guntur District, 1920–1940," *Indian Church History Review* 5 (1971): 27–41; G. A. Oddie, "Christian Conversion in Telugu Country, 1860–1900: A Case Study of One Protestant Movement in the Godavery-Christian Delta," *Indian Economic and Social History Review* 12 (1975): 61–79; and Duncan B. Forrester, *Caste and Christianity: Attitudes and Policies on Caste of Anglo-Saxon Protestant Missions in India* (London: Curzon Press, 1980).

4 Rowena Robinson, *Conversion, Continuity, and Change: Lived Christianity in Southern Goa* (New Delhi: Sage, 1998); R. L. Stirrat, *Power and Religiosity in a Post-colonial Setting: Sinhala Catholics in Contemporary Sri Lanka* (Cambridge: Cambridge University Press, 1992); Susan Bayly, *Saints, Goddesses and Kings: Muslims and Christians in South Indian Society, 1700–1900* (Cambridge: Cambridge University Press, 1989); Susan Visvanathan, *The Christians of Kerala: History, Belief, and Ritual among the Yakoba* (Madras: Oxford University Press, 1993). See also Ines G. Zupanov, *Disputed Mission: Jesuit Experiments and Brahmanical Knowledge in Seventeenth-Century India* (New Delhi: Oxford University Press, 1999).

5 David Scott, "Conversion and Demonism: Colonial Christian Discourse on Religion in Sri Lanka," *Comparative Studies in Society and History* 34 (1992): 331–65; and Anthony Copley, *Religions in Conflict: Ideology, Cultural Contact and Conversion in Late Colonial India* (Delhi: Oxford University Press, 1997). See also Koji Kawashima, *Missionaries and a Hindu State: Travancore, 1858–1936* (Delhi: Oxford University Press, 1998); Gerald Studdert-Kennedy, *Providence and the Raj: Imperial Mission and Missionary Imperialism* (New Delhi: Sage, 1998); Sathianathan Clarke, *Dalits and Christianity: Subaltern Religion and Liberation Theology in India* (Delhi: Oxford University Press, 1998); John C. Webster, *The Dalit Christians: A History* (Delhi: ISPCK, 1994); Richard Eaton, "Conversion to Christianity among the Nagas, 1876–1971," *Indian Economic and Social History Review* 21 (1984): 1–44; and Gauri Viswanathan, *Outside the Fold: Conversion, Modernity, Belief* (Princeton: Princeton University Press, 1998).

6 Ussama Makdisi, "Reclaiming the Land of the Bible: Missionaries, Secularism, and Evangelical Modernity," *American Historical Review* 102 (1997): 680–713; Comaroff, *Images of empire*; Comaroff and Comaroff, "Christianity and Colonialism"; Nicholas Thomas, "Colo-

nial Conversions: Difference, Hierarchy and History in Early Twentieth Century Evangelical Propaganda," *Comparative Studies in Society and History* 34 (1992): 366–89. See also Thomas O. Beidelman, *Colonial Evangelism: A Socio-historical Study of an East African Mission at the Grass Roots* (Bloomington: Indiana University Press, 1982); Cooper and Stoler, *Tensions of Empire*; Johannes Fabian, *Language and Colonial Power: The Appropriation of Swahili in the Former Belgian Congo, 1880–1938* (Cambridge: Cambridge University Press, 1986); Mignolo, *The Darker Side of the Renaissance*; and Vicente Rafael, *Contracting Colonialism: Translation and Christian Conversion in Tagalog Society under Early Spanish Rule* (Ithaca: Cornell University Press, 1988).

7 Comaroff and Comaroff, *Of Revelation and Revolution*, vol. 1: 250.

8 See, for example, Larson, "Capacities and Modes of Thinking"; Meyer, *Translating the Devil*; Geoffrey White, *Identity through History: Living Stories in a Solomon Islands Society* (Cambridge: Cambridge University Press, 1991); Robert Hefner, ed., *Conversion to Christianity: Historical and Anthropological Perspectives on a Great Transformation* (Berkeley: University of California Press, 1993); Comaroff and Comaroff, *Of Revelation and Revolution*, vol. 2; Derek Peterson, "Translating the Word: Dialogism and Debate in Two Gikyu Dictionaries," *Journal of Religious History* 23 (1999): 31–50; J. D. Y. Peel, "For Who Hath Despised the Day of Small Things? Missionary Narratives and Historical Anthropology," *Comparative Studies in Society and History* 37 (1995): 581–607; and Paul Landau, *The Realm of the Word: Language, Gender, and Christianity in a Southern African Kingdom* (London: Heineman, 1995). See also Diane Austin-Broos, *Jamaica Genesis: Religion and the Politics of Moral Orders* (Chicago: University of Chicago Press, 1997); Rafael, *Contracting Colonialism*; and Hunt, *A Colonial Lexicon*.

9 I hope to address these issues more fully in my larger project on evangelical entanglements—a project straddling North American cultural histories and central Indian ethnographic past. Consider, too, Dube, *Genealogías del presente*; and "Conversion to Translation."

10 "Autobiography of Oscar Lohr," 1; Seybold, *God's Guiding Hand*, 1.

11 "Autobiography of Oscar Lohr," 2.

12 *DDM*, 2, 12 (December 1867), p. 86, EAL.

13 Seybold, *God's Guiding Hand*, 6.

14 Ibid., 8.

15 "Autobiography of Oscar Lohr," 2.

16 Ibid., 3–4.

17 Even before moving to Bisrampur, Lohr had set up a school in Raipur in order to instruct the Satnamis in elementary subjects and Christian truths and to find out more about their sect. This contact had led to the missionary's first encounter with the Satnami guru, discussed in the last chapter. Some of Lohr's Satnami students moved with him from Raipur to Bisrampur. They were among the first to consider conversion.

18 The janeu is of course a mark of the twice-born castes in the Hindu social order and as such was denied to the Satnamis, an untouchable community. However, Balakdas, the second guru of the Satnampanth, distributed the sacred thread among the Satnamis in the 1850s. Satnami myths rehearse the tale of Balakda's wearing and distribution of the janeu as a simultaneous challenge to upper-caste authority and colonial power. See Dube, "Myths, Symbols and Community," 151–54.

19 Seybold, *God's Guiding Hand*, 21–22; *Der Friedensbote* 79, no. 21 (1928): 325–31, EAL.

20 In December 1869, a cautious Lohr reported to the Home Board: "I have not baptised anyone but . . . what is required is a deeper understanding of Christian truth and a thorough grounding in the same than what the sons of wilderness can grasp in three or four months" (*DDM*, 6, 4 [April 1870], p. 1, EAL).

21 A few years ago, I discovered during fieldwork that one of these Satnamis, Anjori Paulus, was actually a Gond. He had been incorporated into Satnampanth after he married a Satnami woman.

22 Report of the Chuttesgurh Mission, June 1870–July 1871, pp. 5–6, ARM, EAL.

23 Ibid., p. 5.

24 DDM, 8, 4 (April 1872), p. 25, EAL.

25 Report of the Chuttesgurh Mission, June 1871–July 1872, pp. 8–9, ARM, EAL.

26 DDM, 8, 4 (April 1872), pp. 25–26; DDM, 9, 2 (February 1873), p. 10; DDM, 9, 11 (November 1873), p. 83, EAL. By 1883, the number of converts at Bisrampur had grown to 175, and other relatives of these families were awaiting baptism. This process of slow growth went on until 1890, when the number of converts stood at 258 (Report of the Chuttesgurh Mission, 1883, p. 17, ARM, EAL; Bisrampur Baptismal Register, 1870–90, EAL).

27 The situation of the converts in Bisrampur (and other mission stations) contrasts with what obtained in other villages of Chhattisgarh. In the 1860s, the proprietary rights conferred by the colonial government strengthened the hand of the newly styled malguzars and left the vast majority of cultivators, occupancy tenants, and tenants at will with few defenses. The Brahman and Marwari malguzars squeezed out the tenants by a variety of means and increased their own holdings. Generally, lower-caste cultivators and malguzars lost out. At the turn of the century, the combined effects of the famine compounded these circumstances. The converts to Christianity at the mission stations were sheltered from these adverse economic processes. See Dube, Untouchable Pasts, 48–57.

28 Annual Reports of the Chuttesgurh Mission, 1870–71, pp. 5–6; 1871–72, pp. 4–8; 1874–75, pp. 8–13; 1876–77, pp. 8–10; 1878–80, pp. 6–11, 15–16; 1880–81, p. 6, 13; 1881–82, pp. 11–12; 1882–83, pp. 5–7, 8–10, p. 15, ARM, EAL. This picture is also confirmed by the missionary reports from Bisrampur published in DDM, 1870–90, EAL.

29 Bisrampur Kalasiya ki Vishesh Agyayen (Bisrampur: n.p., 1890).

30 Today the stone press fashioned by Oscar Lohr stands in the Eden Archives in Missouri, a mute memorial to evangelical desires.

31 Ibid., 2–3.

32 On churi in Chhattisgarh, see Dube, Untouchable Pasts, 108–15; and chapter 3.

33 Annual Report of the Chuttesgurh Mission, 1876–77, pp. 2–3, ARM, EAL. DDM, 11, 11 (November 1875), pp. 81–3; DDM, 13, 2 (February 1877), pp. 18–19; DDM, (n.s.) 4, 4 (April 1887), pp. 29–31, EAL.

34 Bisrampur Kalasiya ki Vishesh Agyayen, 5.

35 Ibid.; DDM, 9, 8 (August 1873), p. 57; DDM, (n.s.), 4, 9 (September 1886), pp. 68–70, EAL.

36 Concerning the debate on the nature of caste, I have argued that purity/pollution and ritual kingship were not opposed principles but twin ritual schemes of meaning and power. In the nineteenth and twentieth centuries, these schemes worked together with the forms of power derived from colonial governance to define patterns of domination and subordination in the caste order (Dube, Untouchable Pasts). Here I wish to emphasize that schemes of purity/pollution and cultural kingship, in modified and reworked ways, also shaped the patterns, practices, and perceptions of Christian congregations in colonial central India. This once more questions the authoritative assumption, discussed earlier, that converts to Christianity in South Asia made a clean break with the past in the image of the evangelists.

37 During my fieldwork in Chhattisgarh in the mid-1990s, this description of the mission-

ary as *raja log* cropped up repeatedly among different individuals and groups of rural Christians as they recalled past times.

38   *DDM*, 9, 8 (August 1873), pp. 57–58; Annual Report of the Chuttesgurh Mission, 1876–77, pp. 2–3. The arguments of the last three paragraphs also draw on information contained in several issues of *DDM* between 1870 and 1900, EAL.

39   Immanuel Church, Bisrampur, to P. A. Menzel, Secretary, American Evangelical Mission, U.S.A., 25 October 1933, BMF, EAL. The letter had 168 signatures. A number of the applications, notes, and letters written by the converts are in Hindi. The translations are mine.

40   The India Mission District of the Evangelical Synod of North America, formed in 1924 as a self-governing church body in India, was comprised of missionaries of the American Evangelical Mission at six mission stations. See Seybold, *God's Guiding Hand*, 75–76.

41   J. C. Koenig, Bisrampur, to F. A. Goetsch, St. Louis, 22 January 1935, BMF, EAL.

42   Premdas Jacob, Bisrampur, to Chairman, Evangelical Synod of North America, Detroit, 17 April 1935, BMF, EAL; J. C. Koenig, Bisrampur, to F. A. Goetsch, St. Louis, 22 January 1935, BMF, EAL.

43   Premdas Jacob, Bisrampur, to Chairman, Evangelical Synod of North America, Detroit, 17 April 1935, BMF EAL; Noordass and Powel, Christian members, Ganeshpur (near Bisrampur), to Chairman Saheb (?), 29 March 1934, BMF, EAL.

44   Miller, Survey of Bisrampur, 1925, p. 4, BMF, EAL. Another survey conducted by the missionaries in 1943 revealed that about 96 percent of the Christians of Bisrampur and Ganeshpur had descended from "Satnami-Chamar" families. Moreover, the congregation at Bisrampur comprised about 42.5 percent of the total native membership of the American Evangelical Mission. See A study of Christian descendants from Chamars and Satnamis (handwritten and typed note), 1943, pp. 1–5, FS, MPDP, EAL.

45   Miller, Survey of Bisrampur, p. 4, BMF, EAL.

46   Miller's survey report stated that "out of a communicant membership of 575 [185 families]—176 families own their houses, 112 own land, 85 own teams of cows or buffaloes while perhaps 80 have savings in some form or other than those mentioned or other than regular household equipment" (ibid., p. 5).

47   Ibid., 4–5; P. M. Konrad, Annual Report, Bisrampur, 1925, p. 2, ARM; Mrs. T. Twente, Report on Bible-women's work, Annual Report, Bisrampur, 1927, pp. 1–2, ARM; Note on Christian descendants from Satnami families, 1940, pp. 1–5, FS, MPDP, EAL; E. W. Menzel, Annual Report, Bisrampur, 1951, pp. 2–7, ARM, EAL.

48   According to Seybold, Pandit Gangaram, Oscar Lohr's faithful coworker, had paid the missionary the finest compliment when he called him "Apostle to the Satnamis" (*God's Guiding Hand*, 57). See E. W. Menzel, Note on sixtieth anniversary celebrations at Bisrampur, Annual Report, Bisrampur, 1928, 1–2, ARM, EAL; M. M. Paul, *Evangelical Kalasiya ka Sankshipt Itihas* (Allahabad: Mission Press, 1936), 7–9, 22–23; Rev. Hagenstein, *Satmat ka Updesh* (Allahabad: Mission Press, 1934), 4.

49   The missionary was "the civic authority (through the Malguzari), the employer or landlord of most people, the legal guardian of many or the legal guardian of [villagers'] children or other relatives, as well as the symbol in which ecclesiastical moral authority and charitable enterprises was more or less vested" (E. W. Menzel, Note on Bisrampur, 1940, 2–3, BMF, EAL).

50   Ibid.; J. Purti, Annual congregational report, Bisrampur, 1929, ARM, EAL.

51   During the interwar period in Chhattisgarh, cultivators had to extend their holdings in order to assure profits from agriculture. The increased occupation of land and the system of high *nazranas* (consent money) made this difficult for poorer cultivators.

Although the situation of the converts at Bisrampur was decidedly better, they could not escape the wider constraints of the agrarian economy in Chhattisgarh. The threats to the Bisrampur cultivators resulting from the measures taken by the missionaries from the 1920s onward require understanding in this light. See Saurabh Dube, *Caste and Sect in Village Life: Satnamis of Chhattisgarh, 1900–1950* (Shimla: Indian Institute of Advanced Study, 1993), 7–21.

52 By the early 1920s, the difficult economic situation of the people of Bisrampur had become evident, facts noted by the missionaries. See F. A. Goetsch, Annual Report, Bisrampur, 1922, pp. 2–4, ARM, EAL.

53 Interview with Mr. Daulat, Bisrampur, March 1996.

54 E. W. Menzel, Annual Report, Bisrampur, 1938, p. 6, ARM, EAL.

55 T. Twente, Annual Report, Bisrampur, 1929, p. 3, ARM, EAL; J. C. Koenig, Baitalpur, to T. Twente, Bisrampur, 21 June 1929, BMF, EAL.

56 T. Twente, Annual Report, Bisrampur, 1929, p. 3, ARM, EAL.

57 J. C. Koenig, Note regarding the Bisrampur jungle, Bisrampur, 5 May 1929, p. 1, BMF, EAL.

58 Noordass and Powel, Christian members, Bisrampur, to Chairman Saheb (?), 29 March 1934, BMF, EAL.

59 Dube, *Untouchable Pasts*.

60 E. W. Menzel, Note on Bisrampur, 1940, p. 3, BMF, EAL.

61 Ibid., 4.

62 M. P. Davis, Report of the Bisrampur church trouble, 28 February 1934, p. 1, BMF, EAL.

63 Ibid.

64 Application from Immanuel Church, Bisrampur, to P. A. Menzel, Secretary, American Evangelical Mission, U.S.A., 25 October 1933, p. 1, BMF, EAL.

65 Ibid.

66 Bisrampur congregation to the Home Board in the U.S., 14 December 1933, BMF, EAL.

67 Application from Immanuel Church, Bisrampur, to P. A. Menzel, Secretary, American Evangelical Mission, U.S.A., 25 October 1933, BMF, EAL.

68 E. W. Menzel, Note on Bisrampur, 1940, p. 4, BMF, EAL.

69 For instance, see Shahid Amin, Gandhi as Mahatma: Gorakhpur District, eastern UP, in *Subaltern Studies III: Writings on South Asian History and Society*, edited by Ranajit Guha (Delhi: Oxford University Press, 1984), 1–55. Consider also the discussion in chapters 4 and 5.

70 Herzfeld, As in your own house, 76.

71 On the critical constitution of women as signs in different contexts, see Rosalind O'Hanlon, "Issues of widowhood: Gender and resistance in colonial western India," in *Contesting Power: Resistance and Everyday Social Relations in South Asia*, edited by Douglas Haynes and Gyan Prakash (Delhi: Oxford University Press, 1991), 62–108; and Lata Mani, *Contentious Traditions: The Debate on Sati in Colonial India* (Berkeley: University of California Press, 1998). See also Chatterjee, *The Nation and Its Fragments*, chapters 6 and 7.

72 The annual and quarterly reports of the missionaries frequently referred to this problem. The missionary Goetsch provided a detailed comment. See F. A. Goetsch, Annual Report, Bisrampur, 1925, pp. 2–3, ARM, EAL.

73 Application from Immanuel Church, Bisrampur, to P. A. Menzel, Secretary, American Evangelical Mission, U.S.A., 25 October 1933, BMF, EAL.

74 Bisrampur congregation to the Home Board in the U.S., 14 December 1933, BMF, EAL.

75 Ibid.

76 Ibid.

77 Application from Immanuel Church, Bisrampur, to P. A. Menzel, Secretary, American Evangelical Mission, U.S.A., 25 October 1933, BMF, EAL.

78 Ibid.

79 In using the notions of evangelical governmentality and pastoral power, I am extending Foucault's categories to modalities of missionary authority and their subversion in colonial contexts. See Foucault, "Governmentality."

80 Bisrampur congregation to the Home Board in the U.S., 14 December 1933, BMF, EAL; Note on missionaries, by Premdas Munshi, no date, BMF, EAL.

81 Immanuel Church, Bisrampur, to P. A. Menzel, Secretary, American Evangelical Mission, U.S.A., 25 October 1933, BMF, EAL.

82 Bisrampur congregation to the Home Board in the U.S., 14 December 1933, BMF, EAL; Note on reasons for a split in the Bisrampur congregation, no date, BMF, EAL.

83 Bisrampur congregation to the Home Board in the U.S., 25 October 1933, BMF, EAL.

84 J. C. Koenig, Annual Report, Bisrampur, 1934, p. 3, ARM, EAL.

85 M. P. Davis, Report of the Bisrampur church trouble, p. 1; Minutes of the first meeting of the Immanuel mandli, 10 August 1933, BMF, EAL.

86 Minutes of the first meeting of the Immanuel mandli, 10 August 1933, BMF, EAL.

87 Immanuel Church, Bisrampur, to P. A. Menzel, Secretary, American Evangelical Mission, U.S.A., 25 October 1933, BMF, EAL.

88 J. Gass, Raipur, to F. A. Goetsch, Raipur, 22 March 1934, BMF, EAL.

89 M. P. Davis, Report of the Bisrampur church trouble, 28 February 1934, p. 2, BMF, EAL.

90 On the different missionary bodies, all Protestant, in Chhattisgarh and their cooperation in an organization called the Chhattisgarh Missionary Association, see Seybold, *God's Guiding Hand*, 59–60; and Lapp, *The Mennonite Church in India*, 168–70.

91 Dube, *Untouchable Pasts*.

92 J. C. Koenig, Bisrampur, to F. A. Goetsch, St. Louis, 22 January 1935, BMF, EAL.

93 Ibid; Memo of the deputy commissioner, Raipur, 3 November 1939, CPG Political and Military Department, Confidential, no. 298, 1939, MPSRR.

94 J. Purti, Annual Congregational Report, Bisrampur, 1929, ARM, EAL.

95 J. C. Koenig, Annual Report, Bisrampur, 1930, p. 3, ARM, EAL.

96 J. Purti, Annual Congregational Report, Bisrampur, 1929, ARM, EAL.

97 M. P. Davis, Report of the Bisrampur church trouble, 28 February 1934, p. 1, BMF, EAL.

98 Ibid.

99 J. C. Koenig, First Quarterly Report, Bisrampur, 1935, p. 2, QRM, EAL.

100 Premdas Jacob, Bisrampur, to the Board of Foreign Missions, Evangelical Synod of North America, 17 April 1935, BMF, EAL.

101 Ibid.

102 Ibid.

103 J. C. Koenig, Bisrampur, to F. A. Goetsch, St. Louis, 22 January 1935, BMF, EAL.

104 Ibid.

105 J. C. Koenig, Annual Report, Bisrampur, 1935, p. 2, ARM, EAL.

106 Premdas Jacob, Bisrampur, to F. A. Goetsch, camp Baitalpur, 15 February 1936, BMF, EAL.

107 Earlier, "people had a desire to educate their children and were interested in Church, Sunday School and religious matters, they zealously carried out their duties and wanted the improvement of the congregation." However, "the condition of the present congregation between 1927 and 1935 makes us want to cry, [and] after the workers trained by you die our condition will become like our ancestors before they became Christians"

(S. Tilis, Ganeshpur, to F. A. Goetsch, camp Bisrampur, 4 February 1936). The letter carried 135 other signatures.

108 Ibid.
109 Ibid.
110 Premdas Jacob, Bisrampur, to F. A. Goetsch, camp Baitalpur, 15 February 1936, BMF, EAL.
111 S. Tilis, Ganeshpur, to F. A. Goetsch, camp Bisrampur, 4 February 1936, BMF, EAL.
112 E. W. Menzel, Note on Bisrampur, 1940, p. 7, BMF, EAL.
113 Ibid.; J. C. Koenig, Annual Report, Bisrampur, 1937, p. 3, ARM, EAL; E. W. Menzel, Annual Report, Bisrampur, 1938, p. 6, ARM, EAL.
114 Baur, Annual Report, Bisrampur, 1940, p. 3; Baur, Second Quarterly Report, Bisrampur, 1941, p. 2; Baur, Annual Report, Bisrampur, 1942, pp. 3–4, all in ARM, EAL.
115 J. C. Koenig, Annual Report, Bisrampur, 1937, pp. 3–5, ARM, EAL; E. W. Menzel, Annual Report, Bisrampur, 1940, pp. 2–4, ARM, EAL.
116 Baur, Annual Report, Bisrampur, 1945, pp. 2–6, ARM, EAL. All the annual reports of the missionaries stationed in Bisrampur between 1940 and 1950 mention these problems.
117 E. W. Menzel, Annual Report, Bisrampur, 1951, p. 2, ARM, EAL.
118 Demands of Immanuel Church to American Evangelical Mission, July 1955, BMF, EAL (circular in Hindi).

3 Telling Tales

1 By "rape," Sattar meant illicit sexual relationships between men and women.
2 Simon Schama, The Embarrassment of Riches: An Interpretation of Dutch Culture in the Golden Age (New York: Knopf, 1988), 4.
3 Ranajit Guha, "Chandra's Death," in Subaltern Studies V: Writings on South Asian History and Society, edited by Ranajit Guha (Delhi: Oxford University Press, 1987), 140.
4 Here I am drawing on Ranajit Guha's emphasis on "pick[ing] up the traces of subaltern life in its passage through time" but combining it with a conceptual salience of the "everyday" as a critical analytical perspective (ibid., 138). See David Warren Sabean, Property, Production, and Family in Neckarhausen, 1700–1870 (Cambridge: Cambridge University Press, 1990); David Warren Sabean, Kinship in Neckarhausen, 1700–1870 (Cambridge: Cambridge University Press, 1998); de Certeau, The Practice of Everyday Life; and Alf Ludtke, ed., The History of Everyday Life: Reconstructing Historical Experiences and Ways of Life (Princeton: Princeton University Press, 1995).
5 Carlo Ginzburg has drawn our attention to the significance for historical reconstruction of a gap between a dominant, convicting official voice and wide-ranging subaltern responses and utterances. However, it should be clear that the gaps and discrepancies in my sources are different from those elaborated by him. See Carlo Ginzburg, The Cheese and the Worms: The Cosmos of a Sixteenth Century Miller (Baltimore: Johns Hopkins University Press, 1980); and The Night Battles: Witchcraft and Agrarian Cults in the Sixteenth and Seventeenth Centuries (New York: Penguin, 1983). See also David Warren Sabean, Power in the Blood: Popular Culture and Village Discourse in Early Modern Germany (Cambridge: Cambridge University Press, 1984).
6 Only after presenting my accounts of two village disputes will I offer tentative observations about the exercise of power through the judicial discourse and practices of the colonial state. My main concern is to tell the larger story from a perspective that foregrounds the players and the protagonists in the village dramas.

7   The reconstruction of this dispute is based on *King Emperor v. Samaru and others*, ST 33 of 1927, DSC RR.

8   Judgment, ST 33 of 1927, DSC RR. The records do not specify the precise nature of the kin relations between Chandu and Dukhiram, but both the judgment and the depositions of witnesses emphasized that kinship between them bound the two groups.

9   I have culled the details of the pattern of landholding in Karkhena from Bandobast no. 124, Patwari Halka no. 57, Kharkhena (Karkhena), Group Lakhatpur, 1928–29, BDVSR, BCRR.

10   On churi as a form of secondary marriage, especially among the Satnamis, see Dube, *Untouchable Pasts*, 100–101, 108–13, 132–40. For a discussion of sex and marriage, including churi, in contemporary Chhattisgarh, see Jonathan Parry, "Ankalu's Errant Wife: Sex, Marriage, and Industry in Contemporary Chhattisgarh," *Modern Asian Studies* 35 (2001): 783–820.

11   Deposition of Dukhiram, DPW No. 11, ST 33 of 1927, DSC RR; Deposition of Hagru, DPW No. 5, ST 33 of 1927, DSC RR. According to Dukhiram, Samaru and Chandu had made this statement, while Hagru said that all the male members of Chandu's family—Chandu, Samaru, Sheodayal, and Ramdayal—had made it.

12   Deposition of Dukhiram, DPW No. 11, ST 33 of 1927, DSC RR; Deposition of Kasi, DPW No. 16, ST 33 of 1927, DSC RR. According to Dukhiram, all the male members of Chandu's family—Chandu, Samaru, Shedayal, and Ramdayal—had made the statement, while Hagru said that it was only Samaru and Chandu.

13   Deposition of Kodu, DPW No. 14, ST 33 of 1927, DSC RR.

14   EA Chandu, ST 33 of 1927, DSC RR.

15   EA Samaru, ST 33 of 1927, DSC RR.

16   See, for example, Sabean, *Power in the Blood*; and Gerald Sider, "Christmas Mumming in Outport Newfoundland," *Past and Present* 71 (1976): 102–25.

17   S. C. Dube, "The Folksongs of Chhattisgarh," manuscript.

18   Dube, *Untouchable Pasts*; Guha, "Chandra's Death"; *Kosa: A Village Survey, Census of India 1961*, vol. 8, Madhya Pradesh, part 6, Village Survey Monographs no. 9 (Bhopal: Government Press, 1967).

19   Dube, *Untouchable Pasts*.

20   EA Chandu, ST 33 of 1927, DSC RR.

21   Michel Foucault, *Discipline and Punish: The Birth of the Prison* (London: Penguin, 1977).

22   For related, critical observations, see Martha Kaplan, *Neither Cargo nor Cult: Ritual Politics and the Colonial Imagination in Fiji* (Durham: Duke University Press, 1995), 203–8.

23   Dube, *Untouchable Pasts*.

24   The reconstruction of this dispute is based on *King Emperor v. Balli and thirteen others*, ST 34 of 1940, DSC RR.

25   Table 1 contains the caste, name, father's name and approximate age of the "accused" within the trial. Figure 3 shows the relationships among the accused Satnamis, and figure 4 represents the relationships among the Satnamis who were "assaulted." In figure 3, the names of the accused and in figure 4 the names of prosecution witnesses are underlined, while the names of the other people who feature in these figures often crop up in the narrative. I was unable to trace the names of the women of the two groups of Satnamis from the depositions of witnesses and the judgment, and therefore only the relationships among the men appear in the two figures. Did not the exclusion of women from the colonial judicial narrative stand in the way of its comprehending the relationships among the people it was subjecting to "law and order?" I return to this question later.

26 Details were culled from Bandobast no. 334, Patwari Halka no. 230, Darri (Sarhar), Group Jaijaipur, 1929–30, BDVSR, BCRR.

27 DPW No. 11, Ratan, ST 34 of 1940, DSC RR.

28 In the panchayat, Sahas Satnami, Balaram Teli, Kunjram Nai, Budga Raut, Balli Bhaina, and Balmukund Bhaina acted as the panchas (ibid.).

29 Ibid.

30 DPW No. 1, Awadh, ST 34 of 1940, DSC RR.

31 DPW No. 10, Gajaraj, ST 34 of 1940, DSC RR.

32 DPW No. 1, Awadh, ST 34 of 1940, DSC RR.

33 Ibid.

34 "In the panchayat held over the elopement I was informed by my father, Malikram, that in all ten of us were excommunicated. We considered that we were excommunicated without any fault" (ibid.).

35 Two examples: the 10.93 acres of land owned by Gajaraj Satnami were distributed over forty-three holdings; only three of these were over an acre. Likewise, Balaram Brahman's 19.03 acres comprised sixty-four holdings (Bandobast no. 334, Patwari Halka no. 230, Darri [Sarhar], Group Jaijaipur, 1929–30, BDVSR, BCRR). For a discussion of issues of the fragmentation of landholdings in Chhattisgarh, see Dube, *Untouchable Pasts*, 31, 82–84.

36 DPW No. 11, Ratan, ST 34 of 1940, DSC RR.

37 DPW No. 1, Awadh, ST 34 of 1940, DSC RR.

38 Ibid.

39 DPW No. 12, Gorakh, ST 34 of 1940, DSC RR; DPW No. 1, Awadh, ST 34 of 1940, DSC RR.

40 DPW No. 1, Awadh, ST 34 of 1940, DSC RR.

41 DPW No. 11, Ratan, ST 34 of 1940, DSC RR.

42 DPW No. 9, Bunkuwar, ST 34 of 1940, DSC RR.

43 J, ST 34 of 1940, DSC RR.

44 See, for instance, Erin P. Moore, "Gender, Power, and Legal Pluralism," *American Ethnologist* 20 (1993): 522–42; and Leela Dube, "Conflict and Compromise: Devolution and Disposal of Property in a Matrilineal Muslim Society," *Economic and Political Weekly* 29 (1994): 1273–84.

45 See, for example, Das, *Critical Events*; Saurabh Dube, "Idioms of Authority and Engendered Agendas: The Satnami Mahasabha, Chhattisgarh, 1925–50," *Indian Economic and Social History Review* 30 (1993): 383–411; Dube, *Untouchable Pasts*; and Ishita Banerjee Dube, "Taming Traditions: Legalities and Histories in Twentieth Century Orissa," in *Subaltern Studies X: Writings on South Asian History and Society*, edited by Gautam Bhadra, Gyan Prakash, and Susie Tharu (New Delhi: Oxford University Press, 1999), 98–125. See also Upendra Baxi, "The State's Emissary: The Place of Law in Subaltern Studies," in *Subaltern Studies VII: Writings on South Asian History and Society*, edited by Partha Chatterjee and Gyanendra Pandey (Delhi: Oxford University Press, 1992), 257–64; and Veena Das, "Subaltern as Perspective," in *Subaltern Studies VI: Writings on South Asian History and Society*, edited by Ranajit Guha (Delhi: Oxford University Press, 1989), 310–24.

46 I discuss the crucial place of metaphors of colonial governance and symbols of state in the structuring of caste dominance, the constitution of community, and the making of alternative legalities and moralities in Dube, *Untouchable Pasts*.

47 Dube, "Idioms of Authority and Engendered Agendas."

48 Dube, *Untouchable Pasts*.

49 Bandobast no. 334, Patwari Halka no. 230, Darri (Sarhar), Group Jaijaipur, 1929–30, BDVSR, BCRR.

50 The fight on the morning of 7 May 1940, for example, had brought up the issues of fishing and the washing of buffaloes by Malikram and Awadhram in the pond. Now, while there was no ban on fishing in the pond near Darri due to a proclamation by the malguzar, and other families did fish there, members of Gajaraj's group had not fished in Darri that year. This could have been one of the restrictions imposed on Gajaraj's group.

51 At the panchayat, "the panchas were not consulted and I do not know if they had consulted each other but Kunjbehari gave out that we were fined. The panchas had not gone aside to consult each other" (DPW no. 1, Awadh, ST 34 of 1940, DSC RR).

52 J, ST 34 of 1940, DSC RR.

53 Gayatri Chakravorty Spivak, "Can the subaltern speak?" in *Marxism and the Interpretation of Culture*, edited by Cary Nelson and Lawrence Grossberg (Urbana: University of Illinois Press, 1988), 271–313. See also Kamala Viswesaran, "Small Speeches, Subaltern Gender: Nationalist Ideology and Its Historiography," in *Subaltern Studies IX: Writings on South Asian History and Society*, edited by Shahid Amin and Dipesh Chakrabarty (Delhi: Oxford University Press, 1996), 83–125.

54 Dube, *Untouchable Pasts*.

55 Guha, "Chandra's Death."

56 Leela Dube, "On the Construction of Gender: Hindu Girls in Patrilineal India," *Economic and Political Weekly* 23 (1988): (WS) 11–19; Joyce B. Flueckiger, *Gender and Genre in the Folklore of Middle India* (Ithaca: Cornell University Press, 1996); Gloria G. Raheja and Ann Gold, *Listen to the Heron's Words: Reimagining Gender and Kinship in North India* (Berkeley: University of California Press, 1994); William Sax, *Mountain Goddess: Gender and Politics in a Himalayan Pilgrimage* (New York: Oxford University Press, 1991); Dube, *Untouchable Pasts*; Erin P. Moore, *Gender, Law, and Resistance in India* (Tucson: University of Arizona Press, 1998).

4 Entitlements and Enmities

1 See for example, Shahid Amin, "Approver's Testimony, Judicial Discourse: The Case of Chauri Chaura," in *Subaltern Studies V: Writings on South Asian History and Society*, edited by Ranajit Guha (Delhi: Oxford University Press, 1987), 166–203; Banerjee Dube, "Taming Traditions"; Baxi, "The State's Emissary"; Bernard Cohn, "Law and the Colonial State in India," in *History and Power in the Study of the Law: New Directions in Legal Anthropology*, edited by June Starr and Jane Collier (Ithaca: Cornell University Press, 1989), 131–52; Das, *Critical Events*; Leela Dube, "In the Mother's Line: Structure and Change in Lakshadweep," report prepared for the Indian Council of Social Science Research, New Delhi, 1991; Guha, "Chandra's Death"; Kunal M. Parker, "A Corporation of Superior Prostitutes: Anglo-Indian Legal Conceptions of Temple Dancing," *Modern Asian Studies* 32 (1998): 559–633; Moore, *Gender, Law, and Resistance*; Singha, *A Despotism of Law*; Anand Yang, ed., *Crime and Criminality in British India* (Tucson: University of Arizona Press, 1985); Anupama Rao, "Problems of Violence, States of Terror: Torture in Colonial India," in *Discipline and the Other Body*, edited by Anupama Rao and Steven Pierce, special issue of *Interventions: Journal of Postcolonial Studies* 3 (2001): 186–205; and Chatterjee, *A Princely Impostor*. See also Alavi, *The Sepoys and the Company*, 95–154; Amin, *Event, Metaphor, Memory*; Ishita Banerjee Dube, *Divine Affairs: Religion, Pilgrimage and the State in Colonial and Postcolonial India* (Shimla: Indian Institute of Advanced Study, 2001); Dube, *Untouchable Pasts*; and Bernard Cohn, *An Anthropologist among the Historians and Other Essays* (Delhi: Oxford University Press, 1987), 463–82, 554–631.

2 These analyses follow on my discussions of colonial cultures in the previous chapters

while intersecting with work in the anthropology of the law concerning the multilayered encounters between distinct but connected matrices of legalities and illegalities, elaborating emphases on processes and power. See, for example, Sally Engle Merry, "Anthropology, Law, and Transnational Processes," *Annual Review of Anthropology* 21 (1992): 357–79; Merry, *Colonizing Hawai'i*; Starr and Collier, *History and Power in the Study of the Law*; John Comaroff and Simon Roberts, *Rules and Processes: The Cultural Logic of Dispute in an African Context* (Chicago: University of Chicago Press, 1981); and Sally Falk Moore, *Social Facts and Fabrications: Customary Law in Kilimanjaro, 1880–1980* (Cambridge: Cambridge University Press, 1986).

3 Dube, *Untouchable Pasts*.

4 The reconstruction of this dispute is based on *King Emperor v. Rendhia and six others*, ST 22 of 1932, DSC RR.

5 Bandobast No. 613, Patwari Halka No. 249, Murlidih, Jaijaipur Group, Janjgir Tahsil, 1929–30, BDVSR, BCRR.

6 DPW No. 2, Govinda, ST 22 of 1932, DSC RR.

7 *Report on the Resettlement of the Khalsa of the Bilaspur District, 1927–32* (Nagpur: Government Press, 1932), 32.

8 Ibid., 29, emphasis mine.

9 DPW No. 1, Jagat, ST 22 of 1932, DSC RR.

10 J, ST 22 of 1932, DSC RR.

11 Ibid.

12 DPW No. 6, Baijnathdass, ST 22 of 1932, DSC RR. Baijnathdass was one of the two approvers in the trial (see table 2). The conclusion to this chapter discusses the wider implications of the "approver's testimony" within judicial discourse in the context of colonial cultures.

13 DPW No. 1, Jagat, ST 22 of 1932, DSC RR.

14 J, ST 22 of 1932, DSC RR.

15 DPW No. 6, Baijnathdass, ST 22 of 1932, DSC RR.

16 DPW No. 5, Mohan, ST 22 of 1932, DSC RR.

17 Ibid.

18 *Report on the Resettlement of the Khalsa of the Bilaspur District, 1927–32*, 32.

19 DPW No. 2, Govinda, ST 22 of 1932, DSC RR.

20 DPW No. 5, Mohan, ST 22 of 1932, DSC RR.

21 DPW No. 13, Balakram, ST 22 of 1932, DSC RR.

22 Ibid.

23 Ibid.

24 On the "centrality" of malguzars, their relationships with the service castes, and the nature of their power in the caste order within village life in Chhattisgarh, see Dube, *Untouchable Pasts*, 87–99.

25 DPW No. 10, Budga, ST 22 of 1932, DSC RR.

26 DPW No. 13, Balakram, ST 22 of 1932, DSC RR.

27 See J. P. Sharma, "A Study of the Nationalist Movement in Chhattisgarh, 1920–47," Ph.D. diss., Ravi Shankar University, Raipur, 1974, chapter 5; Ashok Shukla, "History of the Freedom Movement in Chhattisgarh, 1857–1947," Ph.D. diss., Ravi Shankar University, Raipur, 1972, chapter 6.

28 Amin, "Gandhi as Mahatma"; Gyanendra Pandey, "Peasant Revolt and Indian Nationalism: The Peasant Movement in Awadh, 1919–22," in *Subaltern Studies I: Writings on South Asian History and Society*, edited by Ranajit Guha (Delhi: Oxford University Press, 1982), 143–97. See also Dube, "Introduction: Terms That Bind."

29 DPW No. 5, Mohan, ST 22 of 1932, DSC RR.

30 Antonio Gramsci, *Selections from Cultural Writings* (London: Lawrence and Wishart, 1985), 193.

31 DPW No. 1, Jagat, ST 22 of 1932, DSC RR.

32 DPW No. 5, Mohan, ST 22 of 1932, DSC RR.

33 DPW No. 13, Balakram, ST 22 of 1932, DSC RR.

34 DPW No. 5, Mohan, ST 22 of 1932, DSC RR.

35 DPW No. 2, Govinda, ST 22 of 1932, DSC RR.

36 DPW No. 1, Jagat, ST 22 of 1932, DSC RR.

37 DPW No. 2, Govinda, ST 22 of 1932, DSC RR.

38 DPW No. 1, Jagat, ST 22 of 1932, DSC RR.

39 Ibid.

40 DPW No. 5, Mohan, ST 22 of 1932, DSC RR.

41 J, ST 22 of 1932, DSC RR.

42 EA, Rendhia, ST 22 of 1932, DSC RR.

43 The reconstruction of this dispute is based on *King Emperor v. Santram*, ST 1 of 1939, DSC RR.

44 At issue are not absolute and inalienable rights to private property in land. Under the tenurial and property arrangements in agrarian Chhattisgarh, the village proprietor(s) notionally owned the village, and he or she paid the revenue demand made on the village to the agencies of the colonial state. The village proprietors' absolute rights to property, however, extended only to their own farms. As for the other agriculturalists—except for a very small number of "absolute occupancy tenants"—they "owned" their land and could sell and mortage it, albeit under particular rules and conditions. Yet they had to pay rent to the village proprietor. These facts help explain this dispute. More details on the property and tenurial arrangements in Chhattisgarh are contained in Crispin Bates, "Regional Dependence and Rural Development in Central India, 1820–1930," Ph.D. diss., University of Cambridge, 1984; and Dube, *Untouchable Pasts*, 47–57, 79–87.

45 Bandobast No. 59, Patwari Halka No. 229, Kapisda, Birra Group, Janjgir Tahsil, 1929–30, BDVSR, BCRR.

46 This account draws on the depositions of witnesses for the prosecution and the judgment, ST 1 of 1939, DSC RR.

47 EA, Santram, ST 1 of 1939, DSC RR.

48 The entire set of DPW, ST 1 of 1939, DSC RR, agreed on this account.

49 EA, Santram, ST 1 of 1939, DSC RR.

50 DA, Santram, ST 1 of 1939, DSC RR.

51 The receipt passed by Sahasram in favor of Bisram was Exhibit P–11. The unregistered deed of sale by means of which Santram sold the tenancy rights to his fields to Bisram was Exhibit P–4. The court documents delivering Santram's fields to the Dhimar brothers were Exhibits P–16 and P–17. All are in ST 1 of 1939, DSC RR.

52 This pattern of migration—particularly characteristic of the Satnamis during the interwar period—is discussed in Dube, *Untouchable Pasts*, 85–88.

53 For a discussion of the wide-ranging politics of "pieces of paper" in a different context, see John D. Kelly, *A Politics of Virtue: Hinduism, Sexuality, and Countercolonial Discourse in Fiji* (Chicago: University of Chicago Press, 1991), particularly 27–29.

54 EA, Santram, ST 1 of 1939, DSC RR.

55 DPW No. 5, Patiram, ST 1 of 1939, DSC RR.

56 DPW No. 6, Judawan, ST 1 of 1939, DSC RR.

57 DPW No. 2, Bidyaram, ST 1 of 1939, DSC RR.
58 Ibid.
59 DPW No. 3, Santram, ST 1 of 1939, DSC RR.
60 J, ST 1 of 1939, DSC RR.
61 For wider considerations of the exclusions and binds between reason and emotion, see Catherine Lutz, *Unnatural Emotions: Everyday Sentiments on a Micronesian Atoll and Their Challenge to Western Theory* (Chicago: University of Chicago Press, 1988). See also Renato Rosaldo, *Culture and Truth: The Remaking of Social Analysis* (Boston: Beacon Press, 1987); Owen M. Lynch, ed., *Divine Passions: The Social Construction of Emotions in India* (Berkeley: University of California Press, 1990); and William Reddy, "Emotional Liberty: Politics and History in the Anthropology of Emotions," *Cultural Anthropology* 14 (1999): 256–88.
62 However, in two essays of 1965 Dumont also points out that even in Euro-American social systems individualism is central largely to politico-economic institutions and aspects of holism exist as underemphasized elements in other arenas. Moreover, it was Dumont's recognition of the difference between South Indian kinship systems of alliance and affinity and anthropological systems of genealogical kinship of descent that first led him to explore the contrasts between Western and Indian cultural systems. See Louis Dumont, "World Renunciation in Indian Religions," in *Religion/Politics and History in India* (Paris: Mouton, 1970), 33–60; "Religion, Politics and Society in the Individualistic Universe," *Proceedings of the Royal Anthropological Institute* (1970): 33; *Homo Hierarchicus: The Caste System and Its Implications* (Chicago: University of Chicago Press, 1970); "The Modern Conception of the Individual: Notes on its Genesis," *Contributions to Indian Sociology* 8 (1965): 13–61; and "The Functional Equivalents of the Individual in Caste Society," *Contributions to Indian Sociology* 8 (1965): 85–99.
63 McKim Marriott, "Hindu Transactions: Diversity Without Dualism," in *Transaction and Meaning: Directions in the Anthropology of Exchange and Symbolic Behavior*, edited by Bruce Kapferer (Philadelphia: Institute for the Study of Human Issues, 1976), 109–42; McKim Marriott and Ronald Inden, "Toward an Ethnosociology of South Asian Caste Systems," in *The New Wind: Changing Identities in South Asia*, edited by Kenneth David (The Hague: Mouton, 1976), 227–38.
64 Carter himself imaginatively discussed "ranked varieties of personhood" in Maharashtra—relating these closely to rites of passage—a discussion complemented by Madan's exploration of personhood in the context of kinship. See Steve Barnett, "Coconuts and Gold," *Contributions to Indian Sociology*, n.s., 10 (1976): 133–56; Lina Fruzzetti, Akos Ostor, and Steve Barnett, "The Cultural Construction of the Person in Bengal and Tamilnadu," in *Concepts of Person: Kinship, Caste and Marriage in India*, edited by Akos Ostor, Lina Fruzzetti, and Steve Barnett (Delhi: Oxford University Press, 1983), 8–30; Lina Fruzzetti and Akos Ostor, "Bad Blood in Bengal," in Ostor, Fruzzetti, and Barnett, *Concepts of Person*, 31–55; Anthony Carter, "Hierarchy and the Concept of the Person in Western India," in Ostor, Fruzzetti, and Barnett, *Concepts of Person*, 118–42; and T. N. Madan, "The Ideology of the Householder among the Kashmiri Pandits," in Ostor, Fruzzetti, and Barnett, *Concepts of Person*, 99–117.
65 Valentine Daniel, *Fluid Signs: Being a Person the Tamil Way* (Berkeley: University of California Press, 1983), 2–3 and passim.
66 Margaret Trawick, *Notes on Love in a Tamil Family* (Berkeley: University of California Press, 1990).
67 Mattison Mines, *Public Faces, Private Voices: Community and Individuality in South Asia* (Berkeley: University of California Press, 1994), 12 and passim.

68 Guha, *Dominance without Hegemony*, 100 and passim.
69 Consider Eugene Irschick, *Dialogue and History: Constructing South India, 1795–1895* (Berkeley: University of California Press, 1994).
70 Amin, "Approver's Testimony, Judicial Discourse."
71 Consider, too, Baxi, "The State's Emissary."

5 Subaltern Subjects

1 See also, Prakash, "Subaltern Studies as Postcolonial Criticism, 1476–79"; and Ranajit Guha, "Introduction" to *A Subaltern Studies Reader, 1986–1995*, edited by Ranajit Guha (Minneapolis: University of Minnesota Press, 1997), ix–xv.
2 From the early 1980s to the mid-1990s, the subaltern studies editorial collective consisted of Shahid Amin, David Arnold, Gautam Bhadra, Dipesh Chakrabarty, Partha Chatterjee, Ranajit Guha, David Hardiman, Gyanendra Pandey, and Sumit Sarkar. A few years ago, after the reorganization of the collective, Shahid Amin, Gautam Bhadra, Partha Chatterjee, and Gyanendra Pandey became its core members. David Arnold, Dipesh Chakrabarty, and David Hardiman continue as advisory editors, joined in this capacity by Sudipta Kaviraj, Shail Mayaram, M. S. S. Pandian, Ajay Skaria, Gayatri Chakravorty Spivak, and Susie Tharu.
3 See the first six volumes of *Subaltern Studies*, edited by Ranajit Guha; Chatterjee and Pandey, *Subaltern Studies VII*; David Arnold and David Hardiman, eds., *Subaltern Studies VIII: Essays in Honor of Ranajit Guha* (Delhi: Oxford University Press, 1994); Amin and Chakrabarty, *Subaltern Studies IX*; and Bhadra, Prakash, and Tharu, *Subaltern Studies X*. See also Ranajit Guha and Gayatri Chakravorty Spivak, eds., *Selected Subaltern Studies* (New York: Oxford University Press, 1988); and Guha, *A Subaltern Studies Reader*.
4 Ranajit Guha, Preface to Guha, *Subaltern Studies I*, viii.
5 For the finest of these earlier critiques, see Rosalind O'Hanlon, Recovering the subject: *Subaltern Studies* and histories of resistance in colonial South Asia, *Modern Asian Studies* 22 (1988): 189–224. As is generally known, writing on subaltern studies has become an academic industry, and I only provide the most important indicative references here. Several significant critical interventions in subaltern studies are introduced and brought together in David Ludden, ed., *Reading Subaltern Studies: Perspectives on History, Society, and Culture in South Asia* (New Delhi: Permanent Black, 2001), a book that also contains a bibliography of writings related to subaltern studies from the early 1980s through the late 1990s.
6 Sumit Sarkar, "The Decline of the Subaltern in Subaltern Studies," in *Writing Social History* (Delhi: Oxford University Press, 1996), 88–102; Ramchandra Guha, "Subaltern and Bhadralok Studies," *Economic and Political Weekly* 30 (1995): 2056–58. See also Ludden, *Reading Subaltern Studies*, chaps. 8, 12, and 13.
7 Within the project, theoretical and critical discussions of subaltern as a category and of the orientations in subaltern studies more generally include Veena Das, "Subaltern as Perspective," in Guha, *Subaltern Studies VI*, 310–24; Gayatri Chakravorty Spivak, "Subaltern Studies: Deconstructing Historiography," in Guha, *Subaltern Studies IV*, 330–63; Dipesh Chakrabarty, "Invitation to a Dialogue," in Guha, *Subaltern Studies IV*, 364–76; Dipesh Chakrabarty, "Marx after Marxism: A Subaltern Historian's Perspective," *Economic and Political Weekly* 28 (1993): 1094–96; Dipesh Chakrabarty, "Minority Histories, Subaltern Pasts," *Economic and Political Weekly* 33 (1998): 473–79; Partha Chatterjee, "Peasant, Politics and Historiography: A Response," *Social Scientist* 11 (1985): 58–65; and

Guha, "Introduction" to *A Subaltern Studies Reader, 1986–1995*, ix–xxii. See also Prakash, "Writing Post-orientalist Histories," 353–88.

8   Sarkar, "The Decline of the Subaltern"; Prakash, "Subaltern Studies as Postcolonial Criticism." While the very nature of the discussion in this chapter distinguishes my understanding of subaltern studies from the emphases of these key writings, it also reveals critical continuities with the orientations highlighted by Gyan Prakash.

9   Throughout this chapter, I use the terms *people's history* and *history from below* interchangeably.

10 See particularly David Lloyd, "Outside History: Irish New Histories and the 'Subalternity Effect,'" in Amin and Chakrabarty, *Subaltern Studies IX*, 261–80; Cooper, "Conflict and Connection"; Florencia Mallon, "The Promise and Dilemma of Subaltern Studies: Perspectives from Latin America," *American Historical Review* 99 (1994): 1495–1515; Saurabh Dube "Introducción: Temas e intersecciones de los pasados pocoloniales," in Dube, *Pasados poscoloniales*, 17–98; Rodríguez, *The Latin American Subaltern Studies Reader*; and Beverley, *Subalternity and Representation*.

11 Arguably, such a shift is indexed on somewhat different registers by recent writings within subaltern studies that elaborate the politics and cultures of subordinate groups. For example, Banerjee Dube, "Taming traditions"; Mayaram, "Speech, Silence and the Making of Partition Violence in Mewat," in Amin and Chakrabarty, *Subaltern Studies IX*, 126–164; and Skaria, "Writing, Orality and Power." See also Indrani Chatterjee, "Colouring Subalternity: Slaves, Concubines, and Social Orphans in Early Colonial India," in Bhadra, Prakash, and Tharu, *Subaltern Studies X*, 49–97.

12 Dipesh Chakrabarty, "Subaltern Studies and postcolonial historiography," *Nepantla: Views from South* 1 (2000): 15; Ranajit Guha, *Elementary Aspects of Peasant Insurgency in Colonial India* (Delhi: Oxford University Press, 1983).

13 Peter Burke, *Popular Culture in Early Modern Europe* (New York: Harper and Row, 1978). See also Peter Burke, "People's History or Total History," in *People's History and Socialist Theory*, edited by Raphael Samuel (London: Routledge and Kegan Paul, 1981), 4–9.

14 Burke, "People's History or Total History," 5–6.

15 Histories from below have found diverse manifestations. Indicative, recent writings that discuss the genres of oral history, feminist history, microhistory, and historical anthropology, including the intersections of these orientations with emphases of histories from below, are contained in Peter Burke, ed., *New Perspectives on Historical Writing* (University Park: State University of Pennsylvania Press, 1992), particularly 1–66, 93–139; and Lynn Hunt, ed., *The New Cultural History* (Berkeley and Los Angeles: University of California Press, 1989). See also Aletta Biersack, ed., *Clio in Oceania: Toward a Historical Anthropology* (Washington, D.C.: Smithsonian, 1991); Bernard Cohn, *An Anthropologist among Historians and Other Essays* (Delhi: Oxford University Press, 1987), 18–77; and Edward Muir and Guido Ruggiero, eds., *Microhistory and the Lost Peoples of Europe*, translated by Eren Branch (Baltimore: Johns Hopkins University Press, 1991).

16 Two qualifications are pertinent to these examples. On one hand, I admit to following the authors that I discuss in positing a sharp contrast between their writing and earlier historical work. On the other, I am aware that the analytical emphases and historical claims of these historians have been variously questioned and exceeded by subsequent scholarship. Indeed, not only this chapter but all of *Stitches on Time* bears witness to rather distinct orientations toward questions of culture and issues of agency. This acknowledged, my effort here is to present the terms of debate and substantive achievements of such writing as a specific juncture in historiography.

17 The discussion of eighteenth-century popular culture in England that follows is based largely on the work of E. P. Thompson and Hans Medick. See E. P. Thompson, "Patrician Society, Plebian Culture," *Journal of Social History* 7 (1974): 382–405; E. P. Thompson, "Eighteenth Century English Society: Class Struggle Without Class," *Social History* 3 (1978): 133–65; E. P. Thompson, "Time, Work-discipline and Industrial Capitalism," *Past and Present* 38 (1967): 56–97; E. P. Thompson, "The Moral Economy of the English Crowd in the Eighteenth Century," *Past and Present* 50 (1971): 76–136; E. P. Thompson, *Whigs and Hunters* (Harmondsworth: Penguin, 1977); Hans Medick, "Plebian Culture in the Transition to Capitalism," in *Culture, Ideology and Politics*, edited by Raphael Samuel and Gareth Stedman Jones (London: Routledge and Kegan Paul, 1983), 84–113; and Hans Medick, "The Proto-industrial Family Economy," in *Industrialization before Industrialization*, edited by Peter Kriedte, Hans Medick, and Jürgen Schlumbohm (Cambridge: Cambridge University Press, 1981), 38–73.

18 Thompson, "Patrician Society, Plebian Culture," 393.

19 Thompson, "Eighteenth Century English Society," 163. See also Thompson, "Patrician Society, Plebian Culture."

20 Thompson, "The Moral Economy of the English Crowd in the Eighteenth Century."

21 Medick, "Plebian Culture in the Transition to Capitalism"; "The Proto-industrial Family Economy."

22 Specifically, I am arguing against the spectacular confrontation that Thompson sets up between a "tradition-bound" plebian culture and the "modern" force of a market economy. Here I draw on Medick's emphasis on the need to attend to plebian adaptations to the market even as I consider it imperative that we think through the pervasive tradition-modernity dichotomy.

23 Eugene D. Genovese, *Roll Jordan Roll: The World the Slaves Made* (New York: Pantheon, 1974).

24 Lawrence Levine, *Black Culture and Consciousness* (New York: Oxford University Press, 1977). For a more recent, related discussion, see Henry Louis Gates Jr., *The Signifying Monkey: A Theory of African-American Literary Criticism* (New York: Oxford University Press, 1988).

25 The notion of a "living space" is that of Genovese (*Roll Jordan Roll*).

26 See, particularly, Saidiya Hartman, *Scenes of Subjection: Terror, Slavery, and Self-Making in Nineteenth Century America* (New York: Oxford University Press, 1997).

27 T. L. Jackson Lears, "The Concept of Cultural Hegemony: Problems and Possibilities," *American Historical Review* 90 (1985): 567–93.

28 For example, E. P. Thompson wrote his seminal study of how the English working-class made itself, a work exemplifying orientations of histories from below, in the context of the emergence of journals such as the *Socialist Register* and the *New Left Review* and the emergent political struggles for nuclear disarmament, ventures in which Thompson participated. These were all attempts to forge alternative terms for an intellectual and practical politics of democratic socialism after the deep disenchantment with the Soviet invasion of Hungary in 1956. See E. P. Thompson, *The Making of the English Working Class* (New York: Vintage, 1963); and *The Poverty of Theory and Other Essays* (New York: Monthly Review Press, 1978).

29 Significant examples include the efforts centered around the History Workshop in the 1970s in Britain and the histories of "everyday life" in Germany. See Raphael Samuel, ed., *People's History and Socialist Theory* (London: Routledge and Kegan Paul, 1981); and Lüdtke, *The History of Everyday Life*. Challenges of "minority" histories today are discussed, for example, in Chakrabarty, "Minority Histories, Subaltern Pasts."

30 For example, see Ravinder Kumar, ed., *Essays on Gandhian Politics: The Rowlatt Satyagraha of 1919* (Oxford: Clarendon Press, 1971); Gyanendra Pandey, *The Ascendancy of the Congress in Uttar Pradesh, 1926–1934: A Study in Imperfect Mobilization* (Oxford: Clarendon Press, 1978); David Hardiman, *Peasant Nationalists of Gujarat: Kheda District, 1917–1934* (Delhi: Oxford University Press, 1981); Majid Siddiqi, *Agrarian Unrest in North India: The United Provinces, 1918–22* (New Delhi: Vikas, 1978); Kapil Kumar, *Peasants in Revolt: Tenants, Landlords, Congress and the Raj* (Delhi: Manohar, 1984); and Sarkar, *Modern India, 1885–1947*.

31 Ramchandra Guha, "Forestry and Social Protest in British Kumaun, c. 1893–1921," in Guha, *Subaltern Studies IV*, 54–100.

32 For example, see David Arnold, "Rebellious Hillmen: The Gudem-Rampa Uprisings," in Guha, *Subaltern Studies I*, 88–142; Stephen Heningham, "Quit India in Bihar and the Eastern United Province: The Dual Revolt," in Guha, *Subaltern Studies II*, 130–79; and Swapan Dasgupta, "Adivasi Politics in Midnapur, c. 1760–1924," in Guha, *Subaltern Studies IV*, 101–35. See also Gautan Bhadra, Two frontier uprisings in Mughal India, in Guha, *Subaltern Studies II*, 43–59.

33 Pandey, "Peasant Revolt and Indian Nationalism."

34 The background of the movement lay in a complex process of changes in agrarian relations in Awadh since 1856 (ibid., 144–47).

35 Ibid., 171.

36 Ibid., 166.

37 Ibid., 175.

38 Ibid., 166.

39 Sumit Sarkar, "The Conditions and Nature of Subaltern Militancy: Bengal from Swadeshi to Non-cooperation, c. 1905–22," in Guha, *Subaltern Studies III*, 305.

40 Ibid., 316.

41 Tanika Sarkar, "Jitu Santal's Movement in Malda, 1924–1932: A Study in Tribal Protest," in Guha, *Subaltern Studies IV*, 136–64.

42 On sanskritization, see M. N. Srinivas, *Religion and Society among the Coorgs of South India* (Oxford: Clarendon Press, 1952); M. N. Srinivas, *Social Change in Modern India* (Berkeley: University of California Press, 1966), 1–45; David Hardiman, *Coming of the Devi: Adivasi Assertion in Western India* (Delhi: Oxford University Press, 1987), 157–65; and Dube, "Myths, Symbols and Community." See also Dube, *Untouchable Pasts*.

43 Tanika Sarkar, "Jitu Santal's Movement in Malda, 1924–1932," 157–62.

44 Ibid., 163.

45 Shahid Amin, "Gandhi as Mahatma."

46 Ibid., 27–47.

47 Ibid., 48.

48 For example, see David Hardiman, "Adivasi Assertion in South Gujarat: The Devi Movement," in Guha, *Subaltern Studies III*, 196–230; David Hardiman, "From Custom to Crime: The Politics of Drinking in Colonial Gujarat," in Guha, *Subaltern Studies IV*, 165–228; Gautam Bhadra, "Four Rebels of Eighteen-Fifty-Seven," in Guha, *Subaltern Studies IV*, 229–75; and Gautam Bhadra, "The Mentality of Subalternity: Kantanama or Rajdharma," in Guha, *Subaltern Studies VI*, 54–91.

49 Guha, *Elementary Aspects of Peasant Insurgency in Colonial India*.

50 Ibid., 18.

51 A few examples of such visual signs include the *chappatis* (bread made of unleavened flour) circulated during the *jacquries* (rebellions) of 1857, the arrow of war used by the Kols, and the branch of the Sal tree circulated during the Santal rebellion, all in the 1850s.

52 For a critique of Guha's conception of rumor as speech, see Spivak, "Subaltern Studies: Deconstructing Historiography," 351–56. See also Skaria, "Writing, Orality, and Power," 14–18.

53 Guha, *Elementary Aspects of Peasant Insurgency in Colonial India*, 330.

54 For example, see Ranajit Guha, "The Prose of Counter-insurgency," in Guha, *Subaltern Studies II*, 1–42; Guha, "Chandra's Death"; Guha, *Elementary Aspects of Peasant Insurgency in Colonial India*; Shahid Amin, "Approver's Testimony, Judicial Discourse"; and Dipesh Chakrabarty, "Conditions for the Knowledge of Working-class Conditions: Employers, Government and the Jute Workers of Calcutta, 1890–1940," in Guha, *Subaltern Studies II*, 259–310.

55 This is forcefully underscored by the programmatic nature of Guha's initial formulations on the purpose of subaltern studies. See Guha, "Preface" to *Subaltern Studies I*, vii–viii; and Guha, "On Some Aspects of the Historiography of Colonial India," in Guha, *Subaltern Studies I*, 1–7.

56 Of course, the inertia of a large part of the Indian history establishment made for indifference toward these developments, while others, better informed, often chose to be hostile to the new steps.

57 For such tendencies within the folds of the project, see Bernard Cohn, "The Command of Language and the Language of Command," in Guha, *Subaltern Studies IV*, 276–329; Julie Stephens, "Feminist Fictions: A Critique of the Category 'Non-Western Woman' in Feminist Writings on India," in Guha, *Subaltern Studies IV*, 92–125; Susie Tharu, "Response to Julie Stephens," in Guha, *Subaltern Studies IV*, 126–31; Das, "Subaltern as Perspective"; and Spivak, "Subaltern Studies: Deconstructing Historiography." See also Nirmal Chandra, "Agricultural Workers in Burdwan," in Guha, *Subaltern Studies II*, 228–58.

58 Significantly, *Selected Subaltern Studies* was not only jointly edited by Ranajit Guha and Gayatri Spivak, but the volume also carried a foreword by Edward Said that was enormously appreciative of the project (Guha and Spivak, *Selected Subaltern Studies*).

59 Sarkar, *Modern India*, 290.

60 Among others, Tanika Sarkar has questioned the manner in which women's "politicization"—in the sense of their participation in organized political endeavors—and their "emancipation" are used as interchangeable categories challenging the underlying assumptions in the context of anticolonial nationalism in Bengal in the late 1920s and early 1930s. At the same time, she retains an implicit public-private distinction in her use of the terms *politics* and *politicization*. See Tanika Sarkar, "Politics and Women in Bengal: The Conditions and Meaning of Participation," *Indian Economic and Social History Review* 21 (1984): 91–101.

61 Ibid. I recognize that this is a complex issue. Clearly, the participation of women—far from an undifferentiated category—in the nationalist movement could have contributed to perceptible and imperceptible changes in the ways women of different social groups came to look on themselves and in the way men began to view them. But these might also have been unintended consequences of their actions, which are a regular feature of social life. My point is that a teleological construct such as the "struggle for the emancipation of Indian womanhood" externalizes the conditions of possibility and the wider understandings of women's participation in anticolonial nationalism.

62 Here I am drawing on the critical emphases contained in Viswesaran, "Small Speeches, Subaltern Gender."

63 Guha, "Aspects of Historiography of Colonial India," 7, emphasis in the original.

64 In Ranajit Guha's earlier programmatic writings within the subaltern studies endeavor, the Chinese and French revolutions are implicitly projected as the model communist

revolution and the classic bourgeois revolution, respectively. Such an understanding plays a critical, structuring role in Guha's narratives.

65 For a related discussion, see Dipesh Chakrabarty, "Postcoloniality and the Artifice of History."

66 We have noted that through its evocation of diverse relations of domination and subordination the concept-metaphor of subaltern carries *and* contains possibilities of discussing the terms of gender in the work of history. However, as has been incisively discussed, this possibility remained underrealized in the early writing within the project and Guha's text is indicative of these tendencies. See, for example, Spivak, "Subaltern Studies: Deconstructing Historiography"; O'Hanlon, "Recovering the Subject"; and Viswesaran, "Small Speeches, Subaltern Gender."

67 Partha Chatterjee, *The Nation and Its Fragments.*

68 Ibid., 4–13; Anderson, *Imagined Communities.*

69 Chatterjee, *The Nation and Its Fragments,* 237.

70 Ibid., 237–38.

71 Dube, *Untouchable Pasts.*

72 Chakrabarty, "Postcoloniality and the Artifice of History."

73 I take this term for Heidegger's revolution in social thought from the exegesis in Bauman, *Intimations of Postmodernity,* ix–x.

74 Chakrabarty, "Postcoloniality and the Artifice of History," 6.

75 Ibid., 23.

76 Partha Chatterjee, "Claims on the Past: The Genealogy of Modern Historiography in Bengal," in Arnold and Hardiman, *Subaltern Studies VIII,* 1–49.

77 Ibid., 2.

78 Chakrabarty, "The Difference-deferral of (a) Colonial Modernity."

79 Ibid., 58.

80 Ibid., 81.

81 Ibid., 83.

82 Ibid., 87.

83 Ibid., 88.

84 Ibid., 51–55.

85 Chatterjee, "Claims on the Past," 14, 17 (emphasis mine).

86 Ibid., 43.

87 Consider this extract from a lecture by Bholanath Chakravarti articulating elements of modern history: "There are limits to everything. When the oppression of the Musalman became intolerable, the Lord of the Universe provided means of escape. . . . The resumption of good fortune was initiated on the day the British flag was first planted on this land . . . it is to bless us that *isvara* has brought the English to this country. . . . There can be no comparison between Yavana rule and British rule: the difference seems greater than between darkness and light or misery and bliss" (quoted in ibid., 20). To my mind, the criteria of the divine will, religious values, and norms of right conduct in judging the rise and fall of kingdoms are all present here.

6 Pilgrims' Progress

1 This is neither to deny the differences within Hindutva nor to suggest that current Hindu cultural nationalism is only an "elite conspiracy." Rather, my efforts keep in view the centrality of institutionalized power relations of the state in the wider dissemination of Hindutva as a political imaginary. Here I acknowledge Peter Van der Veer's emphasis on

the state as "a series of often conflicting disciplines of ordering society" while attending to Michael Herzfeld's injunction to look behind national facades, unraveling other lives of the nation-state. On one hand, it is crucial to attend to processes through which power relations appear to be reified as external structures and simultaneously emerge internalized as disciplines in both academic models and social worlds. On the other hand, it is critical to recognize that such processes of internalization and externalization are never fully finished, not only because of the inherent instability of power but considering the reworking of power through other bound but distinct filters of subjects/communities. See Amrita Basu, "Mass Movement or Elite Conspiracy? The Puzzle of Hindu Nationalism," in *Making India Hindu: Religion, Community, and the Politics of Democracy in India*, edited by David Ludden (Delhi: Oxford University Press, 1996), 55–80; Peter Van der Veer, "Writing Violence," in Ludden, *Making India Hindu*, 261, 263; and Herzfeld, *Cultural Intimacy*.

2 Thus, the Hindu Right has sought assiduously to revise and rewrite textbooks and rework the public debate on history, which has enormous implications for the academy and far beyond.

3 For this chapter, I consulted a variety of tracts of the Vishwa Hindu Parishad, collected in the mid-1990s. At the time, I also conducted brief fieldwork in Nagpur among middle-class supporters of Hindutva, including my own relatives, eliciting opinions—which generally were readily offered—on Ayodhya and its history, Hindutva, and Indian politics. (The degree to which a homogenized history of Ayodhya constituted these oral accounts was chilling.) The tracts consulted range from collections of true stories for children and teenagers and discussions of Hindu *rashtra* (nation), distortions of secularism, and rights of Hindus to various statements about the history of Ayodhya. While keeping their lessons in mind, including the internal tensions within Hindutva, in this chapter I cite only a few of the tracts that I have consulted.

4 To foreground this connection is not to overlook the fact that Hindutva equally embodies a profound ambivalence toward modernity, expressed for example, in its articulation of an alternative Hindu universalism, which is not a mere critique of the West. As Thomas Hansen has argued, this alternative universalism forms "part of a strategy to invigorate and stabilize a modernizing national project through a disciplined and corporatist cultural nationalism that can earn India recognition and equality (with the West and other nations) through assertion of difference." Within Hindu nationalism, the linkages between its production of a homogenized history and its fetish of the modern nation stand closely connected to such ambivalence, at once animating and utilizing ideological control and disciplinary strategies. The assertion of the difference and purity of Hindu civilization and the salience of a strong and powerful modern nation go hand in hand. See Hansen, *The Saffron Wave*, 90, 231, and passim. See also Dube, "Introduction: Enchantments of Modernity."

5 Anuradha Kapur, "Deity to Crusader: The Changing Iconography of Ram," in *Hindus and Others: The Question of Identity in India Today*, edited by Gyanendra Pandey (New Delhi: Penguin, 1993), 74–109. But consider, too, Chris Pinney, "The nation (Un)pictured? Chromolithography and "Popular" Politics in India, 1878–1995," *Critical Inquiry* 23 (1997): 834–67. See also Richard H. Davis, "The Iconography of Ram's Chariot," in Ludden, *Making India Hindu*, 27–54; Hansen, *The Saffron Wave*, 172–181; Arvind Rajagopal, "Ram Janmabhoomi, Consumer Identity and Image-based Politics," *Economic and Political Weekly* 29 (1994): 1659–68; Philip Lutgendorf, "Ramayan: The Video," *Drama Review* 34 (1990): 127–76; and Peter Van der Veer, *Religious Nationalism: Hindus and Muslims in India* (Berkeley: University of California Press, 1994), 165–91.

6   Gyanendra Pandey, "Modes of History Writing: New Hindu History of Ayodhya," *Economic and Political Weekly* 29 (1994): 1523–28. I have rearranged the arguments and materials presented by Pandey, reading them alongside different tracts of the Hindu Right, and state my differences with his analyses at appropriate points. Moreover, I keep in view the contents of a violent pamphlet, Ramjanambhumi ka Rakt Ranjit Itihas (The blood-soaked history of the birthplace of Ram), which has been discussed in insightful ways in Pradip Dutta, "VHP's Ram: The Hindutva Movement in Ayodhya," in Pandey, *Hindus and Others*, 46–73.

7   For anthropological and historical reflections on "monumental" time, see Michael Herzfeld, *A Place in History, Social and Monumental Time in a Cretan Town* (Princeton: Princeton University Press, 1991).

8   I broadly agree with Pandey's contrast between the "metaphorical quality" of the earlier Hindu account of Ayodhya and the excess of "literalism" and "positivism" that inheres in the new Hindu histories. At the same time, simply reiterating this contrast can overlook the play of tropes within the new Hindu accounts of Ayodhya. Thus, the very literalism and the precise "scientificity"—the rehearsal and recitation of dates and numbers and clearly identified geographical space(s)—that characterize these histories transform the metaphor of Ayodhya by imbuing it with metonymic and synecdochal attributes. Today Ayodhya and its association with Ram, shored up by an excess of facts and facticity, endlessly articulate the story of "foreign aggression" and "native valor," of endemic Muslim misogyny and villainy versus eternal Hindu heroism and sacrifice, a story that forms the core of the new Hindu histories. This is evident, for example, in writings such as R. P. Sharma, *Tithiyan jo Itihas ban Gayi: Shriramjanmabhumi Mukti Sangharsh* (New Delhi: Shriram Janmabhumi Nyas, n.d.). Yet it is also true of more general tracts such as N. H. Palkar, *Bhagwa Dhwaj* (Lucknow: Lokhit Prakashan, 1991), 67–72. Pandey, "Modes of History Writing." On the transformations of metaphor, and the importance of other tropes in social analysis, see, for instance, James W. Fernandez, ed., *Beyond Metaphor: The Theory of Tropes in Anthropology* (Stanford: Stanford University Press, 1991).

9   Pandey, "Modes of History Writing."

10 Also see, for example, Sharma, *Tithiyan jo Itihas ban Gayi*, particularly 4–6.

11 See also Ashok Singhal, "Prakathan," in R. P. Sharma, *Shriram Kar Seva Banam 18 din ka Mahasmar* (New Delhi: Shriram Janmabhumi Nyas, n.d.), vi–viii.

12 Here Pandey is following E. P. Thompson in describing history as a discipline of "context" and "process." At the same time, it is not enough to merely point out the "ahistorical" nature of these histories, for this might be to beg significant questions, a few of which are outlined below. See E. P. Thompson, "Folklore, Anthropology, and the Discipline of History," *Indian Historical Review* 3 (1977): 247–66.

13 For example, Singhal, "Prakathan," in Sharma, *Tithiyan jo Itihas ban Gayi*, 2.

14 Here it is important to keep in mind how in the new Hindu account of Ayodhya strategies intended to authenticate the narrative and assume a collective authoritative voice are linked to wider modes of understanding of texts and the construction of pasts in North India. Such modalities are rooted in reasons of epic narratives of the nation and in different middle-class conventions of reading and writing—and apprehension and consumption—that configure modern Hinduism but equally in several popular forms of religious discourse. The point is that analysis in this direction can help us explore how the Hindu's Right's circular narrative turns on itself yet tells a story with a beginning, middle, and end.

15 These overlapping movements underscore critical issues relating to both the spatializa-

tion of time and territory and the temporalization and territorialization of space, each closely bound to narrative strategies and political practices surrounding the nation. Let me raise two questions here. First, how might we articulate David Harvey's argument holding that "time-space compression" within modern regimes at once undergirds the universality and undermines the particularity of nationalism *with* the simultaneously specific and metonymic attributes of Ayodhya in the "spatial strategies" of Hindutva, part of the fabrication of an "alternative" Hindu universality bearing upon the nation-state? Second, while hierarchical relationships among past, present, and future are seen (following Mikhail Bakhtin) as central to the epic as a nationalist genre and are considered (following Homi Bhabha) as critical for monumental narratives of the nation, how are such scholarly projections complicated by constructions within Hindutva of the national epic past as the relentless struggle against the coeval other, flowing into the present and present for the future? Put another way, the very pasts shaped within Hindutva suggest the importance of reconsidering discussions of the nation in the shadow of universal history and the image of a singular modernity. It follows that exclusive histories—as well as political rituals and techniques of rule—fabricated by Hindutva, when read as forms of "moral regulation," can reveal shifts and ruptures in the imagining and institution of the postcolonial nation-state in India. In different ways, Thomas Hansen and Satish Deshpande address related issues, though by setting up a primary distinction between "places of essence" (e.g., Ayodhya) and "areas of intimacy" (discrete neighborhoods). Deshpande's typology runs the risk of overlooking the interpenetration in the spatial strategies of Hindutva between the "intimacy" of Ayodhya and the "essence" of neighborhoods. See David Harvey, *The Condition of Postmodernity* (Oxford: Basil Blackwell, 1989), 24–70; Mikhail Bakhtin, *The Dialogic Imagination*, translated by C. Anderson and M. Holquist (Austin: University of Texas Press, 1981), particularly 13–16; Homi Bhabha, "DissemiNation: Time, Narrative, and the Margins of the Modern Nation," in *Nation and Narration*, edited by Homi Bhabha (London: Routledge, 1990), 291–322; Hansen, *The Saffron Wave*; and Satish Deshpande, "Hegemonic Spatial Strategies: The Nation-space and Hindu Communalism in Twentieth-century India," *Public Culture* 10 (1998): 249–84. The notion of "moral regulation" derives from Philip Corrigan and Derek Sayer, *The Great Arch: English State Formation as Cultural Revolution* (Oxford: Basil Blackwell, 1985), 4.

16 In this section, I discuss representative writings that have pointedly addressed the recent Hindu extremist construction of the past.

17 At the same time, the nature of the leftist-liberal response as a form of "public debate" is constrained by its confinement to a few English-language newspapers and even fewer scholarly magazines.

18 Sarvepalli Gopal et al., *The Political Abuse of History* (New Delhi: Centre for Historical Studies, Jawaharlal Nehru University, 1989), reprinted in *Babri-Masjid Ramjanambhoomi Controversy*, edited by Asghar Ali Engineer (Delhi: Ajanta Publications, 1990), 231–37; Sarvepalli Gopal, ed., *The Anatomy of a Confrontation: The Babri Masjid-Ramjanmabhumi Issue* (New Delhi: Penguin, 1991). But see also J. C. Aggarwal and N. K. Chowdhry, eds., *Ram Janmabhoomi through the Ages: Babri Masjid Controversy* (New Delhi: S. Chand, 1991); and Devendra Swarup, Arun Shourie, Narendra Mohan, K. R. Malkani, and Suryakant Bali, *Ayodhya ka Sach* (Nagpur: Bharatiya Vichar Sadhna, n.d.).

19 The problems with such procedures are acute, particularly since they underplay the debated and contested nature of nation and history. In other words, the endorsement of an exclusive, disciplinary conception of history as the touchstone of truth can accede to the taken for granted terms of the nation. Such a conception may also have little place for

the inherent variability of forms of historical consciousness and modes of representing the past within and across national spaces, except perhaps as abiding curiosity. See Ana Maria Alonso, "The Effects of Truth: Re-presentations of the Past and the Imagining of Community," *Journal of Historical Sociology* 1 (1988): 33–57; Richard Handler, *Nationalism and the Politics of Culture in Quebec* (Madison: University of Wisconsin Press, 1988); Skaria, *Hybrid Histories*; and Dube, *Untouchable Pasts*.

20 For a longer treatment of these issues, see Van der Veer, *Religious Nationalism*, 157–64.

21 For arguments with somewhat different emphases within the dominant democratic response to Hindu histories, see Neeladri Bhattacharya, "Myth, History and the Politics of Ramjanmabhumi," in Gopal, *The Anatomy of a Confrontation*, 122–40; and Romila Thapar, "Epic and History: Tradition, Dissent and Politics in India," *Past and Present* 125 (1989): 1–26.

22 Partha Chatterjee, "Claims on the Past"; and *Itihaser Uttaradhikar, Baromas* (Calcutta) 12 (1991): 1–24. See also Gyanendra Pandey, "Which of Us Are Hindus?" in Pandey, *Hindus and Others*, 238–72; Tapan Basu et al., *Khaki Shorts and Saffron Flags: A Critique of the Hindu Right* (Delhi: Orient Longman, 1993); Hansen, *The Saffron Wave*; and Christophe Jaffrelot, *The Hindu Nationalist Movement in India* (New York: Columbia University Press, 1996).

23 Walter Benjamin, "Theses on the Philosophy of History," in *Illuminations*, translated by Harry Zohn, edited by Hannah Arendt (New York: Schocken Books, 1969), 253, emphasis mine.

24 "Benjamin was also arguing fellow Marxists to ponder more deeply their own implicit faith in a messianic view of history, to face up to that faith in a conscious fashion, and to consider for their activism the power of social experience, imagery, and mood in constructing and deconstructing political consciousness and the will to act politically" (Taussig, *Shamanism, Colonialism, and the Wild Man*, 368). But see also Roger N. Lancaster, *Thanks to God and the Revolution: Popular Religion and Class Consciousness in the New Nicaragua* (New York: Columbia University Press, 1988), 207–8 and passim.

25 Saurabh Dube, "Ayodhya ke ateet," in *Ayodhya aur Uske Aage*, edited by Rajkishore (Delhi: Vani Prakashan, 1993), 30–36.

26 True to the struggle over the past and containing its many ironies, after Indian independence, this public space was renamed Tulsi Park to commemorate Tulsidas, the late medieval saint-poet who popularized the story of Ram in the vernacular.

27 Peter Van der Veer, *Gods on Earth: The Management of Religious Experience and Identity in a North Indian Pilgrimage Centre* (Delhi: Oxford University Press, 1989). The extent of my debt to this impressive historical ethnography centered on Ayodhya should be evident throughout this section.

28 Ibid., 20–21.

29 See Van der Veer, *Religious Nationalism*, 161.

30 Cited in Van der Veer, *Gods on Earth*, 211.

31 Ibid., 211–14.

32 Bayly, *Rulers, Townsmen and Bazaars*; Bernard Cohn, "The Role of Gosains in the Economy of Eighteenth and Nineteenth Century, Upper India," *Indian Economic and Social History Review* 1 (1964): 175–82. See also David Lorenzen, "Warrior Ascetics in Indian History," *Journal of the American Oriental Society* 98 (1978): 61–75; and William Pinch, "Soldier Monks and Militant Sadhus," in Ludden, *Making India Hindu*, 140–61.

33 Richard Burghart, "The Founding of the Ramanandi Sect," *Ethnohistory* 25 (1978): 121–39; "The Disappearance and Reappearance of Janakpur," *Kailash: A Journal of Himalayan Studies* 6 (1978): 257–84; "Wandering Ascetics of the Ramanandi Sect," *History of Religion* 22 (1984): 361–80.

34 Charlotte Vaudeville, "Braj, Lost and Found," *Indo-Iranian Journal* 18 (1976): 195–213.

35 Van der Veer, *Gods on Earth*, 142–43.

36 Ibid., 37–38, 143–59. See also Juan Cole, *Roots of North Indian Shi'ism: Religion and State in Awadh* (Berkeley: University of California Press, 1988), particularly 242–50; Richard Barnett, *North India between Empires: Awadh, the Mughals and the British, 1720–1801* (Berkeley: University of California Press, 1980); and Michael Fisher, *A Clash of Two Cultures: Awadh, the British and the Mughals* (New Delhi: Manohar, 1987).

37 See, for instance, Dirks, *The Hollow Crown*.

38 Mayaram, *Resisting Regimes*, chap. 3.

39 Van der Veer, *Gods on Earth*, 38–40.

40 We have noted that after the annexation of Awadh in 1856 the British built a railing around the Babri mosque and raised a platform outside the fence. The Muslims worshiped inside the mosque, and the Hindus made their offerings from the platform. This situation continued through to the early years of Indian independence. Until just after the partition and independence of India, Ayodhya was not a center of Hindu-Muslim sectarian strife, although it did witness two major riots—both involving attacks on the Babri mosque by Hindus—in 1912 and 1934. All of this was part of the wider deterioration of Hindu-Muslim relations in the first half of the twentieth century.

The decisive change came at the end of 1949 when an image of Ram appeared rather suddenly inside the mosque, put there to press home Hindu claims to the site. For the Hindus, this was a miracle. For the Muslims, their sacred space had been defiled. Riots followed, but the image remained. Afterward, members of both religious groups were prevented from entering the mosque, which was guarded by the police. Both Hindu and Muslim leaders started litigation to claim the place as their own. Yet nothing much happened until 1984. In that year, the Vishwa Hindu Parishad began an agitation to claim the site for the "Hindu nation." Although the campaign did not catch on immediately, this organization continued to exert pressure on politicians.

In 1986, several decades after the issue had lain quietly in the law courts, the District and Sessions Court of the area handed down a decision opening the "disputed site" to the public. The issue now became central to the platforms of different political parties and was turned into a virtual one-point agenda by the Bharatiya Janata Party. In 1989, the Vishwa Hindu Parishad began a program for the worship of the "bricks of Ram," which were carried in processions to Ayodhya to build the temple of Ram. A year later the Bharatiya Janata Party began a ritual procession, led by its leader L. K. Advani posturing as Ram, that was intended to pass through ten provinces of the Indian union and culminate in the building of the Ram temple at Ayodhya on 30 October 1990. Advani was arrested before he could enter Ayodhya, but an attempt to build the temple on 30 October by volunteers of the Hindu Right led to clashes with the police.

The forces of Hindutva turned this campaign and its casualties into a highly organized audiovisual spectacle that led to the victory of the Bharatiya Janata Party in the provincial elections of 1991. Then a rally organized by the Vishwa Hindu Parishad and the Bharatiya Janata Party in Ayodhya led to the destruction of the Babri mosque on 6 December 1992. This event and Ayodhya itself continue to influence the politics of India today. See Van der Veer, *Religious Nationalism*, x–xi, 1–11; *Gods on Earth*, 40–42; and "God Must be Liberated: A Hindu Liberation Movement in Ayodhya," *Modern Asian Studies* 21 (1987): 283–303. See also Pradip Datta, "VHP's Ram." More recent discussions of the politics of Hindutva are contained in Christophe Jaffrelot, *Hindu Nationalism in India*; and Hansen, *The Saffron Wave*.

41 Van der Veer, *Gods on Earth*, 42.

42   Gyanendra Pandey, "In Defense of the Fragment: Writing About Hindu-Muslim Riots in India Today," in Guha, *A Subaltern Studies Reader*, 3.

7   The Enchanted and the Modern

1   Most of the presentations at the roundtable in Orlando, along with a few other contributions, were considered for publication in a special issue of the *Journal of the American Academy of Religion*. The essay that I submitted for the special issue, based on my presentation in Orlando, a shorter version of this chapter, was rejected, since it was not sufficiently "reader friendly," even though the verdict was that it raised important issues. I mention this fact primarily in the manner of a clarification.

2   This is not to simply dismiss the claims of politics of identities. Rather, my effort is to raise a few questions around the insistence on authenticity and the claims of authority, which take different forms. On such complexities and questions, see Craig Calhoun, ed., *Social Theory and the Politics of Identity* (Oxford: Blackwell, 1994); Ruth Frankenberg and Lata Mani, "Crosscurrents, Crosstalk: Race, 'Postcoloniality,' and the Politics of Location," in *Contemporary Postcolonial Theory: A Reader*, edited by Padmini Mongia (London: Arnold, 1996), 347–64; and, especially, Povinelli, *Cunning of Recognition*.

3   See, for example, Richard King, *Orientalism and Religion: Postcolonial Theory, India and the "Mystic East"* (London: Routledge, 1999); Christopher Minkowski, "Pandit as Public Intellectual," in *The Pandit: Traditional Sanskrit Scholarship in India*, edited by Axel Michaels (New Delhi: Manohar, 2001); and Ann Gold and Bhoju Ram Gujar, *In the Time of Trees and Sorrows: Nature, Power, and Memory in Rajasthan* (Durham: Duke University Press, 2002).

4   For example, see Mongia, *Contemporary Postcolonial Theory*; and Dube, *Untouchable Pasts*.

5   For example, see Spivak, "Can the Subaltern Speak?"; Chakrabarty, "Postcoloniality and the Artifice of History"; Paul Gilroy, *Between Camps: Race, Identity and Nationalism at the End of the Colour Line* (London: Allen Lane, 2000); and Gilroy, *The Black Atlantic*. See also Bhabha, *The Location of Culture*; and Chandra Talpade Mohanty, "Under Western Eyes: Feminist Scholarship and Colonial Discourses," in *Third World Women and the Politics of Feminism*, edited by Chandra Mohanty, Ann Russo, and Lourdes Torres (Bloomington: Indiana University Press, 1991), 51–80.

6   At particular points, this problem characterizes Said's analyses in his enormously influential *Orientalism*.

7   On related questions, see particularly Spivak, "Can the Subaltern Speak?"

8   Consider here the critical spirit of Sara Suleri, "Women Skin Deep: Feminism and the Postcolonial Condition," in Mongia, *Contemporary Postcolonial Theory*, 335–46.

9   To pose issues of voice and authority in this manner is to think through the tension between "liberal" demands for the inclusion and representation of the widest possible number of voices, on one hand, and "radical" claims that since particular, dominant voices have long (mis)represented disadvantaged groups members of these groups alone can represent their traditions and realities on the other. If in different ways questions of representation and authority remain central to both these sets of positions, it is also true that no easy resolution can be proposed here. Rather, these divergent positions may both have something to offer in the institutional context of academe, and more than a priori assertions it is the particular nature of issues and questions under debate that bear attention. At the same time, turning to academic discussion, in a context saturated with the politics of location and emphasizing preconfigured identities, I can only confess to my deep unease with na(t)ive claims to voice and agency, including moves that stage alterity to claim authority. However, this does not rule out the possibilities of

seeking alternative locations, other sites for shaping intellectual dialogue at once based on the renunciation of the privilege of categorical identities and an engagement with the terms of minority discourses. Such dialogue can base itself on forms of reading and writing that eschew rapid rebuttals and quick dismissals but equally shun eclectic endorsements and bland affirmations of competing theoretical and textual tendencies and different epistemological and political positions.

10 Chakrabarty, "Postcoloniality and the Artifice of History."

11 Ibid., 2.

12 In the essay, Chakrabarty goes on to construct an alternative reading of history by discussing the pasts of a colonial modernity in Bengal and also outlines a wider proposal to "provincialize Europe" (ibid.).

13 See, for example, Coronil, *The Magical State*; Comaroff and Comaroff, *Ethnography and the Historical Imagination*; Dube, *Untouchable Pasts*; Lutz, *Unnatural Emotions*; and Michael Taussig, *The Magic of the State* (London: Routledge, 1997). See also Brown, *Life against Death*; and Michael Taussig, *The Nervous System* (New York: Routledge, 1992).

14 This is not to deny important exceptions within and significant overlaps across these academic endeavors or to overlook the significant changes that have been under way in humanist and social scientific conceptions. Rather, I seek only to indicate the wider formative dispositions of these disciplines, with lasting legacies over time. Moreover, it bears pointing out that the enduring binaries under discussion have critically informed analyses of religions in the modern West founded on the dominant assumption that since the Christian Reformation religion in the West has undergone a profound transformation, becoming a largely tolerant and broadly private affair. Here the traditions, rituals, and beliefs of these religions in the West have often been implicitly cast as at once outside of and encompassed by processes of modernity, disenchantment, and secularization. Finally, approaches inclined toward establishing a "universal grammar of religions" have tended to mark out a separate domain of the "sacred" before and beyond all that lies outside this heuristically privileged domain. See Asad, *Genealogies of Religion*; and Russell McCutheon, *Manufacturing Religion: The Discourse on Sui Generis Religion and the Politics of Nostalgia* (New York: Oxford University Press, 1997).

15 Asad, *Genealogies of Religion*, 269.

16 See, for example, Hartman, *Scenes of Subjection*; Uday Mehta, Liberal strategies of exclusion, in Cooper and Stoler, *Tensions of Empire*, 59–86; and Gyan Prakash, *Bonded Histories: Genealogies of Labor Servitude in Colonial India* (Cambridge: Cambridge University Press, 1990).

17 For example, see Amin, *Event, Metaphor, Memory*; Chatterjee, *The Nation and Its Fragments*; and Prakash, *Another Reason*.

18 Chatterjee, *The Nation and Its Fragments*; Prakash, *Another Reason*. At the same time, both Chatterjee and Prakash tend to underplay the critical implications of the presence of such binaries.

19 Some of these questions are discussed in interesting ways in McClintock, *Imperial Leather*.

20 Many of the issues that I raise here find critical elaboration in Dube, *Enduring Enchantments*.

Afterword

1 Benjamin, "Theses on the Philosophy of History," 257–58.

2 See Michael Taussig, *Defacement: Public Secrecy and the Labor of the Negative* (Stanford: Stanford University Press, 1999).

Glossary

adalat. law court
adawat. enmity
adivasi. original inhabitant
aghan. November–December
asad. June–July
ashwin. September–October
athgawana. committee of eight villages
bali. ornament worn in the ear
balwa. revolution
banjara. gypsy, pack trader
barcha. land adjoining a village pond used to
    grow sugarcane
begar. unremunerated labor
behatri. compensation for bride-price
bhauji. brother's wife
bhet-bega. free labor
buchadkhana. slaughter-house for cattle
chekbandi. consolidation of landholdings
chura. ornament worn above the wrist
churi. bangle, also secondary marriage
dadaria. genre of folk songs in Chhattisgarh
dand. punitive fine
dewar. husband's younger brother
dhan. unhusked paddy
diku. outsider or foreigner—usually refers to
    a non-tribal person
falgun. February–March
faqir. Muslim saint, mendicant
gawahi. testimony
grihalakshmi. housewife

gochar. village waste
guddi. village meeting place
guru puja. worship of guru
hool. rebellion
jajman. patron of the sacrifice
janeu. sacred thread
jati. caste
jat sayan. elders of a caste
kanun. law
kashtkar. cultivator
koalari. coalfields
kotwar. village law and order functionary
kula. lineage
lathi. stick, usually stout
lakhabata. periodic redistribution of land
lambardar. man in charge of village proprie-
    tory holdings
lugda. short sari
ma-bap. mother-father, paternalistic master
malguzar. village owner-proprietor
malguzari. village proprietorship
mandli. congregation
memsaheb. white woman
mukhtiyar. man in charge of village proprie-
    tory holdings
nagar. plow
nawab. Muslim ruler
paithoo. secondary marriage
pancha. member of a village and/or caste
    council

panchayat. village and/or caste council
panda. hereditary priest
para. neighborhood
parampara. tradition
parcha. paper
patwari. village accountant
prachin. elder, ancient
praja. ruled
puja. ritual worship
pus. December–January
raja. ruler, king
raja-praja. ruler-ruled
rawat. village grazier
raja log. kingly person
rashtra. nation
sadhu. Hindu ascetic

saheb. white official, master
sarkar bahadur. colonial government
sarpanch. head of a caste and/or village
    council
satnam. true name
savan. July–August
sayan. elder
satyanam. true name
swatantrata. freedom
swaraj. freedom/independence
tahsil. administrative unit
thanedar. subinspector of police
tirthankar. preceptor
tutari. stick with a sharp tip used to drive
    bullocks

Bibliography

Unpublished Records

District and Sessions Court Record Room, Raipur, Chhattisgarh
King Emperor v. Samaru and others, Sessions Trial 33 of 1927.
King Emperor v. Rendhia and six others, Sessions Trial 22 of 1932.
King Emperor v. Santram, Sessions Trial 1 of 1939.
King Emperor v. Balli and thirteen others, Sessions Trial 34 of 1940.

Bilaspur Collectorate Record Room, Bilaspur, Chhattisgarh
Bilaspur District Village Settlement Records, Bandobast no. 124, Patwari Halka no. 57, Kharkhena (Karkhena), Group Lakhatpur, 1928–29.
Bilaspur District Village Settlement Records, Bandobast no. 334, Patwari Halka no. 230, Darri (Sarhar), Group Jaijaipur, 1929–30.
Bilaspur District Village Settlement Records, Bandobast no. 613, Patwari Halka no. 249, Murlidih, Jaijaipur Group, Janjgir Tahsil, 1929–30.
Bilaspur District Village Settlement Records, Bandobast no. 59, Patwari Halka no. 229, Kapisda, Birra Group, Janjgir Tahsil, 1929–30.

Madhya Pradesh Secretariat Record Room, Bhopal
Central Provinces Government Political and Military Department, Confidential Records.

Eden Archives and Library, Webster Groves, Missouri
Annual Reports of Missionaries by Name of Station and Missionary, 1868–83 (bound volumes), 1883–1956.
Baptismal Register, Bisrampur, 1870–90.
Bisrampur Malguzari File.
Correspondence of Missionaries, 1905–50.
Day-Book of a Catechist (not named), Manuscript, 83–5.
Manuscript Biographies and Autobiographies of Missionaries.
Manuscript Histories of the Mission and Mission Stations.
Missionary M. P. Davis Papers.
Quarterly Reports of Missionaries by Name of Station and Missionary, 1905–56.

Archives of the American Mennonite Church, Goshen, Indiana
Correspondence of Missionaries, 1898–1965.
Manuscript Biographies and Autobiographies of Missionaries.
Manuscript Histories of the Mission and Mission Stations.
Reports of Missionaries by Name of Missionary and Station, 1899–1956.

Archives of the General Conference Mennonites, Newton, Kansas
Manuscript Biographies and Autobiographies of Missionaries.
Manuscript Histories of the Mission and Mission Stations.
Reports of Missionaries by Name of Missionary and Station, 1905–55.

Oral Accounts

Several of the chapters of this book have been shaped by accounts heard and collected during fieldwork. Fieldwork on aspects of the evangelical encounter was conducted among Indian converts to Christianity in Chhattisgarh in the winter of 1994–95 and March 1996 and among American missionaries and their descendants in Goshen, Indiana, and Newton, Kansas, between August and October 1993 and in April 1997. Fieldwork on aspects of the law and legalities was conducted in Chhattisgarh in the early 1990s and during several subsequent visits to the region. Fieldwork among middle-class supporters of Hindutva was primarily conducted in Nagpur in October and November 1994 and September 1998.

Newspapers

Christian Monitor, selected issues.
Der Deutsche Missionsfreund, 1866–1905.
Evangelical Herald, selected issues.
Der Friedensbote, selected issues.

Government Publications

C. P. Ethnographic Survey XVII: Draft Articles on Hindustani Castes, First Series. Nagpur: Government Press, 1914.
Kosa: A Village Survey, Census of India 1961, vol. 8, Madhya Pradesh, part 6, Village Survey Monographs no. 9. Bhopal: Government Press, 1967.
Report on the Resettlement of the Khalsa of the Bilaspur District, 1927–32. Nagpur: Government Press, 1932.

Hindi Tracts

Bisrampur Kalasiya ki Vishesh Agyayen. Bisrampur: n.p., 1890.
Hagenstein, Sadhu. *Satma Ka Updesh*. Allahabad: Mission Press, 1934.
Palkar, N. H. *Bhagwa Dhwaj*. Lucknow: Lokhit Prakashan, 1991.
Paul, M. M. *Evangelical Kalasiya ka Sankshipt Itihas*. Allahabad: Mission Press, 1936.
——. *Satyanami Panth aur Shri Gosain Ghasidas Girodvasi*. Raipur: Mission Press, 1936.
Sharma, R. P. *Shriram Kar Seva Banam 18 Din ka Mahasmar*. New Delhi: Shriram Janmabhumi Nyas, n.d.

——. *Tithiyan jo Itihas ban Gayi: Shriramjanmabhumi Mukti Sangharsh*. New Delhi: Shriram Jan-mabhumi Nyas, n.d.

Singhal, Ashok. Prakathan. In *Shriram Kar Seva Banam 18 din ka Mahasmar*, by R. P. Sharma. New Delhi: Shriram Janmabhumi Nyas, n.d.

Swarup, Devendra, Arun Shourie, Narendra Mohan, K. R. Malkani, and Suryakant Bali. *Ayodhya ka Sach*. Nagpur: Bharatiya Vichar Sadhna, n.d.

Books and Articles

Afzal-Khan, Fawzia, and Kalpana Seshadri-Crooks, eds. *The Pre-occupation of Postcolonial Studies*. Durham: Duke University Press, 2000.

Aggarwal, J. C., and N. K. Chowdhry, eds. *Ram Janmabhoomi through the Ages: Babri Masjid Controversy*. New Delhi: S. Chand, 1991.

Alavi, Seema. *The Sepoys and the Company: Tradition and Transition in Northern India, 1770–1830*. Delhi: Oxford University Press, 1995.

Alonso, Ana Maria. The effects of truth: Representations of the past and the imagining of the community. *Journal of Historical Sociology* 1 (1988): 33–57.

——. The politics of space, time, and substance: State formation, nationalism, and ethnicity. *Annual Review of Anthropology* 23 (1994): 379–400.

Amin, Shahid. Approver's testimony, judicial discourse: The case of Chauri Chaura. In *Subaltern Studies V: Writings on South Asian History and Society*, edited by Ranajit Guha, 166–203. Delhi: Oxford University Press, 1987.

——. *Event, Metaphor, Memory: Chauri Chaura, 1922–1992*. Berkeley: University of California Press, 1996.

——. Gandhi as Mahatma: Gorakhpur District, Eastern UP, 1921–22. In *Subaltern Studies III: Writings on South Asian History and Society*, edited by Ranajit Guha, 1–61. Delhi: Oxford University Press, 1984.

Amin, Shahid, and Dipesh Chakrabarty, eds. *Subaltern Studies IX: Writings on South Asian History and Society*. Delhi: Oxford University Press, 1996.

Anderson, Benedict. *Imagined Communities: Reflections on the Origin and Spread of Nationalism*. London: Verso, 1983.

Appadurai, Arjun. *Modernity at Large: Cultural Dimensions of Globalization*. Minneapolis: University of Minnesota Press, 1996.

Apter, Andrew. *Black Critics and Kings: The Hermeneutics of Power in Yoruba Society*. Chicago: University of Chicago Press, 1993.

Arnold, David. *Colonizing the Body: State Medicine and Epidemic Disease in Nineteenth-Century India*. Berkeley: University of California Press, 1993.

——. Rebellious hillmen: The Gudem-Rampa uprisings. In *Subaltern Studies I: Writings on South Asian History and Society*, edited by Ranajit Guha, 88–142. Delhi: Oxford University Press, 1982.

Arnold, David, and David Hardiman, eds. *Subaltern Studies VIII: Essays in Honor of Ranajit Guha*. Delhi: Oxford University Press, 1994.

Asad, Talad. *Genealogies of Religion: Discipline and Reasons of Power in Christianity and Islam*. Baltimore: Johns Hopkins University Press, 1993.

Austin-Broos, Diane. *Jamaica Genesis: Religion and the Politics of Moral Orders*. Chicago: University of Chicago Press, 1997.

Axel, Brian K. *The Nation's Tortured Body: Violence, Representation, and the Formation of the Sikh "Diaspora."* Durham: Duke University Press, 2001.

Bakhtin, Mikhail. *The Dialogic Imagination*. Translated by C. Anderson and M. Holquist. Austin: University of Texas Press, 1981.

Bannerjee Dube, Ishita. *Divine Affairs: Religion, Pilgrimage, and the State in Colonial and Postcolonial India*. Shimla: Indian Institute of Advanced Study, 2001.

———. Taming traditions: Legalities and histories in twentieth-century Orissa. In *Subaltern Studies X: Writings on South Asian History and Society*, edited by Gautam Bhadra, Gyan Prakash, and Susie Tharu, 98–125. New Delhi: Oxford University Press, 1999.

Barnett, Richard. *North India between Empires: Awadh, the Mughals and the British, 1720–1801*. Berkeley: University of California Press, 1980.

Barnett, Steve. Coconuts and gold. *Contributions to Indian Sociology*, n.s., 10 (1976): 133–56.

Basu, Amrita. Mass movement or elite conspiracy? The puzzle of Hindu nationalism. In *Making India Hindu: Religion, Community and the Politics of Democracy in India*, edited by David Ludden, 55–80. Delhi: Oxford University Press, 1996.

Basu, Aparna. Mary Anne Cooke to Mother Teresa: Christian missionary women and the Indian response. In *Women and Missions, Past and Present: Anthropological and Historical Perceptions*, edited by Fiona Bowie, Deborah Kirkwood, and Shirley Ardener, 187–208. Oxford: Berg Publishers, 1993.

Basu, Tapan, et al. *Khaki Shorts and Saffron Flags: A Critique of the Hindu Right*. Delhi: Orient Longman, 1993.

Bates, Crispin. Regional dependence and rural development in central India, 1820–1930. Ph.D. diss., University of Cambridge, 1984.

Bauman, Zygmunt. *Intimations of Postmodernity*. London: Routledge, 1992.

Baxi, Upendra, "The state's emissary": The place of law in subaltern studies. In *Subaltern Studies VII: Writings on South Asian History and Society*, edited by Partha Chatterjee and Gyan Pandey, 257–64. Delhi: Oxford University Press, 1992.

Bayly, C. A. *Empire and Information: Intelligence Gathering and Social Communication in India, 1780–1870*. Cambridge: Cambridge University Press, 1997.

———. *Indian Society and the Making of the British Empire*. Cambridge: Cambridge University Press, 1988.

———. *Rulers, Townsmen and Bazaars: North Indian Society in the Age of British Expansion, 1770–1870*. Cambridge: Cambridge University Press, 1983.

Bayly, Susan. *Saints, Goddesses and Kings: Muslims and Christians in South Indian Society, 1700–1900*. Cambridge: Cambridge University Press, 1989.

Benjamin, Walter. Theses on the philosophy of history. In *Illuminations*. Translated by Harry Zohn, edited by Hannah Arendt, 155–65. New York: Schocken Books, 1969.

Beverley, John. *Subalternity and Representation: Arguments in Cultural Theory*. Durham: Duke University Press, 1999.

Bhabha, Homi. DissemiNation: Time, narrative, and the margins of the modern nation. In *Nation and Narration*, edited by Homi Bhabha, 291–322. London: Routledge, 1990.

———. *The Location of Culture*. New York: Routledge, 1994.

———. Signs taken for wonders: Questions of ambivalence and authority under a tree outside Delhi, May 1817. In *The Location of Culture*, 102–22. New York: Routledge, 1994.

Bhadra, Gautam. Four rebels of Eighteen-Fifty-Seven. In *Subaltern Studies IV: Writings on South Asian History and Society*, edited by Ranajit Guha, 229–75. Delhi: Oxford University Press, 1985.

———. The mentality of subalternity: Kantanama or Rajdharma. In *Subaltern Studies VI: Writings on South Asian History and Society*, edited by Ranajit Guha, 54–91. Delhi: Oxford University Press, 1989.

———. Two frontier uprisings in Mughal India. In *Subaltern Studies II: Writings on South Asian History and Society*, edited by Ranajit Guha, 43–59. Delhi: Oxford University Press, 1983.

Bhadra, Gautam, Gyan Prakash, and Susie Tharu, eds. *Subaltern Studies X: Writings on South Asian History and Society*. New Delhi: Oxford University Press, 1999.

Bhattacharya, Neeladhi. Myth, history and the politics of Ramjanmabhumi. In *The Anatomy of a Confrontation: The Babri Masjid-Ramjanmabhumi Issue*, edited by Sarvepalli Gopal, 122–40. New Delhi: Penguin, 1991.

Biersack, Aletta, ed. *Clio in Oceania: Toward a Historical Anthropology*. Washington, D.C.: Smithsonian, 1991.

Bourdieu, Pierre. *Pascalian Meditations*. Translated by Richard Nice. Cambridge: Polity Press, 2000.

Breckenridge, Carol, and Peter Van der Veer, eds. *Orientalism and the Postcolonial Predicament: Perspectives on South Asia*. Philadelphia: University of Pennsylvania Press, 1993.

Brown, Norman. *Life against Death: The Psychoanalytical Meaning of History*. London: Routledge and Kegan Paul, 1959.

Burghart, Richard. The disappearance and reappearance of Janakpur. *Kailash: A Journal of Himalayan Studies* 6 (1978): 257–84.

——. The founding of the Ramanandi sect. *Ethnohistory* 25 (1978): 121–39.

——. Wandering ascetics of the Ramanandi sect. *History of Religions* 22 (1983): 361–80.

Burke, Peter. People's history or total history. In *People's History and Socialist Theory*, edited by Raphael Samuel, 4–8. London: Routledge and Kegan Paul, 1981.

——. *Popular Culture in Early Modern Europe*. New York: Harper and Row, 1978.

Burke, Peter, ed. *New Perspectives on Historical Writing*. University Park: State University of Pennsylvania Press, 1992.

Butalia, Urvashi. *The Other Side of Silence: Voices from the Partition of India*. New Delhi: Viking Penguin, 1998.

Calhoun, Craig. *Nationalism*. Minneapolis: University of Minnesota Press, 1997.

Calhoun, Craig, ed. *Social Theory and the Politics of Identity*. Oxford: Blackwell, 1994.

Carter, Anthony. Hierarchy and the concept of the person in western India. In *Concepts of Person: Kinship, Caste and Marriage in India*, edited by Akos Ostor, Lina Fruzzetti, and Steve Barnett, 118–42. Delhi: Oxford University Press, 1983.

Chakrabarty, Dipesh. Conditions for the knowledge of working-class conditions: Employers, government and the jute workers of Calcutta, 1890–1940. In *Subaltern Studies II: Writings on South Asian History and Society*, edited by Ranajit Guha, 259–310. Delhi: Oxford University Press, 1983.

——. The difference-deferral of a colonial modernity: Public debates on domesticity in British India. In *Subaltern Studies VIII: Essays in Honor of Ranajit Guha*, edited by David Arnold and David Hardiman, 50–88. Delhi: Oxford University Press, 1994.

——. *Habitations of Modernity: Essays in the Wake of Subaltern Studies*. Chicago: University of Chicago Press, 2002.

——. Invitation to a dialogue. In *Subaltern Studies IV: Writings on South Asian History and Society*, edited by Ranajit Guha, 364–76. Delhi: Oxford University Press, 1985.

——. Marx after Marxism: A subaltern historian's perspective. *Economic and Political Weekly* 28 (1993): 1094–96.

——. Minority histories, subaltern pasts. *Economic and Political Weekly* 33 (1998): 473–79.

——. *Provincializing Europe: Postcolonial Thought and Historical Difference*. Princeton: Princeton University Press, 2001.

——. Postcoloniality and the artifice of history: Who speaks for "Indian" pasts? *Representations* 37 (winter 1992): 1–26.

—— Subaltern Studies and postcolonial historiography. *Nepantla: Views from South* 1 (2000): 9–32.

Chandra, Nirmal. Agricultural workers in Burdwan. In *Subaltern Studies II: Writings on South*

Asian History and Society, edited by Ranajit Guha, 228–58. Delhi: Oxford University Press, 1983.

Chatterjee, Indrani. Colouring subalternity: Slaves, concubines, and social orphans in early colonial India. In *Subaltern Studies X: Writings on South Asian History and Society*, edited by Gautam Bhadra, Gyan Prakash, and Susie Tharu, 49–97. Delhi: Oxford University Press, 1999.

Chatterjee, Partha. Claims on the past: The genealogy of modern historiography in Bengal. In *Subaltern Studies VIII: Essays in Honor of Ranajit Guha*, edited by David Arnold and David Hardiman, 1–49. Delhi: Oxford University Press, 1994.

———. Itihaser uttaradhikar. *Baromas* 12 (1991): 1–24.

———. *The Nation and Its Fragments: Colonial and Postcolonial Histories*. Princeton: Princeton University Press, 1993.

———. *Nationalist Thought and the Colonial World: A Derivative Discourse?* London: Zed Press, 1986.

———. Peasant, politics and historiography: A response. *Social Scientist* 11 (1985): 58–65.

———. *A Princely Impostor? The Strange and Universal History of the Kumar of Bhawal*. Princeton: Princeton University Press, 1994.

Chatterjee, Partha, and Gyanendra Pandey, eds. *Subaltern Studies VII: Writings on South Asian History and Society*. Delhi: Oxford University Press, 1992.

Chawla Singh, Maina. *Gender, Religion, and "Heathen Lands": American Missionary Women in South Asia (1860s–1940s)*. New York: Garland, 2000.

Clarke, Sathianathan. *Dalits and Christianity: Subaltern Religion and Liberation Theology in India*. Delhi: Oxford University Press, 1998.

Clastres, Pierre. *Society against the State: Essays in Political Anthropology*, translated by Robert Hurley. New York: Zone Books, 1989.

Cohn, Bernard. *An Anthropologist among the Historians and Other Essays*. Delhi: Oxford University Press, 1987.

———. Anthropology and history in the 1980s: Towards a rapprochement. In *An Anthropologist among the Historians and Other Essays*, 50–77. Delhi: Oxford University Press, 1987.

———. *Colonialism and Its Forms of Knowledge: The British in India*. Princeton: Princeton University Press, 1996.

———. The command of language and the language of command. In *Subaltern Studies IV: Writings on South Asian History and Society*, edited by Ranajit Guha, 276–329. Delhi: Oxford University Press, 1985.

———. History and anthropology: The state of play. *Comparative Studies in Society and History* 22 (1980): 198–221.

———. Law and the colonial state in India. In *History and Power in the Study of the Law: New Directions in Legal Anthropology*, edited by June Starr and Jane Collier, 131–52. Ithaca: Cornell University Press, 1989.

———. The role of Gosains in the economy of eighteenth and nineteenth century, upper India. *Indian Economic and Social History Review* 1 (1964): 175–82.

Cole, Juan. *Roots of North Indian Shi'ism: Religion and State in Awadh*. Berkeley: University of California Press, 1988.

Comaroff, Jean, and John Comaroff. Christianity and colonialism in South Africa. *American Ethnologist* 13 (1986): 1–22.

———. *Of Revelation and Revolution: Christianity, Colonialism, and Consciousness in South Africa*. Vol. 1. Chicago: University of Chicago Press, 1991.

Comaroff, John. Images of empire, contests of conscience: Models of colonial domination in South Africa. *American Ethnologist* 16 (1989): 661–85.

Comaroff, John, and Jean Comaroff. *Ethnography and the Historical Imagination.* Boulder: Westview, 1992.

——. *Of Revelation and Revolution: The Dialectics of Modernity on the South African Frontier.* Vol. 2. Chicago: University of Chicago Press, 1997.

Comaroff, John, and Simon Roberts. *Rules and Processes: The Cultural Logic of Dispute in an African Context.* Chicago: University of Chicago Press, 1981.

Cooper, Frederick. Conflict and connection: Rethinking colonial African history. *American Historical Review* 99 (1994): 1516–45.

Cooper, Frederick, and Ann Stoler, eds. *Tensions of Empire: Colonial Cultures in a Bourgeois World.* Berkeley: University of California Press, 1997.

Copley, Anthony. *Religions in Conflict: Ideology, Cultural Contact and Conversion in Late Colonial India.* Delhi: Oxford University Press, 1997.

Coronil, Fernando. *The Magical State: Nature, Money, and Modernity in Venezuela.* Chicago: University of Chicago Press, 1997.

Corrigan, Philip, and Derek Sayer. *The Great Arch: English State Formation as Cultural Revolution.* Oxford: Basil Blackwell, 1985.

Cusicanqui, Silvia Rivera, and Rosa Barragan, eds. *Debates PostColoniales: Una Introduccion a los Estudios de la Subalternidad.* La Paz: Ediciones Aruwiyiri, 1997.

Daniel, Valentine. *Fluid Signs: Being a Person the Tamil Way.* Berkeley: University of California Press, 1983.

Das, Veena. *Critical Events: An Anthropological Perspective on Contemporary India.* Delhi: Oxford University Press, 1995.

——. Subaltern as perspective. In *Subaltern Studies VI: Writings on South Asian History and Society,* edited by Ranajit Guha, 310–24. Delhi: Oxford University Press, 1989.

Dasgupta, Swapan. Adivasi politics in Midnapur, c. 1760–1924. In *Subaltern Studies IV: Writings on South Asian History and Society,* edited by Ranajit Guha, 101–35. Delhi: Oxford University Press, 1985.

Datta, Pradip. vhp's Ram: The Hindutva movement in Ayodhya. In *Hindus and Others: The Question of Identity in India Today,* edited by Gyanendra Pandey, 46–73. New Delhi: Penguin, 1993.

Davin, Anna. Imperialism and motherhood. *History Workshop* 5 (1978): 9–65.

Davis, Richard. The iconography of Ram's chariot. In *Making India Hindu: Religion, Community, and the Politics of Democracy in India,* edited by David Ludden, 27–54. Delhi: Oxford University Press, 1996.

de Certeau, Michel. *The Practice of Everyday Life,* translated by Steven Rendall. Berkeley: University of California Press, 1984.

Dening, Greg. *Performances.* Chicago: University of Chicago Press, 1997.

Desai, Gaurav. *Subject to Colonialism: African Self-Fashioning and the Colonial Library.* Durham: Duke University Press, 2001.

Deshpande, Satish. Hegemonic spatial strategies: The nation-space and Hindu communalism in twentieth-century India. *Public Culture* 10 (1998): 249–84.

Dirks, Nicholas B. *Castes of Mind: Colonialism and the Making of Modern India.* Princeton: Princeton University Press, 2001.

——. Foreword to *Colonialism and Its Forms of Knowledge: The British in India,* by Bernard Cohn, ix–xvii. Princeton: Princeton University Press, 1996.

——. *The Hollow Crown: Ethnohistory of an Indian Kingdom.* Cambridge: Cambridge University Press, 1987.

Dirlik, Arif. The postcolonial aura: Third World criticism in the age of global capitalism. In

Contemporary Postcolonial Theory: A Reader, edited by Padimini Mongia, 294–320. London: Arnold, 1996.

Donham, Donald. *Marxist Modern: An Ethnographic History of the Ethiopian Revolution*. Berkeley: University of California Press, 1999.

Duara, Prasenjit. *Rescuing History from the Nation: Questioning Narratives of Modern China*. Chicago: University of Chicago Press, 1996.

Dube, Leela. Conflict and compromise: Devolution and disposal of property in a matrilineal Muslim society. *Economic and Political Weekly* 29 (1994): 1273–84.

—. On the construction of gender: Hindu girls in patrilineal India. *Economic and Political Weekly* 23 (1988): (WS) 11–19.

—. In the mother's line: Structure and change in Lakshadweep. Report prepared for the Indian Council of Social Science Research, New Delhi, 1991. Manuscript.

Dube, S. C. The folksongs of Chhattisgarh. Manuscript.

Dube, Saurabh. Auguring art: The iconography of a radical imagination. Manuscript.

—. Ayodhya ke ateet. In *Ayodhya aur Uske Aage*, edited by Rajkishore, 30–36. Delhi: Vani Prakashan, 1993.

—. *Caste and Sect in Village Life: Satnamis of Chhattisgarh, 1900–1950*. Shimla: Indian Institute of Advanced Study, 1993.

—. Conversion to translation: Unbound registers of a vernacular Christianity. In *Enduring Enchantments*, edited by Saurabh Dube. Special issue of *South Atlantic Quarterly* 101, no. 4 (2002): 807–37.

—. *Genealogías del presente: Conversión, colonialismo, cultura*. Mexico City: El Colegio de México, 2003.

—. Idioms of authority and engendered agendas: The Satnami Mahasabha, Chhattisgarh, 1925–50. *Indian Economic and Social History Review* 30 (1993): 383–411.

—. Introducción: Temas e intersecciones de los pasados poscoloniales. In *Pasados poscoloniales: Colección de ensayos sobre la nueva historia y etnografía de la India*, edited by Saurabh Dube, 17–98. Mexico City: El Colegio de México, 1999.

—. Introduction: Colonialism, modernity, colonial modernities. In *Critical Conjunctions: Foundations of Colony and Formations of Modernity*, edited by Saurabh Dube, Ishita Banerjee Dube, and Edgardo Lander. Special issue of *Nepantla: Views from South* 3, no. 2 (2002): 197–219.

—. Introduction: Enchantments of modernity. In *Enduring Enchantments*, edited by Saurabh Dube. Special issue of *South Atlantic Quarterly* 101, no. 4 (2002): 729–55.

—. Introduction: Terms that bind—colony, nation, modernity. In *Postcolonial Passages: A Handbook of Contemporary History-Writing on India*, edited by Saurabh Dube. New Delhi: Oxford University Press, 2004.

—. Issues of Christianity in colonial Chhattisgarh. *Sociological Bulletin* 41 (1992): 37–63.

—. Myths, symbols and community: Satnampanth of Chhattisgarh. In *Subaltern Studies VII: Writings on South Asian History and Society*, edited by Partha Chatterjee and Gyanendra Pandey, 121–56. Delhi: Oxford University Press, 1992.

—. Native witness: Colonial writings of a vernacular christianity. Manuscript.

—. Presence of Europe: An interview with Dipesh Chakrabarty. In *Enduring Enchantments*, edited by Saurabh Dube. Special issue of *South Atlantic Quarterly* 101, no. 4 (2002): 859–68.

—. *Sujetos subalternos: Capítulos de una historia antropólogica*. Translated by Germán Franco and Ari Bartra. Mexico City: El Colegio de México, 2001.

—. *Untouchable Pasts: Religion, Identity, and Power among a Central Indian Community, 1780–1950*. Albany: State University of New York Press, 1998.

Dube, Saurabh, ed. *Enduring Enchantments*. Special issue of *South Atlantic Quarterly* 101, no. 4 (2002).

———. *Pasados poscoloniales: Colección de ensayos sobre la nueva historia y etnografía de la India*. Translated by Germán Franco. Mexico City: El Colegio de México, 1999.

———. *Postcolonial Passages: A Handbook of Contemporary History-Writing on India*. New Delhi: Oxford University Press, 2004.

Dube, Saurabh, and Ishita Banerjee Dube. Spectres of conversion: Transformations of caste and sect in India. In *Conversion in India: Modes, Motivations, and Meanings*, edited by Rowena Robinson and Sathianathan Clarke, 322–54. New Delhi: Oxford University Press, 2003.

Dube, Saurabh, Ishita Banerjee Dube, and Edgardo Lander, eds. *Critical Conjunctions: Foundations of Colony and Formations of Modernity*. Special issue of *Nepantla: Views from South* 3, no. 2 (2002).

Dumont, Louis. The functional equivalents of the individual in caste society. *Contributions to Indian Sociology* 8 (1965): 85–99.

———. *Homo Hierarchicus: The Caste System and Its Implications*. London: Weidenfeld and Nicholson, 1970.

———. The modern conception of the individual: Notes on its genesis. *Contributions to Indian Sociology* 8 (1965): 13–61.

———. Religion, politics and society in the individualistic universe. *Proceedings of the Royal Anthropological Institute* (1970): 31–41.

———. World renunciation in Indian religions. In *Religion/Politics and History in India: Collected Papers in Indian Sociology* 33–60. Paris: Mouton, 1970.

Dussel, Enrique. Eurocentrism and modernity. *Boundary 2* 20 (1993): 65–76.

———. *The Invention of the Americas: Eclipse of "the Other" and the Myth of Modernity*. New York: Continuum, 1995.

———. World-system and "trans"-modernity. In *Critical Conjunctions: Foundations of Colony and Formations of Modernity*, edited by Saurabh Dube, Ishita Banerjee Dube, and Edgardo Lander. Special issue of *Nepantla: Views from South* 3, no. 2 (2002): 221–44.

Eaton, Richard. Conversion to Christianity among the Nagas, 1876–1971. *Indian Economic and Social History Review* 21 (1984): 1–44.

Errington, Shelly. *The Death of Authentic Primitive Art and Other Tales of Progress*. Berkeley: University of California Press, 1998.

Fabian, Johannes. *Language and Colonial Power: The Appropriation of Swahili in the Former Belgian Congo, 1880–1938*. Cambridge: Cambridge University Press, 1986.

———. *Out of Our Minds: Reason and Madness in the Exploration of Central Africa*. Berkeley: University of California Press, 2000.

———. *Time and the Other: How Anthropology Makes Its Object*. New York: Columbia University Press, 1983.

Ferguson, James. *Expectations of Modernity: Myths and Meanings of Urban Life on the Zambian Copperbelt*. Berkeley: University of California Press, 1999.

Fernández, James W., ed. *Beyond Metaphor: The Theory of Tropes in Anthropology*. Stanford: Stanford University Press, 1991.

Fisher, Michael. *A Clash of Two Cultures: Awadh, the British and the Mughals*. Delhi: Manohar, 1987.

Florida, Nancy. *Writing the Past, Inscribing the Future: History as Prophecy in Colonial Java*. Durham: Duke University Press, 1995.

Flueckiger, Joyce B. *Gender and Genre in the Folklore of Middle India*. Ithaca: Cornell University Press, 1996.

Forrester, Duncan B. *Caste and Christianity: Attitudes and Policies on Caste of Anglo-Saxon Protestant Missions in India*. London: Curzon Press, 1980.

Foucault, Michel. *Discipline and Punish: The Birth of the Prison*. Translated by Alan Sheridan. London: Penguin, 1977.

——. Governmentality. In *The Foucault Effect: Studies in Governmentality*, edited by Graham Burcell, Colin Gordon, and Peter Miller, 87–104. Chicago: University of Chicago Press, 1992.

Frankenburg, Ruth, and Lata Mani. Crosscurrents, crosstalk: Race, "postcoloniality" and the politics of location. In *Contemporary Postcolonial Theory: A Reader*, edited by Padmini Mongia, 347–64. London: Arnold, 1996.

Fruzzetti, Lina, and Akos Ostor. Bad blood in Bengal. In *Concepts of Person: Kinship, Caste and Marriage in India*, edited by Akos Ostor, Lina Fruzzetti, and Steve Barnett, 31–55. Delhi: Oxford University Press, 1983.

Fruzzetti, Lina, Akos Ostor, and Steve Barnett. The cultural construction of person in Bengal and Tamil Nadu. In *Concepts of Person: Kinship, Caste and Marriage in India*, edited by Akos Ostor, Lina Fruzzetti, and Steve Barnett, 8–30. Delhi: Oxford University Press, 1983.

Fuller, C. J., and Véronique Bénéï, eds. *The Everyday State and Society in Modern India*. New Delhi: Social Science Press, 2000.

Gaonkar, Dilip P., ed. *Alternative Modernities*. Durham: Duke University Press, 2001.

Gates, Henry Louis, Jr. *The Signifying Monkey: A Theory of African American Literary Criticism*. New York: Oxford University Press, 1988.

Genovese, Eugene. *Roll Jordan Roll: The World the Slaves Made*. New York: Pantheon, 1974.

Ghosh, Kaushik. A market for aboriginality: Primitivism and race classification in the indentured labour market of India. In *Subaltern Studies X: Writings on South Asian History and Society*, edited by Gautam Bhadra, Gyan Prakash, and Susie Tharu, 8–48. New Delhi: Oxford University Press, 1999.

Gilroy, Paul. *Between Camps: Race, Identity and Nationalism at the End of the Color Line*. London: Allen Lane, 2000.

——. *The Black Atlantic: Modernity and Double Consciousness*. Cambridge: Harvard University Press, 1993.

Ginzburg, Carlo. *The Cheese and the Worms: The Cosmos of a Sixteenth Century Miller*. Translated by John Tedeschi and Anne Tedeschi. Baltimore: Johns Hopkins University Press, 1980.

——. *The Night Battles: Witchcraft and Agrarian Cults in the Sixteenth and Seventeenth Centuries*. Translated by John Tedeschi and Anne Tedeschi. New York: Penguin, 1985.

Gold, Ann G., and Bhoju Ram Gujar. *In the Time of Trees and Sorrows: Nature, Power, and Memory in Rajasthan*. Durham: Duke University Press, 2002.

Gopal, Sarvepalli, ed. *The Anatomy of a Confrontation: The Babri Masjid-Ramjanmabhumi Issue*. New Delhi: Penguin, 1991.

Gopal, Sarvepalli, et al. *The Political Abuse of History*. New Delhi: Centre for Historical Studies, Jawaharlal Nehru University, 1989. Reprinted in Asghar Ali Engineer, ed. *Babri-Masjid Ramjanambhoomi Controversy*, 231–37. Delhi: Ajanta Publications, 1990.

Gramsci, Antonio. *Selections from Cultural Writings*. Translated by William Boelhower, edited by David Forgacs and Geoffrey Nowell-Smith. London: Lawrence and Wishart, 1985.

——. *Selections from the Prison Notebooks of Antonio Gramsci*. Translated and edited by Q. Hoare and N. Smith. London: Lawrence and Wishart, 1971.

Gray, John. *Enlightenment's Wake: Politics and Culture at the Close of the Modern Age*. New York: Routledge, 1995.

——. *Two Faces of Liberalism*. New York: New Press, 2000.

Guha, Ramchandra. Forestry and social protest in British Kumaun, 1893–1921. In *Subaltern*

Studies IV: Writings on South Asian History and Society, edited by Ranajit Guha, 54–100. Delhi: Oxford University Press, 1985.

——. Savaging the Civilized: Verrier Elwin, His Tribals, and India. New Delhi: Oxford University Press, 1999.

——. Subaltern and bhadralok studies. Economic and Political Weekly 30 (1995): 2056–58.

Guha, Ranajit. Chandra's death. In Subaltern Studies V: Writings on South Asian History and Society, edited by Ranajit Guha, 135–65. Delhi: Oxford University Press, 1987.

——. Dominance without Hegemony: History and Power in Colonial India. Cambridge: Harvard University Press, 1997.

——. Elementary Aspects of Peasant Insurgency in Colonial India. Delhi: Oxford University Press, 1983.

——. Introduction to A Subaltern Studies Reader, 1986–1995, edited by Ranajit Guha, ix–xxii. Minneapolis: University of Minnesota Press, 1997.

——. Preface to Subaltern Studies I: Writings on South Asian History and Society, edited by Ranajit Guha, vii–viii. Delhi: Oxford University Press, 1982.

——. The prose of counter-insurgency. In Subaltern Studies II: Writings on South Asian History and Society, edited by Ranajit Guha, 1–42. Delhi: Oxford University Press, 1983.

——. On some aspects of the historiography of colonial India. In Subaltern Studies I: Writings on South Asian History and Society, edited by Ranajit Guha, 1–7. Delhi: Oxford University Press, 1982.

Guha, Ranajit, ed. Subaltern Studies I: Writings on South Asian History and Society. Delhi: Oxford University Press, 1982.

——. Subaltern Studies II: Writings on South Asian History and Society. Delhi: Oxford University Press, 1983.

——. Subaltern Studies III: Writings on South Asian History and Society. Delhi: Oxford University Press, 1984.

——. Subaltern Studies IV: Writings on South Asian History and Society. Delhi: Oxford University Press, 1985.

——. Subaltern Studies V: Writings on South Asian History and Society. Delhi: Oxford University Press, 1987.

——. Subaltern Studies VI: Writings on South Asian History and Society. Delhi: Oxford University Press, 1989.

——. A Subaltern Studies Reader, 1986–1995. Minneapolis: University of Minnesota Press, 1997.

Guha, Ranajit, and Gayatri Chakravorty Spivak, eds. Selected Subaltern Studies. New York: Oxford University Press, 1988.

Gupta, Akhil. Postcolonial Developments: Agriculture in the Making of Modern India. Durham: Duke University Press, 1998.

Handler, Richard. Nationalism and the Politics of Culture in Quebec. Madison: University of Wisconsin Press, 1988.

Hansen, Thomas Blom. The Saffron Wave: Democracy and Hindu Nationalism in Modern India. Princeton: Princeton University Press, 1999.

Hansen, Thomas Blom, and Finn Stepputat, eds. States of Imagination: Ethnographic Explorations of the Postcolonial State. Durham: Duke University Press, 2001.

Hardiman, David. Adivasi assertion in south Gujarat: The Devi movement of 1922–23. In Subaltern Studies III: Writings on South Asian History and Society, edited by Ranajit Guha, 196–230. Delhi: Oxford University Press, 1984.

——. The Coming of the Devi: Adivasi Assertion in Western India. Delhi: Oxford University Press, 1987.

——. From custom to crime: The politics of drinking in colonial Gujarat. In Subaltern Studies IV:

Writings on South Asian History and Society, edited by Ranajit Guha, 165–228. Delhi: Oxford University Press, 1985.

——. *Peasant Nationalists of Gujarat: Kheda District, 1917–1934.* Delhi: Oxford University Press, 1981.

Harootunian, Harry. *Overcome by Modernity: History, Culture, and Community in Interwar Japan.* Princeton: Princeton University Press, 2000.

Hartman, Saidiya. *Scenes of Subjection: Terror, Slavery, and Self-Making in Nineteenth Century America.* New York: Oxford University Press, 1997.

Harvey, David. *The Condition of Postmodernity: An Enquiry into the Origins of Cultural Change.* Oxford: Basil Blackwell, 1989.

Hefner, Robert, ed. *Conversion to Christianity: Historical and Anthropological Perspectives on a Great Transformation.* Berkeley: University of California Press, 1993.

Henningham, Stephen. Quit India in Bihar and the Eastern United Province: The dual revolt. In *Subaltern Studies II: Writings on South Asian History and Society,* edited by Ranajit Guha, 130–79. Delhi: Oxford University Press, 1983.

Hernández Castillo, Rosalva Aída. *La otra frontera: Identidades multiples en el Chiapas poscolonial.* Mexico City: Centro de Investigaciones y Estudios Superiores en Antropología Social, 2001.

Herzfeld, Michael. "As in your own house": Hospitality, ethnography, and the stereotype of the Mediterranean society. In *Honor and Shame and the Unity of the Mediterranean,* edited by David Gilmore, 75–89. Washington, D.C.: American Anthropological Association, 1987.

——. *Cultural Intimacy: Social Poetics in the Nation-State.* New York: Routledge, 1997.

——. *A Place in History: Social and Monumental Time in a Cretan Town.* Princeton: Princeton University Press, 1991.

Hoffenberg, Peter E. *An Empire on Display: English, Indian, and Australian Exhibitions from the Crystal Palace to the Great War.* Berkeley: University of California Press, 2001.

Hunt, Lynn, ed. *The New Cultural History.* Berkeley: University of California Press, 1989.

Hunt, Nancy Rose, *A Colonial Lexicon of Birth Ritual, Medicalization, and Mobility in the Congo.* Durham: Duke University Press, 1999.

Irschick, Eugene. *Dialogue and History: Constructing South India, 1795–1895.* Berkeley: University of California Press, 1994.

Jaffrelot, Cristophe. *The Hindu Nationalist Movement in India.* New York: Columbia University Press, 1996.

Juhnke, James. *A People of Mission: History of the General Conference Mennonite Overseas Mission.* Newton: Faith and Life Press, 1979.

Kaplan, Martha. *Neither Cargo nor Cult: Ritual Politics and Colonial Imagination in Fiji.* Durham: Duke University Press, 1995.

Kapur, Anuradha. Deity to crusader: The changing iconography of Ram. In *Hindus and Others: The Question of Identity in India Today,* edited by Gyanendra Pandey, 74–109. New Delhi: Penguin, 1993.

Kawashima, Koji. *Missionaries and a Hindu State: Travancore, 1858–1936.* Delhi: Oxford University Press, 1998.

Kelly, John. *A Politics of Virtue: Hinduism, Sexuality, and Countercolonial Discourse in Fiji.* Chicago: University of Chicago Press, 1991.

King, Richard. *Orientalism and Religion: Postcolonial Theory, India, and the "Mystic East."* London: Routledge, 1999.

Klein, Kerwin Lee. *Frontiers of the Historical Imagination: Narrating the European Conquest of Native America, 1890–1990.* Berkeley: University of California Press, 1999.

Kraniauskas, John, and Guillermo Zermeño, eds. *Historia y subalternidad*. Special issue of *Historia y grafia* 12 (1999): 7–176.

Kumar, Kapil, *Peasants in Revolt: Tenants, Landlords, Congress and the Raj*. Delhi: Manohar, 1984.

Kumar, Ravinder, ed. *Essays on Gandhian Politics: The Rowlatt Satyagraha of 1919*. Oxford: Clarendon Press, 1971.

Lancaster, Roger. *Thanks to God and the Revolution: Popular Religion and Class Consciousness in the New Nicaragua*. New York: Columbia University Press, 1988.

Landau, Paul. *The Realm of the Word: Language, Gender, and Christianity in a Southern African Kingdom*. London: Heineman, 1995.

Lander, Edgardo, ed. *La Colonialidad del Saber: Eurocentrismo y ciencas sociales, perspectivas latinoamericanas*. Buenos Aires: Consejo Latinoamericano de Ciencias Sociales, 2000.

Lapp, J. A. *The Mennonite Church in India*. Scottsdale: Herald Press, 1972.

Larson, Pier M. "Capacities and modes of thinking": Intellectual engagements and subaltern hegemony in the early history of Malagasy Christianity. *American Historical Review* 102 (1997): 968–1002.

Lears, T. L. Jackson. The concept of cultural hegemony: Problems and possibilities. *American Historical Review* 90 (1985): 567–93.

Levine, Lawrence. *Black Culture and Consciousness: Afro-American Folk Thought from Slavery to Freedom*. New York: Oxford University Press, 1977.

Lewis, Martin, and Karen Wigen. *The Myth of the Continents: A Critique of Metageography*. Berkeley: University of California Press, 1997.

Lloyd, David. Outside history: Irish new histories and the "subalternity effect." In *Subaltern Studies IX: Writings on South Asian History and Society*, edited by Shahid Amin and Dipesh Chakrabarty, 261–80. Delhi: Oxford University Press, 1996.

Lohr, Julius J. *Bilder aus Chhattisgarh und den Ceantral Provinzen Ostindiens*. N.p., 1899.

Lomnitz-Adler, Claudio. *Exits from the Labyrinth: Culture and Ideology in Mexican National Space*. Berkeley: University of California Press, 1992.

Lorenzen, David. Warrior ascetics in Indian history. *Journal of the American Oriental Society* 98 (1978): 61–75.

Lowe, Lisa, and David Lloyd, eds. *The Politics of Culture in the Shadow of Capital*. Durham: Duke University Press, 1997.

Ludden, David, ed. *Reading Subaltern Studies: Perspectives on History, Society, and Culture*. New Delhi: Permanent Black, 2001.

Lüdtke, Alf, ed. *The History of Everyday Life: Reconstructing Historical Experiences and Ways of Life*. Translated by W. Templer. Princeton: Princeton University Press, 1995.

Lutgendorf, Philip. Ramayan: The video. *Drama Review* 34 (1990): 127–76.

Lutz, Catherine. *Unnatural Emotions: Everyday Sentiments on a Micronesian Atoll and Their Challenge to Western Theory*. Chicago: University of Chicago Press, 1988.

Lynch, Owen M., ed. *Divine Passions: The Social Construction of Emotions in India*. Berkeley: University of California Press, 1990.

Madan, T. N., The ideology of the householder among the Kashmiri Pandits. In *Concepts of Person: Kinship, Caste and Marriage in India*, edited by Akos Ostor, Lina Fruzzetti and Steve Barnett, 99–117. Delhi: Oxford University Press, 1983.

Makdisi, Ussama. Reclaiming the land of the Bible: Missionaries, secularism, and evangelical modernity. *American Historical Review* 102 (1997): 680–713.

Mallebrein, Cornelia. Constructing a "house within the house": Reading the wall-paintings of the Lanjia Sora from recitations. In *Jagannath Revisited: Studying Society, Religion, and the State in Orissa*, edited by Hermann Kulke and Burkhard Schnepel, 93–122. New Delhi: Manohar, 2001.

Mallon, Florencia. *Peasant and Nation: The Making of Postcolonial Mexico and Peru*. Berkeley: University of California Press, 1994.

———. The promise and dilemma of subaltern studies: Perspectives from Latin America. *American Historical Review* 99 (1994): 1495–1515.

Mamdani, Mahmood. *Citizen and Subject: Decentralized Despotism and the Legacy of Late Colonialism*. Princeton: Princeton University Press, 1996.

Mani, Lata. *Contentious Traditions: The Debate on Sati in Colonial India*. Berkeley: University of California Press, 1998.

Manor, James C. Testing the barrier between caste and outcaste: The Andhra Evangelical Lutheran Church in Guntur District, 1920–1940. *Indian Church History Review* 5 (1971): 27–41.

Marriott, McKim. Hindu transactions: Diversity without dualism. In *Transaction and Meaning: Directions in the Anthropology of Exchange and Symbolic Behavior*, edited by B. Kapferer, 109–42. Philadelphia: Institute for the Study of Human Issues, 1976.

Marriott, McKim, and Ron Inden. Toward an ethnosociology of South Asian caste systems. In *The New Wind: Changing Identities in South Asia*, edited by Kenneth David, 227–38. The Hague: Mouton, 1976.

Mayaram, Shail. *Resisting Regimes: Myth, Memory and the Shaping of a Muslim Identity*. Delhi: Oxford University Press, 1997.

———. Speech, silence, and the making of partition violence in Mewat. In *Subaltern Studies IX: Writings on South Asian History and Society*, edited by Shahid Amin and Dipesh Chakrabarty, 126–64. Delhi: Oxford University Press, 1996.

Mbembe, Achille. The banality of power and the aesthetics of vulgarity in the postcolony. *Public Culture* 4 (1992): 1–30.

———. *On the Postcolony*. Berkeley: University of California Press, 2001.

McClintock, Anne. *Imperial Leather: Race, Gender, and Sexuality in the Colonial Contest*. New York: Routledge, 1995.

McCutheon, Russell. *Manufacturing Religion: The Discourse on Sui Generis Religion and the Politics of Nostalgia*. New York: Oxford University Press, 1997.

McGowan, John. *Postmodernism and Its Critics*. Ithaca: Cornell University Press, 1991.

Medick, Hans. Plebian culture in the transition to capitalism. In *Culture, Ideology and Politics*, edited by Raphael Samuel and Gareth Stedman Jones, 84–113. London: Routledge and Kegan Paul, 1983.

———. The proto-industrial family economy. In *Industrialization before Industrialization*, edited by Peter Kriedte, Hans Medick, and Jürgen Schlumbohm, 38–73. Cambridge: Cambridge University Press, 1981.

Mehta, Uday Singh. Liberal strategies of exclusion. In *Tensions of Empire: Colonial Cultures in a Bourgeois World*, edited by Frederick Cooper and Ann Laura Stoler, 59–86. Berkeley: University of California Press, 1997.

———. *Liberalism and Empire: A Study in Nineteenth-Century British Liberal Thought*. Chicago: University of Chicago Press, 1999.

Menon, Ritu, and Kamla Bhasin. *Borders and Boundaries: Women in India's Partition*. New Delhi: Kali for Women, 1998.

Merry, Sally Engle. Anthropology, law, and transnational processes. *Annual Review of Anthropology* 21 (1992): 357–79.

———. *Colonizing Hawai'i: The Cultural Power of Law*. Princeton: Princeton University Press, 2000.

Meyer, Birgit. *Translating the Devil: Religion and Modernity among the Ewe in Ghana*. Trenton, N.J.: Africa World Press, 1999.

Mignolo, Walter. *The Darker Side of the Renaissance: Literacy, Territoriality, and Colonization*. Ann Arbor: University of Michigan Press, 1995.

———. *Local Histories/Global Designs: Coloniality, Subaltern Knowledges, and Border Thinking*. Princeton: Princeton University Press, 2000.

Mines, Mattison. *Public Faces, Private Voices: Community and Individuality in South Asia*. Berkeley: University of California Press, 1994.

Minkowski, Christopher. The pandit as public intellectual: The controversy over virodha or inconsistency in the astronomical sciences. In *The Pandit: Traditional Sanskrit Scholarship in India*, edited by Axel Michaels, 79–96. New Delhi: Manohar, 2001.

Mitchell, Timothy. The stage of modernity. In *Questions of Modernity*, edited by Timothy Mitchell, 1–34. Minneapolis: University of Minnesota Press, 2000.

Mitchell, Timothy, ed. *Questions of Modernity*. Minneapolis: University of Minnesota Press, 2000.

Mohanty, Chandra Talapade. Under Western eyes: Feminist scholarship and colonial discourses. In *Third World Women and the Politics of Women*, edited by Chandra T. Mohanty, Ann Russo and Lourdes Torres, 51–80. Bloomington: Indiana University Press, 1991.

Moore, Erin P. *Gender, Law, and Resistance in India*. Tucson: University of Arizona Press, 1998.

———. Gender, power, and legal pluralism. *American Ethnologist* 20 (1993): 522–42.

Moore, Sally Falk. *Social Facts and Fabrications: Customary Law in Kilimanjaro, 1880–1980*. Cambridge: Cambridge University Press, 1986.

Muir, Edward, and Guido Ruggiero, eds. *Microhistory and the Lost Peoples of Europe*. Translated by Eren Branch. Baltimore: Johns Hopkins University Press, 1991.

Nader, Laura. *Harmony Ideology: Justice and Control in a Zapotec Mountain Village*. Stanford: Stanford University Press, 1990.

Nandy, Ashis. *An Ambiguous Journey to the City: The Village and Other Odd Remains of the Self in the Indian Imagination*. New Delhi: Oxford University Press, 2001.

———. *The Intimate Enemy: Loss and Recovery of the Self under Colonialism*. Delhi: Oxford University Press, 1982.

———. *The Savage Freud and Other Essays on Possible and Retrievable Selves*. Princeton: Princeton University Press, 1995.

———. *Traditions, Tyranny, and Utopias: Essays in the Politics of Awareness*. Delhi: Oxford University Press, 1992.

Niranjana, Tejaswini. *Siting Translation: History, Post-structuralism and the Colonial Context*. Berkeley: University of California Press, 1992.

O'Hanlon, Rosalind. Issues of widowhood: Gender and resistance in colonial western India. In *Contesting Power: Resistance and Everyday Social Relations in South Asia*, edited by Douglas Haynes and Gyan Prakash, 62–108. Delhi: Oxford University Press, 1991.

———. Recovering the subject: *Subaltern Studies* and histories of resistance in colonial South Asia. *Modern Asian Studies* 22 (1988): 189–224.

Obeyesekere, Gananath. *The Apotheosis of Captain Cook*. Princeton: Princeton University Press, 1992.

Oddie, G. A. Christian conversion in the Telugu country, 1869–1900: A case study of one Protestant movement in the Godavery-Christian Delta. *Indian Economic and Social History Review* 12 (1975): 61–79.

Ong, Aihwa. *Flexible Citizenship: The Cultural Logics of Transnationality*. Durham: Duke University Press, 1999.

Ortner, Sherry. Resistance and the problem of ethnographic refusal. *Comparative Studies in Society and History* 37 (1995): 173–93.

Pandey, Gyanendra. *The Ascendancy of the Congress in Uttar Pradesh, 1926–1934: A Study in Imperfect Mobilization.* Oxford: Clarendon Press, 1978.

——. The colonial construction of "communalism": British writings on Banaras in the nineteenth century. In *Subaltern Studies VI: Writings on South Asian History and Society,* edited by Ranajit Guha, 132–68. Delhi: Oxford University Press, 1989.

——. In defense of the fragment: Writing about Hindu-Muslim riots in India today. In *A Subaltern Studies Reader, 1986–1995,* edited by Ranajit Guha, 1–33. Minneapolis: University of Minnesota Press, 1997.

——. Modes of history writing: New Hindu history of Ayodhya. *Economic and Political Weekly* 29 (1994): 1523–28.

——. Peasant revolt and Indian nationalism: The peasant movement in Awadh, 1919–22. In *Subaltern Studies I: Writings on South Asian History and Society,* edited by Ranajit Guha, 143–97. Delhi: Oxford University Press, 1982.

——. *Remembering Partition: Violence, Nationalism and History in India.* Cambridge: Cambridge University Press, 2001.

——. Which of us are Hindus? In *Hindus and Others: The Question of Identity in India Today,* edited by Gyanendra Pandey, 238–72. New Delhi: Penguin, 1993.

Parker, Kunal M. "A corporation of superior prostitutes": Anglo-Indian legal conceptions of temple dancing. *Modern Asian Studies* 32 (1998): 559–633.

Parry, Jonathan. Ankalu's errant wife: Sex, marriage, and industry in contemporary Chhattisgarh. *Modern Asian Studies* 35 (2001): 783–820.

Peel, J. D. Y. For who hath despised the day of small things? Missionary narratives and historical anthropology. *Comparative Studies in Society and History* 37 (1995): 581–607.

Peterson, Derek. Translating the Word: Dialogism and debate in two Gikuyu dictionaries. *Journal of Religious History* 23 (1999): 31–50.

Pinch, William. Soldier monks and militant sadhus. In *Making India Hindu: Religion, Community, and the Politics of Democracy in India,* edited by David Ludden, 140–61. Delhi: Oxford University Press, 1996.

Pinney, Christopher. Indian magical realism: Notes on popular visual culture. In *Subaltern Studies X: Writings on South Asian History and Society,* edited by Gautam Bhadra, Gyan Prakash, and Susie Tharu, 201–33. Delhi: Oxford University Press, 1999.

——. The nation (un)pictured? Chromolithography and "popular" politics in India, 1878–1995. *Critical Inquiry* 23 (1997): 834–67.

Piot, Charles. *Remotely Global: Village Modernity in West Africa.* Chicago: University of Chicago Press, 1999.

Povinelli, Elizabeth A. *The Cunning of Recognition: Indigenous Alterities and the Making of Australian Multiculturalism.* Durham: Duke University Press, 2002.

Prakash, Gyan. *Another Reason: Science and the Imagination of Modern India.* Princeton: Princeton University Press, 1999.

——. *Bonded Histories: Genealogies of Labor Servitude in Colonial India.* Cambridge: Cambridge University Press, 1990.

——. Science between the lines. In *Subaltern Studies IX: Writings on South Asian History and Society,* edited by Shahid Amin and Dipesh Chakrabarty, 59–82. Delhi: Oxford University Press, 1999.

——. Subaltern studies as postcolonial criticism. *American Historical Review* 99 (1994): 1475–94.

——. Writing post-orientalist histories of the Third World: Indian historiography is good to think. In *Colonialism and Culture,* edited by Nicholas Dirks, 353–88. Ann Arbor: University of Michigan Press, 1992.

Price, Richard. *The Convict and the Colonel: A Story of Colonialism and Resistance in the Caribbean*. Boston: Beacon Press, 1998.

Prins, Gwyn. *The Hidden Hippopotamus: Reappraisals in African History*. Cambridge: Cambridge University Press, 1980.

Quijano, Aníbal. Colonialidad del poder, eurocentrismo y América Latina. In *La Colonialidad del Saber: Eurocentrismo y ciencas sociales, perspectivas latinoamericanas*, edited by Edgardo Lander, 201–46. Buenos Aires: Consejo Latinoamericano de Ciencias Sociales, 2000.

Radhakrishnan, P. Postmodernism and the rest of the world. In *The Pre-occupation of Postcolonial Studies*, edited by Fawzia Afzal-Khan and Kalpana Seshadri Crooks, 37–70. Durham: Duke University Press, 2000.

Rafael, Vicente. *Contracting Colonialism: Translation and Christian Conversion in Tagalog Society under Early Spanish Rule*. Ithaca: Cornell University Press, 1988.

Raheja, Gloria, and Ann Gold. *Listen to the Heron's Words: Reimagining Gender and Kinship in North India*. Berkeley: University of California Press, 1994.

Rajagopal, Arvind. Ram Janmabhoomi, consumer identity and image-based politics. *Economic and Political Weekly* 29 (1994): 1659–68.

Rao, Anupama. Problems of violence, states of terror: Torture in colonial India. In *Discipline and the Other Body*, edited by Anupama Rao and Steven Pierce. Special issue of *Interventions: Journal of Postcolonial Studies* 3 (2001): 186–205.

Rappaport, Joanne. *Cumbe Reborn: An Andean Ethnography of History*. Chicago: University of Chicago Press, 1994.

Reddy, William. Emotional liberty: Politics and history in the anthropology of emotions. *Cultural Anthropology* 14 (1999): 256–88.

Redfield, Peter. *Space in the Tropics: From Convicts to Rockets in French Guiana*. Berkeley: University of California Press, 2000.

Robinson, Rowena. *Conversion, Continuity, and Change: Lived Christianity in Southern Goa*. New Delhi: Sage, 1998.

Rodríguez, Ileana, ed. *The Latin American Subaltern Studies Reader*. Durham: Duke University Press, 2001.

Rofel, Lisa. *Other Modernities: Gendered Yearnings in China after Socialism*. Berkeley: University of California Press, 1998.

Rosaldo, Renato. *Culture and Truth: The Remaking of Social Analysis*. Boston: Beacon Press, 1987.

Roth, Michael. *The Poetics of Resistance: Heidegger's Line*. Evanston: Northwestern University Press, 1996.

Sabean, David Warren. *Kinship in Neckarhausen, 1700–1870*. Cambridge: Cambridge University Press, 1998.

——. *Power in the Blood: Popular Culture and Village Discourse in Early Modern Germany*. Cambridge: Cambridge University Press, 1984.

——. *Property, Production, and Family in Neckarhausen, 1700–1870*. Cambridge: Cambridge University Press, 1990.

Sahlins, Marshall. *How "Natives" Think: About Captain Cook, for Example*. Chicago: University of Chicago Press, 1995.

——. *Islands of History*. Chicago: University of Chicago Press, 1985.

Said, Edward. *Orientalism*. New York: Pantheon, 1978.

Saldaña-Portillo, María Josefina. Reading a silence: The "Indian" in the era of Zapatismo. In *Critical Conjunctions: Foundations of Colony and Formations of Modernity*, edited by Saurabh Dube, Ishita Banerjee Dube, and Edgardo Lander. Special issue of *Nepantla: Views from South* 3, no. 2 (2002): 287–314.

Samuel, Raphael, ed. *People's History and Socialist Theory*. London: Routledge and Kegan Paul, 1981.

Sarkar, Sumit. The conditions and nature of subaltern militancy: Bengal from Swadeshi to non-cooperation, c. 1905–22. In *Subaltern Studies III: Writings on South Asian History and Society*, edited by Ranajit Guha, 271–320. Delhi: Oxford University Press, 1984.

——. The decline of the subaltern in subaltern studies. In *Writing Social History*, 88–102. Delhi: Oxford University Press, 1997.

——. *Modern India, 1885–1947*. Delhi: Macmillan, 1983.

——. *Writing Social History*. Delhi: Oxford University Press, 1997.

Sarkar, Tanika. Jitu Santal's movement in Malda, 1924–1932: A study in tribal protest. In *Subaltern Studies IV: Writings on South Asian History and Society*, edited by Ranajit Guha, 136–64. Delhi: Oxford University Press, 1985.

——. Politics and women in Bengal: The conditions and meaning of participation. *Indian Economic and Social History Review* 21 (1984): 91–101.

Sax, William. *Mountain Goddess: Gender and Politics in a Himalayan Pilgrimage*. New York: Oxford University Press, 1991.

Schama, Simon. *The Embarrassment of Riches: An Interpretation of Dutch Culture in the Golden Age*. New York: Knopf, 1988.

Scott, David. Conversion and demonism: Colonial Christian discourse on religion in Sri Lanka. *Comparative Studies in Society and History* 34 (1992): 331–65.

——. *Refashioning Futures: Criticism after Postcoloniality*. Princeton: Princeton University Press, 1999.

Seshadri-Crooks, Kalpana. At the margins of postcolonial studies, part I. In *The Pre-occupation of Postcolonial Studies*, edited by Fawzia Afzal-Khan and Kalpana Seshadri-Crooks, 3–23. Durham: Duke University Press, 2000.

——. Surviving theory: A conversation with Homi Bhabha. In *The Pre-occupation of Postcolonial Studies*, edited by Fawzia Afzal-Khan and Kalpana Seshadri-Crooks, 369–79. Durham: Duke University Press, 2000.

Seybold, Theodore. *God's Guiding Hand: History of the Central Indian Mission, 1868–1967*. Philadelphia: United Church Board for World Ministries of the United Church of Christ, 1971.

Sharma, J. P. A study of the nationalist movement in Chhattisgarh, 1920–47. Ph.D. diss., Ravi Shankar University, Raipur, 1974.

Shohat, Ella. Notes on the postcolonial. In *Contemporary Postcolonial Theory: A Reader*, edited by Padmini Mongia, 321–34. London: Arnold, 1996.

Shukla, Ashok. History of the freedom movement in Chhattisgarh, 1857–1947. Ph.D. diss., Ravi Shankar University, Raipur, 1972.

Siddiqi, Majid. *Agrarian Unrest in Northern India: The United Provinces, 1918–1922*. New Delhi: Vikas, 1978.

Sider, Gerald. Christmas mumming in outport Newfoundland. *Past and Present* 71 (1976): 102–25.

Singha, Radhika. *A Despotism of Law: Crime and Justice in Early Colonial India*. Delhi: Oxford University Press, 1998.

Sinha, Mrinalini. *Colonial Masculinity: The "Manly Englishman" and the "Effeminate Bengali" in the Late Nineteenth Century*. Manchester: Manchester University Press, 1995.

Sivaramakrishnan, K. *Making Forests: Statemaking and Environmental Change in Colonial Eastern India*. New Delhi: Oxford University Press, 1999.

Skaria, Ajay. *Hybrid Histories: Forests, Frontiers and Wildness in Western India*. New Delhi: Oxford University Press, 1999.

——. Writing, orality, and power in the Dangs, western India, 1800s–1920s. In *Subaltern Studies*

IX: *Writings on South Asian History and Society*, edited by Shahid Amin and Dipesh Chakrabarty, 13–58. Delhi: Oxford University Press, 1996.

Spivak, Gayatri Chakravorty. Can the subaltern speak? In *Marxism and the Interpretation of Culture*, edited by Cary Nelson and Larry Grossberg, 271–313. Urbana: University of Illinois Press, 1988.

——. *A Critique of Postcolonial Reason: Toward a History of the Vanishing Present*. Cambridge: Harvard University Press, 1999.

——. Subaltern studies: Deconstructing historiography. In *Subaltern Studies IV: Writings on South Asian History and Society*, edited by Ranajit Guha, 330–63. Delhi: Oxford University Press, 1985.

Srinivas, M. N. *Religion and Society among the Coorgs of South India*. Oxford: Clarendon Press, 1952.

——. *Social Change in Modern India*. Berkeley: University of California Press, 1966.

Starr, June, and Jane Collier, eds. *History and Power in the Study of Law: New Directions in Legal Anthropology*. Ithaca: Cornell University Press, 1989.

Steinmetz, George. Critical realism and historical sociology. *Comparative Studies in Society and History* 40 (1998): 170–86.

Stephens, Julie. Feminist fictions: A critique of the category "non-Western woman" in feminist writings on India. In *Subaltern Studies IV: Writings on South Asian History and Society*, edited by Ranajit Guha, 95–125. Delhi: Oxford University Press, 1985.

Stirrat, R. L. *Power and Religiosity in a Post-colonial Setting: Sinhala Catholics in Contemporary Sri Lanka*. Cambridge: Cambridge University Press, 1992.

Stoler, Ann Laura. *Carnal Knowledge and Imperial Power: Race and the Intimate in Colonial Rule*. Berkeley: University of California Press, 2002.

——. Perceptions of protest: Defining the dangerous in colonial Sumatra. *American Ethnologist* 12 (1985): 642–58.

——. *Race and the Education of Desire: Foucault's History of Sexuality and the Colonial Order of Things*. Durham: Duke University Press, 1995.

Stoler, Ann Laura, and Frederick Cooper. Between metropole and colony: Rethinking a research agenda. In *Tensions of Empire: Colonial Cultures in a Bourgeois World*, edited by Frederick Cooper and Ann Laura Stoler, 1–56. Berkeley: University of California Press, 1997.

Studdert-Kennedy, Gerald. *Providence and the Raj: Imperial Mission and Missionary Imperialism*. New Delhi: Sage Publications, 1998.

Suleri, Sara. Women skin deep: Feminism and the postcolonial condition. In *Contemporary Postcolonial Theory: A Reader*, edited by Padmini Mongia, 335–46. London: Arnold, 1996.

Tanner, Th. von. *Im Lande der Hindus oder Kulturschilderungen aus Indien*. St. Louis: The German Evangelical Synod of North America, 1894.

Taussig, Michael. *Defacement: Public Secrecy and the Labor of the Negative*. Stanford: Stanford University Press, 1999.

——. *The Magic of the State*. New York: Routledge, 1996.

——. *The Nervous System*. New York: Routledge, 1992.

——. *Shamanism, Colonialism, and the Wild Man: A Study in Terror and Healing*. Chicago: University of Chicago Press, 1987.

Teltscher, Kate. *India Inscribed: European and British Writing on India, 1600–1800*. Delhi: Oxford University Press, 1997.

Thapar, Romila. Epic and history: Tradition, dissent and politics in India. *Past and Present* 125 (1989): 1–26.

Tharu, Susie. Response to Julie Stephens. In *Subaltern Studies IV: Writings on South Asian History and Society*, edited by Ranajit Guha, 126–32. Delhi: Oxford University Press, 1985.

Thomas, Nicholas. Colonial conversions: Difference, hierarchy, and history in early twentieth century evangelical propaganda. *Comparative Studies in Society and History* 34 (1992): 366–89.

——. *Colonialism's Culture: Anthropology, Travel, and Government.* Princeton: Princeton University Press, 1994.

Thompson, Edward P. *Customs in Common: Studies in Traditional Popular Culture.* New York: New Press, 1993.

——. Eighteenth century English society: Class struggle without class. *Social History* 3 (1978): 133–65.

——. Folklore, anthropology and the discipline of history. *Indian Historical Review* 3 (1977): 247–66.

——. *The Making of the English Working Class.* New York: Vintage, 1963.

——. The moral economy of the English crowd in the eighteenth century. *Past and Present* 50 (1971): 76–136.

——. Patrician society, plebian culture. *Journal of Social History* 7 (1974): 382–405.

——. *The Poverty of Theory and Other Essays.* New York: Monthly Review Press, 1978.

——. Time, work-discipline and industrial capitalism. *Past and Present* 38 (1967): 56–97.

——. *Whigs and Hunters.* Harmondsworth: Penguin, 1977.

Thorne, Susan. "The conversion of Englishmen and the conversion of the world inseparable": Missionary imperialism and the languages of class in early industrial Britain. In *Tensions of Empire: Colonial Cultures in a Bourgeois World,* edited by Frederick Cooper and Ann Laura Stoler, 238–62. Berkeley: University of California Press, 1997.

Trawick, Margaret. *Notes on Love in a Tamil Family.* Berkeley: University of California Press, 1990.

Trouillot, Michel-Rolph. North Atlantic universals: Analytical fictions, 1492–1945. In *Enduring Enchantments,* edited by Saurabh Dube. Special issue of *South Atlantic Quarterly* 101, no. 4 (2002): 840–57.

——. *Silencing the Past: Power and the Production of History.* Boston: Beacon Press, 1995.

Van der Veer, Peter. God must be liberated: A Hindu liberation movement in Ayodhya. *Modern Asian Studies* 21 (1987): 283–303.

——. *Gods on Earth: The Management of Religious Experience and Identity in a North Indian Pilgrimage Centre.* Delhi: Oxford University Press, 1988.

——. *Religious Nationalism: Hindus and Muslims in India.* Berkeley: University of California Press, 1994.

——. Writing violence. In *Making India Hindu: Religion, Community, and the Politics of Democracy in India,* edited by David Ludden, 250–69. Delhi: Oxford University Press, 1996.

Vaudeville, Charlotte. Braj, lost and found. *Indo-Iranian Journal* 18 (1976): 195–213.

Visvanathan, Susan. *The Christians of Kerala: History, Belief, and Ritual among the Yakoba.* Madras: Oxford University Press, 1993.

Viswanathan, Gauri. *Outside the Fold: Conversion, Modernity, and Belief.* Princeton: Princeton University Press, 1998.

Viswesaran, Kamala. Small speeches, subaltern gender: Nationalist ideology and its historiography. In *Subaltern Studies IX: Writings on South Asian History and Society,* edited by Shahid Amin and Dipesh Chakrabarty, 83–125. Delhi: Oxford University Press, 1996.

Voloshinov, V. N. [Mikhail Bakhtin]. *Marxism and the Philosophy of Language.* Translated by L. Matejka and I. R. Titunik. Cambridge: Harvard University Press, 1984.

Washbrook, David. Progress and problems: South Asian economic and social history. *Modern Asian Studies* 22 (1988): 57–96.

Webster, John C. *The Dalit Christians: A History.* Delhi: ISPCK, 1994.

White, Geoffrey. *Identity through History: Living Stories in a Solomon Islands Society.* Cambridge: Cambridge University Press, 1991.

White, Luise. *Speaking with Vampires: Rumor and History in Colonial Africa.* Berkeley: University of California Press, 2000.

White, Stephen. *Sustaining Affirmation: The Strengths of Weak Ontology in Political Theory.* Princeton: Princeton University Press, 2000.

Widenthal, Lora. Race, gender and citizenship in the German colonial empire. In *Tensions of Empire: Colonial Cultures in a Bourgeois World,* edited by Frederick Cooper and Ann Laura Stoler, 263–83. Berkeley: University of California Press, 1997.

Williams, Brackette. A class act: Anthropology and the race to nation across ethnic terrain. *Annual Review of Anthropology* 18 (1989): 401–44.

Wolfe, Patrick. *Settler Colonialism and the Transformation of Anthropology: The Politics and Poetics of an Ethnographic Event.* London: Cassell, 1999.

Yang, Anand, ed. *Crime and Criminality in British India.* Tucson: University of Arizona Press, 1985.

Index

143–48, 150–53, 200 n.50, 211 n.4, 218 n.2, 222 nn.52, 55, 58, 64

Gulf War, 3, 193 n.4

Hall, Stuart, xii
Hansen, Thomas Blom, 224 n.4, 225–26 n.15
Hanumangarhi, 174
Hardiman, David, 218 n.2
Haridwar, 172
Harvey, David, 225–26 n.15
Hegemony, 17, 24–25, 33–34, 39–43, 53–54, 124, 134–36, 140
Heidegger, Martin, 156, 181
Heidelberg, 32, 49
Herzfeld, Michael, 17, 65, 202 n.16, 224 n.1
Heterogeneity, 7, 8, 11, 12, 16, 18–21, 24, 130, 157
Hinduism, 170, 177–81, 185, 225 n.14
Hindu Right, 19–20, 27, 157–58, 162, 164–65, 179, 223 n.1, 224 nn.2, 4, 225–26 n.15; histories of Ayodhya of, 165–67, 224 n.3, 225 nn.6, 8, 14; questioning of histories of Ayodhya of, 167–76, 226 n.17
Hindutva. See Hindu Right
History: from below, 27, 130–37, 163, 219 nn.9, 15, 220 n.28; and nation, xiii, 4, 17–20, 27, 130–33, 149–50, 157–58, 161–69, 176, 188–89, 194 n.11, 224 nn.2–4, 225 nn.6, 8, 14, 225–26 n.15, 226–27 n.19 (see also Nationalism); universal, 3, 5, 6, 8–9, 33, 51, 132, 137, 150, 155, 182–84, 189, 225–26 n.15; without warranty, xii, 20–25, 163, 176, 189, 199 nn.44, 45
Honor, 54, 65–66, 75, 77, 98, 104–5, 121–22
Hospitality, 37, 202 n.16
Household: metaphor of, 72–73
Husserl, Edmund, 181
Hutnyk, John, 51
Hybridity, 15, 23, 48, 184, 200 n.46

Identity: politics of, 178, 180–81, 229 n.2, 229–30 n.9
Immanuel congregation, 68–72
Inden, Ron, 122
India Mission District, 60, 66–72, 208 n.40
Indian National Congress, 111, 137–43
Individual. See Personhood
Insurgency, 143–48, 151–53

Intention. See Crime
International Monetary Fund, 184
Inversion, 144, 152

Jagannath Puri, 172
Jains, 170
Janakpur, 173
Jawaharlal Nehru University, 167

Kaviraj, Sudipta, 218 n.2
Khadi, 141
Kingship, 25, 60, 74, 172, 207 n.36
Kinship, 17, 18, 36, 58–59, 77, 79–102, 104, 135, 152, 212 n.8, 217 nn.62, 64
Kisan Sabha, 139–40
Klee, Paul, 187
Kols, 56, 147–48, 221 n.51
Kubrick, Stanley, 3, 192 n.4
Kumaun, 138–39

Land Revenue Resettlement, 106–10
Latin America, 5–6, 194 n.11
Law: colonial and modern, 16, 17, 22, 26, 71, 77–125 passim, 211 n.6, 212 n.25
Legalities: popular and coeval, 16–17, 26, 57, 77–125 passim, 214–15 n.2
Litany, 49
Location, 196 n.20, 229–30 n.9
Lohr, Oscar, 35–37, 42, 50, 55–60, 206 nn.17, 20, 207 n.30, 208 n.48
Ludden, David, 218 n.5

Madan, T. N., 217 n.64
Malguzar: missionary as, 52, 57, 59, 62, 73–75, 208 n.49
Mamdani, Mahmood, 192 n.1
Margins, 2, 15, 32–35, 154, 157, 194 n.11
Marriage, 17, 59, 65, 68, 74–75, 79–80, 85–86, 88–89, 99–100, 212 n.10. See also Kinship
Marriot, McKim, 122
Marwaris, 176
Marx, Karl, 181
Mayaram, Shail, 175, 218 n.2
McGowan, John, 9–10
Medicine, 43, 58, 74
Medick, 220 nn.17, 22
Mehta, Uday Singh, 201 n.4
Memory, 31, 33, 50, 161
Mennonites, 32, 36, 39–40

Saurabh Dube is a professor of History in the Center for
Asian and African Studies at El Colegio de México.

Library of Congress Cataloging-in-Publication Data
Dube, Saurabh.
Stitches on time : colonial textures and postcolonial tangles /
Saurabh Dube.
Includes bibliographical references and index.
ISBN 0-8223-3325-2 (cloth : alk. paper)
ISBN 0-8223-3337-6 (pbk. : alk. paper)
1. South Asia—History. 2. Ethnology—South Asia. 3. Missions—
South Asia—History. 4. Nationalism—South Asia—History. I.
Title.
DS341.D82 2004   954—dc22   2003021427